Life And Deeds Of General Sherman

Including The Story Of His Great March To The Sea

Henry Davenport Northrop

Alpha Editions

This Edition Published in 2021

ISBN: 9789354484988

Design and Setting By
Alpha Editions
www.alphaedis.com
Email – info@alphaedis.com

As per information held with us this book is in Public Domain.
This book is a reproduction of an important historical work. Alpha Editions
uses the best technology to reproduce historical work in the same manner
it was first published to preserve its original nature. Any marks or number
seen are left intentionally to preserve its true form.

Life and Deeds

of

General Sherman

Including the Story of His

Great March to the Sea

BEING A GRAPHIC NARRATIVE OF

His Boyhood and Early Life; Education at West Point; Career
in Florida, California and Louisiana; Daring Deeds
at Shiloh, Corinth and Vicksburg; Sublime
Achievements in the Georgia and Tennessee Campaigns, and Closing
Scenes of the Great
Struggle, etc., etc.,

COMPRISING

Thrilling Descriptions of Battles, Marches, and Victories;
Personal Anecdotes; Life as a Citizen; Last Sickness
and Death; the Nation's Sorrow, and Magnificent Tributes to the

GREAT COMMANDER, HERO and PATRIOT

By Henry Davenport Northrop

SUPERBLY EMBELLISHED WITH STRIKING ILLUSTRATIONS.

MERCANTILE PUBLISHING & ADVERTISING CO.,
CHICAGO, ILLINOIS.

PREFACE.

The story of General Sherman's brilliant career is one of the most interesting ever told. His early life was spent in poverty and obscurity; he rose to the highest pinnacle of fame. Fortune was against him; he conquered it; he was a conqueror throughout his eventful life. Without wealth or outside influence to lift him above his surroundings, he carved his name high before the eye of the world, and died amidst the honors of the nation he defended so nobly.

Like nearly all Americans who have achieved fame, Sherman was a self-made man. He was a patriot who courted sacrifice and death; he was a leader of undaunted bravery, brilliant strategy, and unfaltering resources. His rank is among the world's greatest heroes, and his place is in the hearts of more than sixty millions of people.

The complete story of his life, contained in this volume, gives a graphic account of his boyhood and youth. The reader sees him struggling with early trials; the sturdy boy grows into the manly youth, pressing on in his eager pursuit of an education. He enters the Military Academy; he graduates with honor, and is fully equipped for his magnificent military career.

General Sherman is then seen among the Everglades of Florida, at Fort Moultrie in South Carolina, and on the Pacific Coast. The outbreak of the war finds the gallant leader in Louisiana; he sees that war is inevitable, resigns his position, and appears in Washington.

At the first battle of Bull Run, Sherman is a colonel; he rises to the rank of brigadier of volunteers and is sent to Kentucky. His upward strides are rapid, and the reader next beholds him in command of a division at Shiloh, where he displays consummate generalship and heroism, and saves that famous battle. He is the first to enter Corinth; he takes command at Memphis; he makes a bold attack on Vicksburg; and next appears upon the world-renowned field of Chattanooga. Through the dense smoke and fiery glare of Missionary Ridge the reader sees the commanding figure now prominent before the nation, whose presence on the field is the signal for victory.

These wonderful exploits, this daring heroism, this extraordinary command of men, these magnificent deeds which thrill two hemispheres, are depicted in this work. The theme is brilliant and captivating. Step by step the thrilling history is unfolded; over the pages armies march and charge, and the reader moves amid startling scenes: the old days of heroism and Spartan bravery are brought back.

The crowning achievement of General Sherman,

that which electrified the whole world, that which even military men believed to be impossible, was his celebrated march to the sea. This part of the narrative has an extraordinary interest for the reader, and is told in this volume by General Sherman himself, who was as skilful and fascinating with the pen as he was valiant with the sword. Here the great general showed his remarkable foresight, burned the bridges behind him, pushed into the enemy's country, met and mastered seeming impossibilities, and put the splendid climax upon his marvellous career.

We find him at Atlanta with an army which is compelled to subsist upon the surrounding country. Thence he marches to the Atlantic. This almost miraculous feat, resulting in the capture of Savannah, the retreat of General Hardee from Charleston, and other events of vast importance, is fully portrayed. The grave doubts as to the result all vanished before the masterly generalship, intrepid courage, and perseverance of the illustrious leader.

Next the reader sees the two great generals, Sherman and Grant, face to face. The bloody days are ended, the smoke of battle lifts from the field, the noise of guns is hushed, and the world looks on in wonder at the closing scenes of the greatest struggle of modern times. Conspicuous in this thrilling period of our history, his majestic form standing in the nation's eye, we see the hero and patriot, the invincible commander. He has received the surrender of Johnston, and has acted a part no less remarkable and successful than that of Grant in the Wilderness and before Richmond.

This work also gives a striking picture of General Sherman's life as a citizen. He was a genial man; he was an admirable speech-maker; he was the idol of the nation: he was honored on every public occasion where his commanding figure was seen; his loyalty to the old veterans was sincere and unwavering; his popularity among the army boys was surpassed by that of no other general.

All readers are interested in personal anecdotes and reminiscences concerning great men. In the long life and checkered career of General Sherman many incidents occurred, and account of which the public is anxious to obtain. Stories of camp-life, long marches, hardships of the campaign, and anecdotes concerning General Sherman's private life and intercourse with his old comrades enliven the pages of this volume. Side by side stand with him other brilliant heroes in the nation's struggle, and a picture of him as a man among men is presented.

The demonstration of sympathy and sorrow when his death occurred has scarcely been paralleled in this country. Sherman was loved by everybody, as well as admired. His death struck home to the heart of the nation. All classes of citizens, including the President, members of the Cabinet, army and naval officers, merchants, farmers, professional men, the rich, the poor, vied with each other at his funeral in telling of his glory and in honoring his memory.

THE CATAFALQUE PASSING FIFTY-SEVENTH ST. AND BROADWAY, N. Y. CITY

CONTENTS.

BOOK I.

CHAPTER I.
A REMARKABLE FAMILY.—THE ILLUSTRIOUS COMMANDER'S EARLY LIFE AND STRUGGLES.—BORN TO BE A HERO . . 17

CHAPTER II.
EDUCATION AT WEST POINT.—CHASING SAVAGE SEMINOLES IN THE SOUTH 25

CHAPTER III.
A RECRUITING OFFICER.—STIRRING TIMES IN CALIFORNIA . 32

CHAPTER IV
SHERMAN'S ROMANTIC MARRIAGE.—BANKER IN CALIFORNIA AND NEW YORK.—BECOMES A LAWYER 40

CHAPTER V.
PROPHET AND PATRIOT.—ADVICE TO THE WAR DEPARTMENT TREATED AS A PROOF OF INSANITY 50

CHAPTER VI.
ARMY OF THE TENNESSEE.—SHERMAN CO-OPERATES WITH GRANT.—FORWARD MOVEMENTS 65

CHAPTER VII.
FROM ATLANTA TO THE SEA.—THRILLING STORY OF ONE OF THE GREATEST FEATS IN MILITARY HISTORY . . . 78

CONTENTS.

CHAPTER VIII.

IMPORTANT LETTER OF GENERAL SHERMAN.—THE COUNTRY DELUDED IN THE EARLY PART OF THE WAR.—STRANGE CHARGE OF LUNACY 95

CHAPTER IX.

AFTER THE WAR.—NOT A CANDIDATE FOR THE PRESIDENCY.—SKETCH OF THE HERO.—LIFE IN NEW YORK . . . 113

CHAPTER X.

REMINISCENCES OF THE RENOWNED COMMANDER.—ARDENT FRIENDSHIP FOR GRANT.—INTERESTING FACTS AND ANECDOTES 133

BOOK II.

CHAPTER XI.

SHERMAN AT THE BATTLE OF BULL RUN.—HIS GRAPHIC ACCOUNT OF THE BLOODY CONFLICT 175

CHAPTER XII.

EVENTS PRECEDING THE BATTLE OF SHILOH.—RAPID MOVEMENTS IN THE CUMBERLAND VALLEY AND SOUTH-WEST . 189

CHAPTER XIII.

SHERMAN SAVES THE BATTLE OF SHILOH.—VALLEY OF DEATH.—A WALL OF IRON.—GRANT PRAISES SHERMAN'S HEROISM. 206

CHAPTER XIV.

GENERAL SHERMAN'S GRAPHIC DESCRIPTION OF THE BATTLE OF SHILOH 236

CONTENTS.

CHAPTER XV.

THRILLING PEN-PICTURE OF THE BATTLE OF SHILOH BY AN ARMY SURGEON 254

CHAPTER XVI.

GENERAL SHERMAN'S ACHIEVEMENTS AT VICKSBURG . . 270

CHAPTER XVII.

SHERMAN'S SUPERB VALOR AT CHATTANOOGA 314

CHAPTER XVIII.

GENERAL SHERMAN'S FASCINATING STORY OF THE BATTLE OF CHATTANOOGA 357

CHAPTER XIX.

THE GREAT ATLANTA CAMPAIGN.—GRAND FORWARD MOVEMENT 393

CHAPTER XX.

FROM ATLANTA TO THE SEA.—THE FAMOUS MARCH . . . 417

CHAPTER XXI.

BRILLIANT CAMPAIGN OF THE CAROLINAS 450

CHAPTER XXII.

SURRENDER OF JOHNSTON TO SHERMAN.—CAPTURE OF FIFTY THOUSAND MEN 469

CONTENTS.

BOOK III.

CHAPTER XXIII.

FATAL ILLNESS.—THE GIANT SHORN OF HIS STRENGTH.—ANXIETY THROUGHOUT THE NATION 481

CHAPTER XXIV.

BATTLING WITH THE FOE.—A GALLANT FIGHT FOR LIFE . . 490

CHAPTER XXV.

THE STRUGGLE ENDED.—THE GREAT WARRIOR'S LAST BATTLE 503

CHAPTER XXVI.

A NATION IN MOURNING.—TRIBUTES OF LOVE AND RESPECT . 514

CHAPTER XXVII.

FINAL OBSEQUIES OF GENERAL SHERMAN.—GRAND PROCESSION OF TROOPS AND CIVIC BODIES 529

CHAPTER XXVIII.

GLOWING EULOGIES UPON THE WORLD-RENOWNED COMMANDER 548

PORTRAITS OF SHERMAN AND SOME OF HIS COMMANDERS.

BOOK I.

STORY OF GENERAL SHERMAN'S LIFE AND DEEDS.

CHAPTER I.

A Remarkable Family.—The Illustrious Commander's Early Life and Struggles.—Born to be a Hero.

A PATRIOTIC American, a wise, brave, skilful soldier, a sincere, earnest, friendly man, GENERAL SHERMAN died honored and beloved by numberless personal friends and by millions of his countrymen. In a sense broader than that of a military genius, General Sherman was a great man. He showed in his war correspondence that he had the learning of the scholar and the wisdom of the statesman. Such men do not die; they pass on from among their surviving old comrades of camp and field to a grander life, to the reward of men who are good and great.

Like Grant, Meade, and Sheridan, General Sherman had not only military genius; he had the highest qualities of a citizen of the great Republic. He entered the service of his country as one who was willing, if need be, to die. He gave it no half-hearted, halting service, and the mighty energy he so continuously displayed on the march and in the assault was as much the inspiration of his loyal heart as of his alert mind and vigorous body.

A Brilliant Record.

Sherman's education was unusually liberal and comprehensive before the war began. He was graduated from the West Point Military Academy with distinction; he served in the army with credit and usefulness as second and as first lieutenant and as captain. Subsequently resigning his commission, he became a banker and lawyer, and still later on a railroad president and the superintendent of the Louisiana State Military Institute; which latter position he resigned, when Louisiana seceded from the Union, in a letter that was in the highest degree creditable to his honor and patriotism. He was nearly forty-one years old when the Civil War began, and was then in the fullest vigor of physical and mental health. His fine intelligence, his diverse education, his varied associations and intercourse with men of distinction in different walks of life, had peculiarly fitted him for the great work to which his country called him at the beginning of the war.

The story of his achievements is one of the most glorious and precious records of his country, and most conspicuous in it is that chapter of it known to his countrymen, to the admirers of military genius of all countries—the march through Georgia from the mountains to the sea. It was the grandeur of this great movement, the grandeur of its courage and of its results, which will render it forever remarkable.

No soldier of ancient or modern history more completely burned his bridges behind him than did Sherman when he marched out of Atlanta at the head of that great Union host, the objective point of which was the Atlantic Ocean, the purpose of which was to cut through the Confederacy in its most vital part, and to bring its chief support, the army of Lee, between two fires, that of Grant and Meade and that of Sherman. As it was planned, it was executed—without a single failure at any point. All that was anticipated from it was realized, and history wrote one of its most thrilling chapters that day when Sherman, turning his back upon the mountains, set out upon his march to the sea.

It is impossible to form any just estimate of the value of services such as this illustrious soldier rendered his country in its time of greatest need. He was one of those who stood as an impregnable fortress in defence of national unity. He offered to the cause of Union and freedom all that man has to offer —intellect, strength, and even that for which all things else will be freely sacrificed, life. General Sherman's was the genius of both planning and doing. He thought and he wrought with magnificent courage and effective skill for his country, and his efforts were crowned with success. In the sudden making of splendid names his name became one which inspired armies with confidence and assured the soldierly endeavor which achieved triumphs.

Such men are so truly great that their countrymen can only reverently salute them and resolve to keep their deeds in grateful remembrance as they pass from the world which was better for their living in it.

Sherman's Ancestors.

The Sherman family from which William Tecumseh Sherman sprang was of English descent. In the records of the British Museum there is an account of the Shermans of Laxley, in the county of Suffolk, dating as far back as 1616. There was another branch of the family in Dedham, Essex county. The first Sherman whose name is found recorded in this country was Edmond, who, with his three sons, Edmond, Samuel, and John, was at Boston before 1636. In the *History of Ancient Woodbury, Connecticut*, it is stated that Samuel Sherman, the Rev. John Sherman, and Captain John, his first cousin, arrived from Dedham in 1634. This Captain John was the ancestor of Roger Sherman, the signer of the Declaration of Independence. The Ohio Shermans trace their descent from Samuel Sherman and his brother John, the clergyman.

All these Shermans and their children were men of prominence in their respective places. They were justices, judges, commissioners, representatives in the Assembly, town-clerks—in fact, they were good office-seekers, lucky in getting what they wanted, and pretty deserving men generally. In religion they were rigid Presbyterians. In politics, when the struggle for independence came, they were rebels.

The Family Settles in Ohio.

When James Monroe became President in 1817, he made Lawyer Charles R. Sherman, of Norwalk, Conn., a collector of internal revenue. Two of his deputies robbed the Government, and involved him in financial embarrassment from which he never recovered. In the hope of bettering his condition he went West in 1821, leaving his wife behind him in Connecticut. A year later he sent for her, and under the escort of some friends and neighbors she travelled on horseback over the Alleghanies, holding her infant child on a pillow in front of her. The new home was in Lancaster, O. Mr. Sherman in a short time won great prominence as an able, eloquent, and judicious advocate.

His reputation soon extended over the entire State, and his practice was very large and fairly remunerative. In 1823, when he was only thirty-five years of age, the Legislature of Ohio elected him a judge of the Supreme Court.

This was upon the recommendation of his fellow-citizens, as follows:

"SOMERSET, OHIO, July 6, 1821.

" MAY IT PLEASE YOUR EXCELLENCY:

"We ask leave to recommend to your Excellency's favorable notice Charles R. Sherman, Esq., of Lancaster, as a man possessing in an eminent degree those qualifications so much to be desired in a judge of the Supreme Court.

"From a long acquaintance with Mr. Sherman we are happy to be able to state to your Excellency that our minds are led to the conclusion that that gentleman possesses a disposition noble and generous, a mind discriminating, comprehensive, and combining a heart pure, benevolent, and humane. Manners dignified, mild, and complaisant, and a firmness not to be shaken and of unquestioned integrity.

"But Mr. Sherman's character cannot be unknown to your Excellency, and on that acquaintance without further comment we might safely rest his pretensions.

"We think we hazard little in assuring your Excellency that his appointment would give almost universal satisfaction to the citizens of Perry county."

He was soon after appointed a judge of the Supreme Court, and served in that capacity to the day of his death. Admirably fitted for the bench, his written opinions prove that he possessed a fine legal mind. His manner was kind and considerate, and to know him was to be his friend. The salary attached to the office was barely sufficient to support himself and his large family, so that when he suddenly died at Lebanon, O., June 24, 1829, in the noon of his fame and at the age of forty-one, those dependent on him were almost totally unprovided for, and the family was suddenly thrown on its own resources.

In this emergency the relatives and friends of her

husband came to the assistance of the widow and her eleven children. Two of them were adopted by an aunt. John, afterward United States Senator and ex-Secretary of the Treasury, went to live with an uncle, and Thomas Ewing, who had then been United States Senator and Secretary of the Treasury, took William Tecumseh into his family and educated him as one of his own children.

Adopted by Mr. Ewing.

The story of the adoption is interesting. Mr. Ewing, who was not only a warm friend, but also a distant relative of Judge Sherman, drove across the country to the Sherman home as soon as he heard of the death. He knew the family was large, that they were very poor, and he resolved to take one of the children until the fortunes of the house grew brighter. Mrs. Sherman was unable to decide which one of the little ones to surrender. After a tearful consultation she and her eldest daughter accompanied Mr. Ewing out of doors, where the boys were romping on the grass.

"Well," said Mr. Ewing, "which one of 'em shall I take? They all look alike to me."

The distressed mother was still unable to decide, when the daughter, snatching up one of them in her arms and holding him out, said, "Well, Mr. Ewing, if you must take one, take 'Cump,' because he is the smartest."

"All right, then—'Cump' it is," said Mr. Ewing, taking the child in his arms and placing him in his carriage. Mr. Ewing took him to his family, and, says General Sherman, "ever after treated me as his own son.". "Cump" was then nine years of age, having been born in Lancaster, February 8, 1820. His father knew and admired the Indian chief Tecumseh, which accounts for his middle name.

Young Sherman was sent to the Lancaster Academy by his benefactor. It was the best educational establishment in the place—as good a school, in fact, as any in Ohio at the time. He studied all the ordinary branches, including Latin, Greek, and French. The years passed on, and one day a note came from Senator Ewing, who was in Washington, notifying him to prepare for the Military Academy at West Point. Previous to this, however, Sherman was allowed in 1834 to work during that fall and the following spring as rodman for a surveyor who was making surveys for a canal to connect with the great Ohio one at Carroll, eight miles above Lancaster. He was paid a silver half-dollar for each day's actual work, and this was the first money he earned.

MAJOR-GENERAL HENRY W. SLOCUM.

CHAPTER II.

Education at West Point.—Chasing Savage Seminoles in the South.

DURING the autumn and spring of 1835-36 young Sherman worked hard studying mathematics and French, the chief requisites for admission to West Point. The letter of appointment came early in 1836 from the Secretary of War, Mr. Poinsett. Sherman made the journey to Washington to see Mr. Ewing. A week was spent at the capital. General Jackson was then at the height of his power, and General Sherman has left it on record how he spent an hour looking through the wooden railings which then ran around the White House at "Old Hickory" as he walked up and down inside. In less than thirty years his own fame as a soldier was destined to surpass that of the hero of New Orleans.

The start for the academy was made, and on June 12 he stepped, in New York, on board the steamer Cornelius Vanderbilt, and finished the last stage of his journey.

He joined the class of 1836 and went through the regular course of four years, graduating in June, 1840, No. 6 in a class of forty-three. The class originally was more than one hundred. "At the academy," says the general, "I was not considered a good soldier, for at no time was I selected for any office, but remained a private throughout the whole four years. Then, as now, neatness in dress and form, with a strict conformity to the rules, were the qualifications required for office, and I suppose I was found not to excel in any of these. In studies I always held a respectable reputation with the professors, and generally ranked among the best, especially drawing, chemistry, mathematics, and natural philosophy. My average demerits per annum were about one hundred and fifty, which reduced my final class standing from No. 4 to No. 6."

Early Service in the South.

After graduation and the usual three months' furlough he was commissioned second lieutenant in the Third Artillery, and ordered to report the following September at Governor's Island in New York harbor. There he was placed in command of a company of recruits preparing for service in Florida. In less than a month the company, with three others, was ordered to Savannah, Ga. They embarked in a sailing vessel for that port, where they were transferred to a small steamer and taken to St. Augustine, Fla. General Taylor was then in command in Florida, with headquarters at Tampa Bay.

The Third Artillery, Sherman's regiment, occupied the posts along the Atlantic coast from St. Augustine to Key Biscayne, his own company being stationed at Fort Pierce, on the Indian River. He was detached from the company of recruits and joined his own command. In November preparations were be-

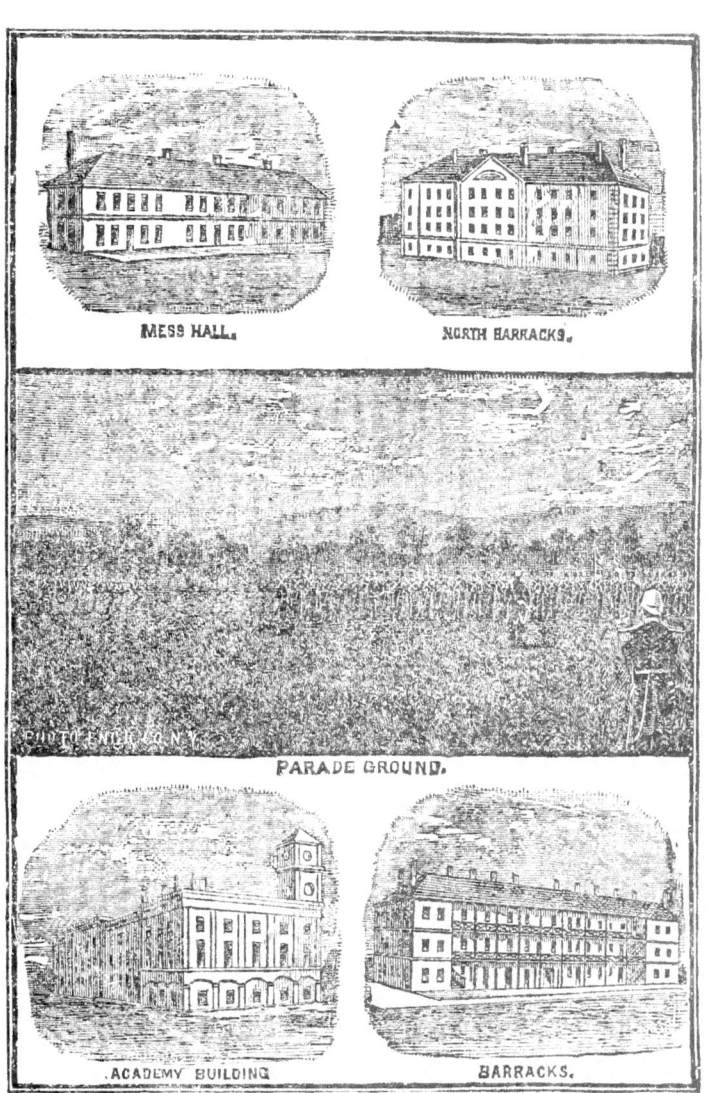

AT WEST POINT.

gun for active operations against the Indians, the object being to catch the scattered bands of Seminoles then on the Peninsula and send them to join their tribe in the newly-established Indian Territory. The life was not without its perils. The Indians did not want to leave, and frequently offered resistance with disastrous consequences to themselves as well as to the military

First Promotion.

In November, 1841, Sherman received his first promotion, being made the first lieutenant of Company G. He left Fort Pierce and joined his new command at St. Augustine. Shortly afterward he was placed in command of a detachment of twenty men at Picolata, on the St. John's River. He remained there only a few months, having been ordered on duty which took him to Pensacola. Thence he was sent to Fort Morgan, Mobile Point.

He was now quartermaster and commissary. The following June found him in Fort Moultrie, the regiment having been changed from the Gulf posts to those on the Atlantic. "We remained at Fort Moultrie," says General Sherman, "nearly five years, until the Mexican war scattered us for ever. Our life there was of strict garrison duty, with plenty of leisure for hunting and social entertainment. We soon formed many and most pleasant acquaintances in the city of Charleston, and it soon happened that many of the families resided at Sullivan's Island in the summer season, where we could reciprocate the hospitalities

FORT MOULTRIE.

extended to us in the winter." This life was interrupted by a brief leave of absence in 1843, which he spent in Ohio and in visiting some of the principal Southern cities.

First March through Georgia.

An order came from the War Department at Washington in January, 1844, which, curiously enough, took him through the country over which he was in after years to sweep at the head of a conquering army on one of the most famous expeditions in all military history—the "march to the sea." It was a detail to assist Colonel Churchill, the inspector-general of the army, in taking depositions in Upper Georgia and Alabama concerning certain losses by volunteers in Florida of horses and equipment by reason of the failure of the United States to provide sufficient forage, and for which Congress had made an appropriation.

The order directed him to go to Marietta, where Churchill was conducting the investigation. It was all over in two months, when Sherman rode south on horseback by way of Rome, Allatoona, Marietta, Atlanta, Madison, and Augusta, Ga. "Thus, by a mere accident," says Sherman, "I was enabled to traverse on horseback the very ground where, in after years, I had to conduct vast armies and fight great battles. That the knowledge thus acquired was of infinite use to me, and consequently to the Government, I have always felt and stated."

Meets with an Accident.

In the winter of 1844 his right shoulder was dislocated by the fall of his horse while hunting deer on the Cooper River. He suffered severely, and spent a short leave of absence which was allowed him in the North. He was back in Fort Moultrie by March, 1845. Congress had about this time passed a joint resolution providing for the annexation of Texas, then an independent republic, and the army and the country looked for an immediate war with Mexico. General Taylor had assembled some regiments of infantry and one of dragoons at Fort Jessup, La., and the orders from Washington were that he should extend military protection to Texas against the Indians or a "foreign country" when the terms of annexation were agreed to. The terms were accepted in July, and he moved his troops to Corpus Christi, at which point during the summer and fall of 1845 was concentrated the army that in the spring of the following year was to begin the Mexican War.

CHAPTER III.

A Recruiting Officer.—Stirring Times in California.

A COMPANY of Sherman's regiment was ordered from Fort Moultrie to Corpus Christi, but it was not his, and before the other companies were directed to follow Sherman was detached for recruiting service, May 1, 1846. That detail took him out of the Mexican War and deprived him of the promotion it brought to so many. Perhaps it also preserved him for the greater work he was to do. The recruiting order brought him back again to Governor's Island. The Pittsburgh district was given to him, and he took up his headquarters at the St. Charles Hotel in that city early in May. Recruits were in very active demand, and he was authorized to open a sub-rendezvous at Zanesville, Ohio.

He had been at Pittsburgh only a few weeks when the stirring news of the battle of Palo Alto excited the entire country. "That I should be on recruiting service," says Sherman, "when my comrades were actually fighting was intolerable, and I hurried to my post at Pittsburgh. I wrote to the adjutant-general at Washington, asking him to consider me as an applicant for any active service, and saying that I would willingly forego the recruiting detail, which I well knew plenty of others would jump at. Impatient to approach the scene of active operations, without authority—and, I suppose, wrongfully—I left my corporal in charge of the rendezvous, and took all the recruits I had made in a steamboat to Cincinnati, turning them over to Major N. C. McCrea, commanding at Newport Barracks. I then reported to Cincinnati, where the superintendent of the Western recruiting service inquired by what authority I had come away from my post. I argued that I took it for granted he wanted all the recruits he could get to forward to the army, and did not know but that he might want me to go along. Instead of appreciating my volunteer zeal, he cursed and swore at me for leaving my post without orders, and told me to go back to Pittsburgh."

He went back, and the following June received orders relieving him from the recruiting business, and assiging him to Company F, then under orders for California. This brought him once more to Governor's Island.

Early Days in California.

Over in Brooklyn the United States storeship Lexington was then being fitted out for the long journey around Cape Horn to California. The Lexington at last was ready, in July, 1846, and they sailed. Among that party of officers were Ord and Halleck. It was a slow, tedious voyage. The first port made was Rio de Janeiro, at the end of sixty days. They had a good time on shore for a week, seeing Dom Pedro and his then young empress, the daughter of the king of Sicily. Throne and empress have passed away, and only Dom Pedro himself remains, the last perhaps of all.

The Lexington resumed her voyage, and in October saw the snows of the Cape. In sixty days from Rio, Valparaiso was reached. There they heard news about the war, the events of which up to that time had been a sealed volume. At last, about the middle of January, the California coast began to loom up, and when the high mountains about Santa Cruz came in view a boat with Lieutenant Henry Wise, master of the Independence frigate, that they had left at Valparaiso, came alongside. He told them that California had broken out into insurrection; that General Kearney had reached the country and been beaten in a severe battle; and much else which was not strictly fact.

Ready to Fight.

When the old Lexington dropped anchor in the Bay of Monterey, Jan. 26, 1847, after a voyage of two less than two hundred days from New York, all on board were ready to fight at once. But when they went on shore, nothing could be more peaceful then Monterey. No fighting was necessary. Sherman was then quartermaster and commissary, and he had abundance of work on his hands for a few weeks. But he soon had leisure enough, and he employed it in learning something about the country in which the chances of war, although it was all peace to him, had thrown him. Sherman was not making much history then, but the vivid story of the scenes and incidents in those distant California days which he tells shows that if he was denied the chance to make history, he knew how to write it.

Making Surveys.

Sherman was acting assistant adjutant-general of the Department of California until February, 1849, when he was transferred to San Francisco on similar duty on the staff of General Persifer Smith, commanding the Division of the Pacific. There was very little to do, and General Smith encouraged Sherman and two or three other officers to go into any business that would enable them to make money. Sherman made a contract to survey Colonel J. D. Stevenson's newly-projected city, which was to be called "New York of the Pacific," at the mouth of the San Joaquin River. The contract embraced also the making of soundings and the marking out of a channel through Suisun Bay. For this work he got five hundred dollars and ten or fifteen lots. Sherman sold enough lots to make an additional five hundred dollars, "and," he tells us, "let the balance go, for the 'City of New York of the Pacific' never came to anything."

Subsequently he made a bargain with a Mr. Hartnett to survey his ranch at Consumnees River in the Sacramento Valley. General Ord was associated with him in this work. It took about a month to make this survey, which, when finished, was duly plotted, and for it they received one-tenth of the land or two sub-divisions. Sherman by the sale of the land subsequently realized three thousand dollars. Ord and he did some work for a man named Dailor, who paid them five hundred dollars a day for the party. He invested these earnings in Sacramento City lots, on which he made fair profit.

General Smith had promised Sherman that he would send him East the first opportunity, and the chance came in December, 1849. Smith was in Oregon, and from there he sent despatches to Sherman, to be delivered in person to General Winfield Scott, who was then in New York. He came back by way of Panama. Scott questioned him closely, he says, in regard to affairs on the Pacific coast, and "startled me with the assertion that 'our country was on the eve of a terrible civil war.' He interested me by anecdotes of my old army comrades in his recent battles around the city of Mexico, and I felt deeply the fact that our country had passed through a foreign war, that my comrades had fought great battles, and yet I had not heard a hostile shot. Of course I thought it the last and only chance in my day and that my career as a soldier was at an end."

Sent to Washington by General Scott.

By order of Scott, Sherman went to Washington to lay before Secretary of War Crawford the despatches he had brought from California. He found Mr. Ewing Secretary of the Interior, and of course his position was in every way assured. Crawford, he says, questioned him on California, but he seemed to be interested in the country chiefly as it related to slavery and the route through Texas. The President, Zachary Taylor, whom he had never met, although he had served under him in Florida in 1840-41, received him with great kindness, told him that he had heard his name mentioned with praise, and that he would be pleased to do him any act of favor. A few years before, if he had spoken these words to the recruiting officer at Pittsburgh, he would have promptly asked him to take him with him into Mexico.

Very wonderful stories are told of these old days in California. Persons are now living who can remember well when gold was first discovered, and how the gold fever swept like wild-fire over the country. Men left home, family, friends, and all their pleasant surroundings in the East to make their fortunes on the Pacific coast. The country was in a craze; men were mad to obtain sudden fortunes.

Eager for Gold.

Life in California at that time was of course rough and wild. Men were their own diggers; hands that had never been hardened by work grew rough by handling the spade; wherever there was gold to be had, a whole host was after it; some men made fortunes, and many others lost the little fortune they had acquired in the East in the vain endeavor to obtain a larger one in the West.

Sherman's life at this time, since it brought him into contact with all grades of men, was well calculated to prepare him for his future career in the service of the

United States. It is particularly important that a general should have a knowledge of men, should know the interests by which they are influenced, and should be able to control them at his will. Only a man of experience who has seen a great deal of the world can do this. One thing is particularly to be noted, however; which is, that General Sherman did not in California make a fortune for himself. However rich the diggings might be, he was not himself a " digger."

Men slept on the ground, and even during the rainy season the sky was their only covering. As a soldier in the service of the United States he had only those comforts which soldiers obtain in the field. The life of a soldier is hard anyway, and the only wonder is that during his brief stay in California Sherman did not break down under it. He was possessed, however, of an iron constitution, which served him admirably through his long life. The fibre of which he was made was oak, not basswood.

A Fine City.

What a contrast between the California of to-day and the California of forty years ago! Now the wave of civilization, sweeping westward, has struck the Golden Gate. San Francisco, one of the great cities of the Republic, has its inviting streets, lofty mercantile establishments, costly public buildings, schools, churches, and financial institutions, and in some respects is the foremost city in the land. At the time when Sherman traversed the vales and climbed the mountains of the country all this was but a dream, if any one dreamed it at all.

As an instance of the kind of life United States officers and soldiers led there, Sherman relates that the servants whom General Smith had brought from New Orleans, and who had pledged their word that they would remain with him faithfully for a year, deserted him one after another. The ladies were left without maid or attendant, and, says Sherman, with an exquisite touch of humor, "The general commanding all the mighty forces of the United States on the Pacific coast had to scratch to get one good meal a day for his family." There was no regular time for breakfast, dinner, or supper; breakfast could generally be had by twelve o'clock, and "dinner according to circumstances," which circumstances varied from day to day, so that the most uncertain thing was the dinner, as no one knew when it was coming nor what it was to be composed of when it did come.

We have been more particular to refer to this experience of Sherman on the Pacific coast in order to bring out the varying struggles of his earlier days. If he had been the scion of wealth he would never have been the world-renowned commander. He was to be a self-made man; he was to make his own way in the world; he was to master the world—was to put the world proudly beneath his feet; he was to rise above men, stretch out his arm over them and give them command, and his early experience qualified him for his magnificent career.

CHAPTER IV.

General Sherman's Romantic Marriage.—A Banker in California and New York.—Becomes a Lawyer.

SHERMAN applied for leave of absence from army duty, which was, of course, immediately granted. His first visit was to the mother whose poverty had compelled her to surrender him so many years before to Mr. Ewing. She was then living at Mansfield, Ohio. All through these years, while he was in Florida and California, they had been in constant correspondence, and he contributed handsomely toward the support of the family. He returned to Washington, and on May 1, 1850, he was married to his old playmate, Miss Ellen Boyle Ewing, the daughter of the man of whom he was the adopted child.

The marriage ceremony was attended by a large and distinguished company. Daniel Webster, Henry Clay, Thomas H. Benton, President Taylor, and the entire Cabinet were among the guests. The ceremony took place at the residence of Mr. Ewing, the old house subsequently owned by Francis P. Blair, on Pennsylvania avenue, opposite the old War Department. The wedding-tour took the young officer— then only thirty years old—and his bride to Baltimore,

ADMIRAL DAVID D. PORTER

New York, Niagara, and Ohio. They returned to Washington in July.

Taylor's death followed in a few days, and Sherman attended the funeral as an aide-de-camp at the request of the adjutant-general of the army. Sherman's rank at this time was only that of first lieutenant of the Third Artillery. In the following September he joined his command at Jefferson Barracks, Mo. He had not been there very long when Congress increased the commissary department by four new captains, and he was made one of them. He was ordered to St. Louis, where he relieved Captain A. J. Smith of the First Dragoons. His commission bore date September 27, 1850. Sherman resided in St. Louis during the year 1851, and in the summer of 1852 his family went to Lancaster, but he remained at his post. In September, 1852, he was ordered to New Orleans, where he remained until March, 1853. He then obtained six months' leave of absence, and resigned from the army September 6, 1853, to engage in the banking business in San Francisco.

From Barracks to Banks.

Sherman sent his family to Ohio, and started for California alone by way of Nicaragua. The captain of the vessel lost his reckoning, and at the end of eighteen days out the ship struck a reef north of San Francisco, the engines stopped, and although it was four o'clock in the morning, the decks were soon crowded with terrified passengers. The sea was calm, and the ship, being already on the bottom, could not sink. The passengers were soon taken on shore and huddled on the beach under a bluff. Sherman started off to make an examination of the country and find out, if possible, where they were. He learned that the ship had struck at Bantinas Creek, and that a schooner was only waiting for the tide to sail to San Francisco. Sherman sent back word to the captain that he would go to San Francisco on the schooner and send assistance. The schooner had not been many hours at sea, however, when she was struck by a squall which sent her over on her side. Sherman, among the others, found himself in the water, but they all managed to escape. He was picked up by a passing boat. Finally, he got to San Francisco, but if the weather had been stormy the chances are that he could never have reached shore.

Bank Failure.

After making all the investigations he desired about the proposed banking business, he returned to New York about July, 1853, and proceeded to Lancaster, O., where his family was living. He explained the offer that had been made, the prospects of success, and other matters connected with the enterprise. Having completed arrangements, he resigned from the army, to take effect six months later. With his family he left New York in September for San Juan del Norte. He had then only one child, Lizzie, who at the time was less than a year old. They reached San Francisco safely on October 15. The ex-soldier now plunged into all the mysteries of banking.

A BANKER.

The banking-house of Page, Bacon & Co. soon became involved in trouble, and there was a run on the San Francisco branch. The failure, of course, involved all the other banks in the city, and the Sherman institution was no exception. This was in 1855. When the doors of the Sherman house were opened one morning, in rushed the crowd. Several gentlemen asked if their money was safe, and on being assured that it was they went away satisfied. Before the day closed seventy-five thousand dollars in gold bullion were paid out, and the bank was kept open until the usual hour for closing, meeting all demands upon it. It still had a respectable amount left. The run was continued the next day, and finally it weathered the crisis and was left with a standing of the very first class. Finally in 1855–56 business in California became depressed. A great many enterprises failed. Foreign capital was withdraw, and, on the suggestion of Sherman, Mr. Lucas gradually drew out of the business, settling all demands and giving due notice to depositors. The house closed in April, 1857, having transacted its business in an honorable way from first to last.

The Old "Vigilance" Days.

Sherman bore a very prominent part in the disorders that arose in San Francisco about this time and which led to the establishment of the Vigilance Committee. But he was on the side of law and order, believing that the courts were abundantly able to purge the city of crime, and that all that was required was a vigorous execution of the law. The governor, Johnson, consulted him about the reorganization of the militia, and offered him a commission as major-general of the second division of militia, which embraced the city of San Francisco. Sherman accepted at first, but while volunteers were numerous enough, there were no arms for them. In this emergency efforts were made to induce General John E. Wood to loan some of the Government rifles. He at first promised, but failed to keep his engagement. Sherman made many unsuccessful efforts to stop the high-handed action of the Vigilance Committee, but finally withdrew from the struggle and allowed things to take their course.

A Banker in New York.

After closing the bank, Sherman, on May 1, 1857, left San Francisco with his family, by way of Panama, for New York. It had been arranged that a branch bank of the St. Louis house was to be established there, with Sherman in charge. Mr. Lucas, Major Turner, and he met in New York in July to make the necessary preparations. An office was rented at No. 12 Wall street, furniture was bought, and a teller, bookkeeper, and porter hired. The new firm was to bear the name of Lucas, Turner & Co. The office was opened July 21, 1857, and at once began to receive accounts from the West and from California. Sherman went to live at No. 100 Prince street.

The Metropolitan Bank and Bank of America were institutions at that time of good repute in New York, and with these he established business relations. For a time prosperity crowned his efforts and his financial success appeared to be assured. The struggles through which he had passed in years gone by, and the misfortunes which had attended some of his ventures, seemed to be over. This, as has already been remarked, was in the year 1857, which was memorable for the greatest financial panic our country ever saw. As a certain Friday which destroyed magnificent fortunes in Wall street has been called "Black Friday," so 1857 might be called the black year.

Financial Disaster.

Suddenly, like a thunderbolt falling from a clear sky, on the 21st of August the failure of the Ohio Life and Trust Company was announced; Wall street was instantly convulsed and the city was in a panic; with terrible swiftness the panic extended from New York to every part of the country. Men went to bed thinking they were rich, and waked up to find they were poor. Colossal fortunes were swept away as the frail cottages in the valley of Johnstown were carried like chips before the awful flood.

General Sherman says the panic was so much like similar ones he had witnessed in San Francisco, that for a time he felt no alarm, considering that he had nothing very valuable at stake. He was simply amused, but the turn of affairs assumed a serious aspect, and affected him as it did all others in the community. Western stocks and securities shrank to almost worthless figures, so that the banks which held them and had borrowed money on them were forced to pay their indebtedness at once or substitute other collaterals of increased value.

Startling News.

The house with which General Sherman was connected was not indebted to parties in New York at all, but its correspondents in the West were deeply involved, and felt extremely anxious concerning their interests, and looked to General Sherman to protect them. Early in September the New York banks were threatened, having caught the general alarm, and grave fears were entertained for their safety.

In the very midst of this panic came the news that the steamer Central America, formerly the George Law, with six hundred passengers and about one million six hundred thousand dollars of treasure, coming from Aspinwall, had foundered at sea off the coast of Georgia, and that about sixty of the passengers had been providentially picked up by a Swedish bark and brought into Savannah. The absolute loss of this treasure went to swell the confusion and panic of the day.

All efforts to save the banks were unsuccessful; the whole country was in the grasp of financial failure. No man lost a single cent by the banking-house with which Sherman was connected, which speaks volumes for the integrity of those who managed its affairs.

After helping to straighten matters out in New York and St. Louis, Sherman again went to San Francisco to see what he could do in the way of collecting old debts due himself and the firm. He advertised that the notes held would be sold at auction and that the real estate would be sold. Having collected all that was possible to be collected, he sailed for home. He got back to Lancaster July 28, 1858, free in every way, but confronted with the serious problem of finding some means of supporting a wife and four children.

A Kansas Lawyer.

He conferred with Mr. Ewing and others as to what he should do—this man who was to be the great soldier of the Republic less than six years later. He wanted to be independent if he could. There were coal and salt mines belonging to Mr. Ewing at Chauncey, O., but Sherman was not attracted toward that part of Ohio. Two of the Ewing boys were at Leavenworth, Kan., where they and their father had bought a good deal of land, some in the town and the greater portion back in the country. Mr. Ewing offered Sherman the management of his interest in the speculation, and the boys were willing to give him an equal copartnership in the law firm. He accepted the offer and was admitted to the bar, not by examination, but on the ground of general intelligence.

On the first day of the new year, 1859, another partner was admitted into the firm, which became Sherman, Ewing & McCook. Business continued to grow, but the income was hardly large enough for the three partners, and Sherman consented to look out for something more permanent and profitable. That spring he undertook to open a farm on a large tract forty miles from Leavenworth for the benefit of Mr. Ewing's grand-nephew, Henry Clark, and his grand-niece, Mrs. Walker. There was only a little money in it, but it helped to pass away the time.

Manager of a Military Academy.

In June, 1859, Sherman sent a note to Major D. C. Buell, assistant-adjutant general, inquiring if there was a vacancy among the paymasters or if he could suggest any other military employment. Floyd was then Secretary of War. Buell sent Sherman the programme of a military college which was about to be organized in Louisiana, and advised him to apply for the position of superintendent. Sherman at once addressed a letter to Governor R. C. Wickliffe at Baton Rouge, La. In July, 1859, Governor Wickliffe notified him that he had been elected superintendent of the proposed college, and asking him to come to Louisiana as soon as possible, as they were anxious to put the college into operation.

"For this honorable position," says Sherman in telling the story of his life, "I was indebted to Major D. C. Buell and General G. Mason Graham. During the Civil War it was reported and charged that I owed my position to the personal friendship of Generals Bragg and Beauregard, and that in taking up arms against the South I had been guilty of a breach of hospitality and friendship. I was not indebted to General Bragg, because he himself told me that he was not even aware that I was an applicant, and had favored the selection of Major Jenkins, another West Point graduate. General Beauregard had nothing whatever to do with the matter."

Sherman reported to Governor Wickliffe, who by virtue of his position was the president of the board of supervisors of the new institution, in the autumn of 1859. The college buildings were near Alexandria, in the parish of Rapides. It was a large and handsome house, surrounded by about four hundred acres of pine lands, with numerous springs. The institution was opened with a good staff of professors January 1, 1860. A series of by-laws for its government had been drawn up and the title of the "Louisiana Seminary of Learning and Military Academy" was given to it. The title grew out of the original grant by Congress of a certain township of public land, to be sold by the State and dedicated to the use of a "seminary of learning."

Sixty cadets appeared on the day of the opening, and everything started on pretty much the same lines as at West Point, but without uniforms or muskets. During the first term there were seventy-three cadets, of whom nearly sixty passed the examination in July, 1860. Defects were found in the act of incorporation, and the legislature, at the suggestion of Sherman, amended it. Handsome appropriations were made for the support of the cadets, the erection of new buildings and the purchase of scientific apparatus. The seminary was made a State arsenal, and was placed in a fair way toward efficiency and prosperity.

CHAPTER V

Prophet and Patriot.—Advice to the War Department Treated as a Proof of Insanity.

SHERMAN, however, could not be happy away from the tap of the drum. As stated, he was made president of the Louisiana State Military Academy with a salary of five thousand dollars, and he stayed there until Louisiana's talk of secession roused his ire, and then penned the following sharp and patriotic letter:

JAN. 18, 1861.

GOVERNOR THOMAS O. MOORE, Baton Rouge, La.:

SIR: As I occupy a *quasi*-military position under this State, I deem it proper to acquaint you that I accepted such position when Louisiana was a State in the Union, and when the motto of the seminary was inserted in marble over the main door: "By the liberality of the General Government of the United States—the Union, *Esto perpetua.*" Recent events foreshadow a great change, and it becomes all men to choose. If Louisiana withdraws from the Federal Union, I prefer to maintain my allegiance to the old Constitution as long as a fragment of it survives, and my longer stay here would be wrong in every sense of the word. In that event I beg you will send or appoint some authorized agent to take charge of the

GENERAL GEORGE B. McCLELLAN.

arms and munitions of war here belonging to the State, or direct me what disposition should be made of them. And furthermore, as president of the board of supervisors I beg you to take immediate steps to relieve me as superintendent the moment the State determines to secede, for on no earthly account will I do any act or think any thought hostile to or in defiance of the old Government of the United States.

With great respect, etc.,

W. T. SHERMAN.

His resignation was accepted, and he removed to St. Louis. Pending the dreadful days of doubt between the inauguration of President Lincoln and the firing upon Sumter, Sherman was at Washington, a close observer of affairs. He held a position as superintendent of a street railway in St. Louis at a salary of two thousand dollars, but his heart was in mightier things than transportation and he was ready to obey the first call of duty.

He Meets with a Cool Reception.

It came in the spring and found Sherman waiting. He met the fate which so often overtakes enthusiastic souls. The Secretary of War received him coldly, saying that he thought the ebullition of feeling would soon subside. Even President Lincoln did not then believe that the nation would be plunged into civil war.

"Humph!" said Sherman in his blunt way; "you might as well try to put out a fire with a squirt gun as expect to put down this rebellion with three months' troops."

He refused to go to Ohio for the purpose of raising three months' troops, declaring that the whole military power of the country should be called out at

ABRAHAM LINCOLN.

once to crush the rebellion in its incipiency. Well would it have been if his advice had been taken. It was worthy of consideration, for his residence in Louisiana had given him an inkling of the tremendous feeling in the South—a feeling which the authorities at Washington did not fully appreciate.

Sherman's patriotic ardor was at last rewarded, and he was appointed by General McDowell a colonel of the Thirteenth Infantry, regular army. At the battle of Bull Run he was in command of the Third brigade of the First division, and his command was the only one in that memorable defeat which retired from the field in good order. For his soldierly qualities in this battle he was promoted to the rank of brigadier-general of volunteers, and was ordered to join Anderson, the hero of Sumter, who was in command of the Department of the Ohio, with headquarters at Louisville. General Anderson's ill-health forced him to resign, and Sherman succeeded to the command.

Good Advice Disregarded.

The affairs of the department were in a bad way. Sherman applied for reinforcements. In reply to a question of Secretary Cameron as to the number of troops required for a successful advance, Sherman said that "to make a successful advance against the enemy—then strongly posted at all strategic points from the Mississippi to Cumberland Gap—would require an army two hundred thousand strong." For this reply he was adjuged to be "crazy." Being thus in discredit with the War Department, he asked to be relieved. General Buell succeeded him, and he retired to the command of Benton Barracks, near St. Louis.

Grant, who still had his spurs to win, stood by Sherman in his opinion, and the latter never forgot it. One day, shortly after the occupation of Savannah by Sherman, a prominent civilian approached Tecumseh and sought to win favor by disparaging Grant.

"It won't do, sir," said Sherman; "it won't do at all. Grant is a great general. He stood by me when I was crazy, and I stood by him when he was drunk, and now, by thunder, sir, we stand by each other."

Not so Crazy as Others.

Subsequent events proved that Sherman was again right and the authorities at Washington wrong. If the Confederates had made good use of their opportunities, General Buckner might have made good his boast of investing Louisville before winter.

What hurt Sherman more than to be called crazy was to have the details of a private conversation with Secretary Cameron and General Thomas, in which he fully reported the condition of his troops, amply repeated in the newspapers, thus giving the enemy invaluable information regarding the weakness of his position. The enemy took advantage of this knowledge, and Sherman was forced to employ strategy to hold his position. He recognized that he was in disfavor with the War Department, and had the good sense to retire from a conflict which must have proved disastrous to him and to the men under his command. Sherman was always a man of rare patience, and it never stood him in better stead than in this instance.

Saved the Day at Shiloh.

His opportunity came in the following year, 1862, when he was early called into the field and assigned to the command of the district of Cairo. In February his headquarters were at Paducah, Ky., and he rendered General Grant invaluable assistance in forwarding troops and supplies to the latter, who was operating on the Tennessee and Cumberland rivers. After the capture of Fort Donelson he was assigned to the command of the Fifth division of the Army of the Tennessee, Major-General Grant commanding.

In the battle of Shiloh he first displayed the hidden merit which, up to that time, had only met with the ridicule of his superiors.

General Grant, always generous in giving praise to those beneath him, paid this tribute to Sherman's work:

"To General Sherman I was greatly indebted for his promptness in forwarding to me, during the siege of Fort Donelson, reinforcements and supplies from Paducah. At the battle of Shiloh, on the last day, he held, with raw troops, the key-point of the landing. It is no disparagement to any other officer to say that I do not believe there was another division commander on the field who had the skill and experience to have done it. To his individual efforts I am indebted for the success of that battle."

Valor and Promotion.

General Halleck, in his despatch to the Secretary of War recommending General Sherman for promotion, said of him: "It is the unanimous opinion here that Brigadier-General W. T. Sherman saved the fortunes of the day on the 6th of April and contributed largely to the glorious victory of the 7th. He was in

MAJOR ANDERSON.

the thickest of the fight on both days, having three horses killed under him and being wounded twice. I respectfully request that he be made a major-general of volunteers, to date from the 6th instant."

With such glorious and gallant tributes as these, who will deny to William Tecumseh Sherman the meed of his deserts? The flaming torch of truth speaks from the battle-field. It is only when men are grown cold and selfish that the spirit of envy detracts from a man's true worth.

On the recommendation of General Halleck, General Sherman was promoted to be a major-general of volunteers, his rank dating from May 1, 1862. He next took part in the operations against Corinth, and his troops were the first to enter the enemy's works upon the morning of May 30.

Sherman's Plan of Campaign.

The summer of 1862 was passed in completely overrunning and subjecting that portion of Tennessee lying west of the Tennessee River. Sherman moved at the head of a column across the country toward Memphis. The city capitulated to the gunboats on June 6, and Sherman occupied it and assumed command July 22.

He found the city under a reign of terror, but his strong arm soon brought order out of chaos. The turbulent element was quelled and Union people in the city once more breathed free.

An interesting glimpse into Sherman's scheme of campaign was given by him in a speech delivered in

St. Louis in the summer of 1865. "Here in St. Louis, probably," he said, "began the great centre movement which terminated the war; a battle-field such as never before was seen, extending from ocean to ocean almost with the right wing and the left wing; and from the centre here. I remember one evening up in the old Planters' House sitting with General Halleck and General Cullum, and we were talking about this, that, and the other. A map was on the table, and I was explaining the position of the troops of the enemy in Kentucky, when I came to this State.

Halleck's Question.

"General Halleck knew well the position here, and I remember well the question he asked me—the question of the school-teacher to his child: 'Sherman, here is the line; how will you break that line?'—'Physically, by a perpendicular force.'—'Where is the perpendicular?'—'The line of the Tennessee River.' General Halleck is the author of that first beginning, and I give him credit for it with pleasure. Laying down his pencil upon the map, he said, 'There is the line, and we must take it.' The capture of the forts on the Tennessee River by the troops led by Grant followed.

"These were the grand strategic features of that first movement, and it succeeded perfectly. General Halleck's plan went farther—not to stop at his first line, which ran through Columbus, Bowling Green, crossing the river at Henry and Donelson, but to push on to the second line, which ran through Memphis and Charleston; but troubles intervened at Nashville and delays followed; opposition to the last movement was made, and I myself was brought an actor on the scene. I remember our ascent on the Tennessee River; I have seen to-night captains of steamboats who first went with us there; storms came and we did not reach the point we desired. At that time General C. F. Smith was in command. He was a man indeed. All the old officers remember him as a gallant and elegant officer, and had he lived probably some of us younger fellows would not have attained our present positions.

"We Fought and Held our Ground."

"We followed the line—the second line—and then came the landing of forces at Pittsburg Landing. Whether it was a mistake in landing them on the west instead of the east bank it is not necessary now to discuss. I think it was not a mistake. There was gathered the first great army of the West, commencing with only twelve thousand, then twenty thousand, then thirty thousand, and we had about thirty-eight thousand in that battle, and all I claim for that is that it was a contest for manhood. There was no strategy. Grant was there and others of us, all young at that time and unknown men, but our enemy was old, and Sidney Johnson, whom all the officers remembered as a power among the old officers, high above Grant, myself, or anybody else, led the enemy on the battle-field, and I almost wonder how we conquered. But, as I remarked, it was a contest for manhood—man to man—soldier to soldier. We fought and we held our

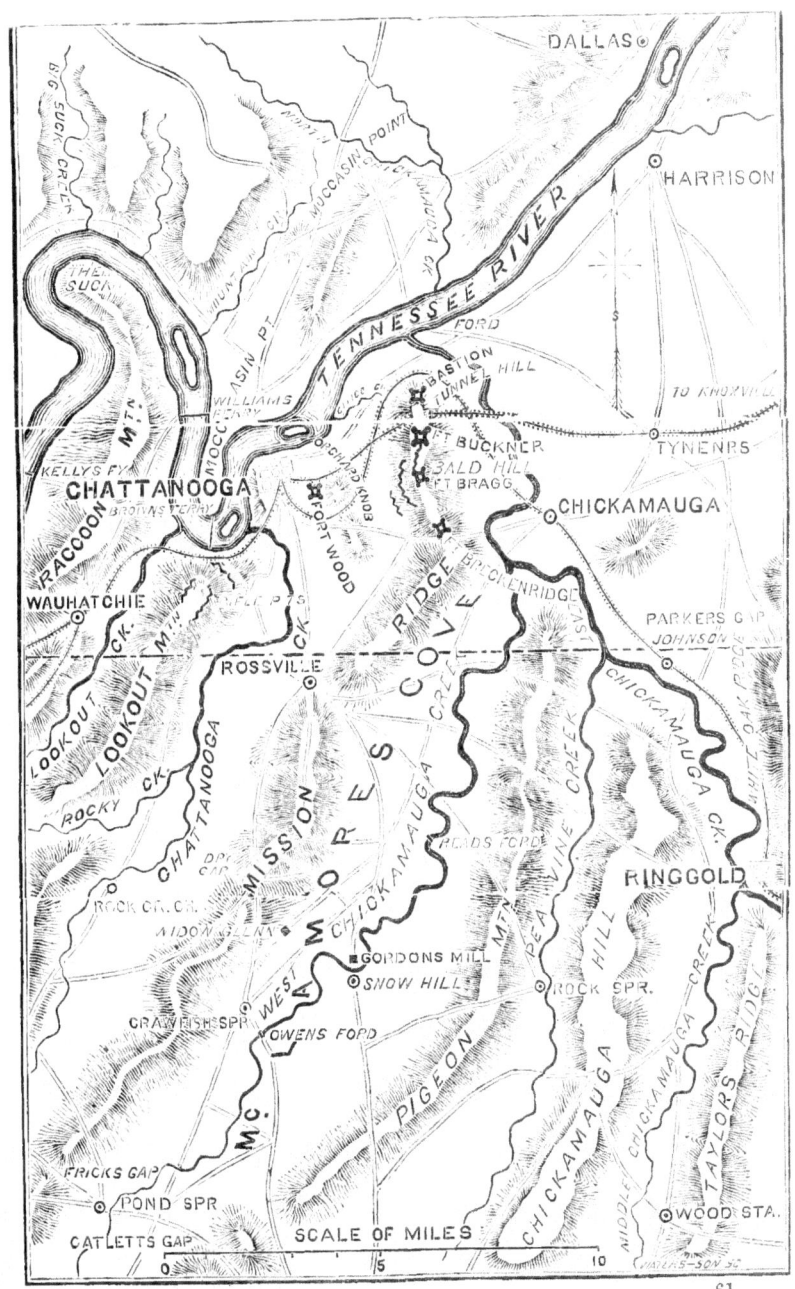

ground, and therefore accounted ourselves victorious. From that time forward we had with us the prestige; that battle was worth millions and millions to us by reason of the fact of the courage displayed by the brave soldiers on that occasion, and from that time to this I never heard of the first want of courage on the part of our Northern soldiers."

Sherman counted the war virtually ended when Vicksburg was taken and "the Mississippi ran unvexed to the sea;" but the Confederates would not have it so, and there had to be more fighting. Jefferson Davis had the Southerners well trained, and he refused to ratify the work of the Union armies, being vexatiously obstinate.

Movements aginst Vicksburg.

In November, Sherman was assigned to the command of the right wing of the Army of the Tennessee, and conducted an expedition threatening the enemy's rear south of the Tallahatchie River, and enabled General Grant to occupy the position without a fight. In December, he, having returned to Memphis, was assigned to the command of the Fifteenth army corps, still continuing, however, in the general command of the right wing of the army. In the middle of the same month he organized an expedition composed of the Thirteenth and Fifteenth corps, and moved down the Mississippi on transports, with a view to an attack upon Vicksburg from the Yazoo River, near Chickasaw Bayou and Haines' Bluff. The surrender of Holly Springs, Miss., enabling the enemy to concentrate at the point of attack, frustrated the efforts of the Union troops.

The terrible fighting of December 27th, 28th, and 29th settled the fact that the place could not be taken by storm, and the troops were withdrawn to consummate the glorious victory of Arkansas Post in Janu

GRANT'S HEADQUARTERS NEAR VICKSBURG.

ary, 1863. In this last action General Sherman was subordinate to General McClellan, having been assigned by that officer to the command of the right wing of the temporary Army of the Mississippi. Upon the concentration of troops preparatory to further movements against Vicksburg, General Sherman was stationed with his corps in the vicinity of

Young's Point. In March, 1863, he conducted the expedition up Steele's Bayou and released Admiral Porter's fleet of gunboats, which, having been cut off and invested by the enemy, was in imminent danger of being captured. This expedition was perhaps one of the most severe ever experienced by his troops. They penetrated through a country cut up by numerous and deep bayous and swamps and overgrown by immense forests of cottonwood and cypress. Sherman, with his usual determination, was not to be thwarted, and pushed ahead and accomplished his object.

CHAPTER VI.

Army of the Tennessee.—Sherman Co-operates with Grant.—Forward Movements.

Upon the inauguration of General Grant's movement across the Peninsula to Grand Gulf and Bruinsburg, during April, 1863, General Sherman made a feint upon Haines' Bluff, on the Yazoo River. His demonstration (April 26th and 29th) was intended to hold the enemy about Vicksburg while the main army was securing a foothold on the eastern shore of the Mississippi below. Having successfully performed this duty, by means of rapid and forced marches he moved down the Louisiana side of the river, crossed at Grand Gulf, and immediately pushed forward and rejoined General Grant's main army.

Sherman, with his corps, accompanied McPherson on his movement against Jackson, the capital of Mississippi. In the battle of Jackson, Sherman took no part, in consequence of the rout of the enemy being effected by McPherson's corps alone. The day after the battle McPherson hurried toward Baker's Creek, while Sherman remained in Jackson some hours longer to complete the destruction of the enemy's stores and the railroad. He then moved on a line parallel with the route of march of McPherson's column, crossed the Big Black River and took possession of Walnut Hills, near Vicksburg, on May 18th.

The occupation of this important position enabled General Grant to open communication with his dépôt of supplies on the Mississippi River, by way of Yazoo

GENERAL ULYSSES S. GRANT.

River, from Chickasaw Bayou. During the siege of Vicksburg, Sherman's corps held the left of General Grant's lines and co-operated in all the combined attacks of the centre and right. During the conference between the rebel commander Pemberton and General Grant in regard to the terms of capitulation for the garrison and city of Vicksburg. Sherman was vigorously engaged in organizing an expedition at the Big Black River. The plan was to carry the war into the enemy's country; hence the preparations for this expedition.

GENERAL JOE JOHNSTON.

No sooner had Vicksburg surrendered than he received orders to throw his force across the river and move out into the country. Vicksburg was occupied on the morning of the 4th of July. The same afternoon troops were converging from all parts of the old lines, and Sherman's advance had already crossed the Big Black.

Two days' march found Sherman investing Joe Johnston in Jackson. Before the beginning of August he engaged the enemy, and, defeating him severely, was about to close in upon his rear when the rebel commander very prudently withdrew.

For his great service in the military operations of 1863, Major-General Sherman was promoted to the rank of brigadier-general in the regular army, to date from July 4, 1863, and was confirmed by the United States Senate February 29, 1864.

Sherman Succeeds Grant.

Upon the assignment of General Grant to the command of the military division of the Mississippi, General Sherman succeeded, by authority of the President, to the command of the Department and Army of the Tennessee, to date from October 27, 1863. After making some necessary changes in the disposition of the troops on the Mississippi River, Sherman concentrated portions of the Fifteenth and Sixteenth corps at Corinth, and in the month of November moved, by way of Tuscumbia and Decatur, Ala., to join and participate with General Grant in his winter campaign against Chattanooga. General Sherman's forces moved up the north side of the Tennessee River, and during the nights of November 23d and 24th established pontoon-bridges and effected a lodgment on the south side, between Citico Creek and the Chickamauga River.

After the development of the plans along other portions of the lines, on the 24th Sherman carried the eastern end of Missionary Ridge up to the tunnel. On the next day the whole of Missionary Ridge, from Rossville to the Chickamauga, was carried after a series of desperate struggles. By the turning of the enemy's right and forcing it back upon Ringgold and Dalton, Sherman's forces were thrown between Bragg and Longstreet, completely severing the enemy's lines. No sooner was this end reached than Thomas and Hooker forced Bragg into Georgia, while Sherman, with his own and Granger's forces, moved off to the succor of Knoxville. Burnside, by a gallant defence of the position, held out against Longstreet, who upon the appearance of Sherman was obliged to raise the siege and effected his escape by withdrawing into Virginia. The enemy being defeated at every point, his army broken and his plans completely disarranged, and Grant's army in winter quarters, General Sherman personally left for Cairo, thence for Memphis, arriving in the beginning of January. After organizing a portion of the Sixteenth corps for the field, he despatched it upon transports to Vicksburg.

Pushes on to Vicksburg.

In the latter part of the month he joined it, and finished the organization of a fine body of troops, composed of portions of the Sixteenth army corps,

Major-General S. A. Hurlbut commanding, and the Seventeenth army corps, Major-General James B. McPherson commanding.

On the third of February the expeditionary army, commanded in person by Sherman, crossed the Big Black, and after continuous skirmishing along the route entered Meridian, Miss., February 14, 1864, driving Polk, with a portion of his army, toward Mobile, another portion toward Selma, and completely cutting off Lovell from the main army, pursuing him with cavalry northward toward Marion. Remaining in possession of Meridian four days, the railroads converging there were destroyed within a radius of twenty miles. The army then returned by a different route, reaching Canton, Miss., February 26.

Turning over the command of his army to McPherson, with instructions to devastate the country and then to continue the return march to Vicksburg, General Sherman, at eight o'clock the next morning, escorted by the Second Iowa Cavalry, pushed through in advance of the army, riding over sixty miles in twenty-four hours, and reached Vicksburg on the morning of February 28th. Remaining in the city but a few hours, he embarked on one of the boats of the Mississippi Marine brigade and left for New Orleans.

At the expiration of eight days he returned to Vicksburg, having during his absence consulted with General Banks upon the Red River expedition, toward which he was to contribute a co-operating column. This force was immediately organized and equipped, and embarked in March for the mouth of Red River, and was commanded by Generals A. J. Smith and Thomas Kilby Smith, both veteran officers of large experience and ability. Sherman now left for Memphis.

On to Atlanta.

The promotion of General Grant to the rank of lieutenant-general and commander-in-chief of the armies of the United States opened a still higher promotion to General Sherman. By authority of the President, expressed in general orders dated March 12th, he was assigned to the command of the military division of the Mississippi. On the 14th of March he received notification of his appointment while at Memphis. He immediately left for Nashville, and held a conference with General Grant upon the subject of the spring operations. Between the two officers there was a full and complete understanding of the policy and plans for the ensuing campaign, which was designed to embrace a vast area of country. On the 25th, General Sherman commenced a tour of inspection of the various armies of his command, visiting Athens, Decatur, Huntsville, and Larkin's Ferry, Ala.; Chattanooga, Loudon, and Knoxville, Tenn.

In the course of his visit he held interviews with Major-General McPherson at Huntsville, Major-General Thomas at Chattanooga and Major-General Schofield at Knoxville. With these officers he arranged in general terms the lines of communication to be guarded, the strength of the several columns and garrisons, and appointed the 1st of May as the time for everything to be in readiness. While these commanders were carrying out their instructions General Sherman returned to Nashville, giving his personal attention to the subject of supplies, organizing a magnificent system of railroad communication by two routes from Nashville, and preparing the way for future operations.

Three Great Armies.

The storehouses and dépôts of Chattanooga soon groaned beneath the weight of abundance. The whole of East Tennessee and Northern Alabama contributed to the general store, while the whole North-west and West poured volumes of sustenance through the avenues of communication from Louisville. On the 27th of April the three great armies of his division were converging at Chattanooga. The 1st of May witnessed over sixty thousand troops and one hundred and thirty guns forming the Army of the Cumberland, Major-General George H. Thomas commanding, encamped in the vicinity of Ringgold, Ga.

McPherson, with a portion of Grant's old veteran and victorious battalions of the Army of the Tennessee, numbering twenty-five thousand troops of all arms and ninety-six guns, lay at Gordon's Mill, on the historic Chickamauga. General Schofield, with over thirteen thousand troops and twenty-eight guns, constituting the Army of the Ohio, lay on the Georgia line, north of Dalton. In the aggregate these three armies formed a grand army of over ninety-eight

GENERAL W. T. SHERMAN.

thousand men and two hundred and fifty-four guns, under the supreme command of General Sherman.

Preparing for Attack.

The enemy, superior in cavalry and with three corps of infantry and artillery, commanded by Hardee, Hood, and Polk, and all under the command of General Joseph E. Johnston, lay in and about Dalton. His position was covered by an inaccessible ridge known as the Rocky Face, through which ran Buzzard Roost Gap. The railroad and wagon-road following this pass the enemy had strongly defended by abattis and well-constructed fortifications. Batteries commanded it in its whole length, and especially from a ridge at its farther end, like a traverse directly across its debouch. To drive the enemy from this position by the front was impossible. After well reconnoitring the vicinity, but one practicable route by which to attack Johnson was found, and that was by Snake Creek Gap, by which Resaca, a point on the enemy's railroad communication, eighteen miles below Dalton, could be reached.

Accordingly, McPherson was instructed to move rapidly from his position at Gordon's Mill, by way of Ship's Gap, Villanow, and Snake Creek Gap, directly upon Resaca. During this movement Thomas was to make a strong feint attack in front, and Schofield was to press down from the north. Thomas occupied Tunnel Hill May 7, facing Buzzard Roost Gap, experiencing little opposition except from cavalry. McPherson reached Snake Creek Gap May 8, surprising a brigade of the enemy while *en route* to occupy it. May 9, Schofield moved down from the north close on Dalton. The same day Newton's division of the

PICKETS ON DUTY.

Fourth corps carried the ridge, Geary of the Twentieth corps crowding on for the summit.

While this was going on at the front the head of McPherson's column made its appearance near Resaca and took position confronting the enemy's works. May 10 the Twentieth corps (Hooker) moved to join

McPherson; the Fourteenth corps (Palmer) followed; the Fourth corps (Howard) commenced pounding Dalton from the front. Meanwhile, Schofield also hastened to join McPherson. May 11 the whole army, with the exception of Howard's corps and some cavalry, was in motion for Snake Creek Gap. May 12, McPherson debouched from the gap on the main road, Kilpatrick with his cavalry in front.

Thomas moved on McPherson's left, Schofield on Thomas' left. Kilpatrick drove the enemy within two miles of Resaca. Kilpatrick having been wounded, Colonel Murray took command, and, wheeling out of the road, McPherson's columns crowded impetuously by, and, driving the enemy's advance within the defences of Resaca, occupied a ridge of bold hills, his right resting on the Oostenaula, two miles below the railroad bridge, and his left abreast of the town. Thomas, on his left, facing Camp Creek, and Schofield, forcing his way through a dense forest, came in on the extreme left.

The enemy had evacuated Dalton and was now concentrated at Resaca. Howard occupied Dalton and hung upon the enemy's rear. May 14 the battle of Resaca commenced: May 15 it continued. The same night the enemy was flying toward the Etowah. The whole army followed in pursuit. May 19, Sherman held all of the country north of the Etowah and several crossings of that stream. May 23 the whole army was moving upon the flank of the enemy's position in the Allatoona Mountains. May 25,

Hooker whipped the enemy near New Hope Church. On May 28, McPherson killed and wounded about five thousand of the enemy near Dallas. June 6 the enemy was in hasty retreat to his next position at Kenesaw Mountains. June 8, Blair arrived at Ackworth with the fresh troops of the Seventeenth corps. June 11 the sounds of Sherman's artillery reverberated among the rugged contortions of Kenesaw. July 3 the enemy was pressing for the Chattahoochee. The mountains and Marietta were occupied by our forces the same day.

The Gallant McPherson's Death.

The enemy had a *tête-du-pont* and formidable works on the Chattahoochee at the railroad crossing. Sherman advanced boldly with a small force on the front. July 7, Schofield had possession of one of the enemy's pontoons and occupied the south side of the Chattahoochee. By July 9, Sherman held three crossings. Johnston abandoned his *tête-du-pont*, and there was no enemy north or west of the Chattahoochee July 10. July 17 the whole army was in motion across the Chattahoochee. July 18, Atlanta was cut off from the east. Rousseau, with an expeditionary cavalry force, was operating within the enemy's lines. July 20 all the armies closed in upon Atlanta. The same afternoon the enemy attacked Hooker and was driven into his intrenchments. On July 22, Johnston was relieved, and Hood, in command of the enemy, suddenly attacked McPherson's extreme left with overpowering numbers. Giles A. Smith held the position first attacked with a division of McPherson s troops. First he fought from one side of the parapet, when, being attacked in the rear, he fought from the other. McPherson's whole army soon became engaged. The battle was the most desperate of the campaign. McPherson was killed when the contest was the thickest. His last order saved the army. Logan succeeded to command. "McPherson and revenge!" rang along the lines. The effect was electric, and victory closed in with the night. The battle footed up nine thousand of the enemy against four thousand of our own troops killed and wounded—a balance in our favor of five thousand dead and mangled bodies.

CHAPTER VII.

From Atlanta to the Sea.—Thrilling Story of One of the Greatest Feats in Military History.

AFTER Vicksburg, Sherman was soon to be heard from among the mountains of Tennessee. Rosecrans, having encountered Bragg in the tremendous battle of Chickamauga, had fallen back into Chattanooga and was virtually under siege. Grant, summoned thither from Vicksburg to take command, hurried Sherman, who had succeeded to the command of the Army of the Tennessee, to the rescue.

Arriving at Chattanooga from the long march, Sherman took post on Grant's left at Tunnel Hill, and when all was ready engaged the enemy hotly; while Thomas, with the Army of the Cumberland, "forming on the plain below with the precision of parade," swept magnificently across Mission Ridge and drove Bragg back into Georgia. Meanwhile, Burnside had been besieged by Longtreet at Knoxville, and was in great stress. Without a pause for rest, Sherman was sent to his relief, but Bragg's disaster had broken up the siege, and Sherman marched back to Chattanooga. Congress voted thanks to him and his men "for their gallant and arduous services in marching to the relief of the

Army of the Cumberland, and for their gallantry and heroism in the battle of Chattanooga, which contributed in a great degree to the success of our arms in that glorious victory."

GENERAL GEORGE H. THOMAS.

Early in 1864, General Sherman was invested with the command of the entire South-west, and on the 19th of April he received his final instructions from General Grant for the movement against Atlanta.

Starting from Ringgold, in front of Chattanooga, with nearly one hundred thousand men, including Thomas's Army of the Cumberland, over sixty thousand strong, McPherson's army of the Tennessee, and Schofield's Army of the Ohio, Sherman drove back his opponent, the wary and skilful General J. E. Johnston, in a series of remarkable movements, now fighting and now flanking him. Sherman came up with Johnston at Dalton, turned his position at Buzzard's Roost, assaulted him at Resaca, flanked him again and threw him back to Cassville and the Etowah, and fought him again at New Hope Church and on the heights of the Kenesaw, finally compelling him to fall back on Atlanta, with all of Northern Georgia at the mercy of the victorious invader.

Thanks from President Lincoln.

In the meantime Hood superseded Johnston, but he lost in quick succession the battles of Peach Tree Creek, Ezra Church, opposite Atlanta, and Jonesboro, twenty miles away, after which the victorious army entered the city, where Sherman received from President Lincoln the thanks of the nation "for the distinguished ability and perseverance displayed in the campaign in Georgia, which, under Divine favor, has resulted in the capture of Atlanta. The marches, battles, sieges, and other military operations that have signalized the campaign must render it famous in the annals of war."

The occasion of this distinguished praise is found

in Sherman's famous march and conquests, which we now proceed to describe.

There was little of the vivid interest then attached to the fiercely-contending armies in Virginia in Sherman's famous march to the sea. However, it was far more brilliant, showed greater mastery of the art of war, and was fraught with more important results than were dreamed of at the time.

Illustrious Commanders.

Sherman had met Grant at Nashville in the middle of March, and had accompanied him to Cincinnati during which time the plans of the campaign were matured. He was in command of the principal Western armies—the Army of the Tennessee, under McPherson; the Army of the Cumberland, under Thomas; and the Army of the Ohio, under Schofield. All were officers of the regular army and graduates of West Point. All had long served with the Western armies, and had received their promotion after distinguished services. Thomas, older than his brother-generals, a Virginian by birth, had never faltered in his allegiance to the Union, and had quickly arrived at high command in the West. At the disastrous battle of Chickamauga he alone had achieved renown when others had suffered defeat and disgrace. McPherson had won each successive step of his promotion by brilliant services from Fort Donelson to Vicksburg. Schofield, the youngest of the three and classmate of McPherson and of his later Confederate opponent, Hood, had shown administrative capacity and military ability of a high order when in command of the Department of the Missouri.

Such were the generals under Sherman's immediate command, in whom he had complete confidence and which they in turn fully reciprocated.

The Confederate forces were also led by men educated at West Point, and who had seen service in the regular army. General Joseph E. Johnston was in chief command, while Hardee, Hood, and Polk commanded the divisions under him. The entire Confederate force throughout Tennessee, Northern Alabama, and Mississippi numbered about one hundred and eighty thousand, while the available force under Johnston at the outset of the great march numbered less than fifty thousand, with headquarters at Chattanooga. Sherman's force started with a total of ninety-eight thousand eight hundred, which a month later was increased by Blair's corps to one hundred and twelve thousand eight hundred men.

The Start for the Sea.

Notwithstanding Johnston's inferiority of force, the authorities at Richmond expected him to assume the offensive, and promised reinforcements as he should advance. Johnston wanted all his reinforcements first, and thus, at the very beginning of the campaign, there was neither harmony nor good feeling between him and President Davis.

Meantime, the 5th of May came, and in accordance with Grant's general orders Sherman set his army in motion for Dalton. And now followed a campaign which has had no parallel in modern war. It resembles more the old "War of Positions" of the days of Gustavus Adolphus and Turenne, when both armies, protecting themselves on their fighting ground, sought for advantage in either outflanking the enemy or cutting off his supplies. From Dalton to Atlanta it was a campaign of siege and counter-siege the whole way. Sherman pressed forward on the principle of an advance against fortified positions. The whole country passed through was an interminable line of forts, connected by fifty miles of trenches, with abattis and finished batteries. Even the skirmishers learned to cover themselves by the simplest and best forms, such as rails or logs piled up to make a simple lunette, covered on the outside by earth thrown up.

In all this work of throwing up intrenchments or making rifle-pits the men of both armies became extremely skilful, because each man could realize its importance to himself. As soon as a brigade fancied a position it would set to work with a will, and would construct an impregnable position in a night. To lighten the labors of his men in this respect Sherman organized a pioneer corps of freedmen, two hundred of whom were assigned to every division, receiving regular pay and rations.

Sherman's greatest problem was to supply his army, and it was a source of continual anxiety to him. The country was entirely impoverished, and he was dependent on the preservation of the railway, which he was obliged to rebuild as he advanced. The displacement of a rail would hinder communication for a considerable time, while the frequent attacks made on the trains by the guerillas necessitated strong guards along the line. Nevertheless, the supplies came and Sherman moved steadily forward.

Hard Fighting.

On the 8th of May the hostile armies first came in contact at Dalton, where heavy skirmishing, followed by an unsuccessful assault under General Thomas against Rock Hill Ridge, convinced General Sherman at the start that direct attacks on intrenched positions could not yield good results. He then moved McPherson around by the right against Johnston's rear, and the latter was obliged to fall back upon Resaca, to fortifications already prepared there. On the 14th of May the Federal forces found nothing in their front at Dalton and moved on to Resaca. Here some hard fighting took place, in which Palmer's corps of Thomas's army and Judah's division of Schofield's played a conspicuous part, but no serious impression could be made on the Confederate lines. Again McPherson moved around by the right, and again Johnston was obliged to retire, nor could he find a suitable place to make a stand until he reached the Etowah River, forty miles south of Resaca and ninety-six miles from Chattanooga. He was immediately followed by Sherman, who sent forward two cavalry divisions in pursuit, supported by a division of infantry, the main army advancing in parallel lines in three columns.

Sherman's march was necessarily slow, because he

was obliged to rebuild the railroads as he advanced. Johnston had crossed the Etowah River, and now held a strong position at Allatoona Pass, in the Etowah Mountains. Here and at New Hope, called by the soldiers "Hell Hole," there was very hard fighting, but again Sherman's flanking movement by the right proved successful, and Johnston on the 4th of June fell back to Marietta, and Allatoona was left in our possession. Before advancing farther Sherman finished the railroad up to Allatoona, and strongly fortified that place and made it a secondary base of supplies. His army, too, needed some rest after nearly a month of incessant fighting and fortifying.

In the Georgia Mountains.

On the 9th of June, Sherman again moved forward in the direction of Marietta. Johnston held an unassailable position in the mountain-ranges which under the names of Kenesaw, Pine Hill, and Lost Mountain divide the tributaries of the Etowah from those of the Chattahoochee. The conical summits of the chestnut-covered mountains were crowned with signal-stations, while along their sides and among the ravines breastworks and abattis completely barred the further progress of the Federal troops.

Here, at last, it seemed that Sherman's farther advance must be stayed. In person he reconnoitred the position, exposing himself fearlessly as he directed the firing of batteries for the purpose of drawing the fire of the enemy to ascertain the strength of the various positions.

A series of engagements now ensued for the possession of these mountains, on one of which General Polk, while overlooking the action, was killed. Thus Louisiana lost its bishop and the Confederates an able soldier. On the 27th of June, Sherman ordered a direct assault against the fortified position on the Kenesaw, but his troops were repulsed with great slaughter. Three thousand fell on that hardly-contested slope, while the defenders lost little more than five hundred. In his memoirs Sherman has justified this assault. "Failure as it was," he says, "and for which I assume the entire responsibility, I yet claim it produced good fruits, as it was demonstrated to General Johnston that I would assault, and that boldly."

Johnston Driven Back.

Satisfied that his former strategy was best adapted to the capabilities of his army, Sherman proceeded to turn the position he had failed to force, and, again extending his right, he threatened Johnston's communications with Atlanta.

These operations were completed by the 3d of July, and Johnston was compelled to retire to the Chattahoochee River. Thomas and Schofield followed his retreat, passing through Atlanta and advancing rapidly with the hope of falling on the retiring army while crossing the river. But the strength of the Confederate defences in front of the river forbade attack, and again Sherman resorted to his accustomed tactics of operating on the flanks. A succession of complicated and well-timed movements of the three Federal armies, successfully executed, secured command of the Chattahoochee, and Johnston again retired and entered the defences of Atlanta. He had retreated over one hundred miles, but he had inflicted heavy losses on his enemy, and had compelled him to consume two months in making his advance.

But his Fabian generalship by no means found favor with the Richmond Government. All through the campaign he had been constantly urged to take the offensive, to throw himself on Sherman's prolonged line, and to force him to retreat. He believed his own policy to be best, and steadfastly adhered to it.

General Hood in Command.

It is said that he intended to try the issue of an offensive battle before the fortifications of Atlanta, and when Sherman should have the Chattahoochee in his rear; but on the same day that the armies of the Ohio, the Cumberland, and the Tennessee poured over the bridges and across the fords of that river Johnston was superseded, and the command of the Western army conferred upon General Hood. He was to take the offensive, and brilliant results at his hand were confidently expected.

Johnston undoubtedly deserves high praise for the conduct of the campaign, and General Grant has approved of his policy and commended his ability. Indeed, it needs but little argument to show that he was right in refusing to rush wildly forward into Tennessee to court such disaster as Hood afterward met with. What he might have accomplished had he been opposed to a less wary and less able commander than Sherman, a commander who would have hurled his troops at impregnable breastworks as Grant did in Virginia, is mere matter of conjecture. As things actually were disposed, and under the circumstances in which he was placed, Johnston merits a place at least in the second rank of great generals.

Before Atlanta at Last.

Atlanta was very strongly intrenched in a complete circle about a mile and a half outside the city. Beyond, there were advanced intrenchments which must be taken before a close siege could be commenced. But Hood did not intend to abide a siege. As the three Federal armies converged on Atlanta he moved out on the 20th of July and attacked the Army of the Cumberland most furiously. Hooker's corps and Newton's and Johnston's divisions were the principal ones engaged in this contest. After a fierce struggle the Confederates were repulsed and retired to their intrenchments, leaving their dead and wounded on the field. It was in this battle that General Gresham, now judge of the United States Circuit Court, was very severely wounded.

But Hood did not intend to abandon offensive operations. On the night of the 21st he moved out again to make an attack on the left of the Federal line. About noon of the 22d the battle commenced with an assault by Hardee upon Blair's corps, which he pressed heavily. Our left was turned, and it was with great difficulty that an immense wagon-train was saved. Sherman and his able lieutenants proved fully equal to the emergency in the end, and, though the fighting was at first very much in favor of the Confederates, before night fell they were driven back into the city. It was during this battle that the brave McPherson was killed. This was the battle of Atlanta, and on the score of having captured thirteen guns and some prisoners Hood claimed a great victory.

Disastrous Victory.

But, nevertheless, Sherman held his ground, and prepared by new combinations to press forward his operations against the city. Hood had suffered the severest losses, and such victories would prove as disastrous as defeats. For the next six weeks he kept mainly on the defensive. To carry the city by an assault was beyond the power of the invading army, and to approach it by regular siege and investment equally impossible.

Sherman's only resource was either to destroy or occupy the great railway arteries which brought supplies to the army and to the people. The work was tedious and the lines to be maintained were very long, but slowly and surely through the months of July and August the work went on. Several extensive cavalry raids were organized. One of these, under General Stoneman, numbering about one thousand men, was captured, and the others did not accomplish nearly so much as was expected. It remained then for the infantry to carry out more slowly the plan of separating Hood's army from its base of supplies.

Daring Cavalry Movements.

Nor was the Confederate cavalry idle. General Wheeler moved upon the railroad north of Resaca and destroyed it nearly up to Dalton, cutting Sherman off from communication with the North for several days. But neither raids nor assaults availed to retard Sherman's movements to seize all the communications leading to Atlanta. Many sharp engagements took place, but Sherman never loosened a grip once firmly taken.

Finally, on August 25, he commenced his last and final flank movement, by which he swung his whole army, except one corps, on Hood's communications south of Atlanta, compelling him to leave his intrenchments and to fight a decisive battle or to retreat. To do this Sherman had to cut loose from his own communications, and to depend for subsistence upon such stores as he could carry or gather from the country. It was bold strategy, but its success proved that the details had been carefully studied out, and that it was a fitting conclusion to the campaign of Atlanta. All the movements of the various corps were made with precision and accomplished as ordered.

On August 30 and 31 sharp engagements occurred with the Confederates under Hardee at Jonesboro, twenty miles south of Atlanta. On September 1,

Sherman had complete possession of the Macon railroad. During that night our army heard great explosions in the direction of Atlanta and Jonesboro. Hood had found himself compelled to yield the city at last. He blew up his military works, and fell back southward, toward Macon. On the following morning General Slocum, who had remained with his corps north of the city, marched in and took possession.

The campaign had lasted four months, and is one of the most memorable of the war. The aggregate loss from the force in killed, wounded, and missing amounted to 31,687 men. During the same period the loss inflicted on the Confederate army amounted to 34,779 men.

This campaign abundantly proved Sherman's commanding genius for war. He could execute as well as conceive. He understood the discipline of armies in its fullest extent. He knew how to select and employ his officers.

Why He did Not go to Augusta.

The question, "Why didn't General Sherman go to Augusta instead of to Savannah when he made the great march through Georgia?" has been often asked and commented upon. General Sherman himself answered it two years ago. "The march to the sea from Atlanta," said he, "was resolved on after Hood had got well on his way to Nashville. I then detached to General Thomas a force sufficient to whip Hood, which he, in December, 1864, very handsomely and conclusively did. Still, I had left a very respectable army and resolved to join Grant at Richmond. The distance was one thousand miles, and prudence dictated a base at Savannah or Port Royal. Our enemy had garrisons at Macon and Augusta. I figured on both, and passed between to Savannah. Then, starting northward, the same problem presented itself in Augusta and Charleston. I figured on both, but passed between.

"I did not want to drive out their garrisons ahead of me at the crossings of the Santee, Catawba, Pedee, Cape Fear, etc. The moment I passed Columbia the factories, powder-mills, and the old stuff accumulated at Augusta were lost to the only two Confederate armies left—Lee's and Hood's. So, if you have a military mind, you will see I made a better use of Augusta than if I had captured it with its stores, for which I had no use. I used Augusta twice as a buffer; its garrison was just where it helped me.

"Sherman's Bummers."

"If the people of Augusta think I slighted them in the winter of 1864–65 by reason of personal friendship formed in 1844, they are mistaken, or if they think I made a mistake in strategy, let them say so, and with the President's consent I think I can send a detachment of one hundred thousand or so of 'Sherman's bummers' and their descendants, who will finish up the job without charging Uncle Sam a cent. The truth is, these incidents come back to me in a humorous vein. Of course the Civil War should have ended with Vicksburg and Gettysburg. Every sensible man on earth must have then seen there could be but one result. The leaders of the South took good care not to 'die in the last ditch,' and left brave men like Walker, Adams, Pat Cleburne, etc., to do that."

After resting at Savannah and refitting his army, he moved northward February 1. Columbia was occupied on the 17th; Cheraw, March 3d; Fayetteville, March 11th; the battle of Averysboro was fought March 16th; that of Bentonville, March 19th, 20th; Goldsboro was occupied March 22d; Raleigh, April 13th; and April 18th, at Durham Station.

By marching through the heart of South Carolina instead of skirting the sea, Sherman pierced the State in its most vital part. It was the boast of Davis and Breckenridge that the sea was not necessary to the South. Their strength lay inland. Sherman marched inland, shutting up one Confederate general in Augusta, another in Branchville, a third in Charleston, and a fourth in Columbia. These generals never knew where the blow would fall, and it never fell where they thought it likely to. As Sherman moved up northward, leaving Charleston on the right, Beauregard was confident that he would have to assault Branchville, a great railway-centre and a post from which he could equally menace Charleston and Augusta. Branchville was accordingly strengthened with guns and occupied in force. But Sherman cut the railway-lines and compelled the enemy to abandon their works and guns. Branchville passed and Columbia gained, Charleston fell.

Sherman accepted the surrender of Johnston's army on a "basis of agreement" which was rejected by the Government, but on the 26th received the surrender on the terms accorded to Lee by Grant. Resuming his march, Washington was reached May 24, 1865, where, after the grand review, his army was dissolved. On the 27th of June, 1865, he was appointed to command the military division of the Mississippi; was promoted to be lieutenant-general July 25, 1866, and August 11 assigned to command the military division of the Missouri. On the accession of General Grant to the Presidency he became general (March 4, 1869). In 1871–72 he made an extended tour in Europe and the East. In October, 1874, the headquarters of the army were removed from Washington to St. Louis, but in April, 1876, were re-established at Washington. He published in 1875 *Memoirs of General W. T. Sherman, by Himself.*

CHAPTER VIII.

Important Letter of General Sherman.—The Country Deluded in the Early Part of the War.—Strange Charge of Lunacy.

A LETTER written by General Sherman while he was at Memphis to his brother, Senator John Sherman, shows how accurately he understood the gravity of the situation, and how crazy they were who pronounced him wild and visionary. The story was actually circulated that he was out of his mind, and so fully was it believed that for a brief period his command was taken away from him. The country soon discovered that no man was more sane on war questions than he was. The letter is as follows:

MEMPHIS, Tenn., Aug. 13, 1862.

MY DEAR BROTHER: I have not written to you for so long that I suppose you think I have dropped the correspondence. For six weeks I was marching along the road from Corinth to Memphis, mending roads, building bridges, and all sorts of work. At last I got here, and found the city contributing gold, arms, powder, salt, and everything the enemy wanted. It was a smart trick on their part thus to give up Memphis, that the desire of gain to our Northern merchants should supply them with the things needed in war. I stopped this at once, and declared gold, silver, Treasury notes, and salt as much contraband of war as powder. I have one man under sentence of death for smuggling arms across the lines, and hope Mr. Lincoln will approve it.

But the mercenary spirit of our people is too much, and my orders are reversed and I am ordered to encourage the trade in cotton, and all orders prohibiting gold, silver, and notes to be paid for it are annulled by orders from Washington. Grant promptly ratified my order, and all military men here saw at once that gold spent for cotton went to the purchase of arms and munitions of war. But what are the lives of our soldiers to the profits of the merchants?

Great Call for Men.

After a whole year of bungling the country has at last discovered that we want more men. All knew it last fall as well as now, but it was not popular. Now one million three hundred thousand men are required, when seven hundred thousand were deemed absurd before. It will take time to work up these raw recruits, and they will reach us in October, when we should be in Jackson, Meridian, and Vicksburg. Still, I must not growl. I have purposely put back, and have no right to criticise, save that I am glad the papers have at last found out we are at war and have a formidable enemy to combat.

Of course I approve the Confiscation Act, and would be willing to revolutionize the Government so as to amend that article of the Constitution which forbids the forfeiture of land to the heirs. My full belief is we must colonize the country *de novo*, beginning with Kentucky and Tennessee, and should remove four million of our people at once south of the Ohio River, taking the farms and plantations of the rebels. I deplore the war as much as ever, but if the thing has to be done let the means be adequate Don't expect to overrun such a country or subdue such a people in one, two, or five years. It is the task of half a century. Although our army is thus far south, it cannot stir from our garrisons. Our men are killed or captured within sight of our lines. I have two divisions here—mine and Hurlbut's, about thirteen thousand men—am building a strong fort, and think this is to be one of the dépôts and bases of operations for future movements.

Too Many Heads.

The loss of Halleck is almost fatal. We have no one to replace him. Instead of having one head, we have five or six, all independent of each other. I expect our enemies will mass their troops and fall upon our detachments before new reinforcements come. I cannot learn that there are any large bodies of men near us here. There are detachments at Holly Springs and Senatobia, the present termini of the railroads from the South, and all the people of the country are armed as guerillas. Curtis is at Helena, eighty miles south, and Grant at Corinth. Bragg's army from Tripoli has moved to Chattanooga, and proposes to march on Nashville, Lexington, and Cincinnati. They will have about seventy-five thousand men.

Buell is near Huntsville with about thirty thousand, and I suppose detachments of the new levies can be put in Kentucky from Ohio and Indiana in time. The weather is very hot, and Bragg can't move his forces very fast; but I fear he will give trouble. My own opinion is, we ought not to venture too much into the interior until the river is safely in our possession, when we could land at any point and strike inland. To attempt to hold all the South would demand an army too large even to think of. We must colonize and settle as we go south, for in Missouri there is as much strife as ever. Enemies must be killed or transported to some other country.

Your affectionate brother, W. T. SHERMAN.

From the outset Sherman looked for a great war, and he regarded President Lincoln's first call for seventy-five thousand men in April, 1861, as trifling with a serious matter. To him the Secessionists were not merely an armed mob to be put down by a few holiday soldiers. Very early in the war he did not hesitate to give his views official expression. Made a brigadier-general of volunteers, he was assigned to the Department of the Cumberland, under General Robert Anderson, whom he soon succeeded, General Anderson's health having failed.

He soon astounded the Washington optimists, who

were going to put down the revolt in sixty days, by declaring that to retake the Mississippi Valley would require two hundred thousand men. It was expected by the Government that all the men needed to keep Kentucky in the Union could be raised in that State, but for that work alone Sherman declared that sixty

GENERAL JOHN A. LOGAN.

thousand would be needed. The country was disposed to look upon this sagacity as lunacy, and the Government shared in the public distrust of Sherman, as was shown by the fact that he was relieved of his command on the 12th of November by General Buell, and ordered to report to General Halleck, by whom he was assigned to the command of Benton Barracks.

This singular proceeding was brought about by Mr. Cameron, Secretary of War, mentioning to General Thomas what he called Sherman's *insane* request for two hundred thousand men. Some newspaper-man got hold of it, and the news was trumpeted abroad that Sherman was " insane, crazy," etc. The occasion of Mr. Cameron's remark was the following letter:

HEADQUARTERS DEPARTMENT OF THE CUMBERLAND,
LOUISVILLE, KENTUCKY, October 22, 1861.

To GENERAL L. THOMAS, *Washington, D. C.:*

SIR: On my arrival at Camp Dick Robinson, I found General Thomas had stationed a Kentucky regiment at Rock Castle Hill, beyond a river of the same name, and had sent an Ohio and an Indiana regiment forward in support. He was embarrassed for transportation, and I authorized him to hire teams and to move his whole force nearer to his advance-guard, so as to support it, as he had information of the approach of Zollicoffer toward London. I have just heard from him that he had sent forward General Schoepf with Colonel Wolford's cavalry, Colonel Steadman's Ohio regiment, and a battery of artillery, followed on a succeeding day by a Tennessee brigade. He had still two Kentucky regiments, the Thirty-eighth Ohio, and another battery of artillery, with which he was to follow yesterday. This force, if concentrated, should be strong enough for the purpose; at all events, it is all he had or I could give him.

I explained to you fully, when here, the supposed

position of our adversaries, among whom was a force in the valley of Big Sandy, supposed to be advancing on Paris, Kentucky. General Nelson at Maysville was instructed to collect all the men he could, and Colonel Gill's regiment of Ohio volunteers. Colonel Harris was already in position at Olympian Springs, and a regiment lay at Lexington, which I ordered to his support. This leaves the line of Thomas's operations exposed, but I cannot help it. I explained so fully to yourself and the Secretary of War the condition of things that I can add nothing new until further developments. You know my views, that this great centre of our field is too weak, far too weak, and I have begged and implored till I dare not say more.

Buckner still is beyond Green River. He sent a detachment of his men, variously estimated at from two to four thousand, toward Greensburg. General Ward, with about one thousand men, retreated to Campbellsburg, where he called to his assistance some partially-formed regiments to the number of about two thousand. The enemy did not advance, and General Ward was at last dates at Campbellsburg. The officers charged with raising regiments must of necessity be near their homes to collect men, and for this reason are out of position; but at or near Greensburg and Lebanon I desire to assemble as large a force of the Kentucky volunteers as possible.

This organization is necessarily irregular, but the necessity is so great that I must have them, and therefore have issued to them arms and clothing during the process of formation. This has facilitated their enlistment; but inasmuch as the Legislature has provided money for organizing the Kentucky volunteers, and entrusted its disbursement to a board of loyal gentlemen, I have endeavored to co-operate with them to hasten the formation of these corps.

The great difficulty is, and has been, that as volunteers offer we have not arms and clothing to give them. The arms sent us are, as you already know, European muskets of uncouth pattern, which the volunteers will not touch.

General McCook has now three brigades—Johnson's, Wood's, and Rousseau's. Negley's brigade arrived to-day, and will be sent out at once. The Minnesota regiment has also arrived, and will be sent forward. Hazzard's regiment of Indiana troops I have ordered to the mouth of Salt Creek, an important point on the turnpike-road leading to Elizabethtown.

I again repeat that our force here is out of all proportion to the importance of the position. Our defeat would be disastrous to the nation, and to expect of new men, who never bore arms, to do miracles, is not right.

I am, with much respect, yours truly,
W. T. SHERMAN,
Brigadier-General commanding.

This letter was characteristic of its author—sagacious, honest, outspoken, and right to the point.

Sherman knew the magnitude of the fight the country had on hand; he wished others to know it too.

The Facts in the Case.

It is important to the unsullied fame of General Sherman that the public should have a plain statement of the facts concerning this remarkable episode in his history. In an interview with Mr. Cameron he urged the necessity of raising more troops, expressing views similar to those stated in his letter to Adjutant-General Thomas. Cameron was astonished at the demand for troops, and exclaimed, "Where are they to come from?" Sherman supposed his conversation with Cameron was confidential, and had occasion to complain afterward that it was made public and was used to his disadvantage.

After the war was over General Thomas J. Wood, then in command of the district of Vicksburg, prepared a statement addressed to the public, describing the interview with the Secretary of War, which he calls a "council of war." Sherman did not then deem it necessary to renew a matter which had been swept into oblivion by the war itself; but, as it is evidence by an eye-witness, it is worthy of insertion here.

Statement of General Wood.

"On the 11th of October, 1861, the writer, who had been personally on mustering duty in Indiana, was appointed a brigadier-general of volunteers and ordered to report to General Sherman, then in command of the Department of the Cumberland, with his headquarters at Louisville, having succeeded General

Robert Anderson. When the writer was about leaving Indianapolis to proceed to Louisville, Mr. Cameron, returning from his famous visit of inspection to General Fremont's department at St. Louis, Missouri, arrived at Indianapolis, and announced his intention to visit General Sherman.

"The writer was invited to accompany the party to Louisville. Taking the early morning train from Indianapolis to Louisville on the 16th of October, 1861, the party arrived in Jeffersonville shortly after midday. General Sherman met the party in Jeffersonville, and accompanied it to the Galt House in Louisville, the hotel at which he was stopping.

Behind Closed Doors.

"During the afternoon General Sherman informed the writer that a council of war was to be held immediately in his private room in the hotel, and desired him to be present at the council. General Sherman and the writer proceeded directly to the room. The writer entered the room first, and observed in it Mr. Cameron, Adjutant-General L. Thomas, and some other persons, all of whose names he did not know, but whom he recognized as being of Mr. Cameron's party. The name of one of the party the writer had learned, which he remembers as Wilkinson or Wilkerson, and who he understood was a writer for the *New York Tribune* newspaper. The Hon. James Guthrie was also in the room, having been invited, on account of his eminent position as a citizen of Kentucky, his high civic reputation, and his well-known devotion to the Union, to meet the Secretary of War in the council. When General Sherman entered the room he closed the door and turned the key in the lock.

"Before entering on the business of the meeting, General Sherman remarked substantially: 'Mr. Cameron, we have met here to discuss matters and interchange views which should be known only by persons high in the confidence of the Government. There are persons present whom I do not know, and I desire to know, before opening the business of the council, whether they are persons who may be properly allowed to hear the views which I have to submit to you.' Mr. Cameron replied, with some little testiness of manner, that the persons referred to belonged to his party, and there was no objection to their knowing whatever might be communicated to him on a matter so important.

The Forces Insufficient.

"Certainly the legitimate and natural conclusion from this remark of Mr. Cameron's was that whatever views might be submitted by General Sherman would be considered under the protection of the seal of secrecy, and would not be divulged to the public till all apprehension of injurious consequences from such disclosure had passed. And it may be remarked, further, that justice to General Sherman required that if, at any future time, his conclusions as to the amount of force necessary to conduct the operations committed to his charge should be made public, the grounds on which his conclusions were based should be made public at the same time, that there might be no misapprehension.

"Mr. Cameron then asked General Sherman what his plans were. To this General Sherman replied that he had no plans; that no sufficient force had been placed at his disposition with which to devise any plan of operations; that before a commanding general could project a plan of campaign he must know what amount of force he would have to operate with.

"The general added that he had views which he would be happy to submit for the consideration of the Secretary. Mr. Cameron desired to hear General Sherman's views.

Sherman Speaks for Kentucky.

"General Sherman began by giving his opinion of the people of Kentucky and the then condition of the State. He remarked that he believed a very large majority of the people of Kentucky were thoroughly devoted to the Union, and loyal to the Government, and that the Unionists embraced almost all the older and more substantial men in the State; but, unfortunately, there was no organization nor arms among the Union men; that the rebel minority, thoroughly vindictive in its sentiments, was organized and armed (this having been done in advance by their leaders), and, beyond the reach of the Federal forces, overawed and prevented the Union men from organizing; that, in his opinion, if Federal protection were extended throughout the State to the Union men, a large force could be raised for the service of the Government.

"General Sherman said that the information in his possession indicated an intention, on the part of the rebels, of a general and grand advance toward the Ohio River. He further expressed the opinion that if such advance should be made and not checked, the rebel force would be swollen by at least twenty thousand recruits from the disloyalists in Kentucky. His low computation of the organized rebel soldiers then in Kentucky fixed the strength at about thirty-five thousand. Add twenty thousand for reinforcements gained in Kentucky, to say nothing of troops drawn from other rebel States, and the effective rebel force in the State, at a low estimate, would be fifty-five thousand men.

Difficulties Ahead.

"General Sherman explained forcibly how largely the difficulties of suppressing the rebellion would be enhanced if the rebels should be allowed to plant themselves firmly, with strong fortifications, at commanding points on the Ohio River. It would be facile for them to carry the war thence into the loyal States north of the river.

"To resist an advance of the rebels, General Sherman stated that he did not have at that time in Kentucky more than some twelve to fourteen thousand effective men. The bulk of this force was posted at Camp Nolin, on the Louisville and Nashville railway, fifty miles south of Louisville. A part of it was in

Eastern Kentucky, under General George H. Thomas, and a very small force was in the lower valley of Green River.

"General Sherman next presented a *résumé* of the information in his possession as to the number of the rebel troops in Kentucky. Commencing with the force at Columbus, Kentucky, the reports varied, giving the strength from ten to twenty thousand. It was commanded by Lieutenant-General Polk. General Sherman fixed it at the lowest estimate, say, ten thousand. The force at Bowling Green, commanded by General A. S. Johnston, supported by Hardee, Buckner, and others, was variously estimated at from eighteen to thirty thousand. General Sherman estimated this force at the lowest figures given to it by his information—eighteen thousand.

The Enemy has the Advantage.

"He explained that for purposes of defence these two forces ought, owing to the facility with which troops might be transported from one to the other by the network of railroads in Middle and West Tennessee, to be considered almost as one. General Sherman remarked also on the facility with which reinforcements could be transported by railroad to Bowling Green from the other rebellious States.

"The third organized body of rebel troops was in Eastern Kentucky, under General Zollicoffer—estimated, according to the most reliable information, at six thousand men. This force threatened a descent, if unrestrained, on the Blue-grass region of Kentucky, including the cities of Lexington and Frankfort, the capital of the State, and, if successful in its primary movements, as it would gather head as it advanced, might endanger the safety of Cincinnati.

"This disposition of the force had been made for the double purpose of watching and checking the rebels and protecting the raising and organization of troops among the Union men of Kentucky.

Defensive Operations Useless.

"Having explained the situation from the defensive point of view, General Sherman proceeded to consider it from the offensive standpoint. The Government had undertaken to suppress the rebellion; the *onus faciendi*, therefore, rested on the Government. The rebellion could never be put down, the authority of the paramount Government asserted, and the union of the States declared perpetual by force of arms, by maintaining the defensive; to accomplish these grand desiderata it was absolutely necessary the Government should adopt and maintain until the rebellion was crushed the *offensive*.

"For the purpose of expelling the rebels from Kentucky, General Sherman said that at least sixty thousand soldiers were necessary. Considering that the means of accomplishment must always be proportioned to the end to be achieved, and bearing in mind the array of rebel force then in Kentucky, every sensible man must admit that the estimate of the force given by General Sherman for driving the rebels out of the State and re-establishing and maintaining the authority of the Government was a very low one. The truth is, that before the rebels were driven from Kentucky many more than sixty thousand soldiers were sent into the State.

Number of Troops Required.

"Ascending from the consideration of the narrow question of the political and military situation in Kentucky, and the extent of force necessary to redeem the State from rebel thraldom, forecasting in his sagacious intellect the grand and daring operations which three years afterward he realized in a campaign, taken in its entirety, without a parallel in modern times. General Sherman expressed the opinion that to carry the war to the Gulf of Mexico and destroy all armed opposition to the Government in the entire Mississippi Valley, at least two hundred thousand troops were absolutely requisite.

"So soon as General Sherman had concluded the expression of his views Mr. Cameron asked, with much warmth and apparent irritation, 'Where do you suppose, General Sherman, all this force is to come from?' General Sherman replied that he did not know—that it was not his duty to raise, organize, and put the necessary military force into the field; that duty pertained to the War Department. His duty was to organize campaigns and command the troops after they had been put into the field.

Sherman's Views Endorsed.

"At this point of the proceedings General Sherman suggested that it might be agreeable to the Secretary to hear the views of Mr. Guthrie. Thus appealed to, Mr. Guthrie said he did not consider himself, being a civilian, competent to give an opinion as to the extent of force necessary to carry the war to the Gulf of Mexico; but, being well informed of the condition of things in Kentucky, he indorsed fully General Sherman's opinion of the force required to drive the rebels out of the State.

"The foregoing is a circumstantial account of the deliberations of the council that were of any importance.

"A good deal of desultory conversation followed on immaterial matters, and some orders were issued by telegraph by the Secretary of War for small reinforcements to be sent to Kentucky immediately from Pennsylvania and Indiana.

"A short time after the council was held—the exact time is not now remembered by the writer—an imperfect narrative of it appeared in the *New York Tribune*. This account announced to the public the conclusions uttered by General Sherman in the council, without giving the reasons on which his conclusions were based. The unfairness of this course to General Sherman needs no comment. All military men were shocked by the gross breach of faith which had been committed.

"TH. J. WOOD, *Major-General Volunteers.*
"VICKSBURG, MISSISSIPPI, *August* 24, 1866."

General Wood's account of what passed between Mr. Cameron and General Sherman shows how baseless were the grounds upon which Sherman was judged to be incompetent and crazy. No man comprehended the appalling situation more fully than he did. Events immediately transpiring proved the correctness of his judgment. He knew the magnitude of the great Southern uprising; his keen eye saw the hosts marshalling for the fray. To be deceived and ignore facts plain and undeniable was lunacy: the lunacy was not his. He was nervous, excited, terribly in earnest; his soul was up in arms. To-day we know what solemn occasion he had for believing that the "unpleasantness" was something more than a bubble soon to burst.

He was relieved of his command for a short time, but his country called; her voice was imperative; the grandest man in the field—in many respects the grandest—must come to the front. He came, and brilliant history in illuminated letters has recorded his deeds.

CHAPTER IX.

After the War.—Not a Candidate for the Presidency.—Sketch of the Hero.—Life in New York.

PRELIMINARY to the disbandment of the national armies they passed in review before President Johnson and Cabinet and Lieutenant-General Grant—the Army of the Potomac on May 23d, and General Sherman's army on the 24th. Sherman was particularly observed and honored. From June 27, 1865, to March 3, 1869, he was in command of the military Division of the Mississippi, with headquarters at St. Louis, embracing the Departments of the Ohio, Missouri, and Arkansas.

Upon the appointment of Grant as general of the army on July 25, 1866, Sherman was promoted to be lieutenant-general, and when Grant became President of the United States, March 4, 1869, Sherman succeeded him as general, with headquarters at Washington. From November 10, 1871, to September 17, 1872, he made a professional tour in Europe, and was everywhere received with the honors due to his distinguished rank and service. At his own request, and in order to make Sheridan general-in-chief, he was placed on the retired list, with full pay and emoluments, on February 8, 1884.

Upon Sherman's retirement from the active list, President Arthur issued an order in which he said: "The announcement of the severance from the command of the army of one who has been for so many years its distinguished chief can but awaken in the minds, not only of the army, but of the people of the United States, mingled emotions of regret and gratitude—regret at the withdrawal from active military service of an officer whose lofty sense of duty has been a model for all soldiers since he first entered the army, in July, 1840, and gratitude, freshly awakened, for the services of incalculable value rendered by him in the war for the Union, which his great military genius and daring did so much to end. The President deems this a fitting occasion to give expression to the gratitude felt toward General Sherman by his fellow citizens, and to hope that Providence may grant him many years of health and happiness in the relief from the active duties of his profession."

General Sherman received many honors, among which may be mentioned the degree of LL.D. from Dartmouth, Yale, Harvard, Princeton, and other universities, and membership in the Board of Regents of the Smithsonian Institution, 1871 to 1883.

Sherman and Blaine.

Every reader will peruse with interest the following, written by General Sherman for the *North American Review* of December, 1888:

In the year of our Lord, 1884, there was to be a sharp contest for the nomination in Chicago for a

Presidential candidate of the Republican party. The press and the people generally believed that Blaine wanted it, and everybody turned to him as the man best qualified to execute the policy to accomplish the result aimed at. Still, abnegating himself, he wrote to me from Washington this letter:

Confidential, strictly and absolutely so.
WASHINGTON, D. C., May 25, 1884.

MY DEAR GENERAL:

This letter requires no answer. After reading it file it away in your most secret drawer or give it to the flames.

At the approaching convention at Chicago it is more than possible—it is, indeed, not improbable—that you may be nominated for the Presidency. If so, you must stand your hand, accept the responsibility, and assume the duties of the place to which you will surely be chosen if a candidate.

You must not look upon it as the work of the politicians. If it comes to you it will come as the groundswell of popular demand, and you can no more refuse than you could have refused to obey an order when you were a lieutenant in the army. If it come to you at all, it will come as a call of patriotism. It would in such an event injure your great fame as much to decline it as it would for you to seek it. Your historic record, full as it is, would be rendered still more glorious by such an administration as you would be able to give the country. Do not say a word in advance of the convention, no matter who may ask you. You are with your friends, who will jealously guard your honor and renown. Your friend, JAMES G. BLAINE.

Sherman's Remarkable Answer.

To which I replied:

912 GARRISON AVE., ST. LOUIS, MO.
May, 28, 1884.

HON. JAMES G. BLAINE, WASHINGTON, D. C.:

MY DEAR FRIEND: I have received your letter of the 25th; shall construe it as absolutely confidential, not intimating even to any member of my family that I have heard from you; and, though you may not expect an answer, I hope you will not construe one as unwarranted. I have a great many letters from all points of the compass to a similar effect, one or two of which I have answered frankly, but the great mass are unanswered.

I ought not to submit myself to the cheap ridicule of declining what is not offered, but it is only fair to the many really able men who rightfully aspire to the high honor of being President of the United States to let them know that I am not, and must not be construed as, a rival. In every man's life occurs an epoch when he must choose his own career, and when he may not throw off the responsibility or tamely place his destiny in the hands of friends. Mine occurred in Louisiana when, in 1861, alone in the midst of a people blinded by supposed wrongs, I resolved to stand by the Union as long as a fragment of it survived on which to cling. Since then, through faction, tempest, war, and peace, my career has been all my family and friends could ask.

We are now in a good house of our own choice, with reasonable provisions for old age, surrounded by kind and admiring friends, in a community where Catholicism is held in respect and veneration, and where my children will naturally grow up in contact with an industrious and frugal people. You have known and appreciated Mrs. Sherman from childhood, have also known each and all the members of my family, and can understand without an explanation from me how their thoughts and feelings should and ought to influence my action. But I will not even throw off on them the responsibility.

I will not in any event entertain or accept a nomination as a candidate for President by the Chicago Republican Convention or any other convention, for reasons personal to myself. I claim that the Civil War, in which I simply did a man's fair share of work, so perfectly accomplished peace that military men have an absolute right to rest, and to demand that the men who have been schooled in the arts and practice of peace shall now do their work equally well.

Any Senator can step from his chair at the Capitol into the White House and fulfil the office of President with more skill and success than a Grant, Sherman, or Sheridan, who were soldiers by education and nature, who filled well their office when the country was in danger, but were not schooled in the practice by which civil communities are and should be governed. I claim that our experience since 1865 demonstrates the truth of this my proposition. Therefore I say that patriotism does not demand of me what I construe as a sacrifice of judgment, of inclination, and of self-interest.

I have my personal affairs in a state of absolute safety and comfort. I owe no man a cent, have no expensive habits, envy no man his wealth or power, no complications or indirect liabilities, and would account myself a fool, a madman, an ass, to embark anew at sixty-five years of age in a career that may become at any moment tempest-tossed by perfidy, the defalcation, the dishonesty, or neglect of any single one of a hundred thousand subordinates utterly unknown to the President of the United States, not to say the eternal worriment of a vast host of impecunious friends and old military subordinates. Even as it is I am tortured by the charitable appeals of poor, distressed pensioners, but as President these would be multiplied beyond human endurance.

I remember well the experience of Generals Jackson, Harrison, Taylor, Grant, Hayes, and Garfield, all elected because of their military services, and am warned, not encouraged, by their sad experiences.

The civilians of the United States should and must buffet with this thankless office, and leave us old soldiers to enjoy the peace we fought for and think we earned. With profound respect, your friend,

W. T. SHERMAN.

These letters prove absolutely that Mr. Blaine, though qualified, waived to me personally a nomination which the world still believes he then coveted for himself.

For copies of these letters I believe I have been importuned a thousand times, but as a soldier I claim the privilege of unmasking my batteries when I please.

In giving to the *North American Review* at this late day these letters, which thus far have remained hidden in my private files, I commit no breach of confidence, and to put at rest a matter of constant inquiry referred to in my letter of May 28, 1884, I here record that my immediate family are strongly Catholic. I am not and cannot be. That is all the public has a right to know; nor do I wish to be construed as departing from a resolve made forty years ago never to embark in politics. The brightest and best youth of our land have been drawn into that maelstrom, and their wrecked fortunes strew the beach of the ocean of time. My memory, even in its short time, brings up names of victims by the hundreds, if not thousands.

W. T. SHERMAN.

Nothing could swerve the general from his purpose to avoid a public life. He had won his fame, and was satisfied. At this time, when his name was prominently mentioned for the Presidency, and when he might have got the nomination, he said to a particular friend, speaking about it: "I wouldn't be devilled by that horde of Congressmen if I could be President for life."

Sketch of the General.

Those three heroes, Grant, Sheridan, and Sherman, after the war lived for many years at the National Capital and became identified with its society. It was here that they were the best known and appreciated. General Sherman came in closer touch with society at large than the other two generals. He was fonder of general company and was more ready to become acquainted with strangers. Grant was companionable only with his intimates. The same could be said of Sheridan. He was even more retiring than Grant. He detested going out in general society, while society was the atmosphere which General Sherman needed in order to live.

The latter was fond of gatherings of any kind. He loved to be the centre of a bright, cheerful group. He had sympathies which reached out in every direction. While he had strong likes and dislikes, he had few prejudices. Like all of the leading men who fought in the Union army, he had more sympathy for the South than any of the Northern politicians. Yet he believed that sterner measures should have been employed during the period of reconstruction.

As a friend to the South he believed that it would have been better if the laws had been more rigidly enforced by the Federal authority, and if the States had not recovered local self-control so early. They should have received back their old rights only when they had given the most solemn guarantee to enforce the laws passed for the protection of the rights of the colored people. Even then this authority should have been granted only temporarily, and only made permanent when it was clear that the State was going to act throughout in good faith.

A Masterly Intellect.

General Sherman had more brilliant intellectual qualities than his two great associates. In this we do not speak of him as a soldier, but as a man. His position as a soldier has been long ago determined by the first military critics of the world. The intellectual advantage that he had over his associates was in his readiness of expression. He was an easy and elegant writer upon almost any topic of the day.

He was also a ready speaker. He had a directness of style and a blunt eloquence which always captivated an audience. He was so direct and so honest as to produce with the simplest phrases the profoundest impression. He was one of the most upright of men. He was patriotic to the verge of passion. No one who has been in the public life of this country was ever more devoted to its highest and best interests. Upon this subject he was always eloquent.

His character was noted for its strong quality of common sense. At the height of his popularity as a general of the army he was never tempted for a moment by any of the flattering offers of the politicians to permit his great name to be used in politics. He said often that this was the mistake which Grant made.

When Grant came out of the war he was at the highest pinnacle of success. When he resigned from the army and became President, General Sherman always said he began a career of misfortune.

Ambition Satisfied.

General Sherman would often say to the politicians: "I am a soldier out and out. For that I am trained, and for that career I am fitted. I have to-day arrived at the climax of my ambition. I am general of the army, and at its head. I desire nothing more. I do not propose to risk my name and fame in the field of partisan politics. I want to leave my reputation free from tarnish to my children."

From this resolution General Sherman never swerved. He was never more sorely tempted than during the period of the Chicago Convention which nominated Mr. Blaine. The politicians then came to him and said: "With your name we can carry the convention."

The combination which came to the general was a strong one. It controlled certainly enough votes to have tempted any man with Presidential ambitions, but General Sherman said "No" from the first. The committee which called on him told him flatly and frankly that they should not consider his refusal, but that they should go ahead and use their own judgment. It was then that the general sat down and dictated that brusque letter which ex-Senator Henderson caused to be read to the convention, and which showed clearly to every one that no possible combination of circumstances could force General Sherman to accept a nomination.

"Go Ahead!"

The general was hot-tempered. He despised petty technicalities. When he was in the War Department the bureau people fretted him with the endless red tape which of necessity came to him when he took charge of the great army machine. He would often write orders for the direction of affairs in the West which would be in direct conflict with the civil law. Once, when his attention was called to this by the adjutant-general in some particular order issued by the general concerning Indian territory, the general replied to the assertion that this was against the law, "So much the worse for the law. Go ahead!"

It was only with difficulty that he was coaxed into changing the order. While he was imperious and high-tempered, he was withal one of the kindest-hearted and most just of men. He would apologize for any hasty word with the earnest vigor of a manly man convicted of having made a mistake. The bureau people apparently took great pleasure in fretting the general, and two or three of them, whom it is needless to name now, were responsible for the celebrated controversy he had with the Secretary of War under Hayes.

"A Plain, Blunt Man."

General Sherman could not reconcile himself to the fact that a civilian Secretary of War should be his superior in purely military matters. It was no wonder that he held this view. Mr. McCrary, who was Secretary of War at that time, was a respectable ex-member of Congress from Iowa. He knew no more about military matters than any one who had always been occupied with civil affairs. When he came into the Department the small bureau people who loved to fret General Sherman were continually forcing the secretary to show his authority. Sherman would say: "What does this Iowa chap mean by always interfering?" He was too blunt and outspoken to get along. He was too impatient to be diplomatic, and so he challenged outright the authority of the secretary. Technically, the Secretary of War was correct, and the President was obliged to sustain him.

If Mr. McCrary had been a greater man, he would undoubtedly have seen some way to avoid a controversy with this distinguished general. Any right-minded secretary would have been only too glad to give General Sherman full sway. Mr. McCrary, however, was of the type, dogged and dull, which is as relentless as fate in adhering to some small technical right, and consequently the breach between him and the general was made complete when the President sustained the secretary. General Sherman never called on him after that. He made one appeal to the President, and that was to be permitted to remove the headquarters of the army to St. Louis. This permission was given him, to the great despair of his staff officers. He packed up the whole establishment, and for the first time since the close of the war the headquarters of the army were in another place than at the Capital.

After several years of exile in St. Louis, where he was unhappy and discontented, General Sherman was persuaded to bring back the headquarters of the army with him, but only after Mr. McCrary had retired. Conflicts have always existed since the war between the general of the army and the Secretary of War. But no one ever made such an energetic protest as General Sherman.

Personal Appearance.

General Sherman was of a tall and spare figure. He had what is called an iron constitution. He never showed signs of fatigue, and was tireless in going about seeking amusement and entertainment when not engaged in the performance of his duties. At the War Department he was a close worker. He had great energy and great decision of character. He could transact business rapidly. He had keen intuitions and formed impressions as rapidly as a woman. He was a strange combination of iron self-control and passionate emotional capabilities.

The general was over six feet in height. He was broad-shouldered. There was a great resemblance between him and his brother, Senator John Sherman. General Sherman had all the ruggedness of feature of a man who lived out of doors, while the Senator's features are refined by indoor life and the study of books. The general had a broad forehead, dark eyes deeply set, a large Roman nose, a face marked and seamed in its upper part and hidden in the lower part by a short, gray beard and mustache. He had a deep voice. He was fond of young people. He loved to go to the theatre.

He rarely prepared himself for any speech-making. Nearly all of his remarks were off-hand, the ideas of which were suggested to him through the stimulus of the occasion. He was fond of attending Grand Army gatherings. At their meetings, called camp-fires, he used to appear at his best. Surrounded by his old associates, he would recount in a most spirited and entertaining manner stories and experiences of his campaigns. He was a man of extreme simplicity of manners, thoroughly devoid of any pretence. He was a manly man. He was in sympathetic touch with the plain people. He knew all parts of this country well. He was especially interested in the West and its development.

Graphic Pictures of the War.

One of the most important chapters of his life after the war was the writing of his memoirs. He wrote this book too soon after the war for his own personal comfort. He had to speak of the actors in the War of the Rebellion while the greater number of them were still living. He wrote as plainly concerning them as if they had been dead and buried. His blunt criticisms brought out many protests. But in the end these memoirs will live as one of the most correct pictures of the period through which he passed. The books written by the three great generals form a splendid basis for an estimate of their characters. Sherman is more brilliant, more slashing, and entertaining. This is his character.

Very Gallant.

He had the reputation of being one of the most gallant men in the army. His gallantry, however, was kindly and commendable throughout his whole long life. His great name was never touched by scandal. He had a fatherly, kindly air which made a welcome for him in every house in Washington. His favorite companion in Washington days was General Van Vliet. Arm in arm they used to go about from one house to another, greeted everywhere with the smiles and bright looks of the young ladies of Washington, who vied with each other in strewing social roses in the path of this most distinguished and most charming veteran.

The resolution and strong purpose and grim gravity exhibited by his features in repose would indicate to the stranger a lack of the softer and more humane qualities, but when he was animated in social conversation such an estimate was changed at once, and in his bright and sympathizing smile one was reminded of Richard's words:

"Grim-visaged War has smoothed his wrinkled front."

His association with his friends and comrades was always exceedingly cordial, and his affection for those allied to him as tender as that of a woman. In May,

1888, when he presided for the last time at a dinner of the Loyal Legion, he declined a re-election, and when he arose at two o'clock in the morning, to say good-bye, an almost death-like stillness prevailed.

A Pathetic Farewell.

The general spoke with feeling of the extraordinary scene. He said it was delightful to see such a body of men together, so strong physically and mentally, and to hear such speeches. He was sure no European country could produce such a gathering, yet he had seen similar meetings all over this land, from Maine to Puget's Sound, even in New Orleans and in Atlanta. The lessons of patriotism and loyalty to the flag inculcated here he begged companions to carry home with them and teach them to their children and grandchildren; and with this he said farewell, asking the commandery to join in singing "America."

General Sherman had to fight some battles after the war, and was attacked repeatedly and in many ways. But he always seemed to take a grim satisfaction in the blows both given and received, and it was never said of him that he ran away from his enemy.

In November, 1871, he obtained leave of absence for twelve months, and travelled extensively in the East and in Europe, being received everywhere with many honors. The Khedive of Egypt caused a good deal of comment by sending to the general's daughter, Minnie, a valuable present of diamonds.

The general's family consisted of his wife, Ellen

Boyle Ewing, and six children, two sons and four daughters. He was married, as already stated, in 1850, when thirty years of age, and his active military life, which began ten years later, involved the necessary separation from his family a great portion of the time until the close of the war. This was not according to his liking, but he was too good a patriot and soldier to grumble or find fault while battles were to be fought and won. On his retirement he removed from Washington to St. Louis, where he had resided at the breaking out of the war. Here he intended to spend the remainder of his life, but two years later was induced by his daughter, Mrs. Fitch, to move to New York, where he continued to reside until his death.

Household Circle.

The first two or three years of his residence in New York he spent with his wife at the Fifth Avenue Hotel, but, preferring home to hotel life, he removed in the latter part of 1888 to a modest house on Seventy-first street, where he passed his closing years. Here his wife died of heart disease November 28, 1888, at the age of sixty-four. After her death his two unmarried daughters, Lizzie and Rachel, presided over the affairs of his househould. His other children are Thomas Ewing Sherman, a Catholic priest; Tecumseh Sherman, a member of the bar in New York City; Elenor M., the wife of Lieutenant Thackara of the navy; and Mrs. T. W. Fitch of Pittsburg

Mrs. Sherman was a devout Catholic, who trained her children in her own faith, and through whose influence her eldest son became a member of the priesthood. His choice of a religious life was a great disappointment to his father, who had marked out for him a brilliant career in another channel. General Sherman was too good a father to oppose his son's choice, while regretting it, as he was too good a husband to oppose his wife, although not a Catholic himself. His own religious faith is best expressed in his own reverent words on one occasion when asked the question. "I believe in God the Almighty; that is as far as I have got," said the grim-visaged soldier.

Army Treasures.

At his home in New York his closing years were far from idle. An early riser, methodical in his habits and work, after a light breakfast he was accustomed to resort at once to the library on the parlor floor of his house. It contained a comparatively large collection of books, not entirely of a military character. There were few men who were better posted on the literary and historical records of this and other lands. A large amount of the space in his library was taken up by the maps which were drawn by himself and his generals during the Civil War.

He had the original copies of the maps, and there was scarcely a day when he was not called upon to settle by reference some disputes as to a military manœuvre made by himself or some other general. These maps were his hobby, and very valuable they are, too, viewed from any standpoint. Then, too, he had an enormous correspondence, made up largely of invitations to speak before Grand Army posts and to contribute to all sorts of periodicals. He passed through the evening of his life in a calm and quiet manner, beloved and honored by the whole country, and blessed with a fuller share of happiness than falls to the lot of most men.

In the summer of 1878 a great disappointment fell upon the general. His eldest son, Thomas Ewing Sherman, named after the kind foster-father and the idol of his father, whom the general had hoped to make a soldier, but finding this impossible had fitted for the study of the law, decided after long hesitation to devote his life to the priesthood. This decision almost broke the general's heart, and he refused to lend the slightest countenance to the step.

In a letter dated June 1, 1878, from young Sherman to his friend Samuel Elbers of St. Louis, which was published with his consent, he stated what he proposed to do and besought his father's friends not to question the latter about it.

"Father," the young man wrote, "gave me a complete education for the Bar at Georgetown College and the Scientific School at Yale. On me rests the entire responsibility for taking this step. I go without his sanction, approval, or consent."

At the same time he expressed his sorrow for causing such grief and disappointment to the father whom he loved. The greatest cross of General Sherman's life was that no son of his followed him into the army. That had always been his first and greatest love.

General Sherman showed his belief in a future life in a letter which he wrote on his return from burying his wife. "I expected to go first," he wrote, "as I am much older and have been more severely tried, but it was not to be. But I expect to resume my place at her side some day."

CHAPTER X.

Reminiscences of the Renowned Commander.—Ardent Friendship for Grant.—Interesting Facts and Anecdotes.

LIKE all men of strong and intense American personality, General Sherman had some peculiarities that were quite his own. Akin to Grant's taciturnity was Sherman's brusqueness. He was not exactly discourteous (though none held in greater contempt the ceremonial insincerities of what is called polite life), but he had the bluntness of the soldier to excess. If anything was said that did not meet with his approval, he was quick to say so in most forcible terms, and he did not care how it was taken. Even in private life he was a fighter, and it was this aggressiveness and pugnacity of his nature and his way of hitting out straight from the shoulder that got him into so many disputes in St. Louis about seeming trifles, and led him to finally shake the dust of the city from his feet for ever.

If he did not like people he did not hesitate to tell them so, and he was very quick and decided in his likes and dislikes. Very often it took strangers some time to get accustomed to him, he was so thoroughly sincere and free from the stereotyped conventionalities. Like many another great soldier, he was forcible in his language and found strong expletives convenient to express his feelings. These usually came thick and fast whenever politics was broached, though it was the subject he did not like. He had an odd antipathy to Congressmen, and as a class spoke of them in terms far from complimentary.

In February, 1862, Grant was assigned to the command of the new military District of West Tennessee, with "limits not defined." At the same time Sherman, who was then a brigadier-general, was put in command of the district of Cairo. They had both been at West Point together, but Sherman had been graduated three years earlier, and up to 1862 no intimacy had existed between them. Fortune, in fact, had set them thousands of miles apart, and besides there was a considerable difference in their worldly condition. Grant was then, as a rule, very poor, while Sherman, if not rich, was at least comfortable.

Congratulating Grant.

The first official intercourse of the two men who were destined to win the highest renown in the army took place during the siege of Fort Donelson, when Sherman sent troops and supplies to Grant with extraordinary rapidity. Sherman was then the senior, but he wrote to Grant: "I will do everything in my power to hurry forward your reinforcements and supplies, and if I could be of service myself would gladly come, without making any question of rank with yourself or General Smith." There was not a particle of envy in Sherman's nature, and he never intrigued for place or position.

When Donelson fell, Sherman was one of the first to congratulate General Grant on his success. "I feel under many obligations to you," wrote General Grant in reply, "for the kind terms of your letter, and hope that should an opportunity occur you will earn for yourself that promotion which you are kind enough to say belongs to me. I care nothing for promotion so long as our arms are successful and no political appointments are made." Many years passed before the pleasant relations that existed then between the two soldiers were disclosed. The war had gone into history, but when at length the story was told the country could understand for the first time why it was there was victory in the West and so much disaster in the East.

"This," says Badeau in the *Military History of U. S. Grant*, "was the beginning of a friendship destined thereafter never to flag; to stand the test of apparent rivalry and public censure; to remain firm under trials such as few friendships were ever subjected to; to become warmer as often as it was sought to be interrupted, and in hours of extraordinary anxiety and responsibility and care to afford a solace and a support that were never lacking when the need arose."

Noble Words from Grant.

Early in 1864, General Grant was made lieutenant-general and assumed command of all the armies of the United States. Immediately on receiving this promotion, with characteristic generosity he wrote as follows to Sherman:

"While I have been eminently successful in this war, in at least gaining the confidence of the public, no one feels more than I how much of this success is due to the energy, skill, and the harmonious putting forth of that energy and skill, of those whom it has been my good fortune to have occupying subordinate positions under me.

"There are many officers to whom these remarks are applicable to a greater or less degree, proportionate to their ability as soldiers; but what I want is to express my thanks to you and McPherson as the men to whom, above all others, I feel indebted for whatever I have had of success. How far your advice and suggestions have been of assistance you know. How far your execution of whatever has been given you to do entitles you to the reward I am receiving you cannot know as well as I do. I feel all the gratitude this letter would express, giving it the most flattering construction."

The reply of General Sherman to what he well called a "characteristic and more than kind" letter is worth quoting in part, to show the relations which existed between these two eminent soldiers fighting in a common cause.

"I repeat, you do General McPherson and myself too much honor. At Belmont you manifested your traits, neither of us being near; at Donelson also you illustrated your whole character. I was not near, and

General McPherson was in too subordinate a capacity to influence you.

"Until you had won Donelson, I confess I was almost cowed by the terrible array of anarchical elements that presented themselves at every point; but that victory admitted the ray of light which I have followed ever since.

"I believe you are as brave, patriotic, and just as the great prototype Washington; as unselfish, kind-hearted, and honest as a man should be; but the chief characteristic in your nature is the simple faith in success you have always manifested, which I can liken to nothing else than the faith a Christian has in his Saviour."

Among General Sherman's photographs was a central group of three pictures. The middle one of these was a full-length likeness of Ulysses S. Grant standing in an easy pose, with the left hand thrust into the breast of a fatigue coat and the right deep down in the trousers pocket. To the left of this was a picture of Phil Sheridan in full uniform, and to the right was a picture of General Sherman himself, also in full uniform. He was especially fond of these pictures of Grant and Sheridan. He was wont to say that he knew of no other likeness of Grant that showed so clearly the repose of the man. It had been taken at the close of the war, when Grant was down to fighting weight, as the general expressed it, and before he had become fleshy and taken on the heavy look that appears in some of his later pictures. The picture of Sheridan had been selected by General Sheridan out of many hundreds, and on this account General Sherman preferred it to all others. He used to say that he loved these pictures because they recalled to him the men as he had known them best. These photographs were among his valuable treasures.

Porter's Description of Sherman.

Admiral Porter got down to Memphis, where Sherman was awaiting him, in a week or ten days, and sent word to Sherman that he would call on him. Admiral Porter, in one of his books, gives a racy account of the meeting and a good portrait of Sherman. They had never before met. "Thinking," says the admiral, "that Sherman would be dressed in full feather, I put on my uniform coat, the splendor of which rivalled that of a drum-major. Sherman, hearing that I was indifferent to appearances and generally dressed in working clothes, thought he would not annoy me by fixing up, and so kept on his blue flannel suit, and we met, both a little surprised at the appearance of the other.

"'Halloo, Porter!' said the general, 'I am glad to see you; you got here sooner than I expected, but we'll get off to-night.' (They were preparing for the second attack on Vicksburg.) 'Devilish cold, isn't it? Sit down and warm up.' And he stirred up the coal in the grate.—'Here, captain,' to one of his aides, 'tell General Blair to get his men on board at once. Tell the quartermaster to report as soon as he has six hundred thousand rations embarked.'—'Here,

Dick,' to his servant, 'put me up some shirts and underclothes in a bag, and don't bother me with a trunk and traps enough for a regiment.'—'Here, captain,' to another aide, 'tell the steamboat captains to have steam up at six o'clock, and to lay in plenty of fuel, for I'm not going to stop every few hours to cut wood. Tell the officer in charge of embarkation to allow no picking and choosing of boats—the generals in command must take what is given them. There! that will do—Glad to see you, Porter; how's Grant?'"

Could not Perform Impossibilities.

The embarkation took place December 19, the boats steaming down to Helena. The failure of that expedition is a matter of history. The obstacles and mishaps were too great for even Sherman to overcome, and he retired, surrendering the command to McClernand, who had been personally appointed by President Lincoln. "My relief on the heels of a failure," says Sherman, "raised the usual cry at the North of 'repulse, failure, and bungling.' There was no bungling on my part, for I never worked harder or with more intensity of purpose in my life, and General Grant, long after, in his report of the operations of the seige of Vicksburg, gave us all full credit for the skill of the movement and described the almost impregnable nature of the ground; and, although in my official reports I assumed the whole responsibility, I have ever felt that had General Morgan promptly and skilfully sustained the lead of Frank Blair's brigade on that day, we should have broken the rebel line and effected a lodgment on the hills behind Vicksburg."

Sherman's wonderful faculty for comprehending topographical details, developed, of course, by his war experience, often astonished those with whom he was well acquainted. He would go for a drive where he had never been before, and startle those around him by telling them where this and that road started, the length of stream, what was planted before growth appeared, and even telling what would be encountered ahead that was not in sight. All this he did by his keen observation, his wonderful intuition and reasoning powers, and the experience he had given to such matters for a lifetime. He said himself once, in speaking of his march to the sea, that he already knew before he started some of the States better than anybody who lived in them.

Living Over Old Campaigns.

General Sherman's house was a war-office in miniature. In his basement he had a big office fitted up with war maps and documents of tremendous value, including duplicates of those in use at Washington. Here he passed many happy hours, living over the old campaigns with the maps before his eyes, and planning how he might have done otherwise if he had it all to do over again, and what the result of this or that movement would have been.

The office was a rendezvous for military men when they were in New York, who always were certain of meeting with a warm welcome, and it was much frequented by historical writers in search of material and documentary evidence.

A friend, in speaking of the general, said: "The old fighter is peculiar in one respect. The girl that opens his door for visitors never has to go and ask him if he is in. At the first she tells one that 'the general is in,' or he is not. That settles it. If he is in he will see you. If you are a bore, as a good many of his callers are, look out for squalls, and under any circumstances it is not well to be prolix. General Sherman likes one to get to the point at once. If the visitor is not able to do this, he is likely to be interrupted.

"There is one sort of caller who is always received with warmth, and that is one of General Sherman's old soldiers, or his 'boys,' as he calls them. Just how much assistance General Sherman gives to old and unfortunate soldiers it would be hard to say. No one but himself knows and he won't tell. But these are among the more numerous of the visitors at his house. Besides them there are all sorts and conditions of callers at his house."

The California Drummer.

General Sherman had a wonderful memory. This was illustrated by an incident that occurred in Philadelphia. He was visiting his daughter, and while sitting at the open window smoking one midsummer night he saw the policeman pass, and as the patrolman halted a moment the general was noticed to give him a keen glance and utter an exclamation.

The next evening he told some one that when the policeman on the beat passed again to say he wanted to speak to him. When the officer entered he straightened up and gave General Sherman the regular military salute.

"Ah, ha!" said the general, "I thought so. Now, where was it I saw you before? Do you know me?"

"Oh yes," said the bearded patrolman, "I knew you when you were a lieutenant. I was your drummer in California."

"Ha, ha, I thought so; and wait a bit. So you were that little drummer-boy, and your name—your name's Hutchinson."

Sure enough, the general of the United States army, who has seen thousands of drummers, had recognized in a passing policeman the drummer-boy who was with his company in the Mexican War.

Dates, names, figures, and the greatest intricacy of details could not escape General Sherman's marvellous memory. He remembered them all, and could call them up after the lapse of many years. He remembered everything about California just before and at the time it was admitted to the Union as though it had been yesterday. He was in command of a portion of the United States forces there then.

Sherman's Humorous Side.

The men who served with or under General Sherman in any of his numerous and brilliant campaigns are now telling anecdotes illustrative of that wonderful personality that has made so deep an impress upon

American history during the third of a century past. It was in the presence of his old army friends, when the civilian world was shut out, that he was at his best, and the flow of his spirits ran unchecked and joke and story ran into each other, sometimes at the expense of his neighbor and as often at the expense of himself. No conceit gave him more amusement than that his friend General Howard was a convivial spirit, given to the bowl and kindred pursuits, whereas the hero of the one arm is the most temperate of men. It was this fact that gave point to the joke, and Sherman was never more happy than when he could corner Howard at one of their little Loyal Legion dinners and lecture him upon the errors of his ways.

That Seidlitz Powder.

Perhaps Sherman never forgot a great practical joke which Howard unconsciously played upon him back in the days when the Union army was resting upon its arms at Goldsborough. Sherman paid a visit to Howard's tent, where neither wine nor anything more invigorating than cold water was kept. As luck would have it, Dr. James Moore, the medical director, dropped into Howard's tent. Here was a man Sherman could depend upon in an emergency like this.

Sherman gave Moore a wink when Howard's back was turned and said, "Doctor, have you a seidlitz powder in your quarters? I don't feel just right, and I know one would do me good." Moore had not supplemented a liberal college education by several years in the army in vain. He was equal to any drug clerk of New York in his knowledge of the meaning of a wink.

"A seidlitz powder, general? Certainly. Come right over to my quarters and I can fix you out immediately."

General Howard sprang to his feet. "That won't be necessary, doctor," he said. "I have plenty of powders here, and good ones, too. I will get the general one."

Sherman had little desire and less need for a seidlitz just then, and he followed Howard to his feet. "Never mind," said he, "I can get along very well without it."

"No trouble at all," Howard answered, as he began to get the powder and the glasses ready. Sherman turned to Moore for relief, but that gentleman was busy in examining the landscape as an aid to keeping his face straight.

When that was accomplished he turned about and gravely said: "By the way, general, I don't believe I have one about the premises, and you had better take the one Howard has prepared." Moore was something of a joker himself, and knew a joke when he saw one.

Sherman was a soldier to the backbone and would not retreat in the face of an enemy. When Howard came up with the glasses he bravely took them and swallowed the foaming stuff. But he never again complained of needing medicine when in Howard's tent.

A Joke on the General.

A joke as good, but of a different character, was that almost unconsciously perpetrated on Sherman by an Indian chief. Out at Fort Bayard there lay for a long time an old cannon of no use to any one, but which had greatly taken the fancy of an old Apache chief. He daily asked the commander for it, but was put off with the excuse that it belonged to the Government and could not be given away. One day General Sherman arrived at the fort, and the request of the chief was referred to him. He examined the cannon, saw that it was worthless, and told the Indian he might have it. Then, putting on a grave air, he said to the chief: "I am afraid you want that gun so that you can turn it on my soldiers and kill them."

"Umph! no," was the unexpected reply. "Cannon kill cowboys. Kill soldiers with club."

General Hickenlooper of Ohio tells a story illustrating Sherman's dry wit, rather at the expense of General Corse. In the fight at Allatoona a rifle-ball took Corse alongside the head, making a slight wound that, at the time, was thought to be a great deal more dangerous than it really was. When the word reached Sherman it had been greatly magnified, and he was informed that Corse's ear and cheek were gone, but that he would still hold his position and fight it out.

Meanwhile, Corse had tied up his head and gone on with the business he had been sent there to do. As soon as possible Sherman hurried over, full of anxiety as to the amount of damage done his officer. Nothing would do but that the bandage must come off, so that he might judge of the damage for himself. The surgeon carefully took off the cloths and revealed a slight gash across the face and a hole through the ear. Sherman looked for a moment and then dryly said: "Why, Corse, they came mighty near missing you, didn't they?"

"Going Just Where I Please."

Many are the stories told of that march to the sea, and occasionally the general would tell one himself. Here is one of his own narration: On one occasion he had halted for rest on the piazza of a house by the roadside, when it came into the mind of an old Confederate who was present that he might pick up a bit of valuable information by a little careful quizzing. He knew by Sherman's dress that he was an officer, but had no suspicion as to his rank. When he heard a staff officer use the title of "General" he turned to Sherman in surprise and said: "Are you a general?"

"Yes, sir," was the response.

"What is your name?"

"Sherman."

"Sherman! You don't mean General Sherman?"

"That's who I mean."

"How many men have you got?"

"Oh, over a million."

"Well, general, there's just one question I'd like to ask, if you have no objection."

"Go ahead."

"Where are youns agoing to go when you go away from here?"

"Well, that's a pretty stiff question to ask an entire stranger under these circumstances, but if you will give me your word to keep it a secret I don't mind telling you."

"I will keep it a secret; don't have no fear of me."

"But there is a great risk, you know. What if I should tell you my plans, and they should get over to the enemy?"

"I tell you there is no fear of me."

"You are quite sure I can trust you?"

"As your own brother."

The general slowly climbed into his saddle and leaned over to the expectant Confederate, who was all eyes and ears for the precious information: "I will tell you where I am going. I am going—just where I please." And he did, and there was not enough power in the South to stop him.

The Brave Drummer-Boy.

Sherman never forgot that little drummer-boy who came to him in the hot fight at the rear of Vicksburg, and when it came in his power he had the youngster appointed to the Naval Academy at Annapolis. The troops were in the heat of the engagement when Sherman heard a shrill, childish voice calling out to him that one of the regiments was out of ammunition, and that the men would have to abandon their position unless he sent to their relief. He looked down, and there by the side of his horse was a mite of a boy with the blood running from a wound in his leg.

"All right, my boy," said the general; "I'll send them all they need, but as you seem to be badly hurt, you had better go and find a surgeon and let him fix you up."

The boy saluted and started to the rear, while Sherman prepared to give the required order for the needed ammunition. But he once more heard the piping voice shouting back at him: "General, calibre fifty-eight! calibre fifty-eight!" Glancing back, he saw the little fellow, all unconscious of his wound, running again toward him to tell of the character of the ammunition needed, as another size would have been of no use and left the men as badly off as before. Sherman never could speak too highly of the little fellow's pluck; he asked him his name, complimented him, and promised to keep an eye upon him; which he did. He often related the story, and always with praises for the little soldier's bravery.

A good story is told of one who was on Kenesaw Mountain during Sherman's advance. A group of Confederates lay in the shade of a tree overlooking the Union camps about Big Shanty. One soldier remarked to his fellows: "Well, the Yanks will have to git up and git now, for I heard General Johnston himself say that General Wheeler had blown up the tunnel near Dalton, and that the Yanks would have to retreat because they could get no more rations."

"Oh, ———!" said a listener. "Don't you know that old Sherman carries a duplicate tunnel along?"

One day, looking back, the men saw a line of bridges in their rear in flames.

"Guess, Charley," said a trooper, "Uncle Billy has set the river on fire."

Charley's reply was, "Well, if he has, I reckon it's all right."

A Capital Host.

General Sherman was always a most delightful host. His welcome was cordial and hospitable, and the guests felt at once at ease while realizing the honor and the privilege of the association. As a *raconteur* he was admirable. He had lived so long, had seen so much, and had done so much, that the least suggestion brought forth from him stories that were both instructive and entertaining. On his seventieth birthday, which he celebrated by a little dinner in his home on the evening of February 8, 1890, he said: "Yes, I am seventy years old to-day, the time allotted for man to live, but I can truly say that I have not felt better at any time within ten years. Seventy years is a long time, and it seems a great while since I was a boy. Still, I can recall incidents that happened when I was not more than four years of age." His memory was astonishing in detail and his mind was wonderful in vigor. He could recall the minutiæ of incidents almost from infancy and throughout his eventful career.

The partiality of the grizzled old war-hero for

ladies' society is well known, and at school reunions and many such occasions his friendly and cordial notice of many a rosy miss who had never seen him before is familiarly remembered.

His love for the theatre was prodigious. He was deeply interested in all that pertained to the stage, and he valued certain actors and actresses as his dearest friends. He used to tell how he had come to New York when he was sixteen years old, and had then visited the old Park Theatre, on Park Row, between Beekman and Ann streets. In those days, he said, there were great star actors, but the general average of theatrical people was not high, and the possibility of an actress being received in social circles was not considered. He gloried in the change that had taken place in the interim, and it was a delight to him to recognize the fact that many of our actresses to-day might grace any parlor with their presence. He maintained that it was the duty of all public men to foster and encourage an institution so worthy as the stage.

Opinion of Dinners.

In attending public dinners, of which he averaged far more than any other man of his age, General Sherman was very particular as to what he ate. He confined himself on such occasions to the plainest dishes, and was wont to drink only a little sauterne or sherry. He never touched champagne, and had no use for the heavier wines. Of all things, he abhorred what he called those mixed-up French dishes which might be anything or nothing. "Half the time," he used to say, "these concoctions are only turkey or chicken hash fixed up with some kind of sauce and called a croquette or something of the kind. I have no use for them." He had his own theories about dining both in private and in public.

He disliked exceedingly the prevalent custom of late dinners. He declared that all private dinners should be given at such an hour as to enable the diners to attend the theatre afterward. His great love for the theatre probably had more to do with this position than his dislike for late dinners. He also advocated plain food for public dinners, and deplored the costliness of modern banquets, declaring that it was absurd to pay twenty-five dollars a plate for a dinner. Most people could not eat such dinners, and those that could paid the penalty of sickness for their rashness. Fond as General Sherman was of public banquets, he loved his home better. He was happiest when he could gather about him a choice circle of intimate friends and entertain them in his own house.

Birthday Episode.

When he attained his seventieth birthday the Union League Club proposed to honor the event by a banquet to him in its club-house. He thanked them for the kindness intended, but refused on the ground that he had arranged and preferred a little dinner in his own dining-room, which could seat but sixteen people. And so he told the members of the Union League that they would have to postpone their proposed banquet or else abandon it altogether. He was going to dine at home that night, and with him he would have his brother John, the United States Senator from Ohio, and General Schofield, General Howard, and General Slocum, who had been his three division commanders at the close of the war. It afforded General Sherman the greatest happiness that these three distinguished soldiers should be with him that night, and all in excellent health. Mr. Depew was very anxious to have General Sherman come around to the Union League Club that night after the dinner in his own house, but the general replied to this suggestion: "How can I do that, Chauncey? I can't hurry up my guests in order to go to somebody else's entertainment. You will have to give up this Union League scheme of yours." And so Mr. Depew submitted gracefully to the inevitable, but a month later a grand banquet was given by the Union League in honor of General Sherman's birthday, and at this banquet were present many of the most noted men in the United States, all eager to honor the old chieftain.

The General's "Fad."

Thousands of his friends have interesting stories to tell of Sherman. So democratic were his manners, and so easy for all sincere travellers was the road to his heart, that of his friends and admirers, numerous as they were, each feel as if he had in his particular custody some bit of history or anecdote of the great commander which the world could not afford to lose.

The general's fondness for kissing pretty girls was the subject for stories innumerable. How that fondness, which may have been latent in his earlier career, for all we know, developed with him into a fad in the satisfaction of which his efforts were untiring, and, it must be confessed, exceedingly popular, is not generally known. Here are the facts as related by himself:

"Some time after Grant was elected President I went to call on him at the White House. I had been struck with the number and speed of his horses, and with the delight it seemed to give him to be in their company. So I said to him, 'General, fine horses seem to have become a fad with you.'

"'Well, Sherman,' said he, 'we all must have our fads these days. It seems to have become the fashionable thing. I have all my life been intensely fond of good horseflesh. In my youth I hadn't the means to indulge this fancy. Later in life I had not the time. Now, when for the first time I have both the money and the leisure, I am indulging it and enjoying it to the full.'

Kissing the Pretty Girls.

"'Well, general,' said I, 'I suppose I'll have to be getting a fad myself. I never have had one, and if I have one now I don't know it. Let me see—let me see: what shall it be? I have it! You may drive your fast horses, and I will kiss all the pretty girls. Ha! ha! that shall be my fad.'"

General Sherman was some years afterward a

guest at Congress Hall, Saratoga, where a well-known lady was a conspicuous figure with her diamonds and her costumes. Not the least interesting of her possessions was a very charming daughter about fifteen years of age, just blushing into the first beauty of maidenhood, and as plump and as fascinating a little creature as the eye might light upon in a long day. There was a children's ball that evening at Congress Hall, and General Sherman, who seemed to be in an excellent humor, strolled into the ball-room about the time the music struck up, in company with the wife of the gentleman who is the authority for these incidents.

Rebuffed by a Little Maid.

There were scores and scores of pretty young misses ranged around the walls and waiting for the dance. As General Sherman, on the arm of his fair companion, promenaded past this array of juvenile pulchritude, a smile of unmistakable satisfaction came to his face, and his eye wandered from one bud to another with intense and respectful appreciation. When he reached the young lady referred to, after having bestowed a series of rattling salutations on the most attractive little maids, he interrupted his triumphal progress and reached out his arms to salute her tempting lips, but she would none of it.

"Thank you, sir," she said with a profound courtesy. "I cannot kiss any one without my mother's permission."

The general was delighted. "My dear young

friend," he said, with a cordial laugh, "you are quite right; but allow me to say that I must insist upon your continuing to keep this excellent rule of conduct. Promise me now that never, as long as you live, will you kiss any man who is not specially designated and approved of by your mother." Whether she did or did not make the promise is not a matter of history, but the incident was an exceedingly diverting one to all who witnessed it.

Florida Experiences.

General Sherman and General Carleton, the father of Henry Guy Carleton, were lieutenants together in the army under General Harney, the famous Indian fighter, down in the Seminole War. General Sherman's experiences at that time in Florida were a fruitful source of anecdote in his after life. One story in particular he told with great gusto of an interview between himself and a very respectable-looking young white man taken prisoner by the troops from the ranks of "Billy Bowlegs's" disreputable followers. He said it showed how accident made or marred a career.

"I said to this young man," General Sherman used to say, "that it was difficult for me to understand how he got into such bad company."

"Lieutenant," said he, "I am here as the victim of one of the most unfortunate accidents that ever happened. My father and mother are excellent citizens of the State of Kentucky, where on the farm near Paris I spent a happy boyhood. The bright dreams of my youth were clouded over by an untoward encounter with a jackass. That whole region in which we live was infested by those half-wild 'jacks' which had been imported into the State by thousands. Kentucky was the great mule-producer among the States, and when the old discarded jacks were turned out worthless we boys used to lasso them and ride them out into the woods on our expeditions after chestnuts and walnuts.

"One day I secured the raggedest, longest-eared, and deepest-voiced brute you ever saw, and hid him in the smoke-house, intending to start off before day the next morning on a nutting expedition. Now, I had a maiden aunt who lived in the family who had a strong and earnest conviction of the existence of a personal devil. The Evil One was to her just such an awful creature as Bunyan showed his to be in his *Pilgrim's Progress*. Down on a farm in Kentucky people get up before day anyway, and when my aunt went out to the smoke-house the next morning to get some bacon to fry for breakfast, it was still pitch dark.

His Satanic Majesty.

"As she opened the smoke-house door, she said afterward, she saw the horrible face of the arch enemy himself popped suddenly out at her through the darkness, set off by two long and hideous 'horns.' No sooner had the jack spied my respected relative than he broke forth into a series of the most diabolic, ear-piercing, nerve-tearing hee-haws that ever desolated the stillness of a country landscape. My aunt went off into a succession of fits, and when she came to, she swore by all that was holy that she had seen the devil. I had slept calmly through the whole disturbance, but the offence was promptly laid at my door, and, entering my room while I was yet asleep, my father wore out a leather strap on me.

"But for this apparently trivial incident I might to-day be a respected citizen of the great State which raises pretty girls, blue grass, mules, and bourbon, for, smarting under a sense of wrong and the lively application of the strap, I put two shirts into a handkerchief, and without waiting to say good-bye, made a bee-line South. I never stopped until I got into the Florida swamps, where I have just been taken prisoner."

"Old Bill."

This was a favorite story of General Sherman's, as showing how a man's whole career could be swerved by a trifling incident. There is another story which he used to tell to his intimates which illustrates the serious side of his mind, and betrays by a touch the gentle and affectionate nature which became toward the end of his life his most marked characteristic.

"When I went back to Washington," he used to say, "after the war was over and took part in the grand review, I was struck during the first day by the disorder and confusion in the procession caused by the antics of some of the fiery chargers ridden by the officers. On the first day the Army of the Potomac filed by. Many gallant troopers had changed off their old war-horses, and that day for the first time rode animals unaccustomed to such surroundings. The immense masses of humanity, the blare of the bands, and the glitter of the landscape in general, frightened these beasts, so that they interfered seriously with the general effect of the spectacle. The morning of the next day, when the Army of the Tennessee was to march by in review, my old body-servant came to me and said:

"'General, what horse do you want to ride to-day?'

"'Old Bill,' said I.

"'Why, general,' said my servant, 'Old Bill isn't the kind of a horse you'd want to ride to-day, sure. Why, he's got no life and spirit about him, and won't make any show at all.'

"Now," continued the general, "that was the very reason why I wanted to ride old Bill. I knew there was no nonsense in him. In fact he might have been called sheepish. A cannonade itself would not have excited him, and I was looking out for my own comfort, not for display. So that morning I got on the old charger and rode quietly along through that impressive scene. The old fellow never phazed and exhibited about as much style as a plough-horse. But we got through very comfortably.

"After passing about one hundred yards beyond the grand stand I rode old Bill to the sidewalk and dismounted. He was led away, where I do not know, and I have never seen the old fellow since. I never knew what they did with him, and it has always been a genuine sorrow to me that I hadn't been able to keep him near me during the rest of our lives."

His Versatility.

Colonel L. M. Dayton, who came on from Cincinnati to attend General Sherman's funeral, was eight years on his staff, serving with him during the entire war and for nearly five years afterward. The intimacy of the relations which Colonel Dayton in such a position necessarily sustained to the great commander gave him a peculiar insight into the operations of his mind. He tells the following story of an incident which could have happened in the military experience of no other general during the war, and which illustrates admirably the boldness of Sherman's military operations and the extraordinary foresight with which he planned out a campaign even beyond what might seem to many its objective point.

"What amazed me most," said Colonel Dayton, "was the varsatility of that extraordinary soldier. I cannot help but believe that as a general he was greater than any other the war produced. He planned a campaign to its uttermost limit before he began active operations. For instance, in the Vicksburg campaign, while General Grant might not have figured out his movements beyond the actual capture of that city itself, General Sherman in his place would have outlined clearly what he would do with his men after the siege and what disposition he would make of the baggage and siege-guns.

"When we started out from Atlanta on the march to the sea, nobody knew what our objective point on the Atlantic coast was, except a few members of the staff and the authorities at Washington. Everybody else simply knew that we were going to march across Georgia to the coast. When General Sherman reached Savannah—which of course was all along known to the authorities as our objective point—he was greatly surprised to find that a gunboat had been despatched down the coast to meet him there.

"I Won't do Anything of the Kind."

"The captain of this gunboat had succeeded in ascending Ossabaw Sound and the Ogeechee River, which lies just back of Savannah, and made instant communication with the general. An important official document which had been brought down in this way was handed to General Sherman in my presence. When he received it he got excited and seemed vexed about something. I noticed his color rising and a look of irritation in his eye, as well as the nervous motion of the left arm which characterized him when anything annoyed him. It seemed, for instance, as if he was pushing something away from him.

"'Come here, Dayton,' said he; and we went into the inner room of the building where he made his headquarters. As soon as we got inside I could see that he was greatly opposed to the suggestions that had apparently been contained in the document.

THE BATTLE OF MANASSAS OR BULL RUN.

GENERALS SHERMAN AND GRANT AT THE BATTLE OF SHILOH.

VICKSBURG, MISSISSIPPI.

GUNBOATS RUNNING PAST VICKSBURG AT NIGHT.

'I won't do it,' he would say to himself several times over—'I won't do anything of the kind.'

"The document was an official order from Secretary Stanton, approved by General Grant, for General Sherman to wait with his army at Savannah for transports which had been sent down the coast to convey them by sea to the mouth of the James, and then to ascend that river to co-operate with Grant. General Sherman had all along intended to march his army up the coast across the country, and he sat down at once and wrote a letter to General Grant explaining to him why he was opposed to taking a sea-voyage with his men; how he thought such an experience would demoralize them with sea-sickness, confinement in close quarters and lack of exercise; and how he had decided to take all the responsibility and march them up by land in accordance with his original plans. He said he would be at Goldsboro, N. C., on the 21st day of March, 1865, and that if any other orders were sent to him there, they would reach him promptly. So closely did he calculate that on the 23d of March he was in possession of Goldsboro.

"As Sherman had at that time practically an army of a hundred thousand men, which could easily annihilate any opposition he might meet with on his march, the wisdom of his course was at once apparent to the authorities, and no attempt was made to interfere with his execution of his plans. As a matter of fact, he did encounter Joe Johnston on the way up the coast and defeated him at Bentonville. That, I believe, was his last battle. No other general would have dared to do what Sherman did in this instance. The boldness of his military genius and his keen insight into the future were admirably illustrated by it.

How He Met Jenny Lind.

"It was in Florence," he said; "I received a card to a *musicale*, as they called it, and Jenny Lind sent me with this card a note saying how much she would feel honored, and all that. So I went.

"Lord! but it was awful!

"They lived on the top floor of an old palace. Jenny Lind looked like a washwoman, and Goldschmidt, her husband, was a little black, weazened fellow. There was a daughter, too, I remember. She was freckled mighty bad!

"It was an awful time. The refreshments were ice-cream and jumbles. I got away as soon as I could —it made my heart ache to remember that woman so different and see her now so contented with the change. I'd have jumped out of a four-story window to have escaped.

"She was a good woman, too," he went on musingly. "They were very poor at this time. She had spent all the money she had made in America in Swedish charities. I think she might better have kept some of it, anyhow."

Hated to be Photographed.

"My! how I hate to be photographed," the general exclaimed one day, "because in pictures by that process I always look stern; don't like to look stern. My mood is pleasant and friendly to all, though I have been told that when I'm in a fight I look like the very devil. That is because my nature is one that concentrates itself, heart and soul, fire and will, into one terrible focus. No half measures for me. I take after my mother in that."

He Tells of a Speech by Grant.

The following characteristic anecdote of General Grant was told, and illustrated with exquisite humor, by General Sherman at a little dinner:

"Grant and I were at Nashville, Tenn., after the battle of Chattanooga. Our quarters were in the same building.

"One day Grant came into the room that I used for an office. I was very busy, surrounded with papers, muster-rolls, plans, specifications, etc., etc. When I looked up from my work I saw he seemed a good deal bothered, and, after standing around a while, with his shoulders thrown up and his hands deep down in his trousers pockets, he said:

"'Look here, there are some men here from Galena.'

"'Well?' I said.

"Looking more uncomfortable every minute, he went on:

"'They've got a sword they want to give me;' and, looking over his shoulder and jerking his thumb in the same direction, he added:

"'Will you come in?'

"He looked quite frightened at the idea of going to face them alone, so I put some weights on my several piles of papers to keep them from blowing around, and went into the next room, followed by Grant, who by this time looked as he might if he'd been going to be court-martialled. There we found the mayor and some members of the board of councilmen of Galena. On a table in the middle of the room was a handsome rosewood box containing a magnificent gold-hilted sword, with all the appointments equally splendid.

Grant Nonplussed.

"The mayor stepped forward and delivered what was evidently a carefully prepared speech, setting forth that the citizens of Galena had sent him to present to General Grant the accompanying sword, not as a testimonial to his greatness as a soldier, but as a slight proof of their love and esteem for him as a man and their pride in him as a fellow-citizen.

"After delivering the speech the mayor produced a large parchment scroll, to which was attached by a long blue ribbon a red seal as big as a pancake, and on which was inscribed a set of complimentary resolutions. These he proceeded to read to us, not omitting a single 'whereas' or 'hereunto.' And after finishing the reading he rolled it up and with great solemnity and ceremony handed it to Grant.

"General Grant took it, looked ruefully at it, and held it as if it burnt him. Mrs. Grant, who had been standing beside her husband, quietly took it from him, and there was dead silence for several minutes. Then Grant, sinking his head lower on his chest and hunching his shoulders up higher and looking thoroughly miserable, began hunting in his pockets, diving first in one and then in another, and at last said: 'Gentlemen, I knew you were coming here to give me this sword, and so I prepared a short speech;' and with a look of relief he drew from his trousers pocket a crooked, crumpled piece of paper and handed it to the mayor of Galena, adding, 'and, gentlemen, here it is!'"

The General and Mrs. Cleveland.

To those who appreciated General Sherman's genial nature it is superfluous to say that he regarded his extensive acquaintance with the "ladies of the White House" with peculiar gratification. This he specially referred to on one occasion when he had been introduced to Mrs. Cleveland, then but a short time a bride. The general said:

"The other day, when I was in Washington, I received a note from Mrs. Endicott telling me that the President and Mrs. Cleveland were to dine at her house that evening, and begging me to join them. I wrote her a very polite reply—said I had two or three engagements I must keep, but if Mrs. Endicott would reserve me a place I would slip in quietly and take up my dinner at the point at which I arrived.

"When I got there they were at the table, and I found that the seat at Mr. Endicott's left had been reserved for me, Mrs. Cleveland being on his right. Well, we just shoved Endicott to one side, and sailed in and had a good time. After a while the ladies left us, and then after a little we went into Endicott's room for a smoke. Then, about 11.30, we went up to the ladies. It was rather late, and very soon Mrs. Cleveland made a move to go, and of course several gentlemen surrounded her, helping her with her wraps; and she turned to me and said very quietly, 'General, I am very glad to have met you, and I want you to come and see me.' I smiled and said, 'You know that such an invitation is a command.' And she smiled back and said, 'When will you come? To-morrow? Shall we say one o'clock?' Well, I went, and she came in to meet me plainly and simply dressed, and was just sweet and girlish—but bright! and shrewd!

The Finest Lady at the White House.

"She wanted to know all about the ladies that have presided in the White House. I have known 'em all since Jackson's time, and she made me tell her about them. I consider Harriet Lane, Buchanan's niece, the finest lady that ever did the honors of the White House, though she was cold and impassive; but her tact and suavity of manner were perfect. I believe Mrs. Cleveland has taken Harriet Lane for her model, and she is as clever and sweet a lady as Miss Lane was.

"The sweetest woman I ever met presiding there was Kitty Taylor, General Taylor's daughter, afterward Mrs. Dr. Dandridge. But none of them was brighter and more beautiful than Mrs. Cleveland."

Youth and beauty General Sherman loved—indeed,

I think the only subject on which I ever heard him speak with deep regret, says a friend, was that of lost youth. One day he remarked, "Ah, how I envy the young their hopes and dreams and aspirations! I envy the beggar on the street if he is young—who can tell what lies before him? Yes, yes, I know, but there's no fun in looking back; it's an old story, you've heard it over and over again, but the future may hold all sorts of surprises. I went into my club the other night, and a young fellow came over to me and said, 'General, I am very proud and happy to meet you; you've been a landmark to me all my life. I've read about you in history.' Lord! he looked at me with reverence and bowed down before me, and it was all I could do to be civil to him. Read about me in his history, indeed! as if I were Moses!"

At the time of the death of General Sheridan he was lamenting the rapid thinning of the ranks of his contemporaries, and, shaking his head, said sadly, "There we go, one after another. Grant and Sheridan, and soon, I suppose, I shall join the procession. Well, that will be the last of the race—there will be no generals left when I'm gone."

Excuses for Swearing.

On one occasion when visiting his sister, Mrs. Ewing, General Sherman met four or five clergyman, and his patience was rather severely tried by their religious discussions, and what seemed to him their intolerant and one-sided views. One of them challenged him to offer any excuse for swearing, meeting him with the clinching statement that there could be no redemption for blasphemers.

"Were you," inquired the young soldier, "ever at sea in a heavy gale, with spars creaking and sails flapping, and the crew cowardly and incompetent?"

"No."

"Did you ever," he continued gravely, "try to drive a five-team ox-cart across the prairie?"

"No."

"Then," said Captain Sherman, "you know nothing of temptations to blasphemy—you know nothing about extenuating circumstances for blasphemers—you are not competent to judge?"

Proud of his Mother.

General Sherman was proud of tracing his powers of endurance to his mother, to whom he also frequently ascribed the heritage of other soldierly characteristics.

"She married very young," said the general, "her husband, who was not very much older, being a lawyer with hope and ambition for his patrimony and all the world before him where to choose. He chose Ohio, leaving his young wife in Jersey City while he made a home for her in what was then a far country, though now comparatively near.

"Soon as he had made a home for her she went to him. She rode on horseback, with her young baby in her arms, from Jersey City to Ohio, the journey occupying twenty-three days! What would a New York bride say to such a journey as that? I'm afraid she'd want to wait until her husband had made money enough to have a railroad built for her."

His Methodical Brother.

"Curious," said the general one day, " to note the differences in the family! I've got a brother out in Wisconsin—cashier in a bank—most methodical man that ever lived—eats and sleeps by rule. He couldn't live in one of these New York palaces. He lives in a nice frame house, and has for twenty years and more gone and come from his office every day at precisely the same hour. The people in the town set their watches by him, and if he were five minutes late there wouldn't be a correct timepiece within a mile. He has sat on one seat in his office and hung his coat on one peg for twenty years, and if anybody gets in before him and gets off a joke on him by using that peg, it sours his temper for the whole day."

General Sherman's "Idolized Soldier-Boy."

Willie Sherman, when about nine years of age, went down to Mississippi, where he became a comrade and favorite of the Thirteenth regulars, who formed General Sherman's personal escort. On the way up the river, after the Vicksburg campaign, he became ill. October 3, 1863, the brave little fellow died. October 4, he had a military funeral at Memphis; at midnight came a letter of thanks from the general to Captain Smith, commanding battalion, one of the most touching letters ever written. In the spring of 1867 the body was removed to St. Louis and buried in Calvary Cemetery. A beautiful marble monument was erected by the officers and soldiers of the battalion.

The above facts suggested the following poem, a copy of which was sent to the general at his home in New York. In the battalion the boy was fondly called:

"Sergeant Willie."

The Thirteenth Regulars, as brave
A regiment as ever gave
Their blood to solder sundered lands,
Of prompt obedience to commands,

Had once a sergeant of the line,
A little fellow aged nine,
Called "Sergeant Willie," Sherman's boy,
His father's pride, his mother's joy.

He—born a soldier—loved the camp;
Of future prowess bore the stamp;
While clinging yet to mother's hand
Had all the air of high command.

The Thirteenth treads to muffled drum;
To some one in its ranks has come
The soldier's fate—to some one small,
Is seen by hearse and little pall.

"Who lies so bravely 'neath the stars,
That wraps a form too young for wars?"
"Our 'Sergeant Willie,' Sherman's boy,
His father's pride, his mother's joy."

"Battalion, halt!"—Battalion weep,
Your dearest comrade sleeps the sleep
That knows no waking:—Dry your tears,
The brave have e'en in death no fears.

Whate'er was mortal, free from guilt,
Rests in the tomb affection built:
His soul has joined the ranks above,
And found a Heavenly Father's love.

GEORGE MORTON.

With military promptitude, the following characteristic letter of acknowledgment was duly sent:

75 West 71st St., New York, Sept. 9, 1889.

G. H. McCabe, Esq., Philadelphia, Pa.:

My Dear Sir: Please accept for yourself, the sender, and for Mr. Morton, the author of the poem "Sergeant Willie," a copy of which is just received, my heartfelt and grateful thanks. The same, I assure you, will be preserved in my archives, together with many other encomiums, mainly from the hands of members of the old Thirteenth, to which regiment he was in life so thoroughly devoted.

Very truly yours,
W. T. Sherman, *General*.

The general's habits of life were simple. He had a keen sense of the beauty of Nature, and never was happier than when his camp was pitched in some forest of lofty pines, where the wind sang through the treetops in melodious measure and the feet were buried in the soft carpeting of spindles. He was the last one to complain when the table fare was reduced to beef and "hard talk," and, in truth, he rather enjoyed poverty of food as one of the conditions of a soldier's life. He apologized to his guest, the Secretary of War, one day at Savannah because certain luxuries, such as canned fruits and jellies, had found their way to his table.

"This," he remarked, "is the consequence of coming

into houses and cities. The only place to live, Mr. Secretary, is out of doors in the woods."

This simplicity of taste, which was so perfectly natural to the general, served well in the campaigns of the war. It is easily seen that in making long marches the most fatal clog to successful operations is excessive transportation, and the tendency of the army was constantly to accretion; but Sherman reduced baggage-trains to the minimum, and himself shared the privations of the common soldier.

Unselfish Patriotism.

General Sherman's patriotism was a vital force. He gave himself and all that he had to the national cause. Personal considerations never influenced him. Doubtless he was ambitious, but it was impossible to discern any selfish or unworthy motive either in his words or deeds. We do not believe it possible for a man more absolutely to subordinate himself and his personal interests than he did. His patriotism was as pure as the faith of a child, and before it family and social influences were powerless. His relatives were the last persons to receive from his hand preferment or promotion. In answer to the request of one nearly allied to him that he would give his son a position on his staff, the general's reply was curt and unmistakable:

"Let him enter the ranks as a soldier and carry a musket a few years."

In all of his pleasant and peaceful old age General Sherman realized fully the necessary infirmities of increasing years and the probability that death might remove him at any time. The contemplation of death had no terrors for him. His position in this matter is best expressed in the reply which he made on his seventieth birthday to a conventional wish that he might have many happy returns of the day. He said then, with a full appreciation of the insecurity of life as well as of the fact that his race was nearly run, "I am too old to hope for many returns of the day. And then life is so uncertain. Death seems to come now-a-days without almost any warning, but many a man has sprung up in readiness when I have had the trumpets sounded, and I am still a soldier. When Gabriel sounds his trumpet I shall be ready."

He was, of course, long past the years when a man can expect vigorous health, and he often spoke about death, and said he did not expect to be much longer on the scene of active affairs. He frequently prefaced remarks about the future by saying, "If I live" and "If I am here." Indeed, for a number of years, especially since the death of his wife, his mind assumed a melancholy mood. The deaths of Hancock, Sheridan, and Grant, with whom he was intimately associated, were to him profound shocks, and had an effect different to the philosophical way in which they were regarded by others.

For some time his hearing had been failing and he had become quite deaf. This troubled him very much, as his senses had been phenomenally keen. It pained him when he could no longer hear the birds sing in the spring or the sparrows twittering in the city, and friends had to be exceedingly careful not to talk before him about things he could not hear. If such a thing occurred he was likely to get up and leave the room.

The Greatest Soldier.

How should the greatest soldier die?
The winds and seas and hills reply:

At peace! The horrid front of War
Smoothed by a smile from every scar;
His sword and spear beat into hooks
To prune his vines; among his books;
His armor rusting on the wall;
Friends thicker than the leaves that fall
In Vallombrosa; with a sigh
Of sweet content—thus let him die.

Where should the greatest soldier lie?
The winds and seas and hills reply
No granite base nor marble pile,
Nor fretted arch nor vaulted aisle,
Nor storied urn nor sculptured stone
Is worthy, now that he is gone.

In every heart where freedom swells,
In every soul where honor dwells,
Till children in their turn impart
Each memory of soul and heart
To others, who still love to hear
The name of him whom all hold dear;
There, of the nation's love possessed
In peace and honor let him rest.

BOOK II.

GENERAL SHERMAN'S GREAT MARCHES AND BATTLES.

CHAPTER XI.

Sherman at the Battle of Bull Run.—His Graphic Account of the Bloody Conflict.

In the Civil War, General Sherman came into the military service of the United States as colonel of the Thirteenth regular infantry. At Bull Run his rank was that of colonel commanding brigade.

The reader will be interested in his own graphic description of the part he acted in the first great onslaught of the war (July 21st, 1861), which is herewith given in his own words:

My brigade was composed of the Thirteenth New York Volunteers, Colonel Quinby; Sixty-ninth New York, Colonel Corcoran; Seventy-ninth New York, Colonel Cameron; Second Wisconsin, Lieutenant-Colonel Peck; and Company E, Third Artillery, under command of Captain R. B. Ayres, Fifth Artillery. We left our camp near Centreville, pursuant to orders, at half-past 2 A. M., taking place in the column of Assistant-Adjutant General Baird, next to the brigade of General Schenck, and proceeded as far as the halt, before the enemy's position, near the stone bridge across Bull Run. Here the brigade was deployed in line along the skirt of timber to the right of the Warrenton road, and remained quietly in position till after 10 A. M. The enemy remained very quiet, but about that time we saw a rebel regiment leave its cover in our front and proceed in double-quick time on the road toward Sudley Springs, by which we knew the columns of Colonels Hunter and Heintzelman were approaching.

The Enemy in Sight.

About the same time we observed in motion a large mass of the enemy below and on the other side of the stone bridge. I directed Captain Ayres to take position with his battery near our right and to open fire on this mass; but Baird had previously detached the two rifle-guns belonging to this battery, and, finding that the smooth-bore guns did not reach the enemy's position, we ceased firing, and I sent a request that Baird would send to me the thirty-pounder rifle-gun attached to Captain Carlisle's battery. At the same time I shifted the New York Sixty-ninth to the extreme right of the brigade. Thus we remained till we heard the musketry-fire across Bull Run, showing that the head of Colonel Hunter's column was engaged. This firing was brisk, and showed that Hunter was driving before him the enemy, till about noon, when it became certain the enemy had come to a stand, and that our forces on the other side of Bull Run were all engaged, artillery and infantry.

BATTLE OF RESACA.

CAVALRY CHARGE.

CHARGE OF THE FEDERALS AT CORINTH.

MAJOR-GENERAL JAMES B. M'PHERSON.

Here Baird sent me the order to cross over with the whole brigade to the assistance of Colonel Hunter. Early in the day, when reconnoitring the ground, I had seen a horseman descend from a bluff in our front, cross the stream, and show himself in the open field on this side, and, inferring that we could cross over at the same point, I sent forward a company as skirmishers, and followed with the whole brigade, the New York Sixty-ninth leading.

Haggerty Shot from his Horse.

We found no difficulty in crossing over, and met with no opposition in ascending the steep bluff opposite with our infantry, but it was impossible to the artillery, and I sent word back to Captain Ayres to follow if possible, otherwise to use his discretion. Captain Ayres did not cross Bull Run, but remained on that side with the rest of the division. Advancing slowly and cautiously with the head of the column, to give time for the regiments in succession to close up their ranks, we first encountered a party of the enemy retreating along a cluster of pines; Lieutenant-Colonel Haggerty, of the Sixty-ninth, without orders, rode out alone and endeavored to intercept their retreat. One of the enemy, in full view, at short range, shot Haggerty, and he fell dead from his horse.

The Sixty-ninth opened fire on this party, which was returned; but, determined to effect our junction with Hunter's division, I ordered this fire to cease, and we proceeded with caution toward the field where we then plainly saw our forces engaged. Displaying our colors conspicuously at the head of our column, we succeeded in attracting the attention of our friends, and soon formed the brigade in the rear of Colonel Porter's.

Here I learned that Colonel Hunter was disabled by a severe wound, and that General McDowell was on the field. I sought him out, and received his orders to join in pursuit of the enemy, who was falling back to the left of the road by which the army had approached from Sudley Springs. Placing Colonel Quinby's regiment of rifles in front, in column by division, I directed the other regiments to follow in line of battle, in the order of the Wisconsin Second, New York Seventy-ninth, and New York Sixty-ninth.

Quinby's Brave Advance.

Quinby's regiment advanced steadily down the hill and up the ridge, from which he opened fire upon the enemy, who had made another stand on ground very favorable to him, and the regiment continued advancing as the enemy gave way, till the head of the column reached the point near which Rickett's battery was so severely cut up. The other regiments descended the hill in line of battle under a severe cannonade, and, the ground affording comparative shelter from the enemy's artillery, they changed direction by the right flank, and followed the road before mentioned. At the point where this road crosses the bridge to our left front the ground was swept by a most severe fire of artillery, rifles, and musketry, and we saw, in succession, several regiments driven from

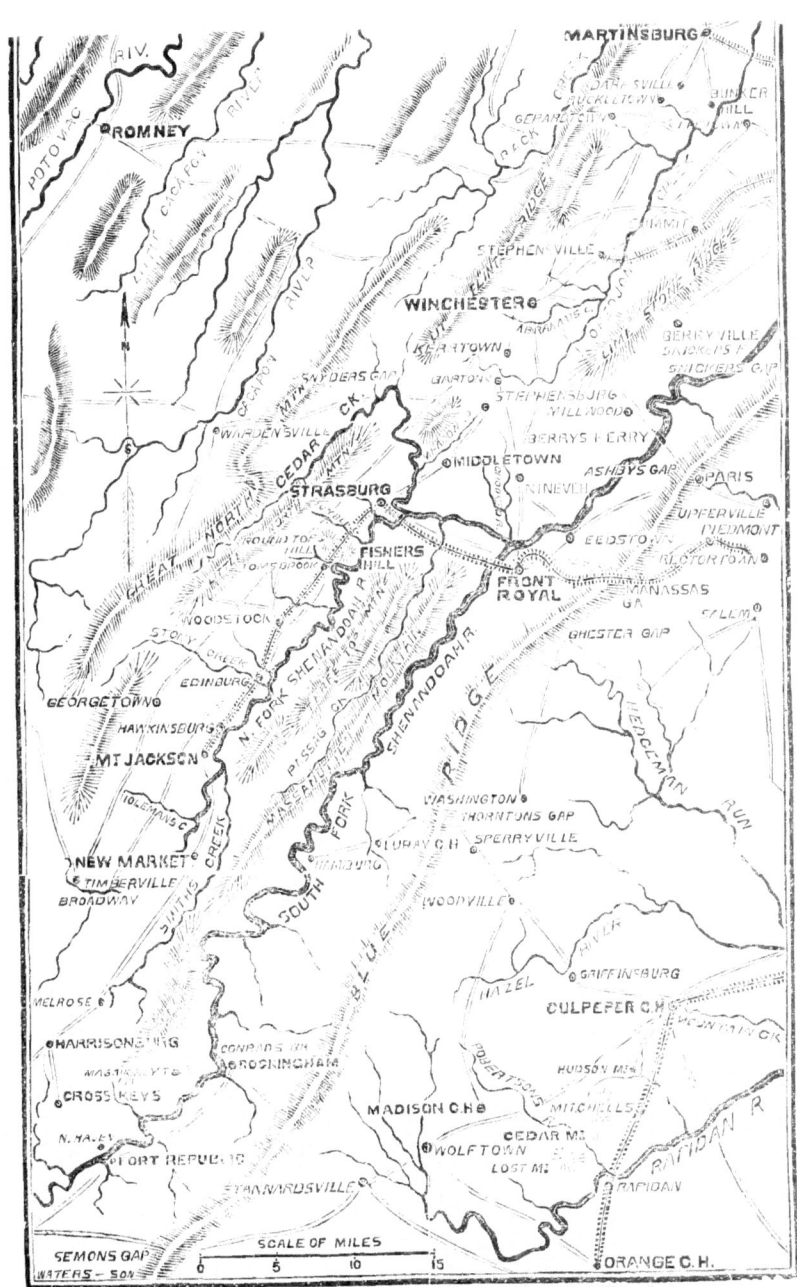

MAP SHOWING THE SHENANDOAH VALLEY.

it; among them the Zouaves and battalion of marines. Before reaching the crest of this hill the roadway was worn deep enough to afford shelter, and I kept the several regiments in it as long as possible; but when the Wisconsin Second was abreast of the enemy, by order of Major Wadsworth, of General McDowell's staff, I ordered it to leave the roadway by the left flank, and to attack the enemy.

Wisconsin Second Repulsed.

This regiment ascended to the brow of the hill steadily, received the severe fire of the enemy, returned it with spirit, and advanced, delivering its fire. This regiment is uniformed in gray cloth, almost identical with that of the great bulk of the Secession army, and when the regiment fell into confusion and retreated toward the road, there was a universal cry that they were being fired on by our own men. The regiment rallied again, passed the brow of the hill a second time, but was again repulsed in disorder. By this time the New York Seventy-ninth had closed up, and in like manner it was ordered to cross the brow of the hill and drive the enemy from cover.

It was impossible to get a good view of this ground. In it there was one battery of artillery, which poured an incessant fire upon our advancing column, and the ground was very irregular, with small clusters of pines affording shelter, of which the enemy took good advantage. The fire of rifles and musketry was very severe. The Seventy-ninth, headed by its colonel, Cameron, charged across the hill, and for a short time the contest was severe; they rallied several times under fire, but finally broke and gained the cover of the hill.

This left the field open to the New York Sixty-ninth, Colonel Corcoran, who in his turn led his regiment over the crest, and had in full open view the ground so severely contested; the fire was very severe, and the roar of cannon, musketry, and rifles incessant; it was manifest the enemy was here in great force, far superior to us at that point. The Sixty-ninth held the ground for some time, but finally fell back in disorder.

Federals Thrown into Confusion.

All this time Quinby's regiment occupied another ridge to our left, overlooking the same field of action and similarly engaged. Here, about half-past 3 P. M., began the scene of confusion and disorder that characterized the remainder of the day. Up to that time all had kept their places, and seemed perfectly cool and used to the shell and shot that fell, comparatively harmless, all around us; but the short exposure to an intense fire of small-arms at close range had killed many, wounded more, and had produced disorder in all of the battalions that had attempted to encounter it. Men fell away from their ranks, talking and in great confusion.

Colonel Cameron had been mortally wounded, was carried to an ambulance, and reported dying. Many other officers were reported dead or missing, and many of the wounded were making their way, with more or less assistance, to the buildings used as hospitals on the ridge to the west.

We succeeded in partially re-forming the regiments, but it was manifest that they would not stand, and I directed Colonel Corcoran to move along the ridge to the rear, near the position where he had first formed the brigade. General McDowell was there in person, and used all possible efforts to reassure the men. By the active exertions of Colonel Corcoran we formed an irregular square against the cavalry which were then seen to issue from the position from which we had been driven, and we began our retreat toward the same ford of Bull Run by which we had approached the field of battle.

Retreat toward Centreville.

There was no positive order to retreat, although for an hour it had been going on by the operation of the men themselves. The ranks were thin and irregular, and we found a stream of people strung from the hospital across Bull Run and far toward Centreville.

After putting in motion the irregular square in person, I pushed forward to find Captain Ayres's battery at the crossing of Bull Run. I sought it at its last position, before the brigade had crossed over, but it was not there; then passing through the woods where, in the morning, we had first formed line, we approached the blacksmith's shop, but there found a detachment of the Secession cavalry, and thence made a circuit, avoiding Cub Run Bridge, into Centreville, where I found General McDowell, and from him understood that it was his purpose to rally the forces and make a stand at Centreville.

But about nine o'clock at night I received from General Tyler, in person, the order to continue the retreat to the Potomac. This retreat was by night and disorderly in the extreme. The men of different regiments mingled together, and some reached the river at Arlington, some at Long Bridge, and the greater part returned to their former camp at or near Fort Corcoran. I reached this point at noon the next day, and found a miscellaneous crowd crossing over the aqueduct and ferries. Conceiving this to be demoralizing, I at once commanded the guard to be increased and all persons attempting to pass over to be stopped. This soon produced its effect; men sought their proper companies and regiments. Comparative order was restored, and all were posted to the best advantage.

Our loss was heavy, and occurred chiefly at the point near where Rickett's battery was destroyed. Lieutenant-Colonel Haggerty was killed about noon, before we had effected a junction with Colonel Hunter's division. Colonel Cameron was mortally wounded leading his regiment in the charge, and Colonel Corcoran has been missing since the cavalry charge near the building used as a hospital.

Lieutenants Piper and McQuesten, of my personal staff, were under fire all day, and carried orders to and fro with as much coolness as on parade. Lieutenant Bagley of the New York Sixty-ninth, a volunteer aide, asked leave to serve with his company during the action, and was among those reported missing. I had intelligence that he was a prisoner and slightly wounded.

"Colonel Coon of Wisconsin, a volunteer aide, also rendered good service during the day."

Lincoln's Humorous Reply.

They were all back near Georgetown by July 23d, and made preparations to defend their position against the Confederates, who they were certain were at their heels. Sherman about this time had trouble with some of his ninety-day men, who wanted to return home. Mr. Lincoln visited the camp one day, when one of the officers stepped up to the President's carriage, in which Sherman was seated with him, and said: "Mr. President, I have a cause of grievance. This morning I went to speak to Colonel Sherman, and he threatened to shoot me." Mr. Lincoln repeated interrogatively the words, "Threatened to shoot you?"—"Yes, sir, he threatened to shoot me." Mr. Lincoln looked at him and then at Sherman, and bending his tall, spare form toward the officer, said to him in a loud stage-whisper, that could be easily heard at some distance, "Well, if I were you, and he threatened to shoot, I would not trust him, for I believe he would do it." The officer disappeared amid the laughter of all who were around.

During the anxious August days after the battle of Bull Run, while Sherman was drilling and disciplining

GENERAL SHERMAN AT THE OUTBREAK OF THE WAR.

the raw regiments under him and getting ready to do his part in repulsing the attack that was almost hourly expected, he received a note from General Robert Anderson asking him to call on him in Washington. Anderson explained that the Administration was becoming alarmed about Kentucky, where matters were rapidly approaching a grave crisis. The Legislature was in session, and was ready, as soon as supported by the General Government, to take measures that would keep the State in the Union. It had been determined, therefore, to organize a new military department, to be known as the Department of the Cumberland, and to embrace Kentucky, Tennessee, etc.

Critical Situation in Kentucky.

Anderson said he had been offered the command, had accepted it, and wanted help. The President agreed that he should select four of the brigadiers, and he wanted Sherman to be one of them and to be his right-hand man. Anderson had been the captain of Sherman's company in the old Fort Moultrie, and knew his splendid abilities as a soldier. The other brigadiers selected for the new department by Anderson were Thomas, D. C. Buell, and Burnside. Sherman always wanted to go West, and he was rejoiced to be given the chance to go with Anderson, whom he so much admired and esteemed.

The situation in Kentucky at this time was exceedingly critical. The State was threatened with invasion by two forces—one from the direction of Nashville, under the command of Albert Sidney Johnston and

Buckner, and the other from the direction of the Cumberland Gap, under the command of Generals Crittenden and Zollicoffer. Anderson saw that the force at his disposal was not sufficient to fight these two columns, and he sent Sherman to Indianapolis and Springfield to confer with the governors of Indiana and Illinois and ascertain what assistance they could give. Sherman found Governor Morton busily engaged equipping regiments and sending them East to McClellan or to Fremont in Missouri. These two generals were then looked upon as the great soldiers who were to put an end to the war and restore the Union. Governor Yates in Illinois was as active as Morton, but the new troops were all going to Fremont or McClellan.

Sherman was not very successful in obtaining help for Kentucky, and he resolved to go to St. Louis and lay the situation before Fremont in person. When he succeeded in obtaining admission to Fremont, which was a work of no small difficulty, owing to the number of guards with whom he surrounded himself, the Western commander was courteous enough, but Sherman could do nothing with him in furtherance of his mission. He returned to Louisville. The city was in the greatest state of excitement. The Legislature had resolved to adhere to the Union, and Johnston had invaded the State, advancing as far as Bowling Green, which he began to fortify. Buckner was despatched by him with a division toward Louisville. Zollicoffer entered the State and advanced as far as Somerset. Columbus was in possession of Generals Polks and Pillow, and General Grant, on the other side, had moved from Cairo to Paducah.

In a few hours the news came that Buckner was rapidly marching on Louisville. All the troops Anderson had to oppose him were Rousseau's division and a few home-guards in Louisville. Sherman was sent out with Rousseau's force to seize Muldraugh's Hill, back of Elizabethtown. As fast as troops reached Louisville they were sent to Sherman, and toward the beginning of October he had a division of two brigades. Anderson in Louisville was rapidly breaking down under mental strain and worry, and relinquished the command. Sherman, as senior, had to fill his place, but he did not desire to serve except in a subordinate capacity. The War Department replied that Brigadier-General Buell would soon arrive from California to relieve him. Sherman in the meantime went vigorously to work raising troops, but it was not an easy matter. The young men, as a rule, sympathized with the South, and the old men wanted to stay at home and defend their property. He succeeded, however, in materially strengthening General George H. Thomas and Brigadier-General A. D. McCook, commanding respectively at Camp Dick Robinson and Elizabethtown.

CHAPTER XII.

Events preceding the Battle of Shiloh.—Rapid Movements in the Cumberland Valley and South-west.—Capture of Island No. 10.

THE fall of Fort Donelson, February 16, 1862, completely broke up the line of defence stretching from Bowling Green to Columbus—a line of defence which the Confederates fondly imagined to be invulnerable. It carried the whole Union front forward two hundred miles. It had the immediate effect of driving the insurgents completely out of Kentucky. It threw them back into the centre of Tennessee, and brought the capital of that State under Union authority. It practically unbound both the Cumberland and Tennessee rivers—an immense gain to the Union commanders, as they fully appreciated the great advantage of gunboats on those inland rivers.

There can now be no doubt in any mind at all familiar with the subject that the Union victories at Forts Henry and Donelson were rendered comparatively easy by the bad management of the Confederate commander-in-chief. Had General Johnston in place of attaching so much importance to the protection of the two forts on the Tennessee and the Cumberland respectively, concentrated his various

FLAG OF TRUCE ON FORT DONELSON.

armies and forced either Grant or Buell or both to risk the chances of battle in the open ground, the result might have been very different. Johnston saw this himself when it was too late, and in a remarkable letter addressed from Murfreesboro to Jefferson Davis, he said, "If I join this corps to the forces of General Beauregard, then those who are declaiming against me will be without an argument." It was the best he could do under the circumstances.

Bowling Green had been evacuated before Fort Donelson fell; for, believing it to be untenable, John-

NASHVILLE, TENNESSEE.

ston had moved on toward the south. Nashville was thrown into a perfect panic by the report of the capture of Donelson, and as Johnston had declared that he fought for that city while endeavoring to save this fort on the Cumberland, the capital of Tennessee fell an easy prey to the troops of General Buell. Six days after the capture of Nashville, General Halleck telegraphed to General McClellan from St. Louis, "Columbus, the Gibraltar of the West, is ours and Kentucky is free. Thanks to the brilliant strategy of the campaign by which the enemy's centre was pierced at Forts Henry and Donelson, his wings isolated from each other and turned, compelling thus the evacuation of his stronghold of Bowling Green first, and now Columbus."

MAJ.-GEN. D. C. BUELL.

Driven from all these strongholds, it became necessary for the Confederates to select some defensive position farther to the south. In obedience to instructions from Richmond, Polk fell back some miles, still clinging to the shores of the Mississippi, and established himself at Island No. 10 and at New Madrid.

Attack on Island No. 10.

These places, although fortified with great strength, Island No. 10 particularly having had the special attention of General Beauregard and being deemed the most impregnable of all the posts on the Mississippi, the Confederates were compelled in succession to evacuate. The attack on Island No. 10 reflected the

THE BATTLE OF SHILOH—SHOWING SHILOH CHURCH.

LOOKOUT MOUNTAIN.

SURRENDER OF GENERAL JOHNSTON—CLOSE OF THE GREAT CIVIL WAR

COMMODORE FARRAGUT.

BEFORE THE BATTLE OF SHILOH.

highest credit on the skill of the Union commanders and on the bravery of the Union troops. It was not until a canal had been cut across Donaldson's Point, between Island No. 8 and New Madrid, that the Nationals had any hope of dislodging the enemy.

ADMIRAL FOOTE.

The canal was twelve miles long and fifty feet wide, and nineteen days were consumed in cutting it from point to point and making it navigable for the largest of the gunboats. Commander Foote reported to his Government that Island No. 10 was "harder to conquer than Columbus, its shores being lined with forts, each fort commanding the one above it."

Beauregard telegraphed to Richmond that the National guns had "thrown three thousand shells and burned fifty tons of gunpowder," his batteries being uninjured and only one man killed. The canal made a complete change in the situation. New Madrid had been evacuated on the 12th of March, and on the 8th of April, four days after the completion of the canal, Island No. 10 had ceased to be a Confederate stronghold.

Federal Victory.

The defenders of the batteries had fled in confusion, but they were pursued by Pope and compelled to surrender. The garrison on the island, learning what had taken place, and believing the situation to be hopeless, sent a flag of truce to Commander Foote, offering to surrender. The immediate fruits of victory were some seven thousand prisoners, including three generals and two hundred and seventy field and company officers, one hundred heavy siege-guns, twenty-four pieces of field artillery, a large quantity of ammunition, several thousand stands of small-arms, with tents, horses, and wagons innumerable. "No single battle-field has yet afforded to the North such visible fruits of victory as have been gathered at Island No. 10." Such was the language used by the

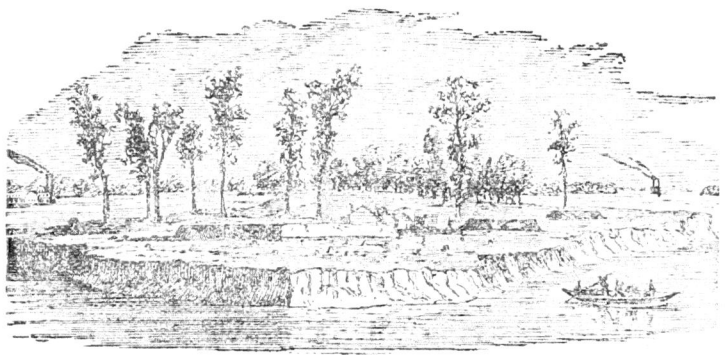

ISLAND NO 10

high officials at Richmond. The Mississippi was now open as far south as Fort Pillow.

While these events were following each other in rapid succession in Middle Tennessee and Western Kentucky, successes of a scarcely less substantial kind were attending the National army in Arkansas, in the grand movement, conducted by Curtis, Sigel, and others, down the Mississippi Valley toward the Gulf. Early in February the Confederate General Price had been compelled to retreat from Missouri into Arkansas.

The Old Flag in Arkansas.

On the 18th of that month he was closely followed by the Nationals under General Samuel R. Curtis of Iowa. On the same day joy was created throughout the Union by a telegram sent by General Halleck to General McClellan. "The flag of the Union," said Halleck, "is floating in Arkansas. The army of the South-west is doing its duty nobly." Curtis foresaw, however, that he was certain soon to be taken at a disadvantage, as the Confederates in retreating had really been falling back upon reinforcements. He therefore took post upon Sugar Creek. His entire force consisted of twelve thousand five hundred men, with forty-nine guns. The enemy, under General Earl Van Dorn, a dashing Confederate officer, was at least twenty thousand strong.

MAJ.-GEN. H. W. HALLECK.

On the morning of the 7th of March the two armies came into collision, and fierce fighting continued throughout the day.

There had been much previous manœuvring, and in consequence of a skilful and successful flank movement made by Van Dorn, Curtis was compelled, almost at the last moment, to change his front.

Carr's Division Driven Back.

When the struggle began the First and Second divisions, under Sigel and Asboth, were on the left, the Third, under Davis, was in the centre, and Carr's Fourth division formed the right. The line extended between three and four miles, from Sugar Creek to Elkhorn Tavern. On the opposite side of a ravine called Cross-Timber Hollow the Confederate line was stretched out before them, with Price on the right, McIntosh in the centre, and McCulloch on the left. The attack fell heavily upon Carr's division, which during the course of the day was driven back nearly a mile, but was not disorganized.

GEN. STERLING PRICE.

An attempt was made by McCulloch, by a movement of his force to the left, to join Van Dorn and Price in their attack on Curtis's right. To arrest this movement, Sigel pushed forward three pieces of artillery, with a body of cavalry to protect and support them. The cavalry were immediately overwhelmed and the guns captured. Davis hurried to the assistance of Sigel; a desperate struggle followed, victory oscillating like a pendulum, the Nationals and Confederates recoiling and recovering alternately; ul-

BEFORE THE BATTLE OF SHILOH.

timately, however, the Confederate right was broken and routed, and among those left on the field were Generals McCulloch and McIntosh, mortally wounded.

At the close of the fighting on the 7th, Price was on the Fayetteville road, in Curtis's rear.

Van Dorn had his headquarters at Elkhorn Tavern. On the right the National army had been defeated; it was cut off from its line of communication; its provisions were all but exhausted. The Confederates, however, had been defeated on their right and nearly driven from the field. During the night the Confederates united their forces on the ground held by their left wing. A change was also effected in the National line, Davis taking the right, Carr the centre, and Sigel the left.

MAJOR-GENERAL F. SIGEL.

A Federal Victory.

At sunrise the battle was resumed, Sigel opening a heavy cannonade and advancing round the enemy's right, Davis at the same time turning the enemy's left. It was a daring and skilful movement, and had all the effects of a surprise. All at once the Confederates found themselves exposed to a destructive cross-fire. They made a brave resistance, but in two hours, such was the precision and rapidity of Sigel's gunners, they were in full retreat through the defiles of Cross-Timber Hollow.

Thus ended what is known as the battle of Pea

Ridge. In two days the Nationals lost over thirteen hundred men. The Confederate loss must have been greater. This battle had no direct connection with the movements more immediately under consideration. It did not result from the fall of Forts Henry and Donelson. It did not in any way affect the impending struggle at Pittsburg Landing.

But inasmuch as the movements of the army under Curtis were part of Halleck's general plan, as that plan contemplated quite as much the opening of the Mississippi from Cairo to the Gulf as the driving of the enemy out of Kentucky and Tennessee, and as the battle of Pea Ridge was noted for skill on the part of the officers and bravery on the part of the men, it has been deemed wise, the more especially as it occurred simultaneously with the events now under review, to give it a place in these pages, which are intended to be preliminary to the most gigantic effort yet made on either side since the commencement of the war.

The Popular Favorite.

After the fall of Donelson it was only natural that General Grant should, for a time at least, become the popular favorite. All over the union his praises were liberally sounded, and by not a few who had acquired an insight into his character he was hailed already as the coming man. His sphere of action had been greatly enlarged. General Halleck, as if to mark his appreciation of Grant's noble services, had assigned him to the command of the new district of

BEFORE THE BATTLE OF SHILOH. 199

West Tennessee, a command which extended from Cairo to the northern borders of Mississippi, and embraced the entire country between the Mississippi and Cumberland rivers.

General Grant took immediate steps to turn to account the victories which he had won and to press the enemy still farther to the south. He established his headquarters at Fort Henry, where General Lewis Wallace was in command. We have seen already

MEMPHIS, TENNESSEE.

that Foote's flotilla was withdrawn from the Cumberland, that part of it had gone up the Tennessee River, and that Foote himself, with a powerful naval armament, had gone down the Mississippi for the purpose of co-operating with the land troops against Columbus, Hickman, Island No. 10, and New Madrid.

General C. F. Smith in Command.

It seems to have been the conviction of all the Union commanders—of Halleck, of Buell, of Grant—that a lodgment should be made at or near Corinth in Northern Mississippi. The possession of Corinth or Florence or Tuscumbia, but particularly Corinth, would give the National forces control of the Memphis and Charleston railroad, the key to the great railway communications between the Mississippi and the East, as well as the border slave States and the Gulf of Mexico.

It would facilitate the capture of Memphis, because it would place it more completely at the mercy of the troops now moving down the Mississippi; and it would render effective assistance to General Curtis, who, as we have seen, was at this moment carrying on important operations in Arkansas. While adopting vigorous measures for the purpose of giving effect to the general plan, Grant had the mortification to receive an order from Halleck instructing him to turn over his command to General C. F. Smith and to remain himself at Fort Henry.

Grant Humiliated.

In such circumstances such an order must have been humiliating in the last degree to General Grant, and it is not surprising that, stung to the quick as he must have been, he should have asked to be entirely relieved from duty. As a general rule, it is unwise to attach too much importance to individuals in a great national contest. No one man is absolutely indispensable. It is undeniable, however, that the retirement of General Grant at this particular juncture might have materially affected the future history of the great national struggle, now fairly begun and already bearing upon it somewhat of the impress of his character and genius.

The story of this short-lived difficulty is easily told. Complying with a request for an interview, Grant had on the 27th of February gone on a visit to Buell, up the Cumberland to Nashville. In the meantime, Halleck had ordered him to ascend the Tennessee, then in full flood, and establish himself on the Memphis and Charleston railroad at or near Corinth. On the 1st of March, Halleck ordered him to fall back from the Cumberland to the Tennessee, with the view of carrying out the orders previously given. It was supposed at this moment that the Confederates had retreated to Chattanooga.

Halleck's Complaints.

Sherman meanwhile received orders to seize all steamboats passing Paducah, and to send them up the Tennessee for the transportation of Grant's army. On hearing that Grant had gone up the Cumberland, Halleck telegraphed to him, "Why don't you obey my orders? Why don't you answer my letters? Turn over the command of the Tennessee expedition to General C. F. Smith, and remain yourself at Fort Henry." At the same time, Halleck wrote complainingly to McClellan at Washington, saying he could get no reports from Grant, whose troops were demoralized by their victory.

To Grant himself Halleck wrote, stating that his repeated neglect of positive orders to report his strength had created great dissatisfaction and seriously interfered with the general military arrangements, and that his going to Nashville when he ought to have been with his troops had given such offence at Washington that it had been considered advisable to arrest him on his return.

Grant's Conduct Explained.

It is possible that, judging by the highest forms of military law, Grant in some of the particulars charged was to blame. It is possible, too, that Halleck, who was a man of the old school and strict to the letter of the law, was officious overmuch. Grant, however, had his explanation ready. He had not received Halleck's orders in time; he had gone to Nashville for the good of the service, and not for personal pleasure or for any selfish motive; he had reported every day, had written on an average more than once a day, and had done his best to obey orders from headquarters; he had not permitted his troops to maraud; on the contrary, he had sent the marauders on to St. Louis. He submitted to instructions by turning the army over to General Smith. He asked, however, that he might be relieved.

The explanations so far satisfied Halleck that he requested the authorities at Washington to allow the

BEFORE THE BATTLE OF SHILOH.

matter to drop. Smith, however, remained in command, but, as the reader will soon discover, only for a brief period.

A Splendid Pageant.

The temporary change of commanders did not allow any intermission of the work. The expedition up the Tennessee was hurried forward. An acquisition was found in Sherman, who, in compliance with orders from Halleck, reported to Smith. It was not many days until seventy transports, carrying over thirty thousand troops, were ready to move to the point agreed upon. As the boats steamed up to Savannah, where the dépôt of supplies was established, bands playing and banners flying, it was perhaps the most splendid pageant seen since the commencement of the war. On the 11th of March the greater portion of the army was debarked at Savannah in perfect safety.

MAJ.-GEN. LEW. WALLACE.

General Lewis Wallace, with his division, disembarked on the west bank of the river at Crump's Landing, about four miles above Savannah, and took post on the road to Purdy. His instructions were to destroy the railroad bridge in the immediate neighborhood of that village. This was a hazardous undertaking, for the Confederates, as was afterward learned, were lying close at hand; but it was successfully accomplished, and that, too, under the inconvenience and discomfort of a series of heavy thunderstorms.

A Confederate train approached while the bridge was burning, and narrowly escaped capture by reversing the engine. Sherman was ordered by Smith to take his own division and the two gunboats Tyler and Lexington, to proceed farther up the river, and to strike the Memphis and Charleston railroad.

Sherman's Command in Peril.

Sherman went up as far as Tyler's Landing, at the mouth of Yellow Creek, just within the borders of Mississippi, but the roads were so flooded by the heavy rains that he found it impossible to reach the railroad. Had the enemy known his opportunity, Sherman's division might have been cut to pieces; for it was with the utmost difficulty, and not until many men and horses had perished in the swollen streams, that he got back to his boats.

On his way up the stream Sherman made one important discovery. On passing Pittsburg Landing the gunboats were fired upon by a Confederate regiment. It had already become known that the Confederate army was concentrating at Corinth, and that two batteries were already posted in advance—one at Eastport, the other just above the mouth of Bear Creek.

Sherman learned that a road led from Pittsburg Landing to Corinth; he conveyed the information at once to Smith, and declared it to be all-important, in his judgment, that Pittsburg Landing should be occupied. The advice was taken and the place became sacred—the name immortal.

After a personal examination of the ground, Smith was satisfied that Sherman's advice was sound; and Hurlbut was ordered to occupy Pittsburg Landing, while Sherman was directed to bring his division on the ground, but to take a position out from the river, leaving space enough behind him as Smith put it, "for a hundred thousand men."

CHAPTER XIII.

Sherman Saves the Battle of Shiloh.—Valley of Death.—A Wall of Iron.—Grant Praises Sherman's Heroism.

PITTSBURG LANDING is about eight or nine miles above Savannah, and lies on the west side of the Tennessee. The river-banks at the landing rise about eighty feet, but are cloven by a number of ravines, through one of which runs the main road to Corinth to the south-west, and branching off to Purdy to the north-west. The landing is flanked on the left by a short but precipitous ravine. On the right and left are Snake and Lick creeks, streams which rise near each other and gradually diverge, falling into the Tennessee some four or five miles apart on either side of the landing. Between these streams, which form a good flanking arrangement, making attack possible only in the front, lies a plateau or table-land rising some eighty feet high, of irregular surface, cleared near the shores, but covered with tall oaks and thick brushwood farther from the river.

About three miles from the landing, and embowered in trees, stood a little log building—a place used occasionally by the Methodists for holding camp-meetings. It had neither doors nor windows, and was only half-floored. Some corn in the husk lay piled on the floor. This was Shiloh Church, destined to give its name to the neighborhood and to the bloody contest which was so soon to disturb its quiet surroundings.

Sherman's Guard of Eight Thousand.

The illness of General Smith, which resulted in death on the 25th of April, brought Grant again to the front. On the 17th of March he arrived at Savannah, established his headquarters at the house of Mr. Cheney, and assumed the command. He found the army already in position, and made no radical changes. The landing was guarded by the gunboats Tyler and Lexington. Sherman's division, eight thousand strong, formed a sort of outlying force, covering all the main roads leading to the landing. There was a gap between his centre and his right, and a still wider gap of about two and a half miles between his centre and his left. Hurlbut's division was put in line on the left of the main Corinth road, and Smith's own division, under General W. H. L. Wallace, was on Hurlbut's right.

Lewis Wallace's division was detached and stationed at Crump's Landing, to observe any movements which might be made by the Confederates at Purdy and to cover the river communications between Pittsburg Landing and Savannah. McClernand's division was about a mile in front of W. H. L. Wallace, with that of Prentiss to his right. These two divisions—that of McClernand and that of Prentiss—formed the real line of battle. The entire force was about thirty-three thousand men. In estimating the possible strength of the Union army the aid which might come from Buell must be taken into account.

Buell on the March.

This general, after repeated solicitations that he might be permitted to abandon Nashville, cross Tennessee, and join his forces to those of Grant with a view to counteract the Confederate concentration at Corinth, had at last obtained Halleck's consent. The Army of the Ohio, which numbered some forty thousand men, was therefore already on its march, and by the 20th of March it had reached Columbia. The roads were bad and the weather stormy in the extreme; but it was not unreasonable to conclude that Buell would be able to accomplish the distance in time. Should this large increase of strength arrive before the commencement of hostilities, Grant could have but small reason for any misgivings as to the issue of the contest.

GEN. P. G. T. BEAUREGARD.

Let us now glance at the position of the Confederates and consider their plans and their prospects. When the first line of the Confederate defence had been swept away by the capture of Fort Donelson, Johnston retired first of all to Murfreesboro:

IRON-CLAD GUNBOAT.

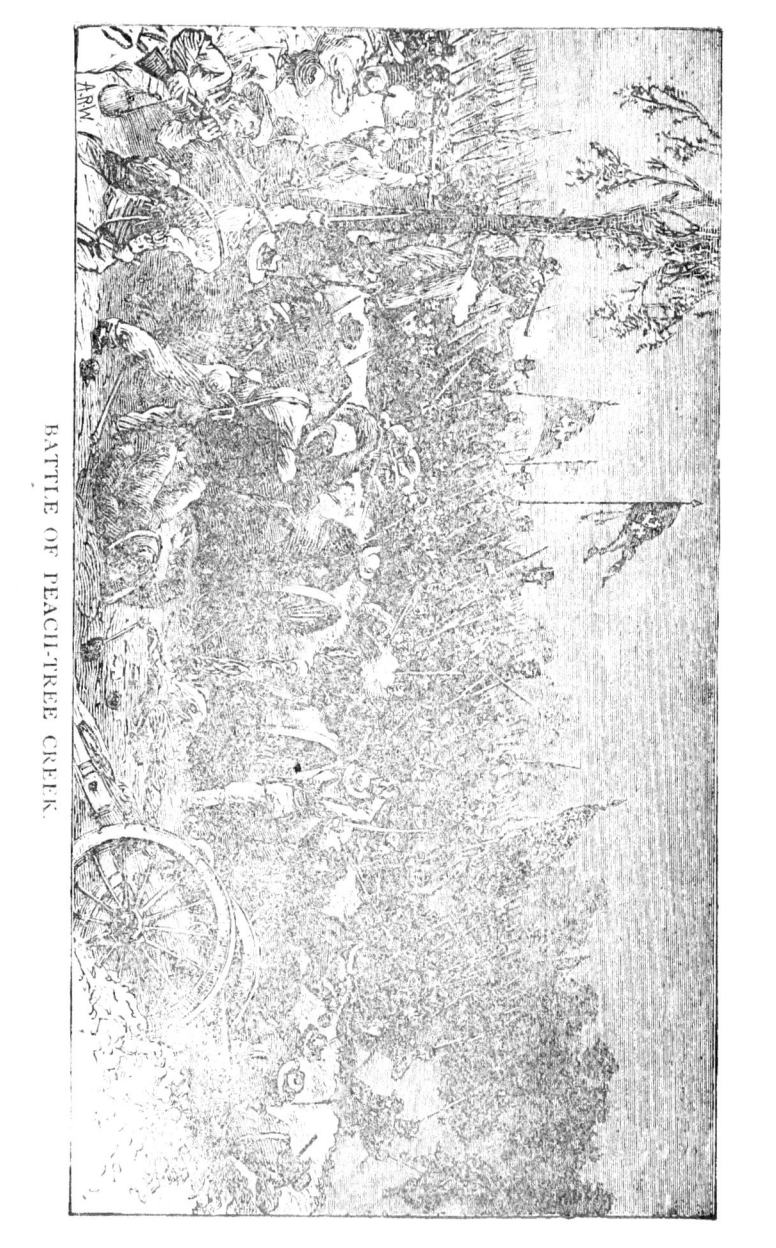

BATTLE OF PEACH-TREE CREEK.

GENERAL SHERMAN AND STAFF IN THE TRENCHES BEFORE ATLANTA.

GENERAL SHERIDAN

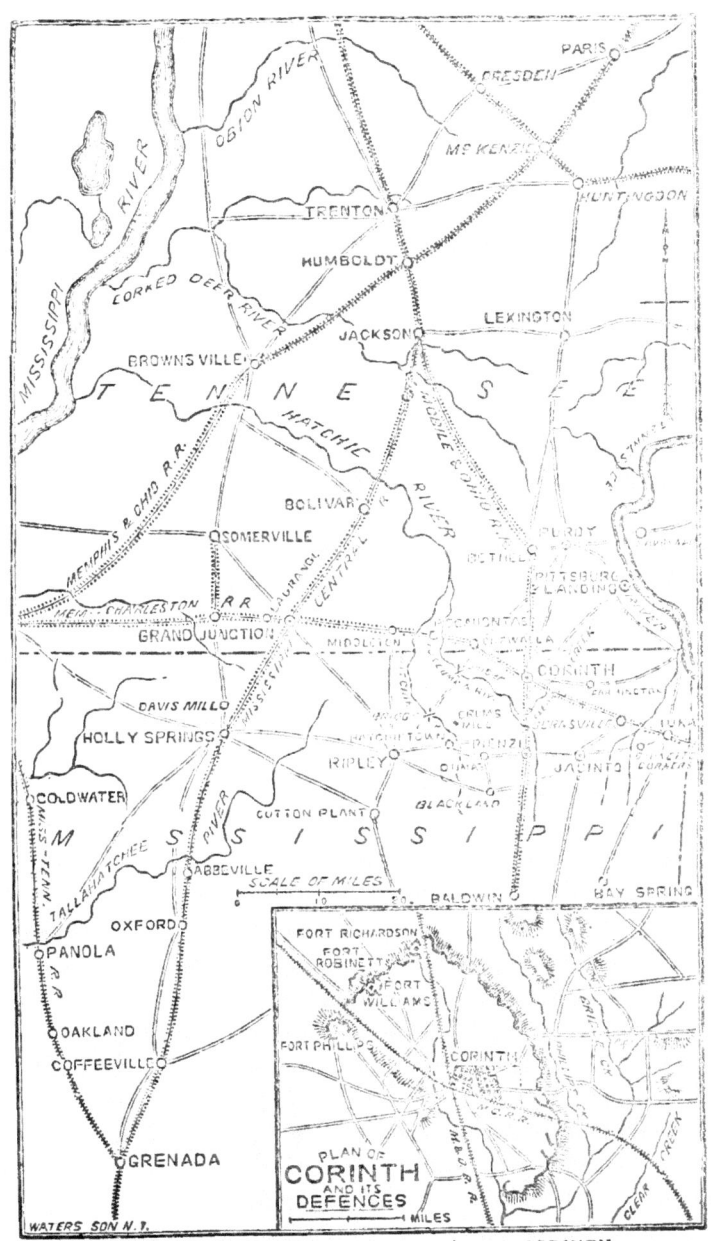

MAP SHOWING PITTSBURG LANDING AND CORINTH.

but the great object aimed at both by him and Beauregard was to concentrate the Confederate forces and establish a second line of defence on the Memphis and Charleston railroad. Concentration had for some time past been the favorite idea of Beauregard. If his advice had been taken in time, Donelson might not yet have fallen. Beauregard selected Corinth as the most desirable point for concentrating the scattered forces of the Confederacy. Here the two great railroads which connect the Gulf of Mexico and the Mississippi with the Atlantic Ocean form a junction. It is the key of the railroad system of Mississippi.

A Great Military Camp.

Orders were issued to the commanders of all the outlying positions, and Beauregard was soon joined by Bragg from Pensacola, by Polk from Mississippi, Johnston also coming up with his entire army from Murfreesboro. Corinth therefore became a great military camp, and in addition to its other advantages it afforded complete protection to Memphis. In three weeks the Confederate strength had risen from eleven thousand to forty-five thousand men. This, however, was not all. Van Dorn and Price were known to be coming up from Arkansas with other thirty thousand men.

GENERAL B. BRAGG.

Since the commencement of the war the Confederates never found themselves in circumstances more favorable for striking a bold and decisive blow. After the junction with Johnston that general took the command, Beauregard being nominally second, but remaining really the soul of the movement.

It had been the intention of Halleck, under whose instructions the entire movement on the part of the Nationals was conducted, to intervene between Johnston and Beauregard. When, therefore, he heard that Johnston had disappeared from Murfreesboro, and that his object was to join Beauregard at Corinth, he ordered Buell to hurry forward to the aid of Grant and counteract, as far as possible, the Confederate concentration.

Confederate Forces United.

There had been unnecessary delay, which permitted the Confederate generals to unite their strength; and now the weather and the roads were such that, although Buell's army was at Columbia on the 20th, it took full seventeen days to reach Pittsburg Landing, a distance of only ninety miles.

To the Confederate general two questions presented themselves: Shall I wait for Van Dorn and Price? or shall I strike Grant at once, before Buell has time to come up? At this time Breckenridge, with the Confederate right, which consisted of eleven thousand men, was stationed at Burnsville; Hardee and Bragg, with more than twenty thousand men, formed the centre at Corinth; and Polk and Hindman, with ten thousand men, were on the left, to the north of the Memphis and Charleston railroad. Johnston, on assuming command, had issued a flaming proclamation. "You are expected," he said to the soldiers, "to show yourselves worthy of your valor and courage, worthy of the women of the South, whose noble devotion in this war has never been exceeded in any time."

LIEUTENANT-GENERAL POLK.

The Foe Advancing.

On the 3d of April their available strength being forty thousand men, the Confederates commenced their onward march. Their plan was first to destroy Grant and then to fall with all their weight on Buell. The roads were in a terrible condition, and in consequence the progress made was slow. It was intended to attack the National army on the 5th, but the attack was delayed in consequence of a heavy rainstorm which fell in the afternoon. They were the less unwilling to delay the attack by reason of information having just reached them that the troops from the West, under Van Dorn and Price, would certainly join them the next morning.

That night they were distant from the National pickets only about three-quarters of a mile. Hardee was in

BATTLE OF SHILOH.

front; Bragg was in a second line behind; Polk was behind Bragg; and Breckenridge brought up the rear. During the course of the evening a council of war was held. There was a disposition to wait for Van Dorn and Price. But there was peril in waiting. If Buell should arrive, Johnston would lose his golden opportunity. It was the general conviction that their forward movement was unknown to Grant, and, after a consultation of some two hours it was resolved to strike a blow before dawn of the coming day. "Gentlemen," said Beauregard at the close of the council, while pointing in the direction of Grant's army, "we sleep in the enemy's camp to-morrow night."

MAJ.-GEN. BRECKENRIDGE.

Sherman at the Front.

The Confederate generals made a mistake in supposing that Grant was ignorant of the fact that they were moving forward upon him with the view of making an attack. That the enemy was massed at Corinth he was well aware, but he was in the enemy's country, and information was not willingly obtained from the people of the neighborhood. That he expected to be attacked is proved by the instructions which he gave to his officers, particularly to Lewis Wallace and Sherman.

But he had no means of knowing the enemy's

strength. He did not know that concentration was taking place so rapidly, and a vague idea prevailed in the Union camp that the force opposed to them did not exceed ten thousand men. Of the forward march

ABATTIS.

of the enemy he could not be ignorant, for on the 4th an infantry picket belonging to Colonel Buckland's brigade having been captured, Sherman took that brigade, with some cavalry, and drove back the Confederate horsemen some six miles from the front of the camp, taking good care not to expose his command to any sudden assault.

The firing of cannon was heard in the evening. On the same day Lewis Wallace reported eight regiments of infantry and twelve hundred cavalry at Purdy, and an equal force at Bethel. It is not to be denied, however, that Grant was in doubt from what direction the onslaught would be made. They might attack his main camp, or they might cross over Snake Creek to the north and west of him, establishing themselves on the Tennessee below, and forcing him to fight or cross to the east side of the river. Grant had his feelers out all around, and, as the result proved, he did best to risk a battle on the ground which had been chosen and on which he stood.

An Eventful Day.

The uncertainty which prevailed in the Union camp as to the point which might first have to bear the shock of battle proved an immense gain to the Confederates. It enabled them to mass themselves in great force and fall with destructive effect on one part of the Union line. So great, indeed, was the advantage which they thus obtained that the wonder is not so much that victory leaned to their standards during the greater part of the first day's fighting, but that they did not succeed in a few hours in completely sweeping the Union army from the field.

Their plan was to penetrate the Union centre, divide the army in two, and cut it up in detail. This done, it would not be difficult to make short, sharp work with Buell. The plan was good enough, but in their calculations the Confederate generals made one mistake: they did not take into account the cool pluck and skill of the Union commanders and the stern courage and determination of the Union men.

The night of the 5th was, as we have seen, wild

and stormy. The next morning (Sunday) rose bright and clear. The recent rains, while they had filled the creeks and streams, had given an air of freshness to the surrounding country. The breath of spring was everywhere. The trees were robed in the most delicate green and the sweet, rich voices of the morning songsters filled the air with melody. In the Union camp it was still unknown toward what point the enemy might be moving, but there was watchfulness everywhere. Prentiss's grand guards had been doubled the night before and his pickets were out one mile and a half.

Sherman's troops had already breakfasted, and were formed into line. With the early dawn Hardee's corps, which formed the first Confederate line, was in motion. Quickly but silently they passed across the ravine of Lick Creek and the ground which separated it from the outlying divisions of the Union army. It was the more easy for them to move noiselessly because the fallen leaves, being soaked with rain, made no rustling sound under the footsteps of the men.

The Terrible Onset.

The onslaught was tremendous. Avalanche-like, it overcame all resistance. The Union outposts were driven like chaff before the wind. On Hardee moved, falling heavily on Sherman's left, and then, as if rebounding from that firm phalanx, his entire force rolled with resistless and crushing weight upon Prentiss's division. The fierce yells of the charging regiments, the sharp shrill sounds of musketry, the booming of cannon, the bursting of shells, the crashing of timber, and the clouds of sulphurous smoke which filled the woods too plainly told that the battle of Shiloh had begun.

When the first shots were fired, Grant, unfortunately, was not on the ground. He had gone down the river to Savannah, some nine miles off, to have an interview with Buell. Soon as he heard the first guns he hastened to the scene of action. Leaving a letter for Buell, and ordering Nelson, who had arrived with a portion of Buell's forces, to hurry forward, he took a steamboat for Pittsburg Landing. Halting at Crump's Landing, he gave directions to Lewis Wallace to follow at once, unless it should turn out that the firing they heard was intended to deceive and that the real attack was to be made upon him. In the latter event he was to defend himself to the utmost, and to rely with confidence on reinforcements being sent him with the least possible delay. The attack had been made at the first streak of early dawn.

Grant on the Field.

It was eight o'clock before Grant reached the field of Shiloh. He saw that he had to fight the combined Confederate force, and without the aid of Buell. What the Confederate strength was Grant could only guess. We know that the combined army was over forty thousand strong. Grant had an available force of thirty-three thousand men. He believed he could depend upon Lewis Wallace, who had five thousand more. Some severe work, however, had already been done.

There was a considerable gap between Prentiss's right and Sherman's left. It was into this gap that Hardee tried to force himself, his object being to outflank and turn both lines. In the beginning of the conflict Sherman's left, as we have indicated, was sorely pressed and suffered terribly.

Sherman in the Thick of the Fight.

But that active and skilful general was present in the thickest of the fight, and by his cheering words and personal bravery, as well as by the admirable manner in which he handled his men, he laid that day the foundation of a fame which the American people will not willingly let die. Hildebrand's brigade, which had been driven from its position by the first onset of the enemy, Sherman tried in vain to rally. While thus engaged he received a severe bullet-wound in the hand. Nothing, however, could daunt his energy or induce him to relax his efforts. McClernand pushed forward a portion of his troops to aid the smitten Hildebrand, and these for a time bore the shock of battle.

All, however, was in vain. In poured the Confederates in ever-increasing numbers. Bragg had come to the aid of Hardee, and Polk, with the third Confederate line, was already moving toward Sherman's rear. By nine o'clock a very large portion of Sherman's division was virtually out of the fight, and before ten Prentiss had been forced from his ground, his camp captured and plundered, his division thrown into confusion, and he himself isolated from his men.

Pluck and Strategy.

But for the pluck and skill of Sherman the battle at this stage might have been lost, although it cannot be said that there was any lack of bravery on the part of any of the Union divisions. Officers and men everywhere vied with each other in deeds of daring. But Sherman showed strategy as well as pluck. Feeling the pressure of the enemy, and in danger of being caught in the rear, he swung round upon his right as upon a pivot, coming out at a right angle and taking entirely new ground. Here he took a firm position and held it tenaciously for several hours, the repeated and vigorous attacks of the enemy falling upon the solid front of his well-arranged battalions as upon a shield of shining steel.

The falling back of Sherman, while it enabled him to prolong the contest and successfully to prevent attack in the rear, left McClernand's division completely exposed. On this, therefore, the Confederate forces fell with tremendous energy. For a time McClernand boldly and even successfully resisted, most effective aid being rendered by Dresser's powerful rifled cannon. Regiment after regiment of the Confederates rushed through the abandoned camps and pressed forward, only to be cut to pieces by the deadly rifle-shot, displaying magnificent courage and the most reckless daring.

Ultimately, however, the force of overwhelming numbers began to tell on McClernand's lines. He was forced to retire, not, however, except in the most perfect order, fighting as he went and bravely contesting every inch of ground. By eleven o'clock this division was on a line with Hurlbut, close to W. H. L. Wallace, with Sherman to the right.

Stewart in Imminent Danger.

Meanwhile, Stewart's brigade of Sherman's division, which was posted on the extreme left of the National line, about two miles from Pittsburg Landing, on the Hamburg road, near Lake Creek, where Buell was expected to land, was, in consequence of the falling back of the other divisions, in an extremely perilous position. The screaming of a shell in its passage through the branches of the trees overhead apprised Stewart of the approach of the enemy in his direction.

It turned out to be a column of cavalry and infantry, composed for the most part of Breckenridge's reserves. They were moving along the road leading from Corinth to Hamburg. Notifying W. H. L. Wallace of his difficulty and calling for aid, he calmly awaited the attack. It was fiercely made and gallantly resisted. Wallace sent McArthur to the aid of Stewart, but McArthur missed his way, and came directly on the Confederates under Withers. It was impossible for Stewart to maintain his position; but so vigorously did McArthur engage the enemy that Stewart managed to avoid capture, and succeeded in reaching a place of comparative safety, where he restored his shattered force to something like order.

Three Divisions Routed.

The battle had raged since the early morning. It was fiercest about ten o'clock. There was but little intermission, however, until two. About ten Grant visited Sherman's camp, and, finding that the supply of cartridges was short, he organized a train of ammunition-wagons to run between the camp and the landing—an arrangement beset with great difficulty in consequence of the large number of fugitives who were forcing their way through the narrow road. By twelve o'clock, noon, the Confederates had possession of the ground occupied in the morning by the first line of the National army, and the camps of Sherman, McClernand, Prentiss, and Stewart had been captured and plundered. Three of the five divisions of that army had been completely routed.

The ground being entirely cleared before them—Prentiss's brigade, as we have seen, being demolished, and Stewart having been compelled to retreat, McClernand, too, and Sherman having both yielded on the right—the Confederates, apparently resolved to push matters to a crisis, rushed with tremendous fury upon Hurlbut, who still maintained his original position, and who had been joined by Prentiss and some two thousand of his men. W. H. L. Wallace flew to the aid of Hurlbut, taking with him the Missouri batteries of Stone, Richardson, and Webber.

Heroic Wallace.

Hurlbut, who had hitherto been in the open fields, now fell back into the woods which lay between his camp and the river, and there, nobly aided by Wallace, who fought like a hero of old, gallantly resisted the foe for several weary hours. Upon this compact body of National troops, who knew that if they had death in front they had certain death in the rear, three most desperate charges were made as if upon a wall of iron.

In one of these encounters General W. H. L. Wallace fell mortally wounded. McArthur took the command, but in spite of their best efforts both he and Hurlbut were compelled to retire a little farther down and toward the river. In the confusion Prentiss and his company, getting isolated, were captured, sent to the Confederate rear, and finally marched to Corinth as prisoners of war.

The situation now seemed desperate. It was between three and four o'clock. Sherman and McClernand, all but utterly exhausted and having lost many of their guns, had fallen back and taken a position in front of the bridge which crosses Snake Creek. It was over this bridge that General Lewis Wallace was momentarily expected to come.

Unaccountable Delays.

Grant had been pressed into a corner of the battle-field, his army at this time occupying a space of not more than four hundred acres on the very verge of the river. As yet there were no signs of Wallace, nor any explanation of his delay. Buell, too, had failed to come to time. Five of the Union camps had been captured, and many guns and prisoners had fallen into the enemy's hands. Fatigue and disorder had done and were still doing their terrible work. Cooped up in this narrow corner of the field, with the triumphant enemy in front and the dark rolling waters of the Tennessee in the rear—death before and death behind—what more can Grant do? Will he surrender? No! The word had no place in his system of tactics.

The Confederates, however, were less strong than they seemed. Success had broken their ranks, and the hard work of the day had produced its natural fruit. The men were completely worn out. Some of their best men had perished.

Death of General A. S. Johnston.

Generals Gladdon and Hindman had been killed, and at about half-past two o'clock, when pressing his men towards the landing and almost recklessly exposing himself, Commander-in-chief Johnston received a rifle bullet in the leg, which proved fatal. There was a lull in the fight after Johnston fell, but Beauregard assumed command, and the struggle for the possession of Pittsburg Landing was resumed with fresh energy. Beauregard felt that there was no time to lose, for night and Buell were coming.

The entire strength of the Confederate army was at this stage being pressed against the National left. It seemed to be the object of Beauregard to turn the National line or force it into the river. In any case, he was determined to seize the landing. Happily, as the result proved, a deep ravine lay between the Confederates and the Nationals, who, cooped up as they were, still covered the landing. This ravine was impassable for artillery and cavalry. In consequence of the heavy rains the bottom was wet and the sides slippery. The ravine led down to the river, and at its mouth the two gunboats, Tyler and Lexington, had taken position, their commanders having obtained permission from General Grant to exercise their discretion in shelling the woods and sweeping the ravine.

A Deadly Battery.

On the brow of his side of the ravine General Grant had hastily flung up some earthworks in the form of a half-moon. To several siege-guns which were parked there Colonel Webster, Grant's chief of staff, added a number of guns which had belonged to light batteries, now broken up, and thus secured a semicircular defence of about fifty cannon. This hurriedly-improvised battery reached around nearly to the Corinth road. The wretched condition to which the National army had been reduced may be gathered from the fact that it was with the utmost difficulty men could be got to work the guns.

The men were exhausted and demoralized. Volunteers were called for, and Dr. Cornyn, surgeon of the First Missouri Artillery, having offered his services, his example was quickly followed. The Confederate assault was led by Chalmers, Withers, Cheatham, Ruggles, Anderson, Stuart, Pond, and Stevens. It

GENERAL J. E. B. STUART.

was a perilous attempt, but it was bravely made. Down the steep sides of the ravine they rushed, uttering their favorite and familiar cry, and with their accustomed dash and fury.

Critical Moment.

For a moment it seemed as if all was lost, and as if Beauregard was about to crown the day's work by a final crushing blow. But no! It was destined to be otherwise. The slippery sides of the ravine and the slush and mud at the bottom greatly hindered the movements of the attacking party. Once in the deadly hollow, there was literally no way of escape. At a signal given Webster's guns from their fifty mouths opened fire in front, while the Tyler and Lexington, striking the Confederates on the flank, swept the ravine with their eight-inch shells.

It was now a most unequal contest. The Confederates had fallen into a trap. Every onward movement was vigorously repulsed. The National troops began to rally, and, finding position, contributed to the work of destruction by the unerring aim of their rifles. Again and again, and yet again, did the Confederates face the terrible fire, rushing across the ravine as if they would storm the battery in front, but it was only to be mowed down like grass or driven back like sheep. The ravine was filled with the wounded and the dead. So dense was the smoke that the entire scene was wrapped in almost midnight darkness—a darkness relieved only by the swift-recurring rifle flash and the cannon's blaze. It was a virtual hell—a real, a veritable valley of death itself.

Union Troops Hold the Field.

The tide had turned. The crisis was past. Beauregard, seeing that it was useless to prolong the struggle, withdrew his men. He professed himself satisfied with what he had done, and, as it was near nightfall, he thought he might rest for the night and give the finishing touch in the morning. The firing now ceased, and Grant was left master of the ground. Before the close of the struggle, Nelson, with Buell's advance, had arrived on the field, and Lewis Wallace, having at last found his way, was coming up with his five thousand men. For the National cause the first day at Shiloh had ended not ingloriously, and with these fresh accessions of strength the prospect was bright for the coming day.

The dreary hours of the night were sufficiently filled with horrors. The gunboats kept up an incessant cannonade, in some places setting the woods on fire. The wounded on both sides vainly sought to escape from the grasp of this new and terrible destroyer. Happily, a heavy rainstorm fell upon the scene of agony and the fire was extinguished.

The Two Commanders Consulting.

Shortly after the firing had ceased Grant visited Sherman, and as it was the opinion of both that the Confederates were exhausted, it was agreed that the attack should be resumed early in the morning. Subsequently, Grant visited each of the division commanders, giving the necessary instructions, and then flung himself on the wet ground and snatched a few hours' rest, with his head resting on the stump of a tree. During the night Lewis Wallace came up and Buell arrived in person. All night through steamboats kept busily plying between Savannah and Pittsburg Landing, bringing up the remaining divisions of Buell's army. Nelson's division was all on the field by nine o'clock P. M. Crittenden's arrived a little later, and by five in the morning McCook's division, which was the last to come up, having had to wait for boats, was all safely disembarked. Twenty-seven thousand men were thus added to the National army.

Second Day at Shiloh.

With the early light of the morning of the 7th, which came in with a drizzling rain, the troops were in position and ready to make the attack. The fresh troops were placed in line as they came upon the field, considerably in advance and upon the ground abandoned by Beauregard after the failure of his last attack. Nelson was on the left, then in order Crittenden, McCook, Hurlbut, McClernand, Sherman, and Lewis Wallace. Thomson of Wallace's division, with his field-guns, was the first to disturb the silence of the morning and to awaken the echoes of the forest.

The response was vigorous, but the fresh troops of Wallace stood bravely to their work. At this moment Grant arrived, and ordered Wallace to press forward and attack the Confederate left under Bragg, who since the death of Johnston was second in command.

BATTLE OF SHILOH.

This was gallantly done, the Confederates being compelled to abandon the high ground, which was soon occupied by Wallace's troops. Here a halt was made, Wallace expecting Sherman to come to his aid.

Booming Guns.

Meanwhile the two armies had come into collision at the other extremities of their lines. From what has been said above it will be seen that Buell's force, which lay nearest to Pittsburg Landing, composed the centre and left of Grant's new line of battle. The divisions of Nelson and Crittenden only were ready when Wallace's guns were heard booming to the right. They moved forward at once, Nelson's division leading. Their artillery had not yet arrived, but the batteries of Mendenhall and Terrill of the regular service were placed at their disposal.

Nelson had moved half a mile at least before he felt the enemy. At the first touch he seemed to yield, but it was only for a moment. At this point Beauregard had gathered up his strength and was resolved to strike a deadly blow. If he could turn the National left he might still accomplish his purpose of yesterday, and make himself master of the landing. His onslaught was tremendous. For a second Nelson's troops wavered, but it was only for a second. Mendenhall's battery was hurried into action, and the advancing Confederates were driven back in confusion by a tempest of grape and canister. Hazen's brigade charged, captured one of Beauregard's batteries, and turned it with deadly effect on the foe. Once more the Confederates came up with redoubled strength, and Hazen fell back before the advancing tide.

The Famous "Brass Twelves."

Terrill's battery of McCook's division was now got into position. Pouring forth shell from his ten-pounders and grape and canister from his brass twelves, Terrill did splendid and effective work. For two hours the artillery conflict raged. Crittenden was on Nelson's right, and McCook was to the right of Crittenden, fronting the Confederate centre. Buell had taken general command of his own troops. The terrible artillery duel began to tell on the Confederate line. Nelson, becoming more daring, began to move forward. Crittenden and McCook advanced abreast at the same time, but every inch of ground was keenly contested, and victory, now leaning to one side and now to the other, seemed undecided as to which to award the palm.

Sherman's captured camp was still in the Confederate rear, and to this as an objective point the National line kept slowly but steadily advancing. Sherman and Wallace, carrying out Grant's instructions to the letter, have advanced under a terrible fire and have reached the ridge occupied by the former on Sunday morning.

Tempest of Battle.

The little log church in Shiloh has again become a conspicuous object in the battle-field. Around it the tempest of battle is again to rage. Beauregard, despairing of success on the left, had, by counter-marching his troops, greatly strengthened himself in front of the enemy's right. The struggle at this point was protracted and severe. Sherman and Wallace held their ground, and it soon became apparent that Beauregard's strength was all but exhausted.

At the same time that the Confederate general had concentrated his troops against the National right he did not neglect an opportunity which seemed to present itself more toward what might be called the National centre. Noticing a slight gap between Crittenden and McCook, he endeavored to force a passage between them. Here he made his last effort, his last decided stand. It was all in vain. McCook's division stood like a wall of iron.

The Confederates Routed.

The Confederate centre now began to yield. All along the line, from Nelson on the left to Sherman and Wallace on the right, the Nationals were pressing forward. Everywhere the enemy was seen retiring. "Cheer after cheer," says Wallace, "rang through the woods, and every man felt that the day was ours." The battle of Shiloh was ended. "Don't," said Beauregard to Breckenridge, as he ordered a retreat—"don't let this be converted into a rout."

It was now half-past five o'clock, and the wearied National troops being in no mood to pursue the foe, the retreat was the more easily conducted. The two days' fighting had resulted in the loss of over twenty thousand men—the Confederate killed and wounded amounting to more than ten thousand, the Nationals to nearly twelve thousand.

General Halleck only did what was right when he thanked Generals Grant and Buell "and the officers and men of their respective commands for the bravery and endurance with which they sustained the general attack of the enemy on the 6th, and for the heroic manner in which on the 7th they defeated and routed the entire rebel army."

Why Wallace was Delayed.

Lewis Wallace was greatly blamed for his non-appearance on the field of battle on the 6th. It was not difficult, however, for that brave officer, who did such effective work on the 7th, to give sufficient and satisfactory explanations. He had, it appeared, obeyed his first orders, which were that he should join the right of the army, but, not knowing that it had fallen back, he had wasted the whole afternoon in a fruitless march.

There has been much useless discussion as to how much Grant was indebted to Buell for the victory at Shiloh. What did happen we know. What might have been we cannot tell. That Grant was largely indebted to Sherman for this brilliant victory his own despatches show, confirmed by the deliberate statements in his *Memoirs*. Some of the facts of the case are plain, and admit of no double interpretation.

During the greater part of Sunday the Confederates marched triumphantly from point to point. The

Nationals were driven back entirely from their original ground; five of their division camps were overrun and captured; and Grant, with his whole army, was pressed into a corner of the field. The situation was desperate. One blow more and it seemed as if Beauregard would reap a glorious victory. Of all this there can be no doubt.

A Desperate Struggle.

It is as little to be denied, however, that at the last moment Grant snatched victory from his triumphant rival. The advancing Confederates were not only successfully resisted, but driven back in confusion and compelled to give up the struggle. All this Grant accomplished before any effective assistance arrived from Buell. It would simply be absurd to deny that the arrival of reinforcements—which, including Wallace's division, amounted in all to twenty-seven thousand men—made victory on the following day comparatively more easy. But we are not at liberty to say that, without the aid of Buell, Grant might not have accomplished his purpose and driven the enemy from the field. We simply cannot tell. We know that both Grant and Buell did their best, and that their best was needed.

From earliest dawn till half-past five in the afternoon the battle raged without intermission. It was no easily-won victory; and if praise is due to the Union commanders, justice compels us to be equally generous to General Beauregard. If for the moment we could forget the cause, and think only of the skill and heroism displayed, we should say that on those two days he covered himself with glory. In Beauregard the Union commanders found a foeman worthy of their steel. He was by far the ablest general who had yet appeared in the Confederate ranks.

Too Late for New Plans.

There is one other point on which it is necessary to make a remark before closing this chapter. It is to be borne in mind that Grant was not responsible either for the selection of the battle-ground or for the disposition of the troops. Whatever praise or blame resulted from the one or the other was due to General C. F. Smith. When Grant was restored to the chief command of the Army of the Tennessee, it was only a few days before the commencement of the fight, and any attempt to make radical changes in the arrangements, carried out, as these must have been, in the presence of a vigilant and powerful enemy, would have been perilous in the extreme. If the battle of the 6th had ended differently, General Grant might have been justified in making some complaint as to the circumstances in which he found the enemy on resuming command. As it was, his mouth was shut. He showed himself a true man by nobly respecting the memory of General Smith—a capable commander and a brave man.

Sherman's Magnificent Deeds.

In his personal *Memoirs*, General Grant pays the following splendid tribute to Sherman: "During the whole Sunday I was continuously engaged in passing from one part of the field to another, giving directions to division commanders. In thus moving along the line, however, I never deemed it important to stay long with Sherman. Although his troops were then under fire for the first time, their commander, by his constant presence with them, inspired a confidence in officers and men that enabled them to render services on that bloody battle-field worthy of the best of veterans. McClernand was next to Sherman, and the hardest fighting was in front of these two divisions. McClernand told me on that day, the 6th, that he profited much by having so able a commander supporting him. A casualty to Sherman that would have taken him from the field that day would have been a sad one for the troops engaged at Shiloh. And how near we came to this! On the 6th, Sherman was shot twice, once in the hand, once in the shoulder, the ball cutting his coat and making a slight wound, and a third ball passed through his hat. In addition to this he had several horses shot during the day."

CHAPTER XIV.

General Sherman's Graphic Description of the Battle of Shiloh.

WE cannot do the reader a greater favor than to insert General Sherman's very interesting account of the important part acted by himself and his division in the celebrated battle of Shiloh. It is a plain statement of facts, free from all self-laudation, and was written at "Camp Shiloh, April 10, 1862." General Sherman's narrative is as follows:

On Friday, the 4th inst., the enemy's cavalry drove in our pickets, posted about a mile and a half in advance of my centre on the main Corinth road, capturing one first lieutenant and seven men; I caused a pursuit by the cavalry of my division, driving them back about five miles and killing many. On Saturday the enemy's cavalry was again very bold, coming well down to our front; yet I did not believe they designed anything but a strong demonstration. On Sunday morning early, the 6th inst., the enemy drove our advance-guard back on the main body, when I ordered under arms all my division, and sent word to General McClernand, asking him to support my left; to General Prentiss, giving him notice that the enemy was in our front in force; and to General Hurlbut, asking him to support General Prentiss. At that time—7 A. M.—my division was arranged as follows:

First brigade, composed of the Sixth Iowa, Colonel J. A. McDowell; Fortieth Illinois, Colonel Hicks; Forty-sixth Ohio, Colonel Worthington; and the Morton battery, Captain Behr, on the extreme right, guarding the bridge on the Purdy road over Owl Creek.

Second brigade, composed of the Fifty-fifth Illinois, Colonel D. Stuart; the Fifty-fourth Ohio, Colonel T. Kilby Smith; and the Seventy-first Ohio, Colonel Mason, on the extreme left, guarding the ford over Lick Creek.

Third brigade, composed of the Seventy-seventh Ohio, Colonel Hildebrand; the Fifty-third Ohio, Colonel Appler; and the Fifty-seventh Ohio, Colonel Mungen, on the left of the Corinth road, its right resting on Shiloh meeting-house.

Fourth brigade, composed of the Seventy-second Ohio, Colonel Buckland; the Forty-eighth Ohio, Colonel Sullivan; and the Seventieth Ohio, Colonel Cockerill, on the right of the Corinth road, its left resting on Shiloh meeting-house.

Two batteries of artillery—Taylor's and Waterhouse's—were posted, the former at Shiloh, and the latter on a ridge to the left, with a front fire over open ground between Mungen's and Appler's regiments. The cavalry, eight companies of the Fourth Illinois, under Colonel Dickey, were posted in a large open field to the left and rear of Shiloh meeting-house, which I regarded as the centre of my position.

The Fire Opens.

Shortly after 7 A. M. with my entire staff I rode along a portion of our front, and when in the open field before Appler's regiment the enemy's pickets opened a brisk fire upon my party, killing my orderly, Thomas D. Holliday, of Company H, Second Illinois Cavalry. The fire came from the bushes which line a small stream that rises in the field in front of Appler's camp and flows to the north along my whole front.

This valley afforded the enemy partial cover, but our men were so posted as to have a good fire at them as they crossed the valley and ascended the rising ground on our side.

About 8 P. M. I saw the glistening bayonets of heavy masses of infantry to our left front in the woods beyond the small stream alluded to, and became satisfied for the first time that the enemy designed a determined attack on our whole camp.

Hot Work along the Whole Line.

All the regiments of my division were then in line of battle at their proper posts. I rode to Colonel Appler, and ordered him to hold his ground at all hazards, as he held the left flank of our first line of battle, and I informed him that he had a good battery on his right and strong support to his rear. General McClernand had promptly and energetically responded to my request, and had sent me three regiments, which were posted to protect Waterhouse's battery and the left flank of my line.

The battle opened by the enemy's battery in the woods to our front throwing shells into our camp. Taylor's and Waterhouse's batteries promptly responded, and I then observed heavy battalions of infantry passing obliquely to the left, across the open field in Appler's front; also, other columns advancing directly upon my division. Our infantry and artillery opened along the whole line, and the battle became general. Other heavy masses of the enemy's forces kept passing across the field to our left, and directing their course on General Prentiss. I saw at once that the enemy designed to pass my left flank and fall upon Generals McClernand and Prentiss, whose line of camps was almost parallel with the Tennessee River and about two miles back from it. Very soon the sound of artillery and musketry announced that General Prentiss was engaged, and about 9 A. M. I judged that he was falling back. About this time Appler's regiment broke in disorder, followed by Mungen's regiment, and the enemy pressed forward on Waterhouse's battery, thereby exposed.

Guns Lost.

The three Illinois regiments in immediate support of this battery stood for some time; but the enemy's advance was so vigorous and the fire so severe that when Colonel Raith of the Forty-third Illinois received a severe wound and fell from his horse, his regiment and others manifested disorder, and the enemy got possession of three guns of this (Waterhouse's) battery.

Although our left was thus turned and the enemy was pressing our whole line, I deemed Shiloh so important that I remained by it, and renewed my orders to Colonels McDowell and Buckland to hold their ground; and we did hold these positions until about 10 A. M., when the enemy had got his artillery to the rear of our left flank and some change became necessary. Two regiments of Hildebrand's brigade—Appler's and Mungen's—had already disappeared to the rear, and Hildebrand's own regiment was in disorder. I therefore gave orders for Taylor's battery—still at Shiloh—to fall back as far as the Purdy and Hamburg road, and for McDowell and Buckland to adopt that road as their new line.

Regiments in Disorder.

I rode across the angle and met Behr's battery at the cross-roads, and ordered it immediately to come into battery, action right. Captain Behr gave the order, but he was almost immediately shot from his horse, when drivers and gunners fled in disorder, carrying off the caisson, and abandoning five out of six guns without firing a shot. The enemy pressed on, gaining this battery, and we were again forced to choose a new line of defence. Hildebrand's brigade had substantially disappeared from the field, though he himself bravely remained. McDowell's and Buckland's brigades maintained their organizations, and were conducted by my aides so as to join on General McClernand's right, thus abandoning my original camps and line.

This was about 10 A. M., at which time the enemy had made a furious attack on General McClernand's whole front. He struggled most determinedly, but finding him pressed, I moved McDowell's brigade directly against the left flank of the enemy, forced him back some distance, and then directed the men to avail themselves of every cover—trees, fallen timber, and a wooded valley to our right. We held this position for four long hours, sometimes gaining and at others losing ground; General McClernand and myself acting in perfect concert and struggling to maintain this line.

Falling Back.

While we were so hard pressed two Iowa regiments approached from the rear, but could not be brought up to the severe fire that was raging in our front; and General Grant, who visited us on that ground, will remember our situation about 3 P. M.; but about 4 P. M. it was evident that Hurlbut's line had been driven back to the river, and, knowing that General Lew Wallace was coming with reinforcements from Crump's Landing, General McClernand and I, on consultation, selected a new line of defence, with its right covering a bridge by which General Wallace had to approach. We fell back as well as we could, gathering, in addition to our own, such scattered forces as we could find, and formed the new line.

During this change the enemy's cavalry charged us, but were handsomely repulsed by the Twenty-ninth Illinois Regiment. The Fifth Ohio Battery, which had come up, rendered good service in holding the enemy in check for some time, and Major Taylor also came up with another battery, and got into position just in time to get a good flank-fire upon the enemy's column as he pressed on General McClernand's right, checking his advance, when General McClernand's division made a fine charge on the enemy and drove him back into the ravines to our front and right.

Night Comes.

I had a clear field, about two hundred yards wide, in my immediate front, and contented myself with keeping the enemy's infantry at that distance during the rest of the day. In this position we rested for the night. My command had become decidedly of a mixed character. Buckland's brigade was the only one that retained its organization. Colonel Hildebrand was personally there, but his brigade was not. Colonel McDowell had been severely injured by a fall off his horse, and had gone to the river, and the three regiments of his brigade were not in line. The Thirteenth Missouri, Colonel Crafts J. Wright, had reported to me on the field and fought well, retaining its regimental organization, and it formed a part of my line during Sunday night and all Monday.

Other fragments of regiments and companies had also fallen into my division and acted with it during the remainder of the battle. Generals Grant and Buell visited me in our bivouac that evening, and from them I learned the situation of affairs on other parts of the field. General Wallace arrived from Crump's

Landing shortly after dark and formed his line to my right rear. It rained hard during the night, but our men were in good spirits, lay on their arms, being satisfied with such bread and meat as could be gathered at the neighboring camps, and determined to redeem on Monday the losses of Sunday.

Deeds of Valor.

At daylight on Monday I received General Grant's orders to advance and recapture our original camps. I despatched several members of my staff to bring up all the men they could find, especially the brigade of Colonel Stuart, which had been separated from the division all the day before; and at the appointed time the division, or rather what remained of it, with the Thirteenth Missouri and other fragments, moved forward and reoccupied the ground on the extreme right of General McClernand's camp, where we attracted the fire of a battery located near Colonel McDowell's former headquarters. Here I remained, patiently waiting for the sound of General Buell's advance upon the main Corinth road.

About 10 A. M. the heavy firing in that direction and its steady approach satisfied me; and General Wallace being on our right flank with his well-conducted division, I led the head of my column to General McClernand's right, formed line of battle, facing south, with Buckland's brigade directly across the ridge and Stuart's brigade on its right in the woods, and thus advanced, steadily and slowly, under a heavy fire of musketry and artillery. Taylor had just got to me from the rear, where he had gone for ammunition, and brought up three guns, which I ordered into position to advance by hand firing. These guns belonged to Company A, Chicago Light Artillery, commanded by Lieutenant P. P. Wood, and did most excellent service.

Awful Rattle of Musketry.

Under cover of their fire we advanced till we reached the point where the Corinth road crosses the line of McClernand's camp, and here I saw for the first time the well-ordered and compact columns of General Buell's Kentucky forces, whose soldierly movements at once gave confidence to our newer and less-disciplined men. Here I saw Willich's regiment advance upon a point of water-oaks and thicket, behind which I knew the enemy was in great strength, and enter it in beautiful style. Then arose the severest musketry-fire I ever heard, and lasted some twenty minutes, when this splendid regiment had to fall back.

This green point of timber is about five hundred yards east of Shiloh meeting-house, and it was evident here was to be the struggle. The enemy could also be seen forming his lines to the south. General McClernand sending to me for artillery, I detached to him the three guns of Wood's battery, with which he speedily drove them back, and, seeing some others to the rear, I sent one of my staff to bring them forward, when by almost providential decree they proved to be two twenty-four-pound howitzers belonging to McAlister's battery, and served as well as guns ever could be.

This was about 2 P. M. The enemy had one battery close by Shiloh, and another near the Hamburg road, both pouring grape and canister upon any column of troops that advanced upon the green point of water-oaks. Willich's regiment had been repulsed, but a whole brigade of McCook's division advanced beautifully, deployed, and entered this dreaded wood.

The Enemy Swept like Chaff.

I ordered my second brigade (then commanded by Colonel T. Kilby Smith, Colonel Stuart being wounded) to form on its right, and my fourth brigade, Colonel Buckland, on its right, all to advance abreast with this Kentucky brigade before mentioned, which I afterward found to be Rousseau's brigade of McCook's division. I gave personal direction to the twenty-four-pounder guns, whose well-directed fire first silenced the enemy's guns to the left, and afterward at the Shiloh meeting-house.

Rousseau's brigade moved in splendid order steadily to the front, sweeping everything before it, and at 4 P. M. we stood upon the ground of our original front line, and the enemy was in full retreat. I directed my several brigades to resume at once their original camps.

Several times during the battle cartridges gave out, but General Grant had thoughtfully kept a supply coming from the rear. When I appealed to regiments to stand fast, although out of cartridges,

I did so because to retire a regiment for any cause has a bad effect on others. I commended the Fortieth Illinois and Thirteenth Missouri for thus holding their ground under heavy fire, although their cartridge-boxes were empty.

Gallant Kentuckians.

I was ordered by General Grant to give personal credit where I thought it due, and censure where I thought it merited. I concede that General McCook's splendid division from Kentucky drove back the enemy along the Corinth road, which was the great centre of this field of battle, where Beauregard commanded in person, supported by Bragg's, Polk's, and Breckenridge's divisions. I think A. S. Johnston was killed by exposing himself in front of his troops at the time of their attack on Buckland's brigade on Sunday morning, although in this I may be mistaken.

My division was made up of regiments perfectly new, nearly all having received their muskets for the first time at Paducah. None of them had ever been under fire or beheld heavy columns of an enemy bearing down on them as they did on that Sunday.

To have expected the coolness and steadiness of older troops would be wrong. They knew not the value of combination and organization. When individual fears seized them the first impulse was to get away. My third brigade did break much too soon, and I am not yet advised where it was during Sunday afternoon and Monday morning. Colonel

Hildebrand, its commander, was as cool as any man I ever saw, and no one could have made stronger efforts to hold his men to their places than he did. He kept his own regiment, with individual exceptions, in hand an hour after Appler's and Mungen's regiments had left their proper field of action.

Heroes of the Fight.

Colonel Buckland managed his brigade well. I commended him as a cool, intelligent, and judicious gentleman, needing only confidence and experience to make a good commander. His subordinates, Colonels Sullivan and Cockerill, behaved with great gallantry; the former receiving a severe wound on Sunday, and yet commanding and holding his regiment well in hand all day, and on Monday until his right arm was broken by a shot. Colonel Cockerill held a larger proportion of his men than any colonel in my division, and was with me from first to last.

Colonel J. A. McDowell, commanding the First brigade, held his ground on Sunday, till I ordered him to fall back, which he did in line of battle; and when ordered he conducted the attack on the enemy's left in good style. In falling back to the next position he was thrown from his horse and injured, and his brigade was not in position on Monday morning. His subordinates, Colonels Hicks and Worthington, displayed great personal courage. Colonel Hicks led his regiment in the attack on Sunday, and received a wound which it was feared would prove mortal. He was a brave and gallant gentleman, and deserves well of his country. Lieutenant-Colonel Walcutt of the Ohio Forty-sixth was severely wounded on Sunday, and was disabled.

Hard-won Laurels.

My second brigade, Colonel Stuart, was detached nearly two miles from my headquarters. He had to fight his own battle on Sunday against superior numbers, as the enemy interposed between him and General Prentiss early in the day. Colonel Stuart was wounded severely, and yet reported for duty on Monday morning, but was compelled to leave during the day, when the command devolved on Colonel T. Kilby Smith, who was always in the thickest of the fight, and led the brigade handsomely.

As I did not receive Colonel Stuart's report of the operations of his brigade during the time he was detached, I was compelled to forbear mentioning names. Lieutenant-Colonel Kyle of the Seventy-first was mortally wounded on Sunday, but the regiment itself I did not see, as only a small fragment of it was with the brigade when it joined the division on Monday morning. Great credit was due the fragments of men of the disordered regiments who kept in the advance. I observed and noticed them, but until the brigadiers and colonels made their reports I could not venture to name individuals, but did in due season notice all who kept in our front line, as well as those who preferred to keep back near the steamboat landing. The following was the result in figures of the killed, wounded, and missing:

Officers killed	16
Officers wounded	45
Officers missing	6
Soldiers killed	302
Soldiers wounded	1230
Soldiers missing	435
Aggregate loss in the division	2034

The enemy captured seven of our guns on Sunday, but on Monday we recovered seven—not the identical guns we had lost, but enough in number to balance the account. At the time of recovering our camps our men were so fatigued that we could not follow the retreating masses of the enemy ; but on the following day I followed up with Buckland's and Hildebrand's brigades for six miles.

Bravery of Staff-officers.

Of my personal staff I could only speak with praise and thanks. I think they smelled as much gunpowder and heard as many cannon-balls and bullets as satisfied their ambition. Captain Hammond, my chief of staff, though in feeble health, was very active in rallying broken troops, encouraging the steadfast, and aiding to form the lines of defence and attack. Major Sanger's intelligence, quick perception, and rapid execution were of very great value to me, especially in bringing into line the batteries that co-operated so efficiently in our movements. Captains McCoy and Dayton, aides-de-camp, were with me all the time, carrying orders and acting with coolness, spirit, and courage. To Surgeon Hartshorne and Dr. L'Hommedieu hundreds of wounded men were indebted for the kind and excellent treatment received on the field of battle and in the various temporary hospitals created along the line of our operations. They worked day and night, and did not rest till all the wounded of our own troops as well as of the enemy were in safe and comfortable shelter.

To Major Taylor, chief of artillery, I felt under deep obligations for his good sense and judgment in managing the batteries, on which so much depended. The cavalry of my command kept to the rear, and took little part in the action; but it would have been madness to expose horses to the musketry-fire under which we were compelled to remain from Sunday at 8 A. M. till Monday at 4 P. M.

Following the Enemy.

With the cavalry placed at my command and two brigades of my fatigued troops I went on the morning of the 8th out on the Corinth road. One after another of the abandoned camps of the enemy lined the roads, with hospital-flags for their protection; at all we found more or less wounded and dead men. At the forks of the road I found the head of General T. J. Wood's division of Buell's army. I ordered cavalry to examine both roads leading toward Corinth, and found the enemy on both. Colonel Dickey, of the Fourth Illinois Cavalry, asking for reinforcements, I ordered General Wood to advance the head of his column cautiously on the left-hand road, while I conducted the head of the third brigade of my division up the right-hand road.

About half a mile from the forks was a clear field, through which the road passed, and immediately beyond a space of some two hundred yards of fallen timber, and beyond that an extensive rebel camp.

CAVALRY CHARGE AT SHILOH.

The enemy's cavalry could be seen in this camp; after reconnoissance, I ordered the two advance companies of the Ohio Seventy-seventh, Colonel Hildebrand, to deploy forward as skirmishers, and the regiment itself forward into line, with an interval of one hundred yards. In this order we advanced cautiously until the skirmishers were engaged. Taking it for granted this disposition would clear the camp, I held Colonel Dickey's Fourth Illinois Cavalry ready for the charge.

The enemy's cavalry came down boldly at a charge, led by General Forrest in person, breaking through our line of skirmishers, when the regiment of infantry, without cause, broke, threw away their muskets, and fled. The ground was admirably adapted for a defence of infantry against cavalry, being miry and covered with fallen timber.

Onset of Cavalry.

As the regiment of infantry broke, Dickey's cavalry began to discharge their carbines, and fell into disorder. I instantly sent orders to the rear for the brigade to form line of battle, which was promptly executed. The broken infantry and cavalry rallied on this line, and, as the enemy's cavalry came to it, our cavalry in turn charged and drove them from the field. I advanced the entire brigade over the same ground and sent Colonel Dickey's cavalry a mile farther on the road. On examining the ground which had been occupied by the Seventy-seventh Ohio, we found fifteen of our men dead and about twenty-five wounded. I sent for wagons and had all the wounded carried back to camp, and caused the dead to be buried, also the whole rebel camp to be destroyed.

Here we found much ammunition for field-pieces, which was destroyed; also two caissons, and a general hospital with about two hundred and eighty Confederate wounded and about fifty of our own wounded men. Not having the means of bringing them off, Colonel Dickey, by my orders, took a surrender, signed by the medical director (Lyle) and by all the attending surgeons, and a pledge to report themselves as prisoners of war; also a pledge that our wounded should be carefully attended to, and surrendered to us as soon as ambulances could go out.

The roads were very bad, and were strewed with abandoned wagons, ambulances, and limber-boxes. The enemy had succeeded in carrying off the guns, but had crippled his batteries by abandoning the hind limber-boxes of at least twenty caissons. I am satisfied the enemy's infantry and artillery passed Lick Creek next morning, after travelling all night, and that he left to his rear all his cavalry, which had protected his retreat; but signs of confusion and disorder marked the whole road. The check sustained by us at the fallen timber delayed our advance, so that night came upon us before the wounded were provided for and the dead buried, and our troops being fagged out by three days' hard fighting, exposure, and privation, I ordered them back to their camps.

CHAPTER XV.

Thrilling Pen-picture of the Battle of Shiloh, by an Army Surgeon.

It requires many eyes to see a great battle in all its details. Eye-witnesses describe what they saw, and each according to his location. While all agree in the general features, changes, and aspects of the contest, each beholder has something new and of vital interest to relate. For this reason we add a striking picture of the terrible fight at Shiloh from the pen of Dr. James Moore, surgeon of the United States army. After detailing the movements preceding the capture of Island No. 10, Dr. Moore says:

Thus the doom of Island No. 10 was sealed. The batteries on the Kentucky shore were soon silenced by the gunboats, and Pope's army crossed. The Confederate army scattered in the woods, and five thousand were at last captured. The Confederate commander on the island, General William D. McCall, then capitulated with a few hundred men. A hundred heavy guns, several field batteries, small-arms in abundance, tents, wagons, horses, and provisions, were the fruit of the victory.

LIEUT.-GEN. W. HARDEE.

Great joy was diffused throughout the North. The great Mississippi was now open as far as Forts Wright and Pillow, sixty miles above Memphis, and Foote prepared to attack these also.

Meanwhile a great battle was in progress at Pittsburg Landing, on the banks of the Tennessee. Thus, on the same Sunday night on which the steamer Pittsburg ran the enemy's batteries, the two armies lay on the field where they had fought desperately the entire day; and when our troops were crossing to victory on the Kentucky shore, our army was struggling to recover the field which it had lost the preceding day. The battle of Pittsburg Landing, or Shiloh, lasted two days. It commenced on the 6th of April.

The Confederate general, Johnston, after retreating south through Tennessee, proceeded toward Memphis, and subsequently massed his army at Corinth, in Mississippi, near the Tennessee line, ninety-three miles from Memphis.

Position of the Union Army.

General Ulysses S. Grant had moved up the Tennessee River, and placed his army on the west bank at Pittsburg Landing, where he awaited Buell's corps from Nashville. The design was to combine their forces and advance on the rebel camp at Corinth. Johnston moved his entire army on the 4th of April, intending to assault Grant on Saturday, but bad roads detained him until Sunday morning. There is a road from Pittsburg Landing to Corinth, distant twenty miles. This road two miles from the Tennessee River divides, and while one fork continues right on in its course, the other runs to lower Corinth. From Hamburg Landing, some miles up the river, a road crosses that before mentioned. Two roads branch off on the right, in the direction of Purdy. It was on these several roads, and between them, at a distance of from two to five miles from Pittsburg Landing, that the Federal army lay encamped. The divisions farthest advanced were those of Prentiss, Sherman, and McClernand. Hurlbut's and Smith's divisions lay between them and the river. Smith being sick, his division wes commanded by W. H. L. Wallace. Sherman's brigade held the right, Prentiss the centre, and Colonel Stuart the left. The extreme left was deemed sufficiently protected by precipices and a ravine.

On the rebel side, General A. S. Johnston commanded and had especial charge of the centre; Generals Braxton Bragg and T. P. G. Beauregard commanded the two wings; and Hardee, Polk, and Breckenridge held subordinate positions. Their plan was to make an attack on the Federal centre, and then on each of the wings, front and flank. The rebel troops numbered seventy thousand men.

Sudden Attack.

The enemy attacked the Federals as some were at breakfast and others lying around. It was a complete surprise. The pickets had been driven in suddenly, and the enemy's artillery cast shot and shell among the regiments. So unexpected was the assault that officers were bayonetted before they rose from their beds. There was a general panic before any line of battle could be formed. The attack on Buckland's brigade of Sherman's division was made so suddenly that the officers had not time to dress. The men, snatching up their muskets as best they could, ran to the other portion of the division in the utmost disorder.

Sherman Falls Back.

Sherman made herculean efforts to get the division in position to abide the coming shock. McClernand meanwhile was trying to fill up the gap caused by Buckland's disordered flight, and was gallantly stemming the tide of battle amid the rolling smoke, the crash of muskets, and the roar of artillery. Sherman saw that he could not resist the fearful odds which were hurled against him, and issued the order to fall back.

Meanwhile the division of Prentiss was in a more deplorable plight. It is true that there was time to form in line of battle, but, being drawn up in an open field, they were exposed to a murderous fire poured on them by the enemy from the edge of the woods, and were mowed down with great slaughter. They stood their ground with cool courage, and their volleys were rapid and steady. But Grant was not on the field, and there was little concert of action, as each commander could only take care of his own division, hold his ground, and wait for support. Hence, no regular line of battle could be formed, and while the Federal forces could adopt no connected plan, the rebel army as one machine was hurled on the disorganized troops.

Prentiss's Division Shattered.

Prentiss was outflanked, and saw himself enclosed by the enemy. The disorganized portion of his division, numbering three thousand men, surrendered and were marched to the rear. The insolent foe drove the other regiments of this division before them like a flock of sheep.

One brigade after another was brought up by McClernand to support Sherman. Desperate grew the struggle which ensued, and cannon and musketry rolled their continuous thunders over the bloody field, and the audacious enemy rushed up to the mouth of the cannon and took several. Desperate hand-to-hand fights ensued, and the stubborn resistance of Sherman, though the sacrifice of life was great, kept the army from being driven in dismay into the river. The enemy, if not repulsed, was checked for a while. McClernand held his ground with great pertinacity, but the gap left by Sherman in retiring laid him open to a flank movement, and the head of the enemy's columns was dashing with all their speed at him.

Terrible Havoc.

At this moment the rifled guns from Dresser's battery swept the road with a destructive fire, and the enemy paused. Reinforcements, however, strengthened the forces of the enemy, and one charge repulsed was only succeeded by another more desperate.

Many Federal officers of the line fell. The artillery-horses were shot by scores, and as the guns could not be withdrawn from the field, they fell into the hands of the enemy. The half of Swartz's guns and sixteen horses of the battery were lost. Dresser lost some rifled pieces and thirty-two horses, and McAlister half of his howitzers. The division at eleven o'clock was driven back, and on a line with Hurlbut's, which, though fighting well and at times repelling the enemy, was at last obliged to retreat. Colonel Stuart, in command of a brigade on Sherman's extreme left, would have been cut off, but had been fortunately overlooked by the enemy.

Almost a Rout.

Two Confederate brigades were now sent to attack him, and he fell back. The enemy pursued, and a bloody combat followed. The gallant brigade had to retreat, with its wounded commander, in ten minutes, but made a stand for upward of an hour on a wooded hill. McArthur's brigade, which was sent to its aid, lost its way, and was driven back again and again till it had to be sent to the rear to re-form.

At twelve o'clock the camps of Sherman, Prentiss, and McClernand were in the possession of the enemy, who was still advancing. The arrival of Grant from Savannah, a few miles down the river, could not stay the disorder or prevent a retreat. Wallace's division, at Crump's Landing, had been ordered up in the morning, and would have strengthened the right, but it lost its way, and, had this been known to the enemy, the result would have been fatal.

Hurlbut put his division into position and animated his men. Sherman drew up the remains of his brigade and saw that the crisis was imminent. The Confederate troops now rushed on, flushed with victory, but were forced back. They advanced again with desperate efforts, and were again obliged to flee to the thicket. The leaders led on fresh regiments. Terrible carnage followed, and the Confederate general A. S. Johnston was slain. For a third time the enemy was repelled, but fresh troops always came up, and the wasted Federal forces were compelled to fall back, while the Confederates pressed on, covering the field with the slain.

On the Brink of Destruction.

The entire left wing was forced back to the river, where thousands were crowded, without boats, and were in danger of being massacred by the exultant enemy. Wallace, on the extreme right, nobly held his ground and four times repelled the foe. The reserve line was carried, and the army now contracted into the area of half a mile. The sun was on the decline and the whole army was now on the brink of destruction. Just then a body of cavalry—Buell's advance—was seen. Help was near. Buell's columns were approaching the Tennessee, and the wily foe bore down on the crowded and disorganized Federal columns to crush them, and thus verify the prediction of Beauregard that ere night fell his horse would drink from the Tennessee. The enemy reckoned without his host.

Death-shots from Parrott Guns.

At the critical moment, Colonel Webster, chief of staff, skilled as an artillerist, had collected all the guns, some of large calibre, from the broken batteries, and arranged them in crescent form around the landing. Collecting a force of artillerists, he was ready when the heavy columns of the enemy advanced. Suddenly twenty-one guns sent forth a deadly fire among the closed ranks, and the enemy recoiled, again to advance. The gunboats Tyler and Lexington now moved down the bank, and with their twenty-four-pound Parrott guns and rifled cannon sent the shrieking shells bursting among the terrified ranks of the Confederates. They halted, turned, and retired from the range of these destructive engines.

Meanwhile, General Nelson, commanding Buell's advance, crossed the Tennessee and opened a heavy fire on the enemy with a battery of artillery. The Confederates withdrew and bivouacked on the bloody field. Buell's army was coming up rapidly. Nelson's division was across the river, and Crittenden's was placed in front of Sherman's broken line. McCook's division had reached Savannah, and was waiting to be brought up to the field of battle. The regular batteries, commanded by Captains Mendenhall and Terrell, and an Ohio battery, arrived in the night, and Captain Bartlett brought word that the rest would be up early in the morning. The news of this powerful reinforcement at hand animated the brave men who had fought against such odds and, though defeated, they felt that returning day would turn the scale of victory in their favor.

Second Day at Shiloh.

At five o'clock in the morning, on the 7th of April, Nelson and Crittenden advanced upon the enemy, drove in his pickets, and at seven o'clock neared his line of battle. Crittenden formed on the right of Nelson, with Bartlett's battery in the centre. The sound of cannon shook the field, and told those at the landing that the battle was begun. McCook took position on the right of Crittenden, and Wallace with three brigades held the extreme right, and opened with artillery at seven o'clock.

A grand artillery duel was for some time kept up. Nelson's line first engaged the enemy in a bloody contest. Colonel Hazen, of the Nineteenth brigade, captured a battery, but was compelled to relinquish it. The lines of Nelson, however, still kept steadily advancing, sweeping the field lost the day before, which was yet strewed with the dead of the combatants. Crittenden pressed the enemy back in his front; and Smith's brigade, by a gallant dash, captured a battery, to recover which the enraged foe charged again and again.

The Host's Majestic Tread.

The combat was deadly for half an hour on this spot. The splendid troops of McCook moved on, and now the Federal line, a mile and a half in extent, advanced with slow, majestic tread against the enemy, who, under cover of the thickets, made a desperate rally and hurled such a powerful force on Nelson's division that it recoiled, faltered, and finally fell back. The compact masses of the foe were assailed at this critical moment by Terrell's regular battery, raining shells from the twenty-four-pound howitzers. They staggered, but rallied again, and, undaunted, marched up to the death-dealing guns, and horses and gunners alike went down, till there was not a man remaining at one of the pieces. Terrell and a corporal worked one of the guns till saved by the dash of a regiment. Nelson kept his men well in hand, but the rally of the foe, which at first had caused him to give way, swept on in turn to Crittenden, who had to take up a new position.

The Tide of Battle Turned.

The exultant enemy followed up his success till his ranks were swept by the death-bolts hurled by Mendenhall's and Bartlett's artillery. Meanwhile, Buell, seeing the determined resistance of the enemy, ordered an advance by brigades at the double-quick. The enemy, recoiling from the terrible line of glittering steel and the simultaneous movement of that great host, fell back step by step as the Federal divisions pressed on. They lost all the ground which had been won the day before. The foe was now in confusion, being mowed down in platoons by the musketry and artillery.

On the same spot where the Federal defeat had taken place on the previous day all the guns lost on that part of the field were recaptured, and two of the enemy's captured in turn. A last and desperate stand was made in front of McCook's division, but could not drive him back, though he was exposed to a flank movement.

Wallace had a desperate encounter with a Confederate line, which seemed, as regiment after regiment poured in, to be interminable. Cannonading on both sides extended along the whole front till he sent sharpshooters to pick off the gunners. Waiting for Sherman, at last that leader brought up the remnant of his brave division and advanced on the Confederate lines.

Sherman Cries, "Forward!"

Sherman rode along where the bullets flew thickest, and roused the courage of his men to a high degree. His horse was killed, but he sprang on another and gave the order, "Forward!" The woods were gained, one of the enemy's batteries flanked, and here the scale of victory preponderated to the Federal side. Wallace, seeing the Confederate guns limbering up, was upon them. The whole line heard the order, "Forward!" and pressed on the enemy till he was driven to the woods.

By a determined stand here Sherman's division was forced back; but, though wounded twice and having three horses shot under him, he rallied his brave troops and hurled them on the foe, being distinguished on this hard-fought field as the hero of heroes. The tide of battle, beginning on the left, had rolled like a wave on to the right, The enemy had tried to find an unguarded or weak point, but now fell back slowly till driven beyond the last Federal camp. Three thousand cavalry in reserve were now ordered to charge them. But the enemy retired in order, and, planting his artillery, hurled destruction on the victorious columns which attempted to turn the defeat into a complete rout. Buell gave the order to halt, and the wearied troops bivouacked on the field.

Heavy Losses on Both Sides.

General Johnston, the Confederate leader, and Johnson, the provisional governor of Kentucky, were among the Confederate dead. The losses on both sides were nearly equal. The Federals lost in killed, wounded, and missing, including three thousand prisoners, almost fourteen thousand. The loss of the enemy was estimated at about the same.

The first day was a defeat; the second a victory, but dearly purchased. McClernand lost nearly a third of his whole force.

The field presented a ghastly spectacle The enemy had left his dead. Ten thousand of the same race and nation lay cold in death on this ensanguined field, while twice that number were wounded. The Sanitary Commission here rendered the most invaluable service, the ordinary means of supply being inefficient and nurses as well as physicians too few.

In this battle the Confederate army on the first day was well fought. Want of united action, partly the consequence of surprise, was the cause which, next to overwhelming numbers, caused the Federal reverse.

It was a bloody battle on both sides, and such as this continent had never before witnessed.

Sherman's Magnificent Valor.

Sherman rose at once to the peril of the occasion, and all day long moved like a fabled god over the disastrous field. Clinging to his position till the last moment, fighting as he retired, his orders flying like lightning in every direction, and he himself galloping incessantly through the hottest fire, now rallying his men, now planting a battery, he seemed omnipresent and to bear a charmed life.

Horse after horse sank under him, he himself was struck again and again, and yet he not only kept the field, but blazed like a meteor over it. At noon of that Sabbath day he was dismounted, his hand in a sling and bleeding, giving directions to his chief of artillery, while it was one incessant crash and roar all around him. Suddenly he saw to the right his men giving way before a cloud of Confederates. "I was looking for that," he exclaimed. The next moment the battery he had been placing in position opened, sending death and destruction into the close-packed ranks.

The Confederate commander, glancing at the battery, ordered the cavalry to charge it. Seeing them coming down, Sherman quickly ordered up two companies of infantry, which, pouring in a deadly volley, sent them to the right about with empty saddles. The onset was arrested and our troops rallied with renewed courage.

Thus he acted all that fearful Sabbath day. As Sheridan was the rock that saved Rosecrans at Stone River, and Thomas the one that saved him at Chickamauga, so Sherman was the rock that saved Grant at Shiloh. At its close his old legion met him, and sent up three cheers at the sight of his well-remembered form.

The Battle Depended on Sherman.

Rousseau, in speaking of his conduct in this battle, said, "No man living could surpass him." General Nelson a few days before his death remarked, "During eight hours the fate of the army on the field of Shiloh depended on the life of one man: if General Sherman had fallen the army would have been captured or destroyed." Grant said, "To his individual efforts I am indebted for the success of that battle;" and Halleck in his despatch bore this unqualified testimony: "It is the unanimous opinion here that Brigadier-General W. T. Sherman saved the fortunes of the day on the 6th of April." "He was a strong man in the high places of the field, and hope shone in him like a pillar of fire when it had gone out in all other men."

The next day, when Buell's fresh battalions took the field, Sherman again led his battered regiments into the fight, and enacted over again the heroic deeds of the day before; for, as Rousseau said, he "fights by the week." Untiring to the last, he pushed out the third day, after the victory, and whipped the enemy's cavalry, taking a large supply of ammunition.

In the subsequent advance to Corinth his division bore the most conspicuous part, and was the first to enter the deserted works of the enemy. In the mean time he had been promoted to be major-general of volunteers.

He could Afford now to Laugh.

He could now laugh at the slander that had so annoyed him and joke of it publicly. There were two General Shermans in the army before Corinth, the only difference in their names being a transposition of the initials, W. T. and T. W. T. W. was known as the Port Royal Sherman, on account of his operations there after the capture of the place by DuPont. He was a very unpopular man with his troops on account of a fretful, peevish disposition, exhibiting itself not only in words, but in a disagreeable, nervous manner. He was equally unpopular with the officers, who discussed his peculiarities freely. One day, General W. T. Sherman was calling on Steadman, when some one gave a ludicrous account of the behavior of T. W. Sherman on a certain occasion, which created a great deal of merriment. Sherman joined in it, and jokingly remarked, "Oh, that is the crazy Sherman, is it?"

The Conquerors.

At the close of this chapter it can hardly be deemed out of place to notice the influence of Shiloh and Corinth on the fortunes of some of the principal actors. Among the Confederates, Beauregard was the man principally affected. He had the greatest opportunity. He sustained the greatest loss. The effect of Shiloh and Corinth was undoubtedly injurious, but it was not lasting. Beauregard suffered the less that neither at Shiloh nor at Corinth did any rival of equal capacity come to the front.

On the National side three men shared largely of the favors of fortune—Halleck, Grant, and Sherman. Halleck reaped a glory which was scarcely all his own. Grant, in spite of a treatment which must be pronounced unjust, not only preserved his reputation, but secured the opportunity of making himself what he soon afterward was recognized to be, the leading representative on the field of the Northern cause.

Sherman in the one battle and in the other surpassed himself in deeds of skill and daring, and earned his right and title to a place in the front rank of the great military men whom the war was gradually developing—a place which he never afterward lost.

CHAPTER XVI.

General Sherman's Achievements at Vicksburg.

AFTER the battle of Corinth, which was fought on the 4th of October, 1862, the army under General Grant fell back to the position which it formerly occupied, and remained in comparative inactivity until the beginning of November. It was stationed from Memphis to Bridgeport, Tennessee, along the Memphis and Charleston railroad. Its strong points were Memphis, Grand Junction, and Corinth. The army was arranged in four divisions.

General Sherman, with the first division, was at Memphis; General Hurlbut, with the second, was at Jackson; General C. S. Hamilton, with the third, was at Corinth; and General T. A. Davies, with the fourth, was at Columbus. Grant's headquarters were at Jackson, Tennessee, a point in the West where the Central Mississippi railroad unites with the Mobile and Ohio. That general had not abandoned the plan which was inaugurated at Henry and Donelson. His whole soul was bent on the capture of Vicksburg. A variety of circumstances, however, had necessitated delay. The removal of Halleck to Washington had devolved upon him the entire care of the Department of the Tennessee—a department which included, in addition to Cairo, Forts Henry and Donelson, the whole of Northern Mississippi, and those portions of Tennessee and Kentucky west of the Tennessee River. This, however, was not the only or even the most important reason.

A Weakened Army.

The army which had fought and won at Shiloh, at Corinth, and at Iuka had been greatly weakened, a large proportion of its strength having been sent to Kentucky to resist the invasion of Bragg. It was necessary, therefore, for Grant, while perfecting his plans and rearranging his troops, to wait for reinforcements. As soon as the reinforcements arrived he was ready to move.

The National gunboats had swept the Mississippi from Cairo to Memphis, and between those two points every Confederate stronghold had been deserted or destroyed. Farragut, with a portion of his fleet, had pushed his way up to Vicksburg after the capture of New Orleans. He was accompanied by General F. Williams with an infantry force of four regiments. While Farragut bombarded the city, Williams was cutting a canal with the view of diverting the waters of the Mississippi from their proper channel, thus leaving Vicksburg high and dry on all sides.

Fruitless Siege.

The siege lasted some seventy days. It was all to no purpose. Farragut, who failed to make any serious impression on the Confederate works, began to fear for his own safety. The canal also proved a complete failure. The fleet and the land force both found it necessary to retire, and Vicksburg remained to obstruct the navigation of the great river.

On the 4th of November, Grant began to move. He transferred his headquarters from Jackson to La Grange, some few miles to the west of Grand Junction. He soon discovered that the Confederates, under General John C. Pemberton, a Pennsylvanian, who had superseded Van Dorn, were in considerable strength immediately in his front. Pemberton, in fact, had taken a strong position behind two lines of defences, the outer being the Yallabusha and the inner being the Tallahatchie—two streams which after their junction form the Yazoo River. Both of these streams cross the Mississippi Central railroad between Grand Junction and Grenada. The banks of the Tallahatchie were strongly fortified. Grant's first intention was to offer Pemberton battle, defeat him, and force his way to Vicksburg.

Sherman and Grant Laying Plans.

On the 8th he sent out McPherson with ten thousand infantry and fifteen hundred cavalry, with instructions to drive from Lamar a body of Confederates who were holding the railroad. McPherson accomplished his task in the most effectual manner, the Confederates having been driven back as far as Holly Springs. The time had now come to make a determined effort to open the Mississippi.

About the 17th of November, Grant summoned Sherman to meet him at Columbus, and at the interview which there took place the views of the two

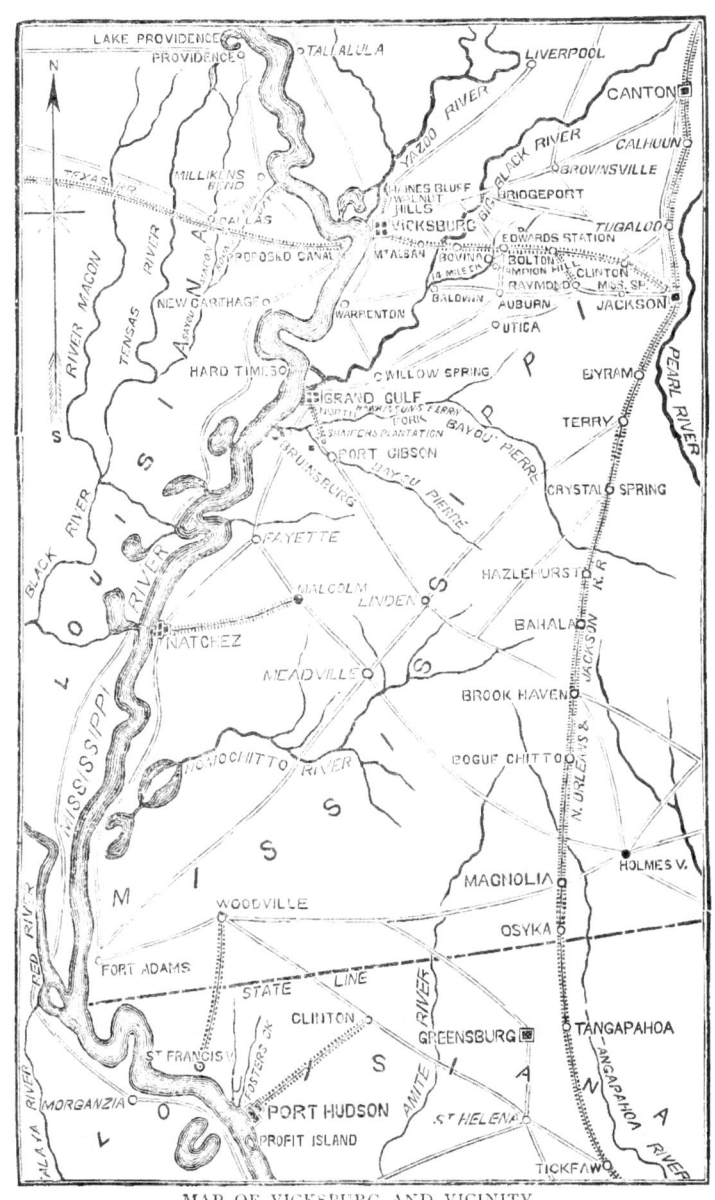

MAP OF VICKSBURG AND VICINITY.

generals were freely exchanged, Grant explaining to Sherman his plan and giving him his orders.

It was Sherman's suggestion that a portion of Curtis's army, which was stationed at Helena, should be brought over to Delta with a view to co-operate with Grant in his general movement toward Vicksburg. These troops which, in the absence of General Curtis, who was at St. Paul, were under the temporary command of General Frederick Steele, were promptly at the place appointed on the eastern bank of the Mississippi. They numbered some seven thousand men, and were under the joint command of Generals A. P. Hovey and C. C. Washburne.

Ordered to scour the country to the south and east in the rear of the Confederate army, to destroy the railroads and bridges so as to cut off supplies, and generally to prepare the way for Grant's advance, they accomplished their task in the most effectual manner, and then returned to the Mississippi.

Confederates Fall Back.

Pemberton, on discovering that the railroads were badly damaged and that the rolling-stock was destroyed, Grant meanwhile pressing on his front, deemed it prudent to fall back on Grenada.

On the 1st of December, Grant was at Holly Springs. On the 5th he was at Oxford, where he established his headquarters. It now became a serious question with General Grant how far he was wise in allowing himself to be tempted to advance into the enemy's country. The State of Mississippi was but sparsely peopled, and he had no means of knowing whether its resources were equal to the wants of a large army possibly cut off from its base of supplies. Had he known what he knew afterward, the caution would have been unnecessary, and he would doubtless have continued his onward march.

On the 5th of December, Sherman, on his way to join Grant and bringing with him from Memphis some sixteen thousand men, arrived at College Hill, about ten miles from Oxford, whence he reported to his chief. On the 8th he received from Grant a letter requesting his immediate presence at Oxford, and enclosing a message from Halleck to Grant authorizing the latter to prosecute the new plan he had just submitted to him, to move his troops as he thought best, to retain till further orders all Curtis's troops now in his department, to telegraph to General Allen in St. Louis for all the steamboats he might need, and to ask Porter to co-operate with his gunboats.

Plan of Land and Naval Attack.

On his arrival at Oxford, Sherman found Grant surrounded by his staff. The new plan was discussed and approved. It will be seen that Grant made up his mind that, for the safety of his men as well as for the final success of the expedition, it was necessary to take full advantage of the river communication with Vicksburg. It was agreed that a large force on transports should proceed down the Mississippi under convoy of Porter's gunboats—that on reaching the mouth of the Yazoo they should open up that water line, and by a joint attack of the land and naval forces attempt to capture Vicksburg in the rear. Grant meanwhile was to press forward toward Jackson, which is only some forty-six miles to the west of Vicksburg, offering Pemberton battle, and following him up close in the event of his retreat, in the hope of finding Sherman on the Yazoo with supplies or in possession of Vicksburg.

Happily, Grant had been left complete control of the whole movement, Halleck having offered no special advice and imposed no conditions. He could move at will, and he could place in prominent command the men of his own choice.

Sherman's Command.

Sherman, who commanded the right wing of Grant's army, was appointed to the command of the river expedition, and received his instructions. Grant had the greater pleasure in appointing Sherman to this command that McClernand, who had great influence with the President, was known to be intriguing for an independent command on the Mississippi. Sherman was therefore ordered to take command of the forces at Memphis, and those also at Helena and Delta under General Steele, to descend the river by transports, with the gunboat fleet, commanded by Admiral Porter, as a convoy, and to attack Vicksburg by the 29th of November.

McClernand was to take the forces at Cairo and to proceed to Vicksburg, so as to be in time to lend Sherman effective aid as soon as he made the attack.

Grant himself, as we have said, was to move rapidly on the Confederates to the north and east of Vicksburg, to follow them if they should retreat toward the city, and to take part with Sherman, if necessary, in the reduction of the place.

Ready for Action.

It was a well-conceived plan. Its success, however, depended on the prompt and faithful execution of all its parts. Grant knew that it was unsafe to trust for supplies solely to the enemy's country. He had therefore repaired the Central Mississippi railroad as far as Oxford, where, for the present, he had established his headquarters, and Holly Springs, which was entrusted to the care of Colonel R. C. Murphy, was retained as a grand dépôt and hospital.

Let us see how this plan was carried out. Grant had taken great care that no misfortune should befall him in his rear. He had left small but adequate garrisons at Columbus, at Humboldt, Trenton, Jackson, Bolivar, Corinth, Holly Springs, Coldwater, Davis's Mills, and Middlebury. He had taken particular care of Holly Springs, for he knew that the treasures at that place presented a powerful temptation to Van Dorn. On the night of the 19th he warned Murphy of his danger, and informed him that he had sent four thousand men to enable him to repel any attack which might be made upon him. Murphy, it would seem, paid little heed to the instructions given him. He made no extra preparations to resist the enemy, and was clearly unequal to the occasion.

On the morning of the 20th, at daybreak, Van Dorn. executing a brilliant cavalry operation, rushed upon the place with tremendous fury. Murphy offered no resistance. The Second Illinois, however, refused to surrender, and gallantly fought their way out with a loss of only seven men. Murphy, with the rest of his men, accepted a parole. Van Dorn seized all the property, valued at over fifteen hundred thousand dollars, taking with him what he could carry and destroying the remainder. He set fire to the buildings, not even sparing the hospital, which was filled with sick and wounded soldiers, and committed an act of inhuman barbarity.

"Cowardly and Disgraceful Conduct."

This was the second time that Murphy had been guilty of such conduct. He did the same thing at Iuka. General Grant was wild with rage. It was his opinion that with "all the cotton, public stores and substantial buildings about the dépôt" Murphy ought to have been able to keep the assailants at bay until relief arrived. It was only four hours after the catastrophe when the four thousand men sent to his aid arrived on the spot. Grant was particularly incensed at Murphy for accepting a parole for himself and his men. A cartel had been agreed to by the rival commanders, and it had been stipulated that each party should take care of his own prisoners.

If Murphy had refused parole for himself and men, Van Dorn would have been "compelled to release them unconditionally or to have abandoned all further aggressive movements for the time being." In a severe order on the 9th of January, General Grant dismissed Murphy from the army, the order to take effect "from December 20th, the date of his cowardly and disgraceful conduct."

The disaster at Holly Springs was ruinous to Grant's plan. It robbed him of supplies which it was intended should sustain the army for several weeks. To replace them it would be necessary to put in operation all the capacity and force of the Columbus railroad, but this railroad had been destroyed, and weeks would be exhausted before it could be put in working order. Ignorant of the resources of the country, and not knowing whether, in the event of his pressing forward, he should find Sherman in the vicinity of Vicksburg, he deemed it his duty to fall back. He immediately recrossed the Tallahatchie.

The Game of War.

Having no other means of subsisting his army, he made requisitions on the inhabitants as he moved along. On the 23d of December he was at Holly Springs, now a scene of wreck and ruin, and a few days later he re-entered La Grange and Grand Junction, where he was once more in communication with Corinth and Memphis. Pemberton made no attempt to pursue. On the contrary, taking advantage of the retreat of his antagonist, he withdrew the greater portion of his forces from Grenada and concentrated toward Vicksburg.

On the same day that Van Dorn made his raid on Holly Springs an attack was made by a Confederate force on Davis's Mills, a little farther to the north. In the neighborhood of Jackson, Tennessee, a vital point in Grant's line of communications, an attack was made by a body of cavalry under Forrest on the 19th. The telegraph wires were cut and the railroad was destroyed.

Hopes Blasted.

On the following day Forrest presented himself before Humboldt and Trenton. These and other stations along the railroad, such as Dyer's, Rutherford, and Kenton, fell an easy prey to the enemy. It seemed to be the purpose of the Confederates to destroy every railroad bridge from Columbus to Corinth, and thus to cut Grant off from all his communications and supplies.

So far, they had carried out their purpose with determination and with not a little success. Never was campaign opened under apparently happier auspicies. The rich bud of promise, however, was cruelly blasted.

Grant's plan of the campaign had failed. Meanwhile, what of Sherman? On the 20th, the very day on which Van Dorn and Forrest struck the blow which compelled Grant to fall back and abandon his part of the joint undertaking, Sherman took his departure from Memphis. Taking with him over twenty thousand troops in transports, he left as a guard to the city a strong force of infantry and cavalry, and the siege-guns in position with a complement of gunners. On the following day, at Friar's Point, he was joined by Admiral Porter in his flag-ship Black Hawk, with the Marmora, Captain Getty, and the Conestoga, Captain Selfridge, which were to act as a convoy. The remainder of Porter's fleet was at the mouth of the Yazoo. On the same evening, the 21st, the troops at Helena embarked in transports and came to Friar's Point. Sherman's force was now at least thirty thousand strong. All the arrangements were completed, and the joint expedition was moving down the river the following morning.

A Strange Story.

Sherman got away just in time to secure for himself the glory or dishonor of the expedition. Had he lingered a day longer he would have been superseded in his command by General McClernand. It is a strange story, and one which, for the sake of all the parties concerned, it would be well if the world could forget. We will not enter into details. It has already been stated that General McClernand was a warm personal friend of President Lincoln, and that he was ambitious of an independent command on the Mississippi.

It is not necessary to say that Sherman was a man according to Grant's own heart. Since that great day at Shiloh their fates had been linked together, and they had been to each other like David and Jonathan. Sherman was also a great favorite with Halleck, the commander-in-chief at Washington. But for the personal wishes of Grant and Halleck, both of whom knew well that Sherman was the man for the position, McClernand would have been appointed by Lincoln in the first instance to the command of the river expedition.

McClernand, however, was not to be put off; and Lincoln, who was always unwilling to disoblige a friend, was weak enough to yield to his entreaties. On the 18th of December an order from the President reached Grant, directing him to divide all his forces into four army corps, to assign one corps to McClernand, and to place him at the head of the troops destined for the attack upon Vicksburg.

Embarrassing Situation.

Grant could hardly fail to see in this order a blow aimed at himself. It was a most awkward circumstance, and reflected little credit on the wisdom and good sense of the President. Good and great as he was, Lincoln was not without his weaknesses. He was vain enough to imagine that he knew quite as much as his generals in the field, and he was disposed to deal with military officers as he was in the habit of dealing with politicians.

It is not much to be wondered at if Grant was staggered by this order and if he was slow to put it in execution. It was not difficult for him to find an excuse. He was in the midst of his preparations for an onward march. The reconstruction of his army, according to the instructions received, occupied him the whole of the 19th. The disaster at Holly Springs, compelling a backward movement, occurred on the

20th, and the raids of Forrest on the same day deprived him of the use of the telegraph.

Every Inch a Soldier.

As it was, Sherman had proceeded down the river before any counter-instructions reached Memphis. If Sherman had any reason to fear a counter-order, his haste to get ready and his prompt departure but revealed the soldierly spirit and true character of the man. As the result proved, it was well for Sherman, well for General Grant, and well for the nation at large that Lincoln's order did not take effect before the 20th of December.

On Christmas Day the expedition under Sherman and Porter had reached Milliken's Bend, when Sherman detached Burbridge's brigade of A. J. Smith's division to break up the railroad leading from Vicksburg to Shreveport, Louisiana. Leaving A. J. Smith's division to await the return, the remaining divisions proceeded on the 26th to the mouth of the Yazoo, and up that river to Johnson's plantation, some thirteen miles, and there disembarked.

Insurmountable Obstacles.

The disembarkation was conducted without any opposition. Steele's division landed farthest up the river, above what is called Chickasaw Bayou; Morgan's division, a little lower down, at the house of Johnson, which had been burned by the gunboats on a former occasion; Morgan L. Smith's division, below that of Morgan; and A. J. Smith's, which arrived next night, below that of M. L. Smith. The ground on which

Sherman now found himself presented obstacles of which formerly he had but a very imperfect conception.

Vicksburg is built on a range of bluffs known as the Walnut Hills. These hills, which take their rise a little below the city, extend for the most part in a north-easterly direction, terminating in Haines' Bluff, a distance of some thirteen or fourteen miles. The configuration of these hills has been compared to the ridge at Inkerman, to which it is said they bear, in some particulars, a striking resemblance. Their average height is about two hundred feet.

Natural Defences.

Where the Mississippi touches their base at Vicksburg, and for some miles both above and below, they are precipitous. Along their entire length, indeed, from Vicksburg to Haines' Bluff, their face is very abrupt and cut up by numerous valleys and ravines. The only approach to the city by land from up the river is by climbing their almost perpendicular front. The ground beyond is high, broken, and somewhat rolling, gradually descending to the Big Black River. The Yazoo, which skirts the ridge at Haines' Bluff, about nine miles above Vicksburg by the road along the foot of the bluffs, flows in a south-western direction, and before discharging its waters into the Mississippi crosses an old arm of the river, which now forms a semicircular lake.

The Yazoo evidently in times gone by clung to the foot of the hills, and traces of its former whereabouts are to be seen in the numerous bayous and channels by which the intervening ground is cut up. One of these bayous puts off from the Yazoo about one-third of the distance below Haines' Bluff, running at right angles with the river until it approaches the bluffs, when it turns and follows their base until it empties itself into the Mississippi. It is called Chickasaw Bayou.

Frowning Batteries.

Between the bayou and the hills there was an irregular strip of land on which the trees had been felled to form an abattis. It was dotted also with rifle-pits. Rifle-trenches abounded, too, along the front of the bluffs, and the heights above were crowned with batteries.

About a mile to the north-east of the bayou, and parallel with it, there is a deep slough, which makes a sharp turn as it approaches the bluffs, and enters Chickasaw Bayou at the point where the latter is checked in its course and turns to flow along the base of the hills. There was thus a fortified line some twelve or thirteen miles in length, formed of abattis and rifle-pits, with an impassable ditch in front, and terminating in the powerful fixed batteries at Haines' Bluff on the one hand, and in the heavy batteries and field-works above Vicksburg on the other.

The land lying between the Yazoo and the Chickasaw was not only low and swampy: it was, except in one or two places where there were plantations, densely wooded. The distance from Johnson's Landing to the Chickasaw was about six miles. Such was the ground over which Sherman proposed to march his men. Such were the obstacles to be overcome before he could enter Vicksburg. To the National commander, however, and to his officers these obstacles were, as yet, but imperfectly known.

Sherman's Valiant Army.

General Sherman's army was organized in four divisions. The First division, comprising three brigades, was under Brigadier-General George W. Morgan; Second division, three brigades, under Brigadier-General Morgan L. Smith; Third division, three brigades, under Brigadier-General A. J. Smith; Fourth division, four brigades, under Brigadier-General Frederick Steele. The brigade commanders of the Fourth division were Generals Frank P. Blair, John M. Thayer, C. E. Hovey, and Colonel Hassendurbel.

According to Sherman's plan of attack, General Steele was to hold the extreme left, General Morgan the left centre, General M. L. Smith the right centre, and General A. J. Smith the extreme right. As the latter general had not yet arrived from Milliken's Bend, where we left him waiting for Burbridge, General Frank P. Blair, with his brigade, was detached from Steele's division and placed on Morgan's right.

Clever Strategy.

The object of this arrangement was to distract the enemy's attention, leading him to expect an attack at a number of different points. Instructions, however, had been given to each of the commanders to converge toward the point of attack, at or near Barfield's plantation. There it had been discovered the bayou could be crossed at two points—at a sand-bar and at a narrow levee.

On the 27th the army began to move. General Steele, who had been ordered to take position on the further side of the slough above this bayou, experienced great difficulty in landing his troops. So soft and slushy was the ground and so dense was the brushwood that he found it necessary to construct roads for moving his wagons and artillery. When night came he had only advanced some two miles from the shore.

During the greater portion of next day he pushed forward his command, but he was compelled to report to Sherman that he found it physically impossible to reach the bluffs from his position, and that to persist in the attempt would inevitably lead to the ruin of his troops and the loss of his field equipage.

Pressing Forward.

He was therefore ordered to leave some of his troops behind him as a show of force, to hasten to the west side of the Chickasaw Bayou, and to take a position on Morgan's left. On the 27th, Blair moved slowly toward the bluffs, his desire being to give Steele time to come into position on the left. He succeeded in silencing one of the enemy's batteries at the point where he expected Steele would be able to join him, and held his ground.

On the 28th the various divisions pressed forward,

and the National troops were in full possession of the Yazoo side of the bayou, with one bridge thrown across and with two bridges partially constructed. During the course of the day, while reconnoitring, General M. L. Smith was severely wounded in the hip, and compelled to retire to his steamboat.

Selecting Positions.

His command devolved on General Stuart; but Sherman, feeling convinced that A. J. Smith could accomplish nothing on the extreme right, because of the heavy fire of the forts immediately in his front, ordered him to leave Burbridge in position at that point, and to come up with a portion of his forces to the point selected for crossing the bayou, and entrusted him with the execution of the task. Such was the state of things on the night of the 28th.

General Morgan was in position on the west, or rather south-west, side of the Chickasaw; General Blair was a little to his right, near the angle of the bayou; General M. L. Smith's division, under General Stuart, was on the right centre; General A. J. Smith's, which was farther to the right, had taken position near the place where the bayou was to be crossed; and General Steele was moving up on the left, to act as a reserve to Morgan.

The Grand Attack.

On the morning of the 29th all things were in readiness for the attack. It was Sherman's object, as he himself has told us, to make a lodgment on the foot-hills and bluffs abreast of his position, while diversions were being made by the navy at Haines' Bluff and by the first division directly toward Vicksburg. We have already mentioned that there were two crossings—one in front of Morgan, and another a little farther to the south-west, in front of M. L. Smith. An attempt was made by A. J. Smith to throw a light flying bridge over the bayou, more to the right. On the extreme left, a little above the angle of the Chickasaw, near the house of Mrs. Lake, Blair's men had succeeded in constructing a bridge, but not without great difficulty and with very considerable loss.

Storm of Fire.

Sherman expected great things from General Morgan, who, as we have seen, commanded the First division and was to lead the attack in person. Sherman pointed out to him the place where he could pass the bayou, and received for answer, "General, in ten minutes after you give the signal I'll be on those hills." His position was one of considerable difficulty. The crossing was narrow, and immediately opposite, at the base of the hills, there was a Confederate battery, supported by infantry posted on the spurs of the hills in the rear. This was the real point of attack, but to distract the attention of the enemy Sherman's instructions were that the initial movements should be made at the flanks.

It was about noon before the signal was given for a general forward movement across the bayou and toward the enemy's position. A heavy artillery fire was opened all along the National line. It recalled the memory of Iuka and Corinth. The Confederate batteries made a prompt reply, and were soon followed by the infantry, which opened a perfect tempest of lead on the advance ranks of Morgan and A. J. Smith.

In the midst of this fierce storm of cannon shot and musketry, DeCourcy's brigade of Morgan's division succeeded in crossing the bayou; but the fire was so terrific that they fled for cover behind the bank, and could not be moved forward. General Blair meanwhile had crossed the Bayou by the bridge above the angle, and had reached the slough, the bottom of which was quicksand and the banks of which were covered with felled trees, these obstacles greatly impeding his advance.

Desperate Assault.

With great difficulty, and not until his ranks were thrown into some disorder, was the crossing of the slough accomplished. This done, it was necessary before reaching the enemy's works to traverse a sloping plateau raked by a direct and enfilading fire from heavy artillery and swept by a storm of bullets from the rifle-pits.

Nothing daunted, Blair and his brave brigade—his own and his officers' horses having been left behind, some of them floundering in the mire and vainly seeking a foothold in the quicksand—went bounding across the plateau. Rushing upon the rifle-pits, they captured the first line, and then the second, and made a desperate effort to gain the crest of the hill on which the batteries were planted.

Colonel Thayer of Steele's division had followed Blair with his brigade over the same bridge. Entering the abattis at the same point, he turned somewhat to the right, and emerged upon the plateau almost simultaneously with Blair and about two hundred yards to his right. Unfortunately, however, Thayer found that he was followed by only one regiment; his second regiment after his movement had commenced having been ordered to the support of Morgan, and the other two regiments having followed this one by mistake. It was a sad blunder, and one which contributed not a little to the disaster of the day.

Thayer discovered the mistake before he had fairly brought his troops into action, but he was too brave a man to halt or hesitate in the circumstances. On he pushed to the right of Blair, and rendered effective aid in the capture of the second line of rifle-pits. The odds were fearfully against him.

An Unequal Struggle.

Leaving his regiment to hold the position it had won, he hurried back, with Blair's consent, to obtain reinforcements. It was a trying interval. The moments seemed hours. "It was a struggle," as has been well said, "between three thousand in the open ground below and ten thousand behind intrenchments above." The hillsides bristled with bayonets and blazed with the fire of musketry, while from the angry mouths of huge cannon destruction was poured forth upon the shattered and rapidly-thinning ranks of the assailants.

Blair, impatient for the return of Thayer, rushed back himself to persuade the advance of more troops. It was all in vain. Both Thayer and himself failed in obtaining reinforcements. No help reached them; no diversion was made in their favor. They had no choice but to order a retreat. Blair and Thayer fell back with a loss of at least one-third of their men, and De Courcy, who had been attacked on the flank by the Seventeenth and Twenty-sixth Louisiana, lost four flags, three hundred and thirty-two men made prisoners, and about five hundred small-arms.

Heroic Bravery.

The attack was a complete failure. Somehow, the signal for attack was imperfectly understood. Either that or it was not heard at all on the right. Two divisions had remained immovable while a handful of men were being crushed in a desperate attempt on the left. A. J. Smith had done nothing. Stuart had managed to push one regiment across—the Sixth Missouri—which had orders to undermine the bluff.

The position of those men was one which severely tried their faith and patience. They were exposed to the vertical fire of the Confederate sharpshooters who occupied the ridge; and a battalion of the Thirteenth regulars, who were stationed opposite, and who attempted to protect them from the Confederate fire, proved equally dangerous with the enemy above. "Shoot higher!" shouted the Nationals below the bluff. "Shoot lower!" cried the Confederates. After dark this regiment was brought back over the bayou. The remainder of Steele's division did not get up in time to be of any assistance to Blair. Morgan failed to make good his promise. He did not even obey his orders.

Disobedience and Disaster.

General Sherman was particularly severe on Morgan. To him and to his conduct he attributed the failure of the attack. "This attack failed," he has since told us in his memoirs, "and I have always felt that it was due to the failure of General G. W. Morgan to obey his orders or to fulfil his promises made in person. He he used with skill and boldness one of his brigades, in addition to that of Blair, he could have made a lodgment on the bluff, which would have opened the door for whole force to follow."

Sherman was naturally mortified at the "lame and impotent conclusion" of a movement which he had fondly and confidently believed would result in a great and decisive victory. Baffled, and even humiliated, he was not dismayed. He resolved to make another attack, and arrangements were made to push forward General Hovey to the position from which Blair had been driven; Morgan's division, with the brigades of Blair and Thayer, to follow and support. For some reason it was not done, and next morning it was found to be impossible, because of the increased strength of the Confederates at the menaced point. Firing was continued on both sides during Tuesday, and on Wednesday, the 31st, a flag of truce was sent in, and the dead were buried and the wounded cared for.

The Sad Burial.

An eye-witness has given us a sad picture of the battle-field on that day of burial: "All across the plain, scattered among the abattis and hid away in little entanglements of bogs or tufts of bushes, they lay, Confederates and Federals side by side, showing how the battle had rolled and surged with the alternate charges of either party.

"But the saddest sight of all was that of the unfortunate wounded, who had lain through all these weary hours since the battle, uncared for, many of them, because the nature of their wounds prevented them from moving; others were held fast by a little knot of corpses which chance had thrown upon them; and still others, perhaps not wounded at all at first, but being caught beneath the horses they rode as they fell, were pinned to the earth. The frantic appeals for water, for food, or other succor of such of these miserable victims of war as could speak at all were most heartrending."

The Great Commander's New Resolve.

Sherman was still dissatisfied, and resolved to make another attack. After consulting with Admiral Porter, it was agreed that a combined naval and land assault should be made on Haines' Bluff, the key of the Confederate position. Porter was to proceed up the Yazoo with his gunboats and open fire on the bluffs, while General Steele was to land his division out of range of the enemy's guns, then to push forward and take the position by storm. The attack was to be made during the dark hours. By two o'clock on the morning of Thursday, the 1st of January, the necessary arrangements were completed. A heavy fog, however, had enveloped the entire district, and so dense was it that Porter found it impossible to steer the boats.

It was utterly out of the question to make any further efforts. On the night of the 29th December there had been a tremendous rainstorm; all the low ground was flooded, and the men, who had been bivouacking for five successive days in those wretched swamps without fire, were suffering cruelly from damp and cold. On the 2d of January, Sherman placed his troops on board the transports, and the fleet sailed down to the mouth of the Yazoo.

Sherman's Disappointment.

Thus ended, somewhat ingloriously, the second campaign against Vicksburg. Sherman had accomplished nothing. He had, however, made great sacrifices, his loss in killed and wounded and prisoners amounting to nearly two thousand men. Such was the battle of Chickasaw Bayou, or, as it is sometimes but less correctly named, the battle of Haines' Bluff.

It was a sad disappointment to the people of the North, and Sherman, from whom great things were expected, came in for a large share of abuse. Several of the correspondents on the spot, ignorant of some of the causes of the failure, and not knowing as yet the fate which had befallen Grant, were unnecessarily severe in their condemnation of Sherman. That he meant well, that he was resolved to win, and that his plan was well conceived, there can be no doubt. But somehow the execution was not equal to the conception.

A Fatal Mistake.

There was some mistake in giving the signal, and the real assault was made by only three thousand men. If Blair had been sustained in his attack, as he ought to have been sustained, the National army would most undoubtedly have effected a lodgment on the heights; and, although hard fighting must have followed, with doubtful success, it is not at all impossible that Sherman might have reaped all the glory due to the capture of Vicksburg. He proved his generalship in the face of impossibilities.

Blair will be remembered as the hero of Chickasaw Bayou. He fought like a warrior of old, face to face and hand to hand with the foe. After Blair praise is due to Thayer, who gallantly sustained his companion in arms. The battle-ground no doubt had much to do with the defeat.

To any one of less daring than Sherman, familiar with the district and well informed as to the strength of the enemy's position, the undertaking might have seemed impracticable from the outset; and it is questionable whether even he, had he possessed a fuller knowledge of the difficulties which beset him, would have imperilled his fame and risked the lives of his soldiers in a task so apparently hopeless

Success Impossible.

It was doubtless a mistake not to have more thoroughly and officially reconnoitred the ground before choosing it as a field of action. After all, however, it was an experiment which might have been successful, and it was not the only unsuccessful experiment which had been made before Vicksburg was captured. As it was, everything might have been well if Grant had been able to carry out his part of the plan. The retreat of the latter from Oxford, leaving, as it did, Pemberton free to concentrate his troops for the defence of Vicksburg, largely diminished Sherman's chances of success.

The Confederates were jubilant after this first victory. It was undoubtedly a great triumph. General Pemberton, not without reason, felt proud that he had baffled Grant in person, compelling him to retreat, and that he had temporarily at least, saved Vicksburg by the defeat of the greatest of Grant's lieutenants. These rejoicings in the South were not unmixed with sorrow. The more thoughtful of the Confederates knew that defeat only intensified the purpose of the North.

We left the transports and the fleet on their way down the Yazoo. At the mouth of that river General McClernand was waiting with orders from the War Department to take command of the entire expedition. That general, it will be remembered, was appointed to this command by the direct influence of President Lincoln. It was a severe blow to Sherman, who felt it keenly. It was some consolation, however, to him to know that the appointment—which had been made weeks ahead, and which had no connection with the recent disaster—was not intended as a disgrace.

With a modesty which became a man of his high spirit he accepted the situation, and explained to McClernand what had been done, accepting the entire responsibility of the failure. Referring to the trains of cars which could be heard coming in to Vicksburg almost every hour, and the fresh troops seen on the bluffs, he gave it as his opinion that Pemberton's army must have been pressed back and that Grant must be at hand.

He then learned, for the first time, what had befallen Grant; McClernand stating that Grant was not coming at all, that the dépôt at Holly Springs had been captured by Van Dorn, that Grant had fallen back from Coffeeville and Oxford to Holly Springs and La Grange, and that when he passed down Quimby's division of Grant's army was actually at Memphis for stores. By common consent, all further attempts against Vicksburg, for the present, were abandoned, and the entire force left the Yazoo and returned to Milliken's Bend on the Mississippi.

On the 4th of January, McClernand issued his General Order No. 1, assuming command of what was to be called the Army of the Missisippi, and, following the plan which had been agreed upon at

Washington, and which had been adopted in the armies of the East, dividing his forces into two corps. The first was to be commanded by General Morgan, and was to be composed of his own and A. J. Smith's divisions, and the second, to consist of Steele's and Stuart's divisions, was to be commanded by General Sherman. The rest of the Army of the Tennessee was similarly divided, General Hurlbut being placed in command of one corps, and General McPherson in command of the other. The supreme command of these four corps was retained by General Grant. On the same day General Sherman issued the following order:

> HEADQUARTERS RIGHT WING ARMY OF TENNESSEE,
> STEAMER FOREST QUEEN, MILLIKEN'S BEND,
> January 4, 1863.

Pursuant to the terms of General Order No. 1, made this day by General McClernand, the title of our army ceases to exist, and constitutes in the future the Army of the Mississippi, composed of two 'army corps,' one to be commanded by General G. W. Morgan, and the other by myself. In relinquishing the command of the Army of the Tennessee and restricting my authority to my own corps, I desire to express to all commanders, to soldiers and officers recently operating before Vicksburg, my hearty thanks for the zeal, alacrity and courage manifested by them on all occasions. We failed in accomplishing one great purpose of our movement, the capture of Vicksburg, but we were part of a whole. Ours was but part of a combined movement in which others were to assist. We were on time; unforeseen contingencies must have delayed the others.

We have destroyed the Shreveport road, we have attacked the defences of Vicksburg and pushed the attack as far as prudence would justify; and, having found it too strong for our single column, we have drawn off in good order and good spirits, ready for any new move. A new commander is now here to lead you. He is chosen by the President of the United States, who is charged by the Constitution to maintain and defend it, and he has the undoubted right to select his own agents.

I know that all good officers and soldiers will give him the same hearty support and cheerful obedience they have hitherto given me. There are honors enough in reserve for all, and work enough, too. Let each do his appropriate part, and our nation must, in the end, emerge from the dire conflict purified and ennobled by the fires which now test its strength and purity. All officers of the general staff not attached to my person will hereafter report in person and by letter to Major-General McClernand, commanding the Army of the Mississippi, on board the steamer Tigress at our rendezvous at Haines' Landing and at Montgomery Point.

By order of
    MAJOR-GENERAL W. T. SHERMAN.
J. H. HAMMOND,
 Assistant Adjutant-General.

Before the arrival of McClernand, Sherman and Porter had agreed upon a plan for the reduction of Fort Hindman, or, as it was called, Arkansas Post. About forty or forty-five miles from the mouth of the Arkansas there is a piece of elevated ground, the first high land on the banks of the river after leaving the Mississippi. At this point the river makes a sharp bend. Here the French had a trading-post and a settlement as far back as 1685.

Sherman Bent on Conquest.

The Confederates had taken advantage of the place to erect some fortifications, the principal work being named Fort Hindman, after the famous guerilla chief. Behind these works they kept several steamboats, which were wont to sweep down the river and intercept supplies.

Sherman had experienced some inconvenience from the existence of this stronghold. He had left Memphis in such haste that he had not been able to take with him a sufficient supply of ammunition for his guns. The Blue Wing, a small steamer carrying a mail, towing some coal-barges, and having with her the necessary supplies, had been sent after him. This boat had been pounced upon at the mouth of the Arkansas, captured, and with all her supplies taken up to Fort Hindman.

It was Sherman's conviction, from the moment he learned of the fate of the Blue Wing, that before any operation could be successfully conducted against Vicksburg by way of the Mississippi it would be necessary to reduce Fort Hindman and make an end of the Arkansas pirates.

The Plan Approved.

Sherman communicated his purpose to McClernand, and asked permission to go up the Arkansas and clear out the post. McClernand, who had not as yet, so far as appearances indicated, formed any plan of his own, went with Sherman on board the Black Hawk to consult with Porter. Porter, who had the highest esteem for Sherman, not only approved of the enterprise, but expressed a desire to go up the river himself, in place of trusting the expedition to any of his subordinates. It was Sherman's expectation that he would be sent with his own corps alone on this business; but McClerand concluded to go himself and to take with him his whole force.

The troops, which had not yet disembarked from the transports, were ordered to remain on board. Sherman's corps was in two divisions. The first, which consisted of three brigades, commanded respectively by Blair, Hovey, and Thayer, was under Brigadier-General Frederick Steele. The second, which consisted of two brigades, commanded by Colonels G. A. Smith and T. Kilby Smith, was under Brigadier-General Stuart. The transports with the troops on board, convoyed by the gunboats, of which three were ironclads, proceeded up the Mississippi.

Expedition against Fort Hindman.

The force under McClernand amounted to some twenty-six thousand or twenty-seven thousand men.

comprising forty regiments of infantry, ten batteries with several guns of heavy calibre, and about fifteen hundred horse. On the 8th of January the expedition was at the mouth of the White River. This river, which is one of the principal streams in Arkansas, rises a few miles east of Fayetteville, flows north-east into Missouri, then returns into Arkansas, and, pursuing a south-easterly course, enters the Mississippi about fifteen miles above the mouth of the Arkansas River. It is navigable by steamboats for about three hundred and fifty miles.

About fifteen miles from its mouth there is a channel or "cut-off," through which it discharges a portion of its waters into the Arkansas. If, as sometimes happens, the Arkansas should be higher than the White River, the state of things is reversed, and the waters of the Arkansas seek the Mississippi through the channel of the White River. The "cut-off" at this season of the year is always well filled and easily navigable.

A Formidable Stronghold.

On the morning of the 9th the expedition, having ascended the White River, had reached the mouth of the "cut-off." There was no delay in making the passage through to the Arkansas, a distance of about eight miles. Steaming up the Arkansas, the boats reached Notrib's farm, about four miles below Fort Hindman, shortly after four o'clock in the afternoon. Here they halted, and during the night the artillery and wagons were got on shore, the troops disembarking in the morning. Arkansas Post is on the north side or left bank of the Arkansas, at a point where the river makes a sharp elbow by flowing north, then east, then again abruptly to the south. The principal work, as we have said, was Fort Hindman. Its guns commanded the river as it stretched to the east and after it bent toward the south. This fort was a regular square bastioned work, one hundred yards each exterior side, with a deep ditch about fifteen feet wide and a parapet eighteen feet high. It was armed with twelve guns, two of which were eight-inch and one nine-inch.

Hold the Fort or Die.

The garrison, which numbered only five thousand men, was under the command of General T. J. Churchill, who was under the direction of General T. H. Holmes, then commanding at Little Rock. Churchill had received instructions to "hold on until help should arrive or all were dead." This order showed the spirit of the enemy.

The disparity of forces was great. It was twenty-six thousand or twenty-seven thousand against five thousand. The strong position held by the Confederates, however, did much to compensate for inferiority of numbers. The fort itself was strong, and its approaches were of the most difficult description. Fronting on the river, it was protected on the west by a bayou, on the east by a swamp which did not quite reach the edge of the water. Between the fort and the swamp there was a ravine which stretched down to the river, and the front of this ravine was well fortified.

The position had thus been approached through the elevated ground which lay between the bayou and the swamp. The encampments of the Confederates were established in front of the fort, in the centre of the plateau dotted with clumps of trees. There was an outer line of intrenchments which stretched across the entire ground.

Vigorous Bombardment.

On the 10th the army was kept busy endeavoring to get a position in rear of the fort, Sherman on the right and Morgan on the left. Some mistakes were made in consequence of a want of knowledge of the ground. In the afternoon, and while the land forces were still seeking position, Porter was making good use of his flotilla. As he moved up the river he shelled the rifle-pits along the levee and drove the Confederates inside the fort. When about four hundred yards from Fort Hindman he brought into action his three iron-clads, the Baron de Kalb, the Louisville, and the Cincinnati, and for half an hour the firing was kept up, the guns of the fort replying vigorously and with rapidity.

On the morning of the 11th, McClernand, who had his quarters still on board the Tigress, had come up and taken a position in the woods to the rear. Early in the forenoon he sent a message to Sherman, asking him why the attack was not begun. It had been understood beforehand that the opening of fire by the gunboats on the fort should be a signal for a general attack.

The Thunder of Guns.

Sherman therefore replied that all was ready; that he was within five or six hundred yards of the enemy's works; that the next movement must be a direct assault along the whole line; and that he was waiting to hear from the gunboats. Half an hour or thereabout afterward was heard the clear, ringing sound of the navy guns, the firing becoming louder and more rapid as they neared the fort.

The National field-pieces opened fire along the whole line. The thunder was terrific. The Confederates, most of whom were Texan volunteers, made a gallant resistance. A regiment of cavalry, abandoning their horses, fought on foot, and rendered for a time effective service in resisting the advance of the Nationals. It was impossible for them to resist the fierce onset made by overwhelming numbers resolved to win or die.

A Storm of Bullets.

Sherman pressed forward on the right, Morgan on the left, each driving the Confederates back and gradually obtaining possession of the wooded ground in front of the newly-erected parapet, but not without considerable loss. The Confederate firing was heavy, but the National soldiers took advantage of the clumps of trees and felled logs to shield themselves from the storm of bullets. Gradually the edge of the woods was reached, the ground was clear, and there was

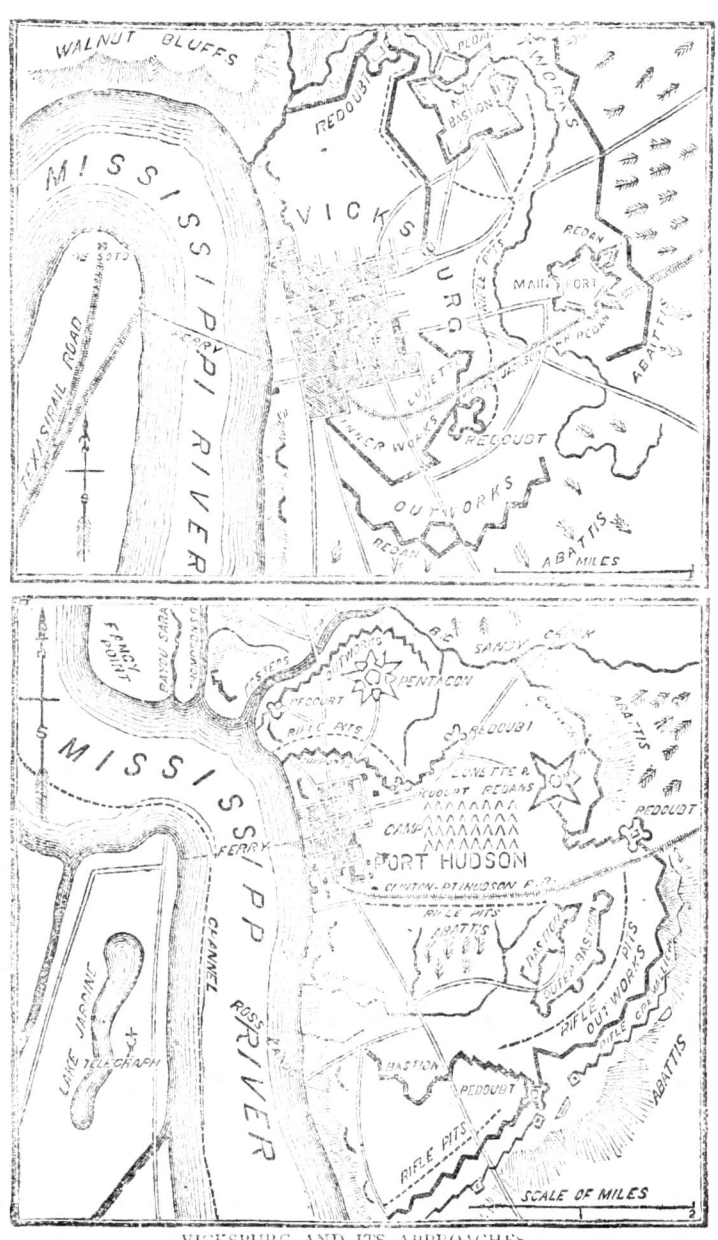

VICKSBURG AND ITS APPROACHES.

nothing to protect them from the decimating fire of the enemy.

Meanwhile, the gunboats were pouring a murderous fire upon the fort and sweeping the adjoining ground above and below with grape and shrapnel. Porter had brought into action not only the iron-clads, but the ram Monarch, Commander Ellet, and even the frailer vessels, as he tells us, that amid the clouds of smoke they might "do the best they could."

The Fort Silenced.

It was not long until the effects of this terrific firing began to be visible. All the adjoining ground was cleared of the foe; nearly all the artillery-horses in the fort were killed; and one by one the guns were being silenced. Shortly after three o'clock the firing from the fort altogether ceased. The cannonading, however, was kept up by the gunboats. Porter, who had taken a regiment on board, was proceeding with the Black Hawk to attempt a landing and to take possession, when a white flag was raised in token of surrender. He immediately ordered the firing to cease.

We left the troops in the clearing at the edge of the woods, fully exposed to the enemy's fire from the parapet outside the fort. This line had three sections of field-guns, and they were handled, according to the testimony of Sherman himself, with great skill and energy. Hovey was wounded; Thayer had his horse shot under him; and so thick and fast were the round-shot falling about Sherman and his staff that they felt it necessary to scatter, Sherman himself dismounting. Morgan at this crisis unfortunately found himself in front of the ravine, beyond which it was impossible to pass.

Prodigies of Valor.

Sherman was now well engaged on the right, and Morgan, finding himself thus hindered, sent a few regiments to his aid. The burden of the fight, as at Chickasaw, had fallen on the brigades which now composed the division of General Steele. Blair and Thayer and Hovey performed prodigies of valor.

On the right the Confederate batteries had been all but silenced. Morgan's men, on the left, had done splendid work before they were brought to a standstill at the ravine. A. J. Smith's brigades had pressed the Confederates back step by step until they were within two hundred yards of the fort. Burbridge expressly distinguished himself. But for the ravine an attempt would have been made by the One-hundred-and-Twentieth Ohio to scale and carry by assault the eastern side of the fort.

Almost at this moment, however, Sherman, as his attention was arrested by the flags of the gunboats visible above the parapet of Fort Hindman, saw a man jump on the nearer parapet at the point where entered the road which divided the peninsula. "Cease firing!" he ordered, and the words were passed along the line with amazing rapidity. The firing soon ceased. Sherman knew that something extraordinary was going on, and so gave this order.

The White Flag.

In a few seconds the fort was invaded on every side by the National troops. Colonel Dayton was ordered forward to the place where was hung out the large white flag, and as soon as his horse was seen on the parapet Sherman advanced with his staff. It appeared afterward that the white flag was hung out without even the knowledge of Churchill. It made little difference. The battle had really been won on the land as well as on the river side of the fort. The surrender was subsequently made in due form—Colonel Dunnington, the commander of the fort, surrendering to Admiral Porter, and Colonel Churchill surrendering to the military authorities.

The National loss in killed, wounded, and missing amounted to nine hundred and seventy-seven men. On the Confederate side there were only sixty killed and eighty wounded. Five thousand soldiers, with their officers, made prisoners, and all the property of the place, including some seventeen guns, constituted the prize of victory. General Burbridge was singled out for the honor of planting the National standard on Fort Hindman. Such was the battle of Arkansas Post.

Sherman Robbed of his Honors.

General Sherman was dissatisfied with the arrangements made by General McClernand immediately after the surrender. The post of honor, the occupation of Fort Hindman, was given to A. J. Smith of Morgan's division, Sherman being ordered to hold the lines outside and go on securing the prisoners and stores. McClernand's reason for so doing was that he did not wish to interfere with the actual state of facts—the *status quo* at the time of surrender.

It is undeniable that it was Sherman's plan throughout; that his corps bore the burden of the fight; that after the surrender his troops were in possession of two of the three brigades which constituted the opposing force; and that he was in possession of all the ground outside the "fort proper." McClernand was proud of his success and manifested not a little vanity. His star, he said, was ever in the ascendant.

In his memoirs Sherman tells us that McClernand was extremely jealous of the navy, and that in his report he ignored altogether the action of Porter's fleet. This was the less to be regretted that Porter told his own story in a very handsome and effective way. It is only simple truth to say that the battle was fought and won by the fleet before the land troops had any certainty of success.

Petty Rivalry.

There was, in fact, a feeling of jealousy among the commanders—a feeling which was not wholly to disappear until the arrival of Grant, in whose presence, and under the influence of whose more commanding genius, jealousy and selfishness gave place to a spirit of honorable rivalry and dutiful obedience.

The day after the battle was devoted to burying the dead. The prisoners were all collected and sent to St. Louis. The victory at Arkansas Post opened the way for a successful expedition to Little Rock, the capital of the State of Arkansas. Sherman expressed a desire to be sent on this expedition. McClernand, however, did not deem it advisable. A combined expedition was therefore sent up the White River as far as St. Charles, Des Arc, and Duval's Bluff under General Gorman and Lieutenant-commanding J. G. Walker. The expedition was completely successful.

Meanwhile, the works at Fort Hindman were dismantled and blown up, and on the 13th the troops were re-embarked and proceeded down the Arkansas to Napoleon. There instructions were received from General Grant, who ordered McClernand to take the entire expedition down the river to Milliken's Bend and await his arrival. This place was reached on the 21st of January.

The Second Assault.

In itself, the movement against Arkansas Post was a small affair; it was so regarded by General Grant; it ought to have been successfully accomplished by one corps and by a portion of the fleet—instead of the combined strength of both—and that was Sherman's idea; but resulting as it did in victory, it served the double purpose of employing troops which would otherwise have been idle, and of cheering the hearts of a people who were somewhat despondent.

In the Vicksburg campaign which succeeded, Sherman bore a prominent part with his command—in the expedition up Steele's Bayou to the Yazoo in March;

the feint upon Haines' Bluff, April 29 to May 1 ; the movement to Grand Gulf, May 1 to 6; the capture of Jackson, May 14; the occupation of Walnut Hills, and subsequent assaults upon the land-defences of Vicksburg, May 19 and 22, in each attempt the colors of the corps being planted on the enemy's works; and in the siege operations which resulted in the surrender of the city July 4, 1863, when Sherman with a detached command was at once ordered to pursue Johnston, who with a relieving force had been lying east of the Big Black, but retreating hastily on the news of the surrender. By the 10th he was driven behind the intrenchments of Jackson. Siege operations were actively pressed, but on the night of the 16th Johnston succeeded in escaping, thus proving himself to be the "hero of retreats." Steele's division pursued to Brandon, and after destroying the railroads in all directions Sherman fell back to the west of the Big Black, along which he lay when summoned, September 22, to the relief of Rosecrans's beleaguered army at Chattanooga. Meanwhile he had been appointed brigadier-general in the regular army, to date from July 4. By the 27th of September the last of his command were embarked at Vicksburg, and by October 4, Memphis was reached, whence he marched eastward, repairing the railroad as he proceeded, until the 27th, when orders reached him at Tuscumbia from General Grant, who had superseded Rosecrans, to abandon all work and hasten on to Chattanooga.

CHAPTER XVII.

Sherman's Superb Valor at Chattanooga.

AFTER Vicksburg came the battle of Chickamauga. It was a Confederate victory, but it was barren of results. The losses on both sides were heavy. The Nationals lost sixteen thousand three hundred and fifty men and fifty-one guns. The Confederates lost about eighteen thousand. Chickamauga was a battle almost without a plan. It resulted to the credit of neither of the generals-in-chief. It made an end of General Rosecrans, and nearly ruined Bragg. It had but one hero, and that was General Thomas. "The Rock of Chickamauga" will live for ever in American history.

After the battle of Chickamauga, Rosecrans proceeded to throw up fortifications around Chattanooga. In this work he found an able and efficient assistant in General James St. Clair Morton. Within twenty-four hours after falling back from Rossville he was strongly intrenched—so strongly that Bragg could not, with safety, venture upon an offensive movement. Bragg, in truth, was in great trouble. He felt bitter disappointment because the late battle had not resulted in more complete success. He was dissatisfied with the conduct of several of his officers. He had not lost the confidence of Jefferson Davis, but with the authorities at Richmond generally he was in bad odor. He was expected by them to perform impossibilities.

The suggestions offered him were as numerous as they were absurd. Bragg, however, had will enough to abide by his own counsel, and sense enough to attempt the one thing which was practicable. If he could not force his way into Chattanooga, he might at least starve the Army of the Cumberland into submission or retreat.

Tactics of Bragg.

With this end in view the Confederate general drew a cordon around the city and interrupted or cut off the various lines of communication. He made himself master of the south bank of the Tennessee, opposite Moccasin Point, and then broke the line of communication between Chattanooga and Bridgeport. He destroyed the bridge at the latter place, and thus severed the communication with Nashville, the base of supplies.

The Army of the Cumberland became a cause of great anxiety to the authorities at Washington. It was felt that if something were not done to relieve it, and that quickly, the army ran the risk of being utterly destroyed, and Chattanooga and East Tennessee would again be brought under Confederate rule. In these circumstances the Government fell back on the conqueror of Vicksburg. Grant was ordered to Chattanooga to take sole command. He was then at New Orleans, confined by an injury sustained in falling from his horse. As soon as he was able he hastened to Indianapolis, where he met Stanton, the Secretary of War, and received from his hands the order appointing him to the command of the new military Division of the Mississippi, compris-

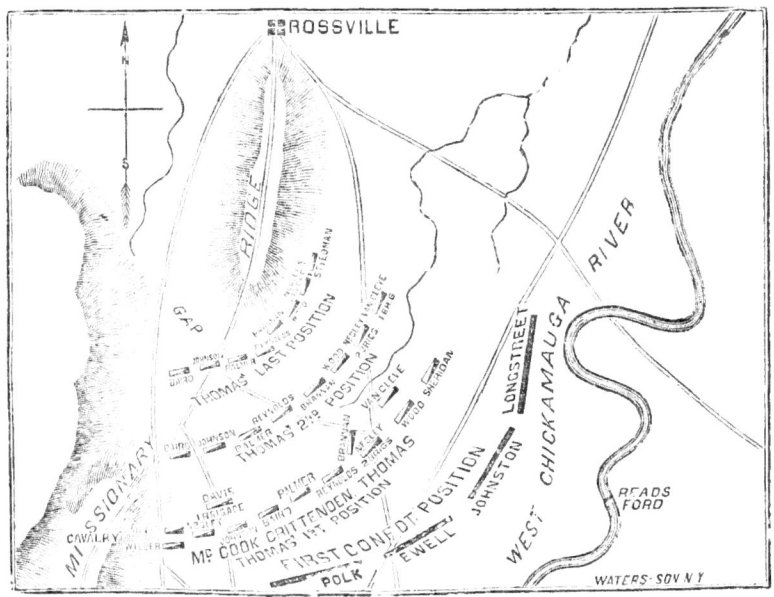

POSITIONS OF THE ARMIES AT THE BATTLE OF CHICKAMAUGA.

ing the three departments and armies of the Ohio, the Cumberland, and the Tennessee. By the same order General Rosecrans was relieved of the command of the Department and Army of the Tennessee.

At the request of General Grant, the Department of the Cumberland was given to Thomas, and that of the

VALOR AT CHATTANOOGA.

Tennessee to Sherman. On the 18th of October, 1863, Grant, having arrived at Louisville, formally assumed the command and issued his first order. Rosecrans on the 19th, after issuing a touching farewell address to the troops, left for Cincinnati. Thither also were ordered Generals McCook and Crittenden, whose corps were now consolidated into one. From Louisville, Grant telegraphed to Thomas, "Hold Chattanooga at all hazards."—" I will hold the town until we starve," was the prompt and characteristic reply.

MAJOR-GEN. W. ROSECRANS.

It was not enough, however, to bring Grant to Chattanooga. It was necessary that he should have under him a competent army. Arrangements had alread. been made for increasing the strength of the National army at Chattanooga. As soon as it became known that General Longstreet had gone to Tennessee, instructions were sent to Grant and other commanders in the South and West to send Rosecrans all possible assistance. Grant was yet at New Orleans, and as Sherman, who represented him at Vicksburg, did not receive the despatch until several days had elapsed, there was some unavoidable delay in sending reinforcements from the neighborhood of Vicksburg.

As early as the 27th of September, Sherman, with the Fifteenth corps, in obedience to the orders from Grant, had set out for Memphis on his way to Chattanooga. Meanwhile, fearful of the consequences which must result if Rosecrans should be tempted to

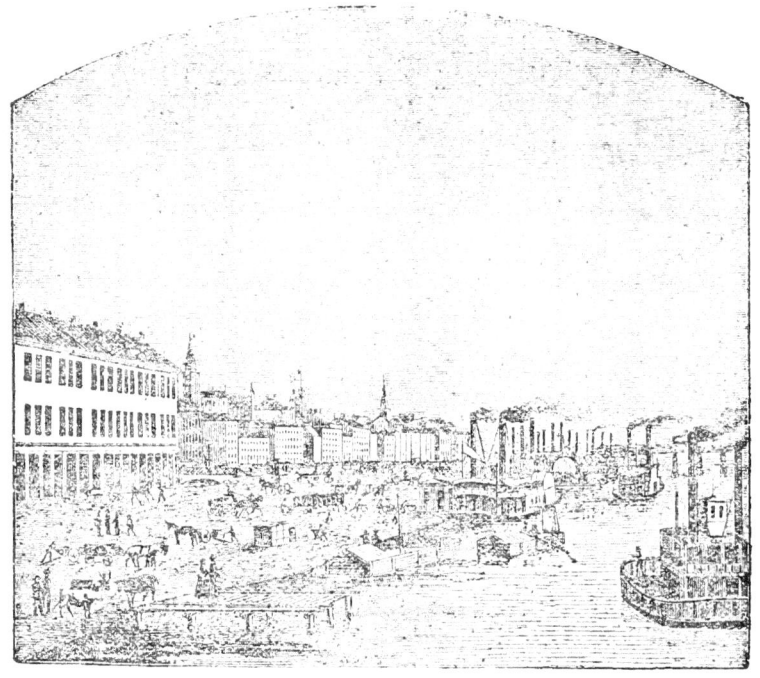

LANDING AT LOUISVILLE, KENTUCKY.

abandon his position and attempt to retreat, the Government had detached the Eleventh and Twelfth corps from the Army of the Potomac, and, placing them in charge of General Hooker, hurried them along by rail to Chattanooga.

VALOR AT CHATTANOOGA.

Never before, not even at Solferino and Magenta, had railroads been more effectively used for transporting troops and all the necessary material of war than on this occasion. It was Stanton's project, and in giving it effect he bent upon it all the energies of his powerful mind and will. In seven days the two corps, some twenty-three thousand strong, with artillery-trains, baggage, and animals, were transferred from the Rapidan to Stevenson, Alabama, a distance of 1192 miles.

The Situation Critical.

Grant reached Nashville on the 21st of October. He there met and had an interview with Rosecrans and Hooker. On the 23d he arrived at Chattanooga. Next morning he made a reconnoissance of the ground and determined on his plan of action. He found that Rosecrans had allowed the enemy to occupy all the heights around his position, and that neither the river nor the railroad could be used. Unless the river or the roads could be opened there was no choice but retreat; and retreat, in the present condition of the army, would be certain ruin.

MAJ.-GEN. JOS. HOOKER.

Thomas and his chief engineer, General William F. Smith, had decided upon a plan by which they hoped to be able to regain possession of Lookout Valley and to re-establish communications with Bridgeport by way of Brown's Ferry. Hooker, by order of Thomas, had already concentrated at the latter place. This plan met the hearty approval of General Grant, who proceeded immediately to put it in execution. Hooker was to cross the Tennessee at Bridgeport

THE PONTOON-BRIDGE.

and push on by the main wagon-road to Wauhatchie in Lookout Valley.

Palmer, who was now opposite Chattanooga, was to move down the north side of the river to a point opposite Whiteside, where he was to cross the river and hold the road passed over by Hooker. W. F. Smith was to go down the river from Chattanooga, under cover of the darkness, with about four thousand troops, to cross at Brown's Ferry and to seize the range of hills at the mouth of Lookout Valley. A pontoon-bridge was to be thrown over the river at Brown's Ferry, so as to open communications between Hooker and Thomas. The movements of Hooker and Palmer might be made in open day, but Smith's success depended largely on secrecy. These movements were promptly and successfully executed and were of great importance.

The Question of Supplies Settled.

The Confederates, unwilling to abandon the position, made a fierce attack; but, finding their efforts useless, they withdrew up the valley toward Chattanooga. The remainder of Smith's force, some twelve hundred strong, under General Turchin, having moved meanwhile down the north bank of the stream, across Moccasin Point, reached Brown's Ferry before daylight. They were rapidly ferried across, and by ten o'clock a pontoon-bridge connected the north and south banks of the Tennessee. On the morning of the 28th, as has been stated, Hooker, with the Eleventh corps, Major-General Howard, and Geary's division of the Twelfth corps, appeared in Lookout Valley at Wauhatchie, his left connecting with Smith at the pontoon-bridge.

These movements secured for the Nationals the possession of the roads and the river, and all fears of starvation in Chattanooga were now abandoned. "General Thomas's plan," said Grant in his telegram to Halleck, "for securing the river and southside road to Bridgeport has proved eminently successful. The question of supplies may now be regarded as settled."

Bragg's Stubborn Resistance.

Bragg was not willing that his antagonist should retain the great advantage he had won without making another attempt to dislodge him. Lookout Valley, which lies between Raccoon and Lookout mountains, and which has an average width of about two miles, is divided toward its centre by a series of wood-crowned heights, some of them rising to an elevation of two hundred and three hundred feet.

These heights, as well as the more commanding positions on Raccoon and Lookout mountains, were in the hands of the Confederates. From these eminences the position and movements of the National army could be easily seen. McLaws, of Longstreet's corps, was on Lookout Mountain, eagerly watching Hooker. It was his determination to fall upon and crush that branch of the National army as soon as he should see a favorable opportunity.

MAJ.-GEN. O. O. HOWARD.

On the night of the 28th, Geary's division, on Hooker's right, was lying at Wauhatchie, Howard's corps, as has been mentioned, having been thrown out in the direction of Brown's Ferry. McLaws, desirous to take Geary by surprise, descended at midnight, and with fierce energy, his men uttering wild screams as they advanced, fell upon Geary's pickets, driving them in.

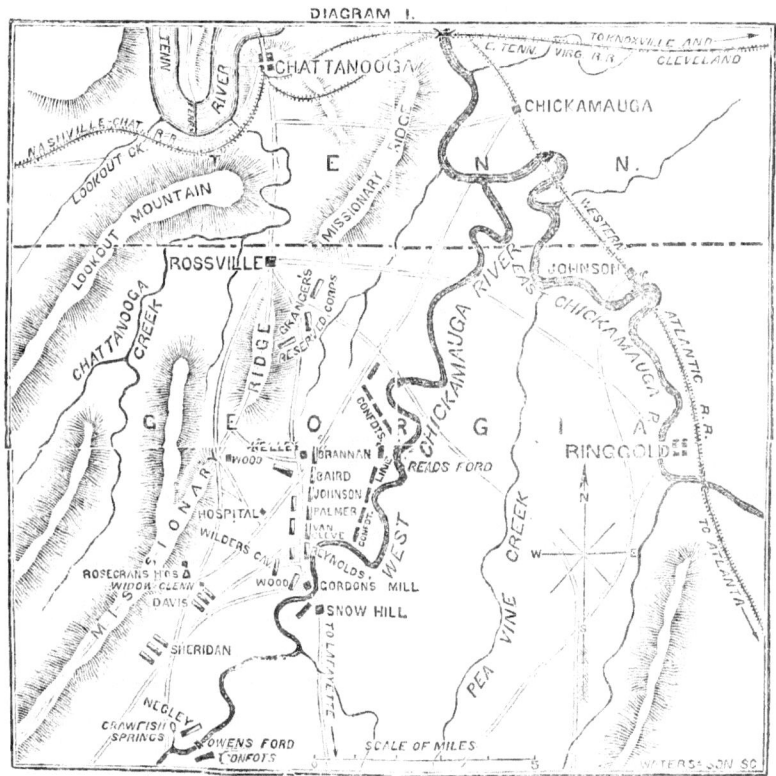

CHATTANOOGA, LOOKOUT MOUNTAIN, AND MISSIONARY RIDGE.

The batteries on Lookout Mountain now opened fire, and while Geary's camp was furiously attacked on three different sides by the on-rushing Confederates, his men were exposed to a very tempest of shot and shell. Geary, however, was not unprepared.

Knowing that he was liable to be attacked at any moment, he had been holding himself in a state of readiness. When, therefore, McLaws' men came up they were warmly received.

Full in the faces of the too-confident Confederates Geary's brave fellows poured a deadly fire of musketry. Such a reception had not been expected. The advancing columns recoiled. Geary, however, was greatly outnumbered, and the battle continued. Hooker was aroused by the booming of cannon and the shrill rattling of musketry. He knew, from the direction whence these sounds issued, that Geary had been attacked. Howard was ordered to double-quick his nearest division, that of Schurz, to the aid of Geary.

"Forward, Boys!"

"Forward to their relief, boys!" shouted Hooker as Schurz's men streamed past him through the darkness. They had advanced but a short distance when, suddenly, there came a blaze of musketry from the hills, showing that the Confederates were close at hand, as well as in force in the neighborhood of Geary's position. Tyndale's brigade was detached and ordered to charge the heights, while Schurz, with the remainder of his troops, moved on toward Geary. A thin brigade of Steinwehr's division, commanded by Colonel Orian Smith of the Seventy-third Ohio, now came up, and it was found that the hill to the rear of Schurz was occupied by the enemy.

This hill Smith was ordered to carry with the bayonet. The moon was shining bright and clear, but the hill was precipitous, seamed with ravines, covered with thick brushwood, and rose to the height of two hundred feet. It was a daring—it seemed almost a foolhardy—experiment; but the order had been given and it must be obeyed. On and up the slope rushed the brave fellows of the Seventy-third Ohio and of the Thirty-third Massachusetts, until they had almost reached the rifle-pits, when they were received by a volley from some two thousand muskets and driven back in confusion to the foot of the hill.

A Grand Charge.

There, however, they re-formed, and, although now fully aware of the nature of the ground and of the difficulties to be encountered, those noble regiments again breasted the hill, and in spite of the destructive volleys which tore through their ranks, and the shouting and yelling and taunting sneers of the men on the summit, they pressed on, without firing a shot, toward the blazing rifle-pits, and then, with one bound, bayonets in hand, swept the enemy before them.

It was not until the enemy was in full retreat and until shouts of victory were rending the midnight air that the first volley was fired. It was a sort of parting salute, given in a species of wild glee by the Nationals, but not particularly agreeable to the retreating foe, and not likely soon to be forgotten by any of the Confederates who survived that moonlight struggle. Geary meanwhile, although contending with vastly superior numbers and sometimes nearly overborne, held his ground with characteristic tenacity, and at length, after three hours' fighting, he hurled his assailants back toward Lookout Mountain.

Historic Deeds.

The charge made by Orlan Smith has been singled out as one of the most brilliant charges of the war. It delighted and astonished Hooker. "No troops," he said, "ever rendered more brilliant service." It won special commendation from so reserved a man as Thomas. "The bayonet charge of Howard's troops," said he in his letter of congratulation to Hooker, "made up the side of a steep and difficult hill over two hundred feet high, completely routing and driving the enemy from his barricades on its top, and the repulse by Geary's division of greatly superior numbers who attempted to surprise him, will rank among the most distinguished feats of arms in this war."

Sherman Pushing Foward.

While these events were taking place at Chattanooga, Sherman was pressing forward from Memphis. He had left Vicksburg for Memphis, on his way to Chattanooga, on the 27th of September. His own corps followed him up the river in steamboats. He had been preceded by the divisions of Osterhaus and John E. Smith. Arriving at Memphis on the 2d of October, he received a letter from Halleck instructing him to move by the line of the Memphis and Charleston railroad to Athens, and to report thence to Rosecrans at Chattanooga.

He was to repair the railroads as he advanced and

VALOR AT CHATTANOOGA.

to depend on his own line for supplies. On his way to Corinth, on Sunday, the 11th, having with him as an escort a battalion of the Thirteenth regulars, he arrived at Colliersville about noon, just in time to save the Sixty-sixth Indiana, Colonel D. C. Anthony, from being overwhelmed and probably destroyed by a body of Confederate cavalry, some three thousand strong with eight guns, under the command of General Chalmers.

Rapid Advances.

He reached Corinth that Sunday evening. Without delay he pushed on to Iuka. At Tuscumbia, on the 27th, his advance, under General Frank Blair, came into contact with a Confederate force some five thousand strong, under General S. D. Lee. The Confederate cavalry were severely punished, and Lee gave no further annoyance to the troops on their march. The National troops had been repairing the roads as they moved along, in obedience to instructions received from Halleck. On the same day on which Blair chastised Lee, Sherman received a despatch from Grant urging him to discontinue his work on the railroad and hasten forward with all possible despatch, with his entire force, to Bridgeport.

ADMIRAL PORTER.

Happily, he had made arrangements with Admiral

Porter to have boats waiting for him at Eastport. By means of these he passed his troops across the Tennessee and hurried eastward, Blair covering his rear, and reached Bridgeport on the 14th. On the day following he joined Grant at Chattanooga, and the two together reconnoitred the ground, Grant explaining his proposed plan of attack so soon as the Army of the Tennessee was forward and ready for action.

"Old Tecumseh" there.

Sherman arrived at Chattanooga at a most opportune moment. It seemed as if the fates were working in the interest of General Grant and the army under his command. The plans of the general commanding had worked to perfection; they had been admirably carried out, and they had been attended, so far, with complete success.

And now, when Sherman, his trusted right arm, came up with his well-trained veterans, Bragg had invited attack by committing a huge and irreparable blunder. It was known to the Confederate commander that Burnside at an earlier date had general instructions to push forward from Knoxville and form a connection with Rosecrans. Believing that if such a connection were now formed it would be fatal to his prospects, and in the vain hope of cutting

MAJ.-GEN. A. E. BURNSIDE.

his rival off and beating him in detail, he detached Longstreet from the army in front of Chattanooga and ordered him to attack Burnside and take possession of Knoxville. A more fatal blunder he could not have committed. He could not, had such been his object, have played more completely into the hands of his antagonist. Grant saw his opportunity, but he resolved to wait until the arrival of Sherman, so as to be able to turn it to full and satisfactory account. He was now ready.

Burnside Hemmed in.

Grant was not insensible to the perilous position in which Burnside was now placed, nor was he indifferent to his calls for help. But he knew that Burnside would be relieved most effectually by the plan which he himself proposed to carry out—that the threatened catastrophe at Knoxville would be best averted by a decisive victory at Chattanooga.

The great battle of Chattanooga—by far the most picturesque battle in the war—was now about to be fought. Grant's plans, as we have seen, were matured and ready for execution. It was now the middle of November. Sherman's corps had arrived at Bridgeport on the 14th. Grant made up his mind to make the general attack on the 21st. He had discovered that the north end of the Missionary Ridge was imperfectly guarded, as also the western bank of the river from the mouth of the South Chickamauga down toward Chattanooga. This point invited attack. This, however, was not all. A successful blow given in that direction would make a junction impossible between Bragg and Longstreet. The northern end of Missionary Ridge therefore he singled out as the special point of attack. While the attack should seem to be general and bearing heavily on the Confederate left, he proposed to mass his converging forces on the point thus indicated.

Sherman's Difficulties.

Sherman, with his own troops and one of Thomas's divisions, was to cross the Tennessee just below the mouth of the South Chickamauga, and secure the heights as far as the railroad tunnel. Thomas was to co-operate with Sherman by concentrating his troops on his own left, leaving a thin line to guard the works on the right and centre. Hooker was to assail the Confederate left and drive it from Lookout Mountain. Grant was the more anxious to make the attack on the 21st that on the day before he received from Bragg a letter suggesting the removal of non-combatants from Chattanooga—a letter intended to convey the idea that an attack on that place was meditated, but which really confirmed the report brought by a deserter, and confirmed Grant in the belief that Bragg was about to retreat.

The general attack which was to be made on the 21st was countermanded. Sherman had experienced unexpected difficulty in passing his troops across Brown's Ferry in consequence of the heavy rains. The pontoon-bridge at last gave way. Osterhaus, whose division was still on the southern side of the

GENERAL JAMES LONGSTREET.

river and without the means of crossing, was ordered to report to General Hooker, with whom he remained. Howard was at the same time called to Chattanooga, and temporarily attached to the command of General Thomas. On the afternoon of the 23d the Fifteenth corps, under the immediate command of General Blair, having flung pontoon-bridges across the Tennessee at the point indicated above, and also across the Chickamauga, were advancing to their position on the extreme left of the National army.

Grant, now impatient of delay, and determined that if Bragg really meant to retire, he should not retire uninjured and in good order, had instructed Thomas on the morning of the 23d to advance and give the enemy an opportunity of developing his lines.

Brilliant Scene.

The day was unusually beautiful. The men, now that they were relieved from their prison-house in Chattanooga and well fed, were in excellent spirits. They were dressed in their best uniforms and accompanied by new bands of music. The neighboring heights were crowded with spectators. The magnificent array, the steady step, the splendid uniforms, the burnished bayonets glittering in the clear November sunlight,—it was a holiday picture. It seemed a dress-parade or review, and was so regarded for a time by the Confederates, who witnessed the spectacle from the side and summit of Missionary Ridge.

Wood's division of Granger's corps moved in advance on the left, Sheridan's division of the same corps being on the right. Palmer of the Fourteenth corps supported Granger's right, with Baird's division refused; Johnson's division of Palmer's remaining under arms in the intrenchments, to be ready to reinforce at any point. Howard's corps was formed in mass behind that of Granger. As soon as Thomas's men began to move forward the heavy guns of Fort Wood opened upon the enemy's first position.

It was the beginning of a decisive battle. The Federal troops were well equipped and splendidly generalled. They had implicit confidence in their commanders, and this went far toward giving them complete confidence in themselves. They felt that the eyes of a nation were on them, that millions of anxious people were waiting to hear of their valor and victory. Under such circumstances hope and courage reigned in every breast, the victory was grasped beforehand, each vied with others in the performance of deeds that should bring renown to the Union arms, and rose to the sublime occasion.

Upon the ramparts of the fort Grant, Thomas, Granger, and Howard stood watching the advance. It was a splendid sight. On moved the mighty mass as if it had been one solid unit. Cheers were heard to arise from the ranks of the advancing columns. The pickets of the enemy were seen to break and fly in confusion before them. In spite of the well-directed fire from its summit, Wood had already reached the base of Orchard Knob, a steep, craggy hill rising above the general level of the valley, midway between the river and the ridge and about a mile from Fort Wood.

Without halting, Wood ordered his men to charge. It was done in gallant style, the rifle-pits on the summit being carried and two hundred men made prisoners. A heavy battery was advanced to the captured position from Fort Wood, and the place was held. This was an important gain to the Nationals and they made the most of it.

Simultaneously with this movement of General Thomas against Orchard Knob, a cavalry brigade by order of General Grant was operating on Bragg's extreme right and rear. No other movement of any consequence took place on the 23d.

Sherman on Missionary Ridge.

Sherman all night through was pushing his troops across the river. As early as daylight on the morning of the 24th he had eight thousand men, with artillery and horses, on the south side of the Tennessee. At one o'clock P. M. the march was taken up by three columns, each head of column covered by a line of skirmishers with supports. It was a dull, drizzly day. The clouds were low, and the movements of the troops could not be easily seen by the enemy.

At half-past three o'clock Sherman had possession of the whole northern extremity of Missionary Ridge, as far almost as the railroad tunnel. In the afternoon and during the night he threw up intrenchments and established himself in a really strong position. Sherman had thus, so far, carried out his part of the general plan. Such was the state of things on the National left at the close of Tuesday, the 24th.

On the National right matters were, if possible, even more favorable. Hooker had performed a brilliant feat of arms on Lookout Mountain. At four o'clock on the morning of the 24th he had reported that his troops were in position and ready to advance. Soon afterward the movement commenced. It had been Hooker's intention to push his men across Lookout Creek and strike the enemy in front. It was a hazardous undertaking, for Lookout Mountain, with its high palisaded crest, its steep, rugged slopes, its numerous rifle-pits, its encircling lines of earthworks and redans, was deemed by Bragg impregnable.

It so happened, however, that Lookout Creek was so swollen by the recent heavy rains that it was impassable. A direct movement by the main road could not be attempted until temporary bridges were constructed. Hooker therefore ordered Geary, with his own division and Whittaker's brigade of Cruft's division, to march to Wauhatchie, to cross the creek there, and move down on the right bank, while he employed the remainder of his forces in throwing bridges across on the main road.

The day was favorable for conducting such operations. A heavy mist enveloped the mountain and spread itself over the adjoining valleys. The attention of the enemy had been drawn to the bridge-builders, of whom an occasional glimpse could be had as the mist drifted with the breeze ; but no notice had been taken of Geary, who reached his appointed place at Wauhatchie unobserved.

The Confederates Surprised.

It was about eight o'clock when he began to cross the creek. Passing over without molestation, he surprised and captured the picket-guard, and, immediately facing to the north, he extended his line on the right to the base of the mountain. The Confederates, caught at once on both flank and rear, offered a stubborn resistance. Meanwhile, the bridges were constructed, and, Osterhaus's division having been brought up from Brown's Ferry, the Nationals were soon in great force on the right bank of the creek. Under cover of the two batteries—the Ohio on Bald Hill, and the New York on the hill in the rear—Hooker's men went dashing down the valley, sweeping everything before them, capturing the rifle-pits, and making a large number of prisoners.

At the same time, the troops to the right, passing directly under the muzzles of the Confederate guns, were rushing up the rugged sides of the hill, leaping over boulders and ledges of rock, cutting their way through the abattis, and gradually forcing position after position until the plateau was cleared and the retreating Confederates were seen plunging themselves down the jagged and precipitous face of the mountain, and flying in confusion and utter rout toward Chattanooga Valley. Hooker had not expected to accomplish so much in the same space of

VALOR AT CHATTANOOGA.

time. Nay, he had been unwilling that his men should attempt so much.

The Men would not Halt.

Not knowing to what extent the enemy might be reinforced, and fearing disaster from the rough character of the ground, he had given directions that the men should halt when they reached the high ground. But aroused to the highest pitch of enthusiasm and with a flying foe before them, a halt was impossible.

It was now about two o'clock in the afternoon, and such was the density of the mist which shrouded the mountain and hung heavily over the valley that it was found necessary, temporarily at least, to suspend operations. Hooker, not deeming it advisable to descend into the valley in pursuit, established his line on the east side of the mountain, his right resting on the palisades, his left near the mouth of Chattanooga Creek.

The battle had literally been fought above the clouds. It was not until nightfall that the sky cleared, and revealed to thousands in the valley below the actual progress which Hooker had made. As soon as it became known that behind that veil of clouds a great battle had been fought and won, and that the National arms had been victorious, the soldiers gave way to the wildest enthusiasm, and loud cheers for "Old Hooker" coming up, resounding from the valley, were echoed and re-echoed among the blood-stained hills.

The night which followed was beautiful in the extreme. The mist disappeared, and a full moon shed her mellow light over a scene of matchless magnificence. It was Hooker's conviction that the enemy would withdraw from the summit of the mountain before daylight. In anticipation of such a movement he detached parties from several regiments with instructions to scale the palisades. When morning came the Confederates were gone.

Frowning Artillery.

Such was the condition of things on the night of the 24th and the morning of the 25th of November. The National army maintained an unbroken line, with open communications from the north end of Lookout Mountain through the Chattanooga Valley, to the north end of Missionary Ridge.

The morning of the 25th rose in beauty. Far almost as the eye could reach the sun fell upon the compact lines of polished steel. In front, towering up, the huge form of Missionary Ridge, its precipitous sides defying attack, its summit swarming with armed men and crowned with artillery; away to the right and standing out clear and well defined the bold outlines of Lookout Mountain; Hooker's men spread out in the valley below to the right, Sherman's massed in compact phalanx above to the left, while Thomas's well-trained bands, eager and ready for the fray, are gathered together in close array around the headquarters of the chief,—such was the sight which met the eye of the beholder as he stood on Orchard Knob on the morning of the day which was to witness the final struggle and the crowning National victory at Chattanooga. It was a magnificent spectacle, and one which it rarely falls to the lot of mortals to witness.

Bragg versus Sherman.

At an early hour the preparations were complete. The sun had arisen, however, before the bugle sounded "Forward!" Hooker had received orders to move on the Confederate left; Sherman was to move against the right; while the centre, under the immediate eye of General Grant, was to advance later in the day and whenever the developments made on either wing should justify the attack. Shortly after sunrise Hooker, who has left a small force on Lookout Mountain, is seen with the mass of his troops moving down the eastern slope of the mountain and sweeping across the valley.

Sherman moved at the same time on the Confederate right, and it soon begins to be evident that Bragg, believing that the main attack is to be made on his right, is massing his troops on Sherman's front. A fierce artillery duel at once commenced between Orchard Knob and Missionary Ridge. Hooker, pressing on toward Rossville Gap, encountered an unexpected obstacle at Chattanooga Creek. The bridge had been destroyed by the Confederates as they retired from the valley in the early morning. It was an unfortunate circumstance, necessitating as it did a delay of three hours.

As soon as the bridge was completed the troops were pushed over. Rossville Gap was quickly occupied, and Hooker, moving Osterhaus along the east side of the ridge, Geary at its base, with the batteries on the west side, and Cruft on the ridge itself, marched northward, driving the enemy before him. Shortly after sunset the victory on the National right was complete. Breckenridge had proved himself no match for Hooker.

The Desperate Struggle.

Let us now see what was going on toward the left and at the centre. On the morning of the 25th, Sherman was in the saddle before it was light. During the night he had strongly intrenched his position. His order of battle was similar to that of Hooker. General Corse, with three of his own regiments and one of Lightburn's, moved forward on the crest of the hill; General Morgan L. Smith, with his command, advanced along the eastern base; while Colonel Loomis, supported by the two reserve brigades of General John E. Smith, advanced along the western base. The brigades of Cockerell and Alexander and a portion of Lightburn's remained behind, holding the position first occupied. Almost from the commencement of the forward movement the advancing columns were exposed to the guns of the enemy.

The tide of battle ebbed and flowed, victory now leaning to the one side and now to the other. It was a desperate grapple and the loss of life was

VALOR AT CHATTANOOGA.

terrible. No decided progress was being made on either side. Corse found it impossible to carry the works in his front; the Confederates were equally unable to drive him from the position he had won. The columns which under Loomis and Smith moved along the sides of the ridge, encountering fewer difficulties, were attended with better success. Smith kept gaining ground on the left spur of Missionary Ridge, while Loomis on his side got abreast of the tunnel and the railroad embankment.

The fire of the one and the other, striking the Confederates on both flanks and slightly in rear of their front, had the effect of withdrawing attention, and thus to a certain extent of relieving the assaulting party on the crest of the hill.

It was now about three o'clock. The battle was raging with tremendous fury. Column after column of the enemy came streaming down upon Sherman's men, gun upon gun pouring upon them its concentrated shot from every hill and spur as they vainly struggled in the valley and attempted to force their way to the farther height. Neither, however, was gaining any advantage.

They Held their Ground.

Almost at the crisis of the fight it seemed to the anxious watchers at Chattanooga as if Sherman was losing ground. There was, indeed, a backward movement. It had seemed to General J. E. Smith that Colonel Wolcott, who now commanded on the crest—Corse having been wounded early in the day—was sorely pressed and in danger of being overpowered.

He therefore sent to his aid the two reserve brigades of Runion and Mathias. Having crossed the intervening fields and climbed the hillside in spite of a most destructive fire of artillery and musketry, they effected a junction with Wolcott. The ridge, however, being narrow, they were forced to take position on the western face of the hill, where, being exposed to attack on right and rear, the enemy, rushing from the tunnel gorge, fell upon them in overwhelming numbers, driving them down the hill and back to the lower end of the field. There they were re-formed, and the Confederates who had ventured to pursue were struck heavily on their flank, and compelled to retire to the shelter of their works on the wooded hills. It was this backward movement of Smith's brigades which, being seen at Chattanooga, created the impression that a repulse had been sustained by the National left.

Impatient for the Fray.

Sherman has taken some pains to correct this false impression, and informs us that the "real attacking columns of General Corse, General Loomis, and General Morgan L. Smith were not repulsed," but, on the contrary, held their ground and struggled "all day persistently, stubbornly, and well."

Long and wearily had Sherman waited for the attack in the centre. An occasional shot from Orchard Knob and some artillery and musketry fire away in the direction of Lookout, were the only signs of activity in the National ranks on his right. It was not until shortly after three o'clock that he saw a white line of smoke in front of Orchard Knob, the line extending farther and farther to the right. It was evident that something decisive was happening. He had faith in the result, for he knew that by his repeated and persistent attacks he had compelled Bragg to concentrate large masses of his troops on his own right. He had thus weakened the Confederate centre and created the opportunity for Grant and Thomas.

During these hours of sore trial and deep anxiety Grant's attention was quite as much directed to the left as was that of Sherman to the centre. Grant's headquarters were at Orchard Knob. He had a commanding view of the entire battle-ground. He knew that Bragg was concentrating on his own right, and, determined to penetrate the National left and force his way to Chattanooga, was hurling against Sherman his well-disciplined legions in overwhelming masses. He feared lest his trusted lieutenant, sorely pressed, should be yielding to impatience because of the continued inaction at the centre.

But it was necessary to wait for Hooker, who, as has been stated, had been delayed three hours in reconstructing the bridge across Chattanooga Creek. It was desirable at least that the Confederate left should be well engaged, as well as the Confederate right, before the decisive blow was dealt at the centre. With any other commander on his left Grant might have risked too much by leaving him so long, unaided or unrelieved, to struggle against the strong position and the ever-increasing numbers of the enemy.

"A Wall of Adamant."

Grant, however, had not forgotten Shiloh. He remembered how on that day, at the foot of the bridge over Snake Creek, Sherman had stood like a wall of adamant, his men massed around him, and presenting to the almost triumphant foe what seemed a huge and solid shield of shining steel, effectually resisting and ultimately turning the tide of battle. What he had done then he had on many a battle-field since proved his ability and willingness to do again. Grant was asking much from his lieutenant, but he felt convinced that Sherman would not be found wanting. Meanwhile, he had the satisfaction of perceiving that his plan was working admirably. Bragg, completely out-generalled, was weakening his own centre and preparing for him his opportunity.

It was now half-past three o'clock. Grant was pacing to and fro on Orchard Knob. Concerned for the welfare of Sherman, seeing his opportunity rapidly ripening, and impatient to strike, yet unwilling by premature action to imperil the hoped-for and what seemed the inevitable result, he kept turning his eyes wistfully in the direction in which Hooker should make his appearance.

The Moment Arrives.

Still there were no signs of his coming. Hooker, as the reader knows, was successfully moving along the ridge and driving the enemy before him. But Grant was as yet ignorant at once of the cause of his delay and of the progress he had made. The opportune moment, however, had come. He saw that Bragg had greatly weakened his centre to support his right, and, having faith that Hooker must be close at hand, he gave Thomas the order to advance.

The thunderbolt was hurled. The signal-guns were fired—one—two—three—four—five—six—and the divisions of Wood, Baird, Sheridan, and Johnson, long since impatient of delay, advanced with firm and steady step. These were preceded by a double line of skirmishers, drawn mostly from the divisions of Wood and Sheridan. The orders were to carry the rifle-pits at the base of the ridge, and then to reform and push their way to the summit.

The whole movement was conducted with the regularity and precision of clockwork. The skirmishers dashed forward, the main body following within easy supporting distance.

The Ridge Ablaze.

Missionary Ridge all at once seems ablaze. On all the forts and batteries the heavy guns open fire, and from their hollow mouths they bellow harsh thunder and vomit forth their missiles of destruction. Full thirty guns are pouring shot and shell into the advancing columns. Nothing, however, can cool the ardor or restrain the impetuosity of the National soldiers. "Rolling on the foe," on moves this "fiery mass of living valor."

The picture of the poet becomes here a living reality. The brigades of Hazen and Willich are already at the base of the mountain. Like "bees out of a hive," to use the expressive words of General Grant, the gray-coated Confederates are seen swarming out of the rifle-pits and rushing up the hillside.

Fired now with the wildest enthusiasm, the brave Nationals, scarcely taking time to re-form, push their way up the steep and rugged sides of the mountain. They are fully exposed now to a terrific fire from the enemy's guns on the heights above them. Shell, canister, shrapnel, bullets, are falling upon them with deadly effect.

The Old Flag climbs Higher.

Nothing daunted, however, on they pressed, and from Orchard Knob the National colors are seen fluttering higher and still higher and gradually nearing the summit. Order now begins to disappear. The brigades, partly because of the nature of the ground and partly because of the severity of the fire, break up into groups. There is, however, neither lack of purpose nor lack of enthusiasm. Every group has its flag, and in wedge-like form, each eager to be first and emulous of the other, is seen pressing onward and upward. It seems as if the color-bearers are running a race. To plant the first color on the summit appears to be the ambition of every brigade, of every group, of every soldier. Now they are clambering over the rugged ledges, now they are seeking momentary shelter in the ravines or behind the overhanging rocks; but they are ever, in spite of the heavy guns and the murderous volleys of musketry from the rifle-pits, nearing the summit.

Down go the Standard-bearers.

Meanwhile, the work of destruction had been terrible. The color-bearers had suffered fearfully. The first to reach the summit was a group of men from the First Ohio and a few others from other regiments under the lead of Lieutenant-Colonel Langdon. Six color-bearers of this party had fallen, when Langdon, waving forward his men and leaping over the crest, was instantly shot down. The breach, however, had been made, and the brigades of Hazen and Willich were soon on the summit. These were quickly followed by the brigades of Sheridan's division, Sheridan himself taking an active part and specially commanding the attention of General Grant, by his wonderful command of his men and his intrepid bearing.

The National advance was within a few hundred yards of Bragg's headquarters. There were still desperate hand-to-hand struggles after the Nationals had reached the summit. But as the shouting victors came pouring into the works, bayonetting the cannoneers at their guns, the bold and resolute front gave way. It was now sunset. The Confederates were in full retreat, their own guns turned upon them by the triumphant Nationals. It was only with difficulty that Bragg was able to make good his escape, along with Breckenridge, who by this time had joined him. Missionary Ridge was now occupied and held by the National troops.

Sherman Drives the Enemy.

Hooker, as we have seen, had been victorious on the right; Sherman had held his ground, and, after a gallant and protracted struggle against superior numbers, had driven the enemy from his front; and now the brave and well-trusted soldiers of the Army of the Cumberland had pierced and routed the Confederate centre. The battle of Chattanooga had been fought and won.

The modesty of Grant, the utter absence of vainglory, is strikingly revealed in the despatch which he sent to General Halleck immediately after the battle. "Although the battle lasted," he says, "from early dawn till dark this evening, I believe I am not premature in announcing a complete victory over Bragg. Lookout Mountain top, all the rifle-pits in Chattanooga Valley, and Missionary Ridge entire have been carried and are now held by us."

The Last Struggle.

The final struggle of the day was in the neighborhood of the tunnel on Thomas's left and in Sherman's front. At that point the Confederates made a most obstinate resistance. This resistance and the darkness which intervened prevented an immediate pursuit. During the night Missionary Ridge blazed with Union camp-fires, the Confederates having fallen back in the direction of Ringgold by the way of Chickamauga Station. Bragg left behind him some six hundred prisoners, besides a large number of stragglers, forty guns, upward of seven thousand small-arms, and a large quantity of ammunition.

Next morning Sherman, Palmer, and Hooker were in eager pursuit. Sherman pushed on toward Graysville, passing Chickamauga Station, where he found everything in flames. The immediate result of the victory at Chattanooga was the relief of Knoxville. Burnside, it will be remembered, after having been relieved of the command of the Army of the Potomac, was assigned on the 26th of March to the command of the Department of the Ohio. His headquarters were at Cincinnati, and his army, about twenty thousand strong, was at Camp Nelson, near Richmond, Kentucky. When Rosecrans commenced his onward movement toward Chattanooga, Burnside, who had been ordered to co-operate with him and to effect a junction between his own right and the left of Rosecrans, commenced on the 16th of August his march for East Tennessee. That district of country was then held by the Confederate general Buckner, whose headquarters were at Knoxville.

The Situation at Knoxville.

Burnside, more intent on restoring the authority of the National Government in East Tennessee, moved in the direction of Knoxville, although repeatedly ordered to reinforce Rosecrans, believing it to be all-important that the place should be permanently occupied by National troops.

If Knoxville was to be taken, it must be taken by

storm. Preparations for a final effort were accordingly hurried forward. The point chosen for attack was Fort Sanders, on the north-west angle of the fortifications and commanding an approach by the river. It was a work of great strength, the ditch being ten feet deep and the parapet of more than ordinary height. Around and in front of it several acres of thick pine timber had been slashed, and a perfect entanglement of wirework had been formed by connecting stump with stump. There were besides numerous rifle-pits and abattis.

The fort was occupied by the Seventy-ninth New York, the Twenty-ninth Massachusetts, two companies of the Second and one of the Twentieth Michigan. The armament consisted of four twenty-pounder Parrott guns, Lieutenant Benjamin, Burnside's chief of artillery; four light twelve-pounders, commanded by Buckley; and two three-inch guns. The assaulting party was composed of three brigades of McLaw's division, with those of Wolford, Humphreys, Anderson, and Bogart. They were picked men, the flower of Longstreet's army.

The Confederate Yell.

In the gray of the morning of the 29th the assault was made, with a vigor and determination not surpassed in the previous history of the war. What with the fierce yells of the Confederates, the rattle of musketry, the screaming of shells, the thunder of artillery, the tumult for a time was awful. The Confederates, as they approached, were received with a deadly fire

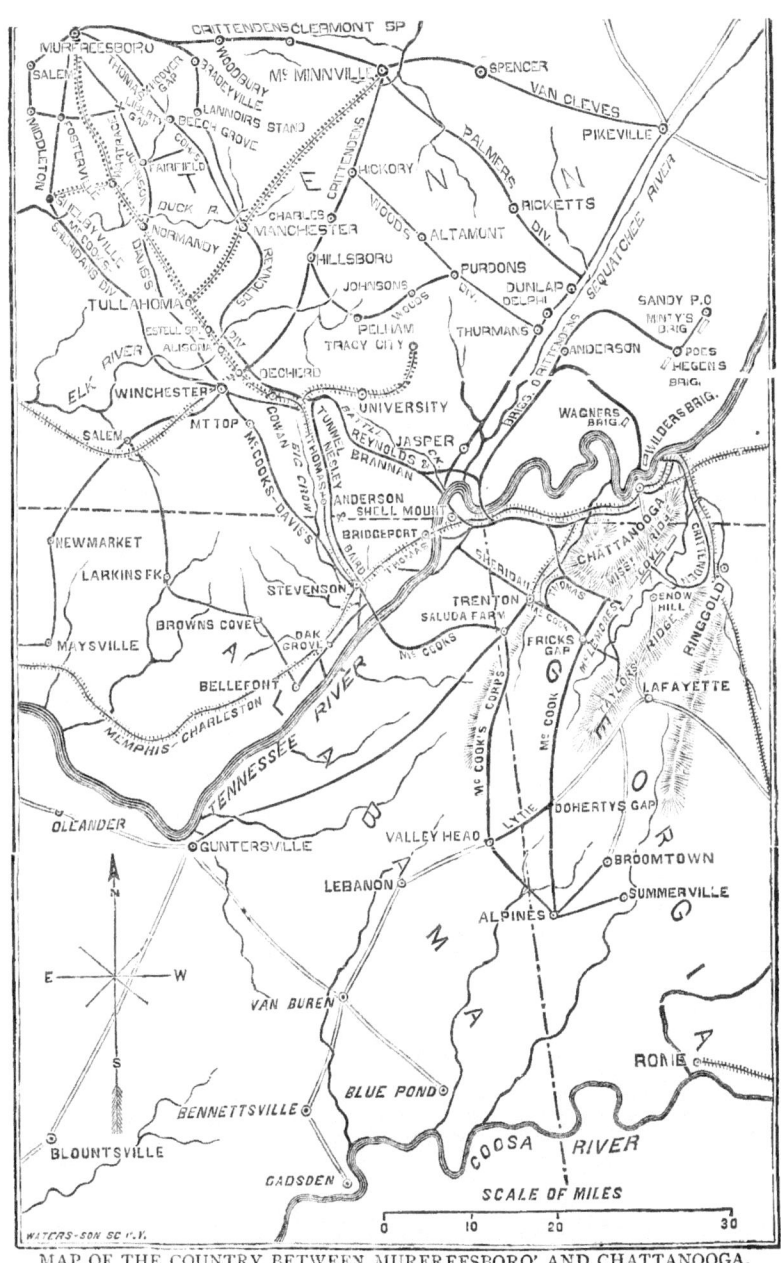

MAP OF THE COUNTRY BETWEEN MURFREESBORO' AND CHATTANOOGA, TENNESSEE.

from the batteries of the fort. Nothing daunted, however, by the destructive missiles which flew thick and fast around them or by the sight of their fallen comrades, on they pressed, through the abattis, across the ditch and up the parapet, some of them forcing their way through the embrasures. The obstacles encountered, the wire network particularly, made their progress slow, and consequently kept them long exposed to the double-shotted guns which Ferrero, the commander of the fort, kept in active play

The Assault Fails.

When the assailants reached the parapet their ranks were greatly thinned, but their spirits were not subdued. One officer actually reached the summit, and, planting upon it the flag of the Thirteenth Mississippi, called for surrender. It was a vain call, for the next moment his body, pierced by a dozen bullets, the flag still in his hand, was rolling into the ditch. Hand-grenades were freely used by the defenders, and they had terrible effect.

The assault, gallant as it was, proved a complete failure. It was tried a second time by another column, but the result was the same. The fighting was discontinued. A truce was granted to the Confederates to carry away their wounded and to bury their dead. Longstreet, still hoping against hope and unwilling to retire, maintained the siege.

The ground in front of the fort was strewn with the dead and wounded. In the ditch alone were over two hundred dead and wounded. "In this terrible ditch," says Pollard, "the dead were piled eight or ten feet deep. In a comparatively short time we lost seven hundred men in killed and wounded and prisoners. Never, excepting at Gettysburg, was there in the history of the war a disaster adorned with the glory of such devout courage as Longstreet's repulse at Knoxville."

Meanwhile, relief was coming from Grant to Burnside. Why was this relief so long delayed? On the evening of the 25th, as soon as success at Chattanooga had been assured, Grant had ordered General Gordon Granger to start for the relief of Knoxville with his own Fourth corps and detachments from others—twenty thousand in all. Granger was to move with four days' rations, arrangements having been made to send after him a steamer with supplies.

"You will Assume Command."

When Grant returned from the front on the 28th he found, much to his astonishment, that Granger had not yet got off, and that he was preparing to move "with reluctance and complaints." Grant fell back upon Sherman, who was ever willing and ever ready. "I am inclined to think," said Grant, in a letter to Sherman, "I shall have to send you. In plain words, you will assume command of all the forces now moving up the Tennessee."

When he received the letter from Grant, Sherman was at Calhoun, at the railroad crossing of the Hiawassee. If he had been less of a soldier he might easily have found cause of complaint. It was only seven days since he had marched his troops from the west side of the Tennessee, with only two days' rations, without change of clothing, with but a single blanket or coat to a man from himself to the private soldier. What provisions they had were picked up by the way.

Sherman Hastening to the Rescue.

Murmur or complaint, however, with Sherman, there was none. To hear was to obey. It was enough for him that twelve thousand of his fellow-soldiers were beleaguered at Knoxville, eighty-four miles away, and that if not relieved within three days they might be at the mercy of the enemy.

With his hardy and untiring veterans Sherman was quickly on his way. The roads were bad, and, as the pontoon-bridge at Loudon had been destroyed, there was unexpected difficulty and consequent delay. After considerable progress had been made the troops were compelled to turn to the east and to trust to General Burnside's bridge at Knoxville. A bridge was flung across the Little Tennessee at Morgantown, and by daybreak on the 5th of December the entire Fifteenth corps was over. Meanwhile, the cavalry command, which had moved forward in advance, had reached Knoxville on the 3d of December, the very day on which Burnside expected his supplies would give out.

The Siege Ended.

On the night of the 5th a messenger from Burnside arrived at Sherman's headquarters, announcing that

Longstreet was in full retreat toward Virginia and that the National cavalry were in pursuit. As soon as Sherman's cavalry appeared, Longstreet, discovering that his flank was turned, raised the siege and retreated toward Russellville in the direction of Virginia. The National cavalry followed for some distance in close pursuit. This ended the siege of Knoxville.

Burnside had offered a noble resistance and had retrieved some of the laurels lost at Fredericksburg. He was not without obligations to Sherman, nor was he ungrateful. In a letter to that general he fully acknowledged those obligations, and thanked both him and his command for so promptly coming to his relief. "I am satisfied," he said, "that your approach served to raise the siege."

Sherman, too, had great reason to be proud of himself and his command. They had been constantly in motion since they left the Big Black in Missisippi. For long periods they had been without regular rations, and the men had marched through mud and over rocks, sometimes barefooted, without a murmur and without a moment's delay.

Marvels of Achievement.

After a march of over four hundred miles, without sleep for three successive nights, they crossed the Tennessee, fought their part in the battle of Chattanooga, pursued the enemy out of Tennessee, and then turned more than one hundred and twenty miles north and compelled Longstreet to raise the siege of Knoxville. After the siege was raised, Sherman, with the consent of Burnside, leaving only Granger's command, fell back to the line of the Hiawassee.

CHAPTER XVIII.

General Sherman's Fascinating Story of the Battle of Chattanooga.

HAVING in the preceding chapter described the great general features of the battle of Chattanooga, having followed the combined Union armies on to their magnificent victory, we now take pleasure in presenting the reader with an intensely interesting account of the sanguinary conflict from General Sherman's own pen. This clear and graphic report relates especially his own part in the terrible yet glorious deeds on that world-renowned battle-field. The report is as follows:

HEADQUARTERS DEPARTMENT AND ARMY OF THE TENNESSEE.
BRIDGEPORT, ALABAMA, December 19, 1863.

Brigadier-General JOHN A. RAWLINS, *Chief of Staff to General* GRANT, *Chattanooga :*

GENERAL: For the first time I am now at leisure to make an official record of events with which the troops under my command have been connected during the eventful campaign which has just closed.

During the month of September last the Fifteenth army corps, which I had the honor to command, lay in camps along the Big Black, about twenty miles east of Vicksburg, Mississippi. It consisted of four divisions. The First, commanded by Brigadier-General

P. J. Osterhaus, was composed of two brigades, led by Brigadier-General C. R. Woods and Colonel J. A. Williamson (of the Fourth Iowa).

The Second, commanded by Brigadier-General Morgan L. Smith, was composed of two brigades, led by Brigadier-Generals Giles A. Smith and J. A. J. Lightburn.

The Third, commanded by Brigadier-General J. M. Tuttle, was composed of three brigades, led by Brigadier-Generals J. A. Mower and R. P. Buckland and Colonel J. J. Wood (of the Twelfth Iowa).

The Fourth, commanded by Brigadier-General Hugh Ewing, was composed of three brigades, led by Brigadier-General J. M. Corse, Colonel Loomis (Twenty-sixth Illinois), and Colonel J. R. Cockerell (of the Seventieth Ohio).

Off for Chattanooga.

On the 22d day of September, I received a telegraphic despatch from General Grant, then at Vicksburg, commanding the Department of the Tennessee, requiring me to detach one of my divisions to march to Vicksburg, there to embark for Memphis, where it was to form a part of an army to be sent to Chattanooga to reinforce General Rosecrans. I designated the First division, and at 4 P. M. the same day it marched for Vicksburg, and embarked the next day.

On the 23d of September, I was summoned to Vicksburg by the general commanding, who showed me several despatches from the general-in-chief, which led him to suppose he would have to send me and my whole corps to Memphis and eastward, and I was instructed to prepare for such orders. It was explained to me that in consequence of the low stage of water in the Mississippi boats had arrived irregularly, and had brought despatches that seemed to conflict in their meaning, and that General John E. Smith's division (of General McPherson's corps) had been ordered up to Memphis, and that I should take that division, and leave one of my own in its stead to hold the line of the Big Black. I detailed my Third division (General Tuttle) to remain and report to Major-General McPherson, commanding the Seventeenth corps, at Vicksburg; and that of General John E. Smith, already started for Memphis, was styled the Third division, Fifteenth corps, though it still belongs to the Seventeenth army corps. This division is also composed of three brigades, commanded by General Mathias, Colonel J. B. Raum (of the Fifty-sixth Illinois), and Colonel J. I. Alexander (of the Fifty-ninth Indiana).

A River Fleet.

The Second and Fourth divisions were started for Vicksburg the moment I was notified that boats were in readiness, and on the 27th of September I embarked in person in the steamer Atlantic for Memphis, followed by a fleet of boats conveying these two divisions. Our progress was slow, on account of the unprecedentedly low water in the Mississippi and the scarcity of coal and wood. We were compelled at places to gather fence-rails and to land wagons and haul wood from the interior to the boats; but I reached Memphis during the night of the 2d of October, and the other boats came in on the 3d and 4th.

On arrival at Memphis, I saw General Hurlbut, and read all the despatches and letters of instruction of General Halleck, and therein derived my instructions, which I construed to be as follows:

To conduct the Fifteenth army corps, and all other troops which could be spared from the line of the Memphis and Charleston railroad, to Athens, Alabama, and thence report by letter for orders to General Rosecrans, commanding the Army of the Cumberland at Chattanooga; to follow substantially the railroad eastward, repairing it as I moved; to look to my own line for supplies; and in no event to depend on General Rosecrans for supplies, as the roads to his rear were already overtaxed to supply his present army.

I learned from General Hurlbut that General Osterhaus's division was already out in front of Corinth, and that General John E. Smith was still at Memphis, moving his troops and material by railroad as fast as its limited stock would carry them. General J. D. Webster was superintendent of the railroad, and was enjoined to work night and day and to expedite the movement as rapidly as possible; but the capacity of the road was so small that I soon saw that I could move horses, mules, and wagons faster by land, and therefore I despatched the artillery and wagons by the road under escort, and finally moved the entire Fourth division by land.

Harassed by the Enemy.

The enemy seems to have had early notice of this movement, and he endeavored to thwart us from the start. A considerable force assembled in a threatening attitude at Salem, south of Salisbury Station, and General Carr, who commanded at Corinth, felt compelled to turn back and use a part of my troops, that had already reached Corinth, to resist the threatened attack.

On Sunday, October 11th, having put in motion my whole force, I started myself for Corinth, in a special train, with the battalion of the Thirteenth United States regulars as escort. We reached Collierville Station about noon, just in time to take part in the defence made of that station by Colonel D. C. Anthony of the Sixty-sixth Indiana against an attack made by General Chalmers with a force of about three thousand cavalry, with eight pieces of artillery. He was beaten off, the damage to the road repaired, and we resumed our journey the next day, reaching Corinth at night.

I immediately ordered General Blair forward to Iuka with the First division, and as fast as I got troops up pushed them forward of Bear Creek, the bridge of which was completely destroyed, and an engineer regiment, under command of Colonel Flad, was engaged in its repairs.

Quite a considerable force of the enemy was assembled in our front, near Tuscumbia, to resist our advance. It was commanded by General Stephen D. Lee, and composed of Roddy's and Ferguson's brigades, with irregular cavalry, amounting in the aggregate to about five thousand.

In person I moved from Corinth to Burnsville on the 18th, and to Iuka on the 19th of October.

Admiral Porter.

Osterhaus's division was in the advance, constantly skirmishing with the enemy; he was supported by General Morgan L. Smith's, both divisions under the general command of Major-General Blair. General John E. Smith's division covered the working-party engaged in rebuilding the railroad.

Foreseeing difficulty in crossing the Tennessee River, I had written to Admiral Porter at Cairo, asking him to watch the Tennessee and send up some gunboats the moment the stage of water admitted; and had also requested General Allen, quartermaster at St. Louis, to despatch to Eastport a steam ferry-boat.

The admiral, ever prompt and ready to assist us, had two fine gunboats at Eastport, under Captain Phelps, the very day after my arrival at Iuka; and Captain Phelps had a coal-barge decked over with which to cross our horses and wagons before the arrival of the ferry-boat.

Still following literally the instructions of General Halleck, I pushed forward the repairs of the railroad, and ordered General Blair, with the two leading divisions, to drive the enemy beyond Tuscumbia. This he did successfully, after a pretty severe fight at Cane Creek, occupying Tuscumbia on the 27th of October.

In the mean time many important changes in command had occurred, which I must note here to a proper understanding of the case.

The Commands Assigned.

General Grant had been called from Vicksburg and sent to Chattanooga to command the military Division of the Mississippi, composed of the three Departments of the Ohio, Cumberland, and Tennessee, and the Department of the Tennessee had been devolved on me, with instructions, however, to retain command of the army in the field. At Iuka I made what appeared to me the best disposition of matters relating to the department, giving General McPherson full powers in Mississippi and General Hurlbut in West Tennessee, and assigned General Blair to the command of the Fifteenth army corps, and summoned General Hurlbut from Memphis and General Dodge from Corinth, and selected out of the Sixteenth corps a force of about eight thousand men, which I directed General Dodge to organize with all expedition, and with it to follow me eastward.

On the 27th of October, when General Blair, with two divisions, was at Tuscumbia, I ordered General Ewing, with the Fourth division, to cross the Tennessee (by means of the gunboats and scow) as rapidly as possible at Eastport, and push forward to Florence, which he did; and the same day a messenger from General Grant floated down the Tennessee over Muscle Shoals, landed at Tuscumbia, and was sent to me at Iuka. He bore a short message from the general to this effect: "Drop all work on the railroad east of Bear Creek; push your command toward Bridgeport till you meet orders," etc.

Crossing the Tennessee.

Instantly the order was executed; the order of march was reversed, and all the columns were directed to Eastport, the only place where we could cross the Tennessee. At first we only had the gunboats and coal-barge; but the ferry-boat and two transports arrived on the 31st of October, and the work of crossing was pushed with all the vigor possible. In person I crossed, and passed to the head of the column at Florence on the 1st of November, leaving the rear divisions to be conducted by General Blair, and marched to Rogersville and Elk River. This was found impassable. To ferry would have consumed too much time, and to build a bridge still more; so there was no alternative but to turn up Elk River by way of Gilbertsboro, Elkton, etc., to the stone bridge at Fayetteville, where we crossed the Elk and proceeded to Winchester and Deckerd.

At Fayetteville, I received orders from General Grant to come to Bridgeport with the Fifteenth army corps, and to leave General Dodge's command at Pulaski and along the railroad from Columbia to Decatur. I instructed General Blair to follow with the Second and First divisions by way of New Market, Larkinsville, and Bellefonte, while I conducted the other two divisions by way of Deckerd; the Fourth division crossing the mountain to Stevenson, and the Third by University Place and Swedon's Cove.

In person I proceeded by Swedon's Cove and Battle Creek, reaching Bridgeport on the night of November 13th. I immediately telegraphed to the commanding general my arrival and the positions of my several divisions, and was summoned to Chattanooga. I took the first steamboat during the night of the 14th for Kelly's Ferry, and rode into Chattanooga on the 15th.

The Arena of Conflict.

\hen learned the part assigned me in the coming drama, was supplied with the necessary maps and information, and rode during the 16th, in company with Generals Grant, Thomas, W. F. Smith, Brannan, and others, to the positions occupied on the west bank of the Tennessee, from which could be seen the camps of the enemy compassing Chattanooga and the line of Missionary Hills, with its terminus on Chickamauga Creek, the point that I was expected to take, hold, and fortify. Pontoons, with a full supply of balks and chesses, had been prepared for the bridge over the Tennessee, and all things had been prearranged with a foresight that elicited my admiration. From the hills we looked down on the amphitheatre of Chattanooga as on a map, and nothing remained but for me to put my troops in the desired position. The plan contemplated that, in addition to crossing the Tennessee River and making a lodgment on the terminus of Missionary Ridge, I should demonstrate against Lookout Mountain near Trenton with a part of my command.

All in Chattanooga were impatient for action, rendered almost acute by the natural apprehensions felt for the safety of General Burnside in East Tennessee.

My command had marched from Memphis, three hundred and thirty miles, and I had pushed them as fast as the roads and distance would admit, but I saw enough of the condition of men and animals in Chattanooga to inspire me with renewed energy. I immediately ordered my leading division (General Ewing's) to march *viâ* Shellmound to Trenton, demonstrating against Lookout Ridge, but to be prepared to turn quickly and follow me to Chattanooga; and in person I returned to Bridgeport, rowing a boat down the Tennessee from Kelly's Ferry, and immediately on arrival put in motion my divisions in the order in which they had arrived.

Preparing for the Attack.

The bridge of boats at Bridgeport was frail, and, though used day and night, our passage was slow, and the road thence to Chattanooga was dreadfully cut up and encumbered with the wagons of the other troops stationed along the road. I reached General Hooker's headquarters during a rain in the afternoon of the 20th, and met General Grant's orders for the general attack on the next day. It was simply impossible for me to fulfil my part in time; only one division (General John E. Smith's) was in position. General Ewing was still at Trenton, and the other two were toiling along the terrible road from Shellmound to Chattanooga. No troops ever were or could be in better condition than mine, or who labored harder to fulfil their part. On a proper representation General Grant postponed the attack. On the 21st I got the Second division over Brown's Ferry bridge, and General Ewing got up; but the bridge broke repeatedly, and delays occurred which no human sagacity could prevent.

All labored night and day, and General Ewing got over on the 23d, but my rear division was cut off by the broken bridge at Brown's Ferry and could not join me. I offered to go into action with my three divisions, supported by General Jeff. C. Davis, leaving one of my best divisions (Osterhaus's) to act with General Hooker against Lookout Mountain. That division has not joined me yet, but I know and feel that it has served the country well, and that it has reflected honor on the Fifteenth army corps and the Army of the Tennessee. I leave the record of its history to General Hooker or whomsoever has had its services during the late memorable events, confident that all will do it merited honor.

Silent Movements.

At last, on the 23d of November, my three divisions lay behind the hills opposite the mouth of the Chickamauga. I despatched the brigade of the Second division commanded by General Giles A.

Smith, under cover of the hills, to North Chickamauga Creek, to man the boats designed for the pontoon-bridge, with orders (at midnight) to drop down silently to a point above the mouth of the South Chickamauga, there land two regiments, who were to move along the river-bank quietly and capture the enemy's river-pickets.

General Giles A. Smith then was to drop rapidly below the mouth of the Chickamauga, disembark the rest of his brigade, and despatch the boats across for fresh loads. These orders were skilfully executed, and every rebel picket but one was captured. The balance of General Morgan L. Smith's division was then rapidly ferried across; that of General John E. Smith followed, and by daylight of November 24th two divisions of about eight thousand men were on the east bank of the Tennessee, and had thrown up a very respectable rifle-trench as a *tête-du-pont*.

As soon as the day dawned some of the boats were taken from the use of ferrying, and a pontoon-bridge was begun under the immediate direction of Captain Dresser, the whole planned and supervised by General William F. Smith in person. A pontoon-bridge was also built at the same time over Chickamauga Creek near its mouth, giving communication with the two regiments which had been left on the north side, and fulfilling a most important purpose at a later stage of the drama. I will here bear my willing testimony to the completeness of this whole business.

All the officers charged with the work were present, and manifested a skill which I cannot praise too highly. I have never beheld any work done so quietly, so well; and I doubt if the history of war can show a bridge of that extent (viz. thirteen hundred and fifty feet) laid so noiselessly and well in so short a time. I attribute it to the genius and intelligence of General William F. Smith. The steamer Dunbar arrived up in the course of the morning, and relieved Ewing's division of the labor of rowing across; but by noon the pontoon-bridge was done, and my three divisions were across, with men, horses, artillery, and everything.

The Columns Formed.

General Jeff. C. Davis's division was ready to take the bridge, and I ordered the columns to form in order to carry the Missionary Hills. The movement had been carefully explained to all division commanders, and at one P. M. we marched from the river in three columns in échelon—the left, General Morgan L. Smith, the column of direction, following substantially Chickamauga Creek; the centre, General John E. Smith, in columns doubled on the centre, at one brigade interval, to the right and rear; the right General Ewing, in column at the same distance to the right rear, prepared to deploy to the right, on the supposition that we would meet an enemy in that direction. Each head of column was covered by a good line of skirmishers, with supports. A light, drizzling rain prevailed and the clouds hung low, cloaking our movement from the enemy's tower of observation on Lookout Mountain.

Pushing to the Top of the Hill.

We soon gained the foot-hills; our skirmishers crept up the face of the hills, followed by their supports, and at 3.30 P. M. we had gained, with no loss, the desired point. A brigade of each division was pushed rapidly to the top of the hill, and the enemy for the first time seemed to realize the movement, but too late, for we were in possession. He opened with artillery, but General Ewing soon got some of Captain Richardson's guns up that steep hill, and gave back artillery, and the enemy's skirmishers made one or two ineffectual dashes at General Lightburn, who had swept round and got a farther hill, which was the real continuation of the ridge.

From studying all the maps I had inferred that Missionary Ridge was a continuous hill, but we found ourselves on two high points, with a deep depression between us and the one immediately over the tunnel, which was my chief objective point. The ground we had gained, however, was so important that I could leave nothing to chance, and ordered it to be fortified during the night. One brigade of each division was left on the hill, one of General Morgan L. Smith's closed the gap to Chickamauga Creek, two of General John E. Smith's were drawn back to the base in reserve, and General Ewing's right was extended down into the plain, thus crossing the ridge in a general line, facing south-east.

The enemy felt our left flank about 4 P. M., and a pretty smart engagement with artillery and muskets ensued, when he drew off; but it cost us dear, for General Giles A. Smith was severely wounded, and had to go to the rear; and the command of the brigade devolved on Colonel Tupper (One-hundred-and-Sixteenth Illinois), who managed it with skill during the rest of the operations. At the moment of my crossing the bridge General Howard appeared, having come with three regiments from Chattanooga along the east bank of the Tennessee, connecting my new position with that of the main army in Chattanooga. He left the three regiments attached temporarily to General Ewing's right, and returned to his own corps at Chattanooga.

Orders for "Dawn of Day."

As night closed in I ordered General Jeff. C. Davis to keep one of his brigades at the bridge, one close up to my position, and one intermediate. Thus we passed the night, heavy details being kept busy at work on the intrenchments on the hill. During the night the sky cleared away bright, a cold frost filled the air, and our camp-fires revealed to the enemy and to our friends in Chattanooga our position on Missionary Ridge. About midnight I received, at the hands of Major Rowley (of General Grant's staff), orders to attack the enemy at "dawn of day," with notice that General Thomas would attack in force *early* in the day. Accordingly, before day I was in the saddle, attended by all my staff; rode to the extreme left of our position near Chickamauga Creek, thence up the hill held by General Lightburn, and round to the extreme right of General Ewing. Catching as accurate an idea of the ground as possible by the dim light of morning, I saw that our line of attack was in the direction of Missionary Ridge, with wings supporting on either flank. Quite a valley lay between us and the next hill of the series, and this hill presented steep sides, the one to the west partially cleared, but the other covered with the native forest. The crest of the ridge was narrow and wooded. The farther point of this hill was held by the enemy with a breastwork of logs and fresh earth, filled with men and two guns.

The Bugle Sounds "Forward!"

The enemy was also seen in great force on a still higher hill beyond the tunnel, from which he had a fine plunging fire on the hill in dispute. The gorge between, through which several roads and the railroad tunnel pass, could not be seen from our position, but formed the natural *place d'armes*, where the enemy covered his masses to resist our contemplated movement of turning his right flank and endangering his communications with his dépôt at Chickamauga Station.

As soon as possible the following dispositions were made: The brigades of Colonels Cockerell and Alexander and General Lightburn were to hold our hill as the key-point. General Corse, with as much of his brigade as could operate along the narrow ridge, was to attack from our right centre. General Lightburn was to despatch a good regiment from his position to co-operate with General Corse; and General Morgan L. Smith was to move along the east base of Missionary Ridge, connecting with General Corse; and Colonel Loomis in like manner to move along the west base, supported by the two reserve brigades of General John E. Smith.

Furious Fighting.

The sun had hardly risen before General Corse had completed his preparations and his bugle sounded the "Forward!" The Fortieth Illinois, supported by the Forty-sixth Ohio, on our right centre, with the Thirtieth Ohio (Colonel Jones), moved down the face of our hill and up that held by the enemy. The line advanced to within about eighty yards of the intrenched position, where General Corse found a secondary crest, which he gained and held. To this point he called his reserves, and asked for reinforcements, which were sent; but the space was narrow, and it was not well to crowd the men, as the enemy's artillery and musketry fire swept the approach to his position, giving him great advantage.

As soon as General Corse had made his preparations he assaulted, and a close, severe contest ensued which lasted more than an hour, gaining and losing ground, but never the position first obtained, from which the enemy in vain attempted to drive him. General Morgan L. Smith kept gaining ground on the left spurs of Missionary Ridge, and Colonel

Loomis got abreast of the tunnel and railroad embankment on his side, drawing the enemy's fire, and to that extent relieving the assaulting-party on the hill-crest. Captain Callender had four of his guns on General Ewing's hill, and Captain Woods his Napoleon battery on General Lightburn's; also, two guns of Dillon's battery were with Colonel Alexander's brigade. All directed their fire as carefully as possible to clear the hill to our front without endangering our own men. The fight raged furiously about 10 A. M., when General Corse received a severe wound, was brought off the field, and the command of the brigade and of the assault at that key-point devolved on that fine young, gallant officer, Colonel Walcutt, of the Forty-sixth Ohio, who fulfilled his part manfully. He continued the contest, pressing forward at all points. Colonel Loomis had made good progress to the right, and about 2 P. M. General John E. Smith, judging the battle to be most severe on the hill, and being required to support General Ewing, ordered up Colonel Raum's and General Mathias's brigades across the field to the summit that was being fought for. They moved up under a heavy fire of cannon and musketry, and joined Colonel Walcutt; but the crest was so narrow that they necessarily occupied the west face of the hill.

"It was Not So."

The enemy, at the time being massed in great strength in the tunnel gorge, moved a large force under cover of the ground and the thick bushes, and suddenly appeared on the right rear of this command. The suddenness of the attack disconcerted the men, exposed as they were in the open field; they fell back in some disorder to the lower edge of the field and re-formed. These two brigades were in the nature of supports, and did not constitute a part of the real attack. The movement, seen from Chattanooga (five miles off) with spy-glasses, gave rise to the report, which even General Meigs has repeated, that we were repulsed on the left. It was *not so*. The real attacking columns of General Corse, Colonel Loomis, and General Smith were not repulsed. They engaged in a close struggle all day persistently, stubbornly, and well. When the two reserve brigades of General John E. Smith fell back as described, the enemy made a show of pursuit, but were in their turn caught in flank by the well-directed fire of our brigade on the wooded crest, and hastily sought cover behind the hill.

Thus matters stood about 3 P. M. The day was bright and clear, and the amphitheatre of Chattanooga lay in beauty at our feet. I had watched for the attack of General Thomas "*early in the day.*"

Column after column of the enemy was streaming toward me; gun after gun poured its concentric shot on us from every hill and spur that gave a view of any part of the ground held by us. An occasional shot from Fort Wood and Orchard Knob, and some musketry-fire and artillery over about Lookout Mountain, was all that I could detect on our side; but about

3 P. M. I noticed the white line of musketry-fire in front of Orchard Knoll, extending farther and farther right and left and on. We could only hear a faint echo of sound, but enough was seen to satisfy me that General Thomas was at last moving on the *centre*. I knew that our attack had drawn vast masses of the enemy to our flank, and felt sure of the result. Some guns which had been firing on us all day were silent or were turned in a different direction.

The Victory Won.

The advancing line of musketry-fire from Orchard Knoll disappeared to us behind a spur of the hill, and could no longer be seen; and it was not until night closed in that I knew that the troops in Chattanooga had swept across Missionary Ridge and broken the enemy's centre. Of course the victory was won, and pursuit was the next step.

I ordered General Morgan L. Smith to feel to the tunnel, and it was found vacant, save by the dead and wounded of our own and the enemy commingled. The reserve of General Jeff. C. Davis was ordered to march at once by the pontoon-bridge across Chickamauga Creek at its mouth and push forward for the dépôt.

General Howard had reported to me in the early part of the day with the remainder of his army corps (the Eleventh), and had been posted to connect my left with Chickamauga Creek. He was ordered to repair an old broken bridge about two miles up the Chickamauga, and to follow General Davis at 4 A. M., and the Fifteenth army corps was ordered to follow at daylight. But General Howard found that to repair the bridge was more of a task than was at first supposed, and we were all compelled to cross the Chickamauga on the new pontoon-bridge at its mouth.

By about 11 A. M. General Jeff. C. Davis's division reached the dépôt just in time to see it in flames. He found the enemy occupying two hills, partially intrenched, just beyond the dépôt. These he soon drove away. The dépôt presented a scene of desolation that war alone exhibits—corn-meal and corn in huge burning piles, broken wagons, abandoned caissons, two thirty-pounder rifled guns with carriages burned, pieces of pontoons, balks and chesses, etc., destined doubtless for the famous invasion of Kentucky, and all manner of things burning and broken. Still, the enemy kindly left us a good supply of forage for our horses, and meal, beans, etc. for our men.

Hot Pursuit.

Pausing but a short while, we passed on, the road filled with broken wagons and abandoned caissons, till night. Just as the head of the column emerged from a dark, miry swamp we encountered the rear-guard of the retreating enemy. The fight was sharp, but the night closed in so dark that we could not move. General Grant came up to us there. At daylight we resumed the march, and at Graysville, where a good bridge spanned the Chickamauga, we found the corps of General Palmer on the south bank, who informed us that General Hooker was on a road still farther south, and we could hear his guns near Ringgold.

As the roads were filled with all the troops they could possibly accommodate, I turned to the east, to fulfil another part of the general plan—viz. to break up all communication between Bragg and Longstreet.

We had all sorts of rumors as to the latter, but it was manifest that we should interpose a proper force between these two armies. I therefore directed General Howard to move to Parker's Gap, and thence send rapidly a competent force to Red Clay, or the Council-Ground, there to destroy a large section of the railroad which connects Dalton and Cleveland. This work was most successfully and fully accomplished that day. The division of General Jeff. C. Davis was moved close up to Ringgold to assist General Hooker if needed, and the Fifteenth corps was held at Graysville for anything that might turn up.

Tennessee Redeemed.

About noon I had a message from General Hooker, saying he had had a pretty hard fight at the mountain-pass just beyond Ringgold, and he wanted me to come forward to turn the position. He was not aware at the time that Howard, by moving through Parker's Gap toward Red Clay, had already turned it. So I rode forward to Ringgold in person, and found the enemy had already fallen back to Tunnel Hill. He was already out of the valley of the Chickamauga, and on ground whence the waters flow to the Coosa. He was out of Tennessee.

I found General Grant at Ringgold, and, after some explanations as to breaking up the railroad from Ringgold back to the State line as soon as some cars loaded with wounded men could be pushed back to Chickamauga dépôt, I was ordered to move slowly and leisurely back to Chattanooga.

On the following day the Fifteenth corps destroyed absolutely and effectually the railroad from a point halfway between Ringgold and Graysville back to the State line; and General Grant, coming to Graysville, consented that, instead of returning direct to Chattanooga, I might send back all my artillery-wagons and impediments and make a circuit by the north as far as the Hiawassee River.

On the March to Knoxville.

Accordingly, on the morning of November 29th, General Howard moved from Parker's Gap to Cleveland, General Davis by way of McDaniel's Gap, and General Blair, with two divisions of the Fifteenth corps, by way of Julien's Gap, all meeting at Cleveland that night. Here another good break was made in the Dalton and Cleveland road. On the 30th the army moved to Charleston, General Howard approaching so rapidly that the enemy evacuated with haste, leaving the bridge but partially damaged, and five car-loads of flour and provisions on the north bank of the Hiawassee.

This was to have been the limit of our operations. Officers and men had brought no baggage or provisions and the weather was bitter cold. I had already reached the town of Charleston, when General Wilson arrived with a letter from General Grant at Chattanooga informing me that the latest authentic accounts from Knoxville were to the 27th, at which time General Burnside was completely invested, and had provisions only to include the 3d of December; that General Granger had left Chattanooga for Knoxville by the river-road, with a steamboat following him in the river; but he feared that General Granger could not reach Knoxville in time, and ordered me to take command of all troops moving for the relief of Knoxville and hasten to General Burnside. Seven days before we had left our camps on the other side of the Tennessee with two days' rations, without a change of clothing—stripped for the fight, with but a single blanket or coat per man, from myself to the private included.

Of course, we then had no provisions save what we gathered by the road, and were ill supplied for such a march. But we learned that twelve thousand of our fellow-soldiers were beleaguered in the mountain-town of Knoxville, eighty-four miles distant—that they needed relief, and must have it in three days. This was enough, and it had to be done. General Howard that night repaired and planked the railroad-bridge, and at daylight the army passed over the Hiawassee and marched to Athens, fifteen miles. I had supposed rightly that General Granger was about the mouth of the Hiawassee, and had sent him notice of my orders—that General Grant had sent me a copy of his written instructions, which were full and complete, and that he must push for Kingston, near which we would make a junction.

Swift Cavalry Movements.

But by the time I reached Athens I had better studied the geography, and sent him orders, which found him at Decatur, that Kingston was out of our way, that he should send his boat to Kingston, but with his command strike across to Philadelphia, and report to me there. I had but a small force of cavalry, which was, at the time of my receipt of General Grant's orders, scouting over about Benton and Columbus. I left my aide, Major McCoy, at Charleston, to communicate with this cavalry and hurry it forward. It overtook me in the night at Athens.

On the 2d of December the army moved rapidly north toward Loudon, twenty-six miles distant. About 11 A. M. the cavalry passed to the head of the column, was ordered to push to Loudon, and, if possible, to save a pontoon-bridge across the Tennessee held by a brigade of the enemy commanded by General Vaughn. The cavalry moved with such rapidity as to capture every picket; but the brigade of Vaughn had artillery in position, covered by earthworks, and displayed a force too respectable to be carried by a cavalry dash, so that darkness closed in before General Howard's infantry got up. The enemy abandoned the place in the night, destroying the pontoons, running three locomotives and forty-eight cars into the Tennessee River, and abandoned much provision, four guns, and other material, which General Howard took at daylight. But the bridge was gone, and we were forced to turn east and trust to General Burnside's bridge at Knoxville. It was all-important that General Burnside should have notice of our coming, and but one day of the time remained.

Surmounting Obstacles.

Accordingly, at Philadelphia, during the night of the 2d of December, I sent my aide (Major Audenried) forward to Colonel Long, commanding the brigade of cavalry at Loudon, to explain to him how all-important it was that notice of our approach should reach General Burnside within twenty-four hours, ordering him to select the best materials of his command, to start at once, ford the Little Tennessee, and push into Knoxville at whatever cost of life and horse-flesh. Major Audenried was ordered to go along. The distance to be travelled was about forty miles and the roads villainous. Before day they were off, and at daylight the Fifteenth corps was turned from Philadelphia for the Little Tennessee at Morgantown, where my maps represented the river as being very shallow; but it was found too deep for fording, and the water was freezing cold—width two hundred and forty yards, depth from two to five feet; horses could ford, but artillery and men could not. A bridge was indispensable. General Wilson (who accompanied me) undertook to superintend the bridge, and I am under many obligations to him, as I was without an engineer, having sent Captain Jenney back from Graysville to survey our field of battle. We had our pioneers, but only such tools as axes, picks, and spades.

Needless Haste.

General Wilson, working partly with cut wood and partly with square trestles (made of the houses of the late town of Morgantown), progressed apace, and by dark of December 4th troops and animals passed over the bridge, and by daybreak of the 5th the Fifteenth corps (General Blair's) was over, and Generals Granger's and Davis's divisions were ready to pass; but the diagonal bracing was imperfect for want of spikes, and the bridge broke, causing delay. I had ordered General Blair to move out on the Marysville road five miles, there to await notice that General Granger was on a parallel road abreast of him, and in person I was at a house where the roads parted, when a messenger rode up, bringing me a few words from General Burnside to the effect that Colonel Long had arrived at Knoxville with his cavalry, and that all was well with him there; Longstreet still lay before the place, but there were symptoms of his speedy departure.

I felt that I had accomplished the first great step in the problem for the relief of General Burnside's army, but still urged on the work. As soon as the bridge was mended all the troops moved forward. General Howard had marched from Loudon, had found a pretty good ford for his horses and wagons at Davis's, seven miles below Morgantown, and had made an ingenious bridge of the wagons left by General Vaughn at Loudon on which to pass his men. He marched by Unitia and Louisville.

"The Deadly Bullet."

On the night of the 5th all the heads of columns communicated at Marysville, where I met Major Van Buren (of General Burnside's staff), who announced that Longstreet had the night before retreated on the Rutledge, Rogersville, and Bristol road, leading to Virginia; that General Burnside's cavalry was on his heels; and that the general desired to see me in person as soon as I could come to Knoxville. I ordered all the troops to halt and rest, except the two divisions of General Granger, which were ordered to move forward to Little River, and General Granger to report in person to General Burnside for orders. His was the force originally designed to reinforce General Burnside, and it was eminently proper that it should join in the stern-chase after Longstreet.

On the morning of December 6, I rode from Marysville into Knoxville, and met General Burnside. General Granger arrived later in the day. We examined his lines of fortifications, which were a wonderful production for the short time allowed in their selection of ground and construction of work. It seemed to me that they were nearly impregnable. We examined the redoubt named "Sanders," where on the Sunday previous three brigades of the enemy had assaulted and met a bloody repulse. Now, all was peaceful and quiet; but a few hours before the deadly bullet sought its victim all around about that hilly barrier.

Burnside's Statement.

The general explained to me fully and frankly what he had done and what he proposed to do. He asked of me nothing but General Granger's command, and suggested, in view of the large force I had brought from Chattanooga, that I should return with due expedition to the line of the Hiawassee, lest Bragg, reinforced, might take advantage of our absence to resume the offensive. I asked him to reduce this to writing, which he did, and I here introduce it as part of my report:

HEADQUARTERS ARMY OF THE OHIO,
KNOXVILLE, December 7, 1863.

Major-General W. T. SHERMAN, *commanding, etc.:*

GENERAL: I desire to express to you and your command my most hearty thanks and gratitude for your promptness in coming to our relief during the siege of Knoxville, and I am satisfied your approach served to raise the siege. The emergency having passed, I do not deem, for the present, any other portion of your command but the corps of General Granger necessary for operations in this section; and, inasmuch as General Grant has weakened the forces immediately with him in order to relieve us (thereby rendering the position of General Thomas less secure), I deem it advisable that all the troops now here, save those commanded by General Granger, should return at once to within supporting distance of the forces in front of Bragg's army. In behalf of my command I desire again to thank you and your command for the kindness you have done us.

I am, general, very respectfully,
Your obedient servant,
A. E. BURNSIDE,
Major-General commanding.

Accordingly, having seen General Burnside's forces move out of Knoxville in pursuit of Longtreet and General Granger's move in, I put in motion my own command to return. General Howard was ordered to move, *via* Davis's Ford and Sweetwater, to Athens, with a guard forward at Charleston to hold and repair the bridge, which the enemy had retaken after our passage up. General Jeff. C. Davis moved to Columbus, on the Hiawassee, *via* Madisonville, and the two divisions of the Fifteenth corps moved to Tellico Plains, to cover a movement of cavalry across the mountains into Georgia to overtake a wagon-train which had dodged us on our way up, and had escaped by way of Murphy.

Return to Chattanooga.

Subsequently, on a report from General Howard that the enemy held Charleston, I diverted General Ewing's division to Athens, and went in person to Tellico with General Morgan L. Smith's division. By the 9th all our troops were in position, and we held the rich country between the Little Tennessee and the Hiawassee. The cavalry, under Colonel Long, passed the mountain at Tellico, and proceded about seventeen miles beyond Murphy, when Colonel Long, deeming his further pursuit of the wagon-train useless, returned on the 12th to Tellico. I then ordered him and the division of General Morgan L. Smith to move to Charleston, to which point I had previously ordered the corps of General Howard.

Conferring with Grant.

On the 14th of December all of my command in the field lay along the Hiawassee. Having communicated to General Grant the actual state of affairs, I received orders to leave on the line of the Hiawassee all the cavalry, and come to Chattanooga with the rest of my command. I left the brigade of cavalry commanded by Colonel Long, reinforced by the Fifth Ohio Cavalry (Lieutenant-Colonel Heath)—the only cavalry properly belonging to the Fifteenth army corps—at Charleston, and with the remainder moved by easy marches, by Cleveland and Tyner's Dépôt, into Chattanooga, where I received in person from General Grant orders to transfer back to their appropriate commands the corps of General Howard and the division commanded by General Jeff. C. Davis, and to conduct the Fifteenth army corps to its new field of operations.

It will thus appear that we have been constantly in motion since our departure from the Big Black in

Mississippi until the present moment. I have been unable to receive from subordinate commanders the usual full, detailed reports of events, and have, therefore, been compelled to make up this report from my own personal memory; but as soon as possible subordinate reports will be received and duly forwarded.

In reviewing the facts I must do justice to the men of my command for the patience, cheerfulness, and courage which officers and men have displayed throughout in battle, on the march, and in camp. For long periods without regular rations or supplies of any kind, they have marched through mud and over rocks, sometimes barefooted, without a murmur.

Courage even to Rashness.

Without a moment's rest after a march of over four hundred miles, without sleep for three successive nights, we crossed the Tennessee, fought our part of the battle of Chattanooga, pursued the enemy out of Tennessee, and then turned more than a hundred and twenty miles north and compelled Longstreet to raise the siege of Knoxville, which gave so much anxiety to the whole country. It is hard to realize the importance of these events without recalling the memory of the general feeling which pervaded all minds at Chattanooga prior to our arrival. I cannot speak of the Fifteenth army corps without a seeming vanity; but, as I am no longer its commander, I assert that there is no better body of soldiers in America than that. I wish all to feel a just pride in its real honors.

To General Howard and his command, to General

Jeff. C. Davis and his, I am more than usually indebted for the intelligence of commanders and fidelity of commands. The brigade of Colonel Bushbeck, belonging to the Eleventh corps, which was the first to come out of Chattanooga to my flank, fought at the Tunnel Hill, in connection with General Ewing's division, and displayed a courage almost amounting to rashness. Following the enemy almost to the tunnel-gorge, it lost many valuable lives, prominent among them Lieutenant-Colonel Taft, spoken of as a most gallant soldier.

In General Howard throughout I found a polished and Christian gentleman, exhibiting the highest and most chivalric traits of the soldier. General Davis handled his division with artistic skill, more especially at the moment we encountered the enemy's rear-guard near Graysville at nightfall. I must award to this division the credit of the best order during our movement through East Tennessee, when long marches and the necessity of foraging to the right and left gave some reason for disordered ranks.

The Test of Fire.

Inasmuch as exception may be taken to my explanation of the temporary confusion during the battle of Chattanooga of the two brigades of General Mathias and Colonel Raum, I will here state that I saw the whole and attach no blame to any one. Accidents will happen in battle, as elsewhere; and at the point where they so manfully went to relieve the pressure on other parts of our assaulting line, they exposed themselves unconsciously to an enemy vastly superior in force and favored by the shape of the ground. Had that enemy come out on equal terms, those brigades would have shown their mettle, which had been tried more than once before and *stood* the test of fire. They re-formed their ranks and were ready to support General Ewing's division in a very few minutes; and the circumstance would have hardly called for notice on my part had not others reported what was seen from Chattanooga, a distance of nearly five miles, from where could only be seen the troops in the open field in which this affair occurred.

I now subjoin the best report of casualties I am able to compile from the records thus far received, which makes our total loss 1949.

Among the killed were some of our most valuable officers: Colonels Putnam, Ninety-third Illinois; O'Meara, Ninetieth Illinois; and Torrence, Thirtieth Iowa; Lieutenant-Colonel Taft of the Eleventh corps, and Major Bushnell, Thirteenth Illinois.

Among the wounded are Brigadier-Generals Giles A. Corse and Mathias; Colonel Raum; Colonel Waugelin, Twelfth Missouri; Lieutenant-Colonel Partridge, Thirteenth Illinois; Major P. I. Welsh, Fifty-sixth Illinois; and Major Nathan McAlla, Tenth Iowa.

Among the missing is Lieutenant Colonel Archer, Seventeenth Iowa.

My report is already so long that I must forbear mentioning acts of individual merit. These will be recorded in the reports of division commanders, which

I will cheerfully indorse ; but I must say that it is but justice that colonels of regiments, who have so long and so well commanded brigades, as in the following cases, should be commissioned to the grade which they have filled with so much usefulness and credit to the public service: Colonel J. R. Cockerell, Seventieth Ohio; Colonel J. M. Loomis, Twenty-sixth Illinois; Colonel C. C. Walcutt, Forty-sixth Ohio; Colonel J. A. Williamson, Fourth Iowa; Colonel G. B. Raum, Fifty-sixth Illinois ; Colonel J. I. Alexander, Fifty-ninth Indiana.

My personal staff, as usual, have served their country with fidelity and credit to themselves throughout these events, and have received my personal thanks.

Inclosed you will please find a map of that part of the battle-field of Chattanooga fought over by the troops under my command, surveyed and drawn by Captain Jenney, engineer on my staff. I have the honor to be, your obedient servant,

W. T. SHERMAN, *Major-General commanding.*

[General Order No. 68.]

WAR DEPARTMENT, ADJUTANT-GENERAL'S OFFICE,
WASHINGTON, February 21, 1864.

PUBLIC RESOLUTION—No. 12.

Joint Resolution tendering the thanks of Congress to Major-General W. T. Sherman and others.

Be it resolved by the Senate and House of Representatives of the United States of America in Congress as-

sembled, That the thanks of Congress and of the people of the United States are due, and that the same are hereby tendered, to Major-General W. T. Sherman, commander of the Department and Army of the Tennessee, and the officers and soldiers who served under him, for their gallant and arduous services in marching to the relief of the Army of the Cumberland, and for their gallantry and heroism in the battle of Chattanooga, which contributed in a great degree to the success of our armies in that glorious victory.

Approved February 19, 1864.

By order of the Secretary of War:

E. D. TOWNSEND, *Assistant Adjutant-General.*

CHAPTER XIX.

The Great Atlanta Campaign.--Grand Forward Movement.

GENERAL GRANT in an open letter to General Sherman, March 2, 1864, acknowledged his gratitude for the co-operation and skill which had so largely contributed to his own success. Congress also tendered its thanks for his services in the Chattanooga campaign. When Grant was made lieutenant-general, he assigned Sherman to the command of the military Division of the Mississippi, including the Departments of the Ohio, the Tennessee, the Cumberland, and the Arkansas, with temporary headquarters at Nashville. Sherman assumed command March 25.

Two weeks later he received instructions for his movements against Atlanta. Then began the great campaign—the march to the sea—which stands in many respects unrivalled in military history. The story still lives, and will ever live in the memory of all men.

The great campaign in Georgia was undertaken without specific orders. There was opposed to Sherman, Joe Johnston's army, numbering sixty-two thousand men. Grant's instructions to Sherman, given April 4, 1864, embraced only these few words:

"You I propose to move against Johnston's army,

to break it up, and to get into the interior of the enemy's country as far as you can, inflicting all the damage you can against their war-resources. I do not propose to lay down for you a plan of campaign, but simply to lay down the work it is desirable to have done, and leave you free to execute it in your own way. Submit to me, however, as early as you can, your plan of operations."

The task assigned Sherman was a part of Grant's great plan of campaign for 1864. Banks, then at New Orleans, was to move on Mobile, Sherman was to strike the enemy near the heart of the Confederacy, while Grant was to engage Lee in Virginia. Each of the three commanders aimed to act so vigorously on the offensive that it would be impossible for the enemy to concentrate his forces against either.

Pushing Johnston.

Neither Atlanta nor Augusta nor Savannah was the objective of Sherman's army, but the army of Joe Johnston, go where it might. Some words from Sherman's loyal response to his superior are worth quoting:

"That we are now all to act upon a common plan, converging on a common centre, looks like enlightened war. Like yourself, you take the biggest load, and from me you shall have thorough and hearty co-operation. I will not let side issues draw me off from your main plans, in which I am to knock Joseph Johnston and to do as much damage to the resources of the enemy as possible. . . . . If Banks can at the same time carry Mobile and open up the Alabama River, he will in a measure solve the most difficult part of my problem—viz. 'provisions.' But in that I must venture. Georgia has a million of inhabitants. If they can live, we should not starve. If the enemy interrupt our communications, I will be absolved from all obligations to subsist on our own resources, and will feel perfectly justified in taking whatever and wherever we can find. I will inspire my command, if successful, with the feeling that beef and salt are all that is absolutely necessary to life, and that parched corn once fed General Jackson's army on that very ground."

Atlanta Threatened.

Never did an army start upon a great invasion with less impedimenta. Tents there were none, even for the officers, and absolutely nothing was carried except food, clothing, arms, and ammunition. The advance began on May 5th, and the enemy was first encountered at Dalton, strongly intrenched. McPherson's troops flanked them by a sudden surprise and threatened their communications. Johnston abandoned Dalton and fell steadily back, fighting several quite serious engagements as he withdrew. Sherman's superior force of ninety-nine thousand men and two hundred and fifty-four guns could not be safely engaged in a general battle except under strong advantages of position and defences.

Sherman, in thus compelling Johnston to evacuate a position of such extraordinary strength as that of

Dalton, demonstrated his ability to make his way to Atlanta, between which and Dalton no position was likely to be held by the Confederates which might not be as easily turned.

On the morning of the 14th the Confederates were in complete readiness to receive an attack, having spent the previous night in strengthening their already formidable earthworks. General Hardee held their right, General Hood their centre, and General Polk their left. At an early hour skirmishing commenced. A body of infantry with cavalry was sent across the Oostanaula to threaten Calhoun in the rear, farther south on the railroad, by which movement General Sherman hoped to turn Johnston's left, and thus cut off his retreat, but this the nature of the ground rendered impossible.

Deadly Fire.

At noon there was heavy firing along the whole line. About one o'clock an attempt was made by Palmer's corps from the left centre to break the enemy's line and force him from an elevated position in the immediate front. To reach the point aimed at it was necessary to descend the slope of a hill commanded by the enemy's artillery, to ford a stream bordered with a thick growth of bushes and vines, and then to cross a space intersected by ditches and otherwise obstructed.

Under a murderous fire of musketry and artillery the hill was descended and the stream crossed; but the troops, becoming confused among the ditches and

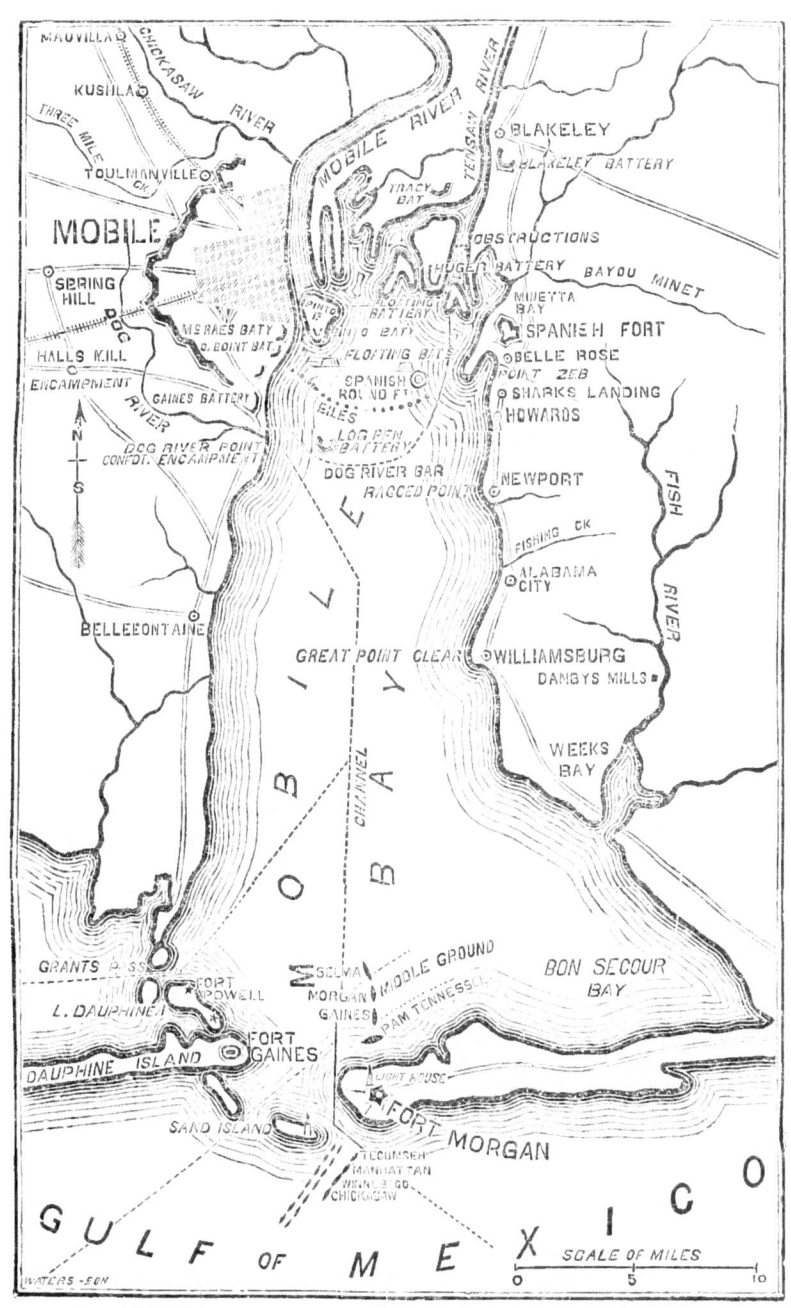

MAP SHOWING THE CITY OF MOBILE AND ITS DEFENCES.

obstructions, and finding no shelter from which the plunging fire of the enemy might be returned, were forced to retire, after losing one thousand of their number. Farther to the left, about the same time, General Judah's division of the Twenty-third corps and Newton's division of the Fourth drove the enemy from an important position on their outer line. By this means, although the position taken was not held, the National line was advanced. Artillery was also got into a position which prevented the enemy from occupying the works. At both extremities of the line heavy skirmishing took place, the density of the woods and undergrowth preventing the use of artillery.

The Gallant Fifteenth.

About three in the afternoon General Johnston massed a heavy force on the road to Tilton, with the view of turning the National left flank, held by Stanley's division of the Fourth corps. The attack was made with overwhelming numbers, who rushed on with loud yells, and with such impetuosity that Stanley's troops were forced in confusion from the hill on which they were posted. The movement ordered by Johnston had been detected early enough to permit of Hooker's corps being moved from the centre to reinforce the National left. The enemy's advance was soon checked, and, Stanley's troops having been rallied, the Confederates were about dusk driven back to their lines with severe loss.

While this movement was going on, General Mc-

Pherson sent the Fifteenth corps, with a portion of the Sixteenth, across Camp Creek, to carry a hill and rifle-pits on the enemy's left in front of Resaca. This was effected, and with loss. As this position commanded the works, the railroad, and the trestle-bridges across the Oostanaula, desperate efforts were made by the enemy after dark to retake it, but in vain. Heavy columns with fixed bayonets moved up to the very crest of the hill, but were compelled to retire in confusion before the steady fire of the National troops. At ten o'clock fighting was over for the day.

"The Troops Rushed in."

Both armies strengthened their positions during the night; and on the morning of the 15th, under cover of severe skirmishing, preparations were made by General Sherman for an assault upon two fortified hills on the enemy's extreme right, the key of the whole position. General Hooker's corps was moved to the extreme left, Howard's, Schofield's, and Palmer's to the right. Soon after one o'clock Hooker sent Butterfield's division forward as the assaulting column, supported by the divisions of Geary and Williams. After several attacks the Confederates were driven from a portion of their lines, and a lodgment was secured under the projecting works of a lunette mounting four guns.

Further advance, however, was found impossible, owing to a severe fire from neighboring rifle-pits, and the troops, seeking such shelter as was available, contented themselves with holding the position gained

Toward the close of the afternoon General Hood's corps made an unavailing effort to dislodge them. Later, under cover of night and in spite of a sharp fire from the Confederates, the ends were dug out of the works and the guns hauled out with ropes. As soon as a breach was made the troops rushed in, and after a fierce struggle made themselves masters of the lunette.

Too Late.

General Johnston abandoned his position during the night, leaving behind another four-gun battery and a quantity of stores, and retreated toward Kingston, thirty-two miles south of Resaca, on the railroad. Resaca was immediately occupied by the troops of General Thomas, who succeeded in saving the wagon-road bridge. The railroad bridge, however, had been burned. Johnston's army owed its escape from Sherman at Resaca to the impracticable nature of the valley between the town and Snake Creek Gap, which greatly retarded the passage of troops, and afforded the Confederate army time to march from Dalton by comparatively good roads, which Johnston with wise foresight had kept in order. Had the National army arrived first at Resaca, nothing could have saved the army of the Confederates.

Once in their strong position at Resaca, it cost much severe fighting to make them abandon it. The total National loss in the two days' fighting was not less than four thousand killed and wounded, while that of the Confederates probably did not exceed two thousand five hundred, as they fought for the most part behind earthworks. The Confederate loss included about one thousand prisoners.

The whole army started in pursuit of Johnston, General Thomas directly on his rear, crossing the Oostanaula at Resaca, General McPherson at Lay's Ferry, a few miles to the south-west, while General Schofield, making a wide détour to the left of Thomas, marched by obscure roads across the Conasauga and Coosawattee rivers, which unite near Resaca to form the Oostanaula. On the 17th the march was continued southward by as many roads as could be found, in a direction parallel with the railroad, but no enemy was seen till within the vicinity of Adairsville, thirteen miles south-west of Resaca, between the railroad and the Oostanaula. There, about sunset, the advance division under General Newton had a sharp skirmish with the enemy's rear-guard. Next morning the Confederates had disappeared, but were found again in force four miles beyond Kingston, on ground comparatively open and well adapted for a grand battle. They held strong works at Cassville, five miles east of Kingston, and on the 19th dispositions were made for a general engagement.

Supplies at Hand.

While, however, Sherman was converging on the Confederate position, Johnston retreated in the night across the Etowah, burning the bridges at Cartersville, thus leaving the country north of the Etowah in the possession of General Sherman. It had, however, been completely stripped of supplies. Sherman now gave his troops a few days' rest, the army of Thomas lying near Cassville, McPherson's about Kingston, and Schofield's at Cassville dépôt and toward the Etowah Bridge. In the mean time, the railroad, which had received but little injury, was restored to running order. Trains laden with supplies arrived at Kingston on the 20th, and the wounded were sent back to Chattanooga, with which place telegraphic communication also was kept up as the army had advanced.

General Jefferson C. Davis had on the 17th marched toward Rome, at the confluence of the Oostanaula and Etowah, fifteen miles west of Kingston. After a sharp fight on the 19th he got possession of the town, several forts, eight or ten large guns, and large quantities of stores, as well as valuable mills and foundries.

Sherman Hurrying Forward.

General Johnston retired upon Allatoona Pass, an almost impregnable position on the railroad, about five miles south of the Etowah River. General Sherman determined not even to attempt the pass in front, but to turn it. Accordingly, on the 23d, leaving garrisons at Rome and Kingston, and carrying with him in wagons supplies for twenty days, he put the army in motion for Dallas, a town about fifteen miles south-south-west of Allatoona Pass and eighteen miles directly west of Marietta, hoping by thus threatening Marietta to compel Johnston to evacuate the pass. The roads through the rugged and densely

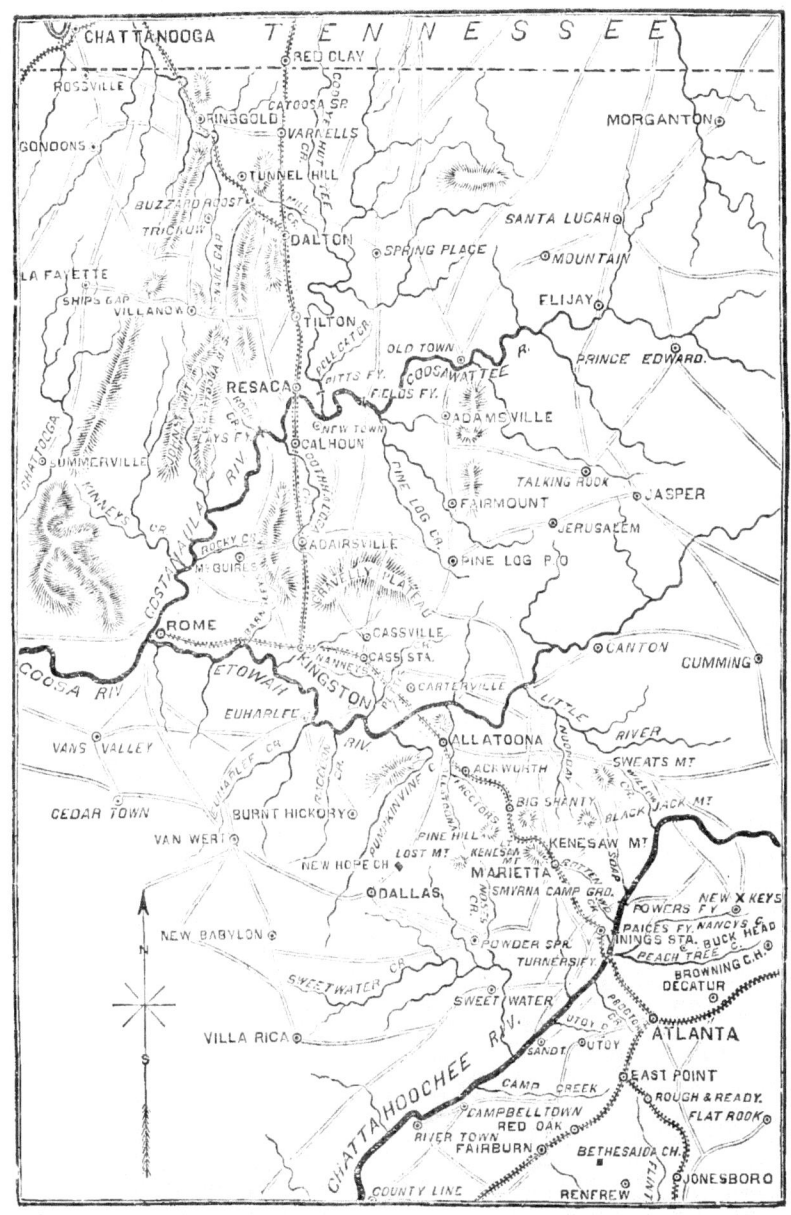

MAP OF COUNTRY BETWEEN CHATTANOOGA, TENN., AND ATLANTA, GA.

wooded region to be traversed were few and bad, and the march was necessarily slow.

The movement and its objects were soon detected by Johnston, who also set his troops in motion toward Dallas to protect the approaches to Marietta. In the march upon Dallas, McPherson, holding the National right, made a détour south-westward by Van Wert, about fourteen miles west of Dallas, while Thomas moved nearly due south, with Schofield on his left. On the 25th, Hooker's corps, the advance of General Thomas, moving on the main road to Dallas, when near Pumpkin Vine Creek met portions of Hood's and Hardee's corps, and a severe contest took place for a position at New Hope Church, where three roads meet from Ackworth, Marietta, and Dallas.

The Enemy Intrenched.

The enemy, however, having hastily thrown up earthworks, and night coming on accompanied by heavy rain, he retained possession of the roads. Hooker lost six hundred men in this affair. Next morning the Confederates were found well intrenched, substantially in front of the road leading from Dallas to Marietta. It was necessary, therefore, to make dispositions on a larger scale. McPherson was moved up to Dallas, Thomas was deployed against New Hope Church, and Schofield moved toward the left, so as to strike and turn the enemy's right.

Owing to the difficult nature of the country, these movements occupied two days and were attended with heavy skirmishing; but as the vicinity was for the most part densely wooded, artillery could not be used, and the casualties were comparatively few. On the 28th, just as McPherson was closing up to Thomas in front of New Hope Church, he was repeatedly and desperately attacked by a large Confederate force, and the contemplated movement was temporarily checked, but the enemy was finally driven back with a loss of two thousand killed and wounded.

The Pass Captured.

After the delay of a few days the movement toward the left was resumed, McPherson taking up the position in front of New Hope Church which Thomas had previously occupied, Thomas and Schofield taking positions still farther to the left. This movement was effected on the 1st of June. All the roads leading back to Allatoona and Ackworth were occupied. General Stoneman's cavalry pushed into the east end of Allatoona Pass, and General Garrard's marched around by the rear to its west entrance. These movements being effected without opposition, the pass fell into Sherman's possession.

Still working toward the left, General Sherman determined on the 4th to leave Johnston in his intrenched position at New Hope Church, and moved toward the railroad above Ackworth, which was reached on the 6th of June.

Between Big Shanty and Marietta intervenes a mountainous district full of defensible positions, covering perfectly the town of Marietta and the railroad as far as the Chattahoochee. Three conical peaks in this region, links in a continuous forest-covered chain, form prominent features in the landscape. These are Kenesaw Mountain, Pine Mountain, and Lost Mountain.

The National lines were gradually advanced toward the Confederate positions. By the 11th the lines were close up, and dispositions were then made to break the enemy's line of defence between Kenesaw and Pine mountains.

Hooker Attacked.

On the 22d the enemy made a sudden attack on portions of Hooker's and Schofield's corps on the National right near the Kulp House. The blow fell mostly on the divisions of Generals Williams and Hascall. The ground was comparatively open; but though the skirmish-lines and an advanced regiment of General Schofield's—sent out to hold the enemy in check until preparations for his reception could be completed—were driven in, yet when the enemy reached the National line of battle he received a terrible repulse. Many prisoners were taken, and the Confederates were compelled to abandon their dead and wounded. The National centre was now established in front of Kenesaw Mountain.

General Sherman determined to assault. His reason for a departure from the course which had hitherto been so successful was, that an army to be efficient must not settle down to one single mode of offence, but must be prepared to execute any plan likely to result in success. The part of the enemy's lines selected to be assaulted was the left centre. A strong column, if thrust through at that point and pushed on boldly two and a half miles, would reach the railroad below Marietta and cut off the enemy's right and centre from the line of retreat, which could then be overwhelmed and destroyed.

Sherman's Assault.

On the 24th of June, therefore, General Sherman ordered that an assault should be made at two points south of Kenesaw Mountain on the 27th, thus affording three days for preparation and reconnoissance. One of these assaults was to be made near Little Kenesaw by General McPherson's troops, the other about a mile farther south by those of General Thomas.

On the morning of the 27th, at the hour and in the manner prescribed, the assaults were made, but both failed, and many valuable lives were lost, including that of General Harker. At six in the morning Blair's corps, holding the extreme left of McPherson's line, moved on the east side of the mountain, while the corps of Dodge and Logan assaulted the adjoining northern slope. The brunt of the attack was borne by three brigades of Logan's corps, which, pushing impetuously up the hill, scattered the Confederate skirmishers and captured some of their rifle-pits, taking also some prisoners. These troops pressed forward till they arrived at the foot of a precipitous cliff thirty feet high, from which the enemy poured a plunging fire and rolled down huge stones. Here the line retired and fortified on the extreme right. For the second and more important attack portions of the divisions of Newton and Davis were selected. When the signal was given the troops charged up the slope of the mountain in face of a murderous fire from a battery on the summit, penetrated two lines of abattis, carried a line of rifle-pits beyond, and reached the works; but a destructive fire of musketry and artillery from the enemy soon made it necessary to recall the men. General Newton's troops returned to their original line, while the brigade of Davis threw up breastworks between those they had carried and the main line of the enemy. The entire contest lasted little more than an hour, but it cost General Sherman three thousand men in killed and wounded, while the enemy, fighting behind breastworks, suffered little.

General Sherman could not rest long under the imputation of defeat or failure. He almost immediately commenced preparations to turn the enemy's left. The effect was instantaneous. The object of the movement was at once detected by General Johnston, who without further delay prepared to evacuate Kenesaw Mountain and fall back to the Chattahoochee. Simultaneously with McPherson's movement, Johnston's rear-guard abandoned the works which for three weeks had been so resolutely defended, and before dawn on the morning of the 3d the National pickets occupied the crest of Kenesaw.

ATLANTA CAMPAIGN.

General Johnston was obliged to leave his new position by another flank movement, and on the night of the 4th he fell back to the Chattahoochee, which he crossed with the main body of his army, leaving Hardee's corps on the right bank.

The sudden abandonment of his formidable line of defences on the left bank of the river by General Johnston occasioned the utmost dissatisfaction with his conduct of the campaign, especially in Atlanta, where it was expected he would make a stand on the Chattahoochee, which it was argued he could easily do, being in the immediate neighborhood of his supplies. His retreat from the Chattahoochee was the crowning offence with the enemies of this able general, whose inferiority of force had made it impossible to avoid Sherman's outflanking movements, but who had nevertheless kept his army in a compact body with insignificant losses of guns or material of war. His removal was loudly demanded, and on the 17th, in accordance with orders from the Confederate War Department, he turned over his command to General Hood, retaining command of one division.

GEN. JOHN B. HOOD.

The whole of General Sherman's army crossed the Chattahoochee on the 17th, with the exception of Davis's division of the Fourteenth corps, left to watch the railroad-bridge and protect the rear, and preparations were made to move upon Atlanta.

Fighting continued at various points, and in one of the bloody combats the gallant McPherson received his death-wound, devolving the command of the Army of the Tennessee upon General Logan. This was July 22d. Sherman's army sustained an irreparable loss in the death of General McPherson. "He was," said Sherman, "a noble youth, of striking personal appearance, of the highest professional capacity, and with a heart abounding in kindness that drew to him the affections of all men." His body was recovered and carried in the heat of battle to General Sherman, who sent it, in charge of his personal staff, back to Marietta, on its way to his Northern home.

Hood was not long in finding out that the army of Sherman was swinging round toward the Macon railroad, and massed troops in the same direction to oppose the movement. At noon on the 28th the Confederates moved out of Atlanta by the Bell's Ferry road, formed in the open fields behind a rising ground, and advanced in parallel lines directly against the Fifteenth corps, expecting to find it detached and unsupported. Fortunately, Logan's troops had thrown up breastworks, and, though the advance of the Confederate columns was "magnificent," as Sherman, who witnessed it, said, it was only to be followed by a recoil before steady volleys of musketry and incessant discharges of grape and canister. In spite of the efforts of their officers the men broke and fled, and though rallied again and again, at some parts of the line as often as six times, they were, about four o'clock in the afternoon, compelled to retire, with a loss of not less than five thousand. Logan's loss was reported at less than six hundred. Had Davis's division come up at

GENERAL SHERMAN DESTROYING THE MACON RAILROAD.

any time before four o'clock, this complete repulse of the enemy might have been made a disastrous rout. Sherman then began the destruction of the Macon railroad, thus cutting off Hood's supplies.

On the 31st the Confederates moved out of their works at Jonesboro and attacked the position of

Howard, but were steadily and repeatedly repulsed. After a contest of two hours' duration they withdrew, losing in killed, wounded, and captured three thousand men, besides general officers, including Major-General Anderson, mortally wounded. Howard's loss was slight, as his men fought behind breastworks. It was observed on this occasion that the Confederate troops had begun to lose the enthusiasm and dash which had hitherto characterized their attacks.

Hearing the sounds of battle about noon, Sherman renewed his orders to push the other movements on the left and centre. Orders were given for the whole army to move on Jonesboro. The troops advanced to the attack across open fields under a withering artillery and musketry fire. After a desperate fight, which lasted two hours, they drove the Confederates from their works, capturing two four-gun batteries—one of them Loomis's, lost at Chickamauga—some battle flags, and a large number of prisoners, including the greater part of Govan's brigade, with its commander, which had formed part of the celebrated "fighting division" of Cleburne.

Repeated orders were sent, urging the rapid advance of Stanley and Schofield, but the want of roads and the difficult nature of the country prevented their coming up and getting into position for attack before further operations were rendered impracticable by the approach of night. Had they been able to close in upon Hardee a few hours earlier, his entire force would in all probability have been captured. As it

GENERAL SHERMAN AT ATLANTA.

was, Hardee had to evacuate the place during the night and fall back seven miles to Lovejoy's, where he intrenched in a naturally strong position. About two o'clock in the morning the watchers in Sherman's camp heard in the direction of Atlanta, about twenty miles distant, the sounds of heavy explosions, followed by a succession of minor reports resembling the rapid firing of cannon and musketry. About four o'clock similar sounds were heard, indicating a night-attack on the city by Slocum, or that Hood was blowing up his magazines and preparing to evacuate. Evidently important events were at hand.

In Atlanta the utmost consternation and excitement had arisen when it became known that the main army of Sherman had got between Hardee's force and the city. Hood immediately gave orders for the evacuation of his works and the removal of as much of the ammunition and stores as was possible with his limited means of transportation, and for the destruction of the rest. Large quantities of provisions in the public store-houses were distributed to the inhabitants and to the troops. The rolling stock of the railroads, consisting of about one hundred cars and six locomotives, was gathered together near the rolling-mill in the evening, by which time all the troops except the rear-guard had got away. The cars were then laden with the surplus ammunition, and, together with the dépôts, store-houses, and all that could be of use to the National army, set on fire about midnight. This occasioned the series of explosions that had been heard in Sherman's camp. Slocum, at the Chattahoochee bridge, also hearing these sounds, sent out early in the morning of the 2d of September a strong reconnoitring column, which, pushing forward without meeting any opposition, arrived at Atlanta about nine o'clock, when the mayor made a formal surrender of the city, only requesting the security of private property and protection for non-combantants, which were readily guaranteed. Sherman's great victory electrified the country. It was a grand military achievement and proved his genius and patriotism.

This success, gained on the 1st of September, 1864, was received throughout the country with great enthusiasm. President Lincoln sent this message of thanks and congratulation:

The national thanks are rendered by the President to Major-General W. T. Sherman and the gallant officers and soldiers of his command before Atlanta for the distinguished ability and perseverance displayed in the campaign in Georgia, which, under divine favor, has resulted in the capture of Atlanta. The marches, battles, sieges, and other military operations that have signalized the campaign must render it famous in the annals of war, and have entitled those who have participated therein to the applause and thanks of the nation.

ABRAHAM LINCOLN,
President of the United States.

General Grant was prompt also in his tribute to

the great exploit, and telegraphed as follows from City Point:

Major-General Sherman:

I have just received your despatch announcing the capture of Atlanta. In honor of your great victory I have ordered a salute to be fired with shotted guns from every battery bearing upon the enemy. The salute will be fired within an hour amid great rejoicing. U. S. Grant,
Lieutenant-General.

CHAPTER XX.

From Atlanta to the Sea.—The Famous March.

It has been a matter of great interest to the American people to obtain the opinion of European generals, men who are considered authority on all military affairs, concerning the relative merits of our commanders who made themselves famous during our sanguinary struggle. By universal consent General Sherman's wonderful march to the sea stands as one of the crowning achievements in the history of modern warfare.

It was unparalleled. No other march can be compared with it, and 'there are good authorities who maintain that it was the boldest, best planned, most important undertaking in our civil war, and one which, being carried to an issue completely successful, stamped the hero of it as the greatest of all our commanders, and one unsurpassed in the annals of war.

In this chapter we favor the reader with General Sherman's own graphic narrative of his famous march to the sea.

The thrilling narrative is as follows:

HEADQUARTERS OF THE MILITARY DIVISION OF THE MISSISSIPPI,
IN THE FIELD, SAVANNAH, GEORGIA, January 1st, 1865.

MAJOR-GENERAL H. W. HALLECK, *Chief of Staff, Washington City, D. C.:*

GENERAL: I have the honor to offer my report of the operations of the armies under my command, since the occupation of Atlanta in the early part of September last up to the present date.

As heretofore reported, in the month of September the Army of the Cumberland, Major-General Thomas commanding, held the city of Atlanta; the Army of the Tennessee, Major-General Howard commanding, was grouped about East Point; and the Army of the Ohio, Major-General Schofield commanding, held Decatur. Many changes occurred in the composition of these armies in consequence of the expiration of the time of service of many of the regiments. The opportunity was given us to consolidate the fragments, reclothe and equip the men, and make preparations for the future campaign. I also availed myself of the occasion to strengthen the garrisons to our rear, to make our communications more secure, and sent Wagner's division of the Fourth corps and Morgan's division of the Fourteenth corps back to Chattanooga, and Corse's division of the Fifteenth corps to Rome. Also a thorough reconnoissance was made of Atlanta, and a new line of works begun, which required a smaller garrison to hold.

During this month the enemy, whom we had left at Lovejoy's Station, moved westward toward the Chattahoochee, taking position facing us, and covering the

LAST TELEGRAM TO THE NORTH BEFORE STARTING ON THE GREAT MARCH

West Point railroad about Palmetto Station. He also threw a pontoon-bridge across the Chattahoochee, and sent cavalry detachments to the woods in the direction of Carrollton and Powder Springs. About the same time President Davis visited Macon and his army at Palmetto, and made harangues referring to an active campaign against us. Hood still remained in command of the Confederate forces, with Cheatham, S. D. Lee, and Stewart commanding his three corps, and Wheeler in command of his cavalry, which had been largely reinforced.

Making Preparations.

My cavalry consisted of two divisions: one was stationed at Decatur, under the command of Brigadier-General Garrard; the other, commanded by Brigadier-General Kilpatrick, was posted near Sandtown, with a pontoon-bridge over the Chattahoochee, from which he could watch any movement of the enemy toward the west.

As soon as I became convinced that the enemy intended to assume the offensive—namely, September 28—I sent Major-General Thomas, second in command, to Nashville, to organize the new troops expected to arrive and to make preliminary preparations to meet such an event.

About the 1st of October some of the enemy's cavalry made their appearance on the west of the Chattahoochee, and one of his infantry corps was reported near Powder Springs, and I received authentic intelligence that the rest of his infantry was crossing to the west of the Chattahoochee. I at once made my orders that Atlanta and the Chattahoochee railroad-bridge should be held by the Twentieth corps, Major-General Slocum, and on the 4th of October put in motion the Fifteenth and Seventeenth corps, and the Fourth, Fourteenth, and Twenty-third corps, to Smyrna camp-ground, and on the 5th moved to the strong position about Kenesaw. The enemy's cavalry had, by a rapid movement, got upon our railroad at Big Shanty and broken the line of telegraph and railroad, and with a division of infantry (French's) had moved against Allatoona, where were stored about a million of rations. Its redoubts were garrisoned by three small regiments under Colonel Tourtellotte, Fourth Minnesota.

The Smoke of Battle.

I had anticipated this movement, and had, by signal and telegraph, ordered General Corse to reinforce that post from Rome.

General Corse had reached Allatoona with a brigade during the night of the 4th, just in time to meet the attack by French's division on the morning of the 5th. In person I reached Kenesaw Mountain about 10 A. M. of the 5th, and could see the smoke of battle and hear the faint sounds of artillery. The distance, eighteen miles, was too great for me to make in time to share in the battle, but I directed the Twenty-third corps, Brigadier-General Cox commanding, to move rapidly from the base of Kenesaw due west, aiming to reach the road from Allatoona to Dallas, threatening the rear of the forces attacking Allatoona. I succeeded in getting a signal message to General Corse during his fight, notifying him of my presence. The defence of Allatoona by General Corse was admirably conducted, and the enemy repulsed with heavy slaughter. His description of the defence is so graphic that it leaves nothing for me to add, and the movement of General Cox had the desired effect of causing the withdrawal of French's division rapidly in the direction of Dallas.

Strategic Movements.

On the 6th and 7th I pushed my cavalry well toward Burnt Hickory and Dallas, and discovered that the enemy had moved westward, and inferred that he would attempt to break our railroad again in the neighborhood of Kingston. Accordingly, on the morning of the 8th I put the army in motion through Allatoona Pass to Kingston, reaching that point on the 10th. There I learned that the enemy had feigned on Rome, and was passing the Coosa River on a pontoon-bridge about eleven miles below Rome. I therefore on the 11th moved to Rome, and pushed Garrard's cavalry and the Twenty-third corps, under General Cox, across the Oostanaula, to threaten the flanks of the enemy passing north. Garrard's cavalry drove a cavalry brigade of the enemy to and beyond the Narrows, leading into the valley of the Chattooga, capturing two field-pieces and taking some prisoners.

The enemy had moved with great rapidity, and made his appearance at Resaca, and Hood had in person demanded its surrender. I had from Kingston reinforced Resaca by two regiments of the Army of the Tennessee. I at first intended to move the army into the Chattooga Valley, to interpose between the enemy and his line of retreat down the Coosa, but feared that General Hood would in that event turn eastward by Spring Place and down the Federal road, and therefore moved against him at Resaca. Colonel Weaver at Resaca, afterward reinforced by General Raum's brigade, had repulsed the enemy from Resaca, but he had succeeded in breaking the railroad from Tilton to Dalton, and as far north as the tunnel.

Arriving at Resaca on the evening of the 14th, I determined to strike Hood in flank or force him to battle, and directed the Army of the Tennessee, General Howard, to move to Snake Tree Gap, which was held by the enemy, while General Stanley, with the Fourth and Fourteenth corps, moved by Tilton across the mountains to the rear of Snake Creek Gap, in the neighborhood of Villanow.

The Army of the Tennessee found the enemy occupying our old lines in the Snake Creek Gap, and on the 15th skirmished for the purpose of holding him there until Stanley could get to his rear. But the enemy gave way about noon, and was followed through the gap, escaping before General Stanley had reached the farther end of the pass. The next day, the 16th, the armies moved directly toward La Fayette with a view to cut off Hood's retreat. We found him intrenched in Ship's Gap, but the leading division (Wood's) of the Fifteenth corps rapidly carried the advanced posts held by two companies of a South Carolina regiment, making them prisoners. The remaining eight companies escaped to the main body near La Fayette.

Hood's Rapid March.

The next morning we passed over into the valley of the Chattooga, the Army of the Tennessee moving in pursuit by La Fayette and Alpine toward Blue Pond; the Army of the Cumberland by Summerville and Melville post-office to Gaylesville; and the Army of the Ohio and Garrard's cavalry from Villanow, Dirttown Valley, and Gooer's Gap to Gaylesville. Hood, however, was little encumbered with trains and marched with great rapidity, and had succeeded in getting into the narrow gorge formed by the Lookout Range abutting against the Coosa River in the neighborhood of Gadsden. He evidently wanted to avoid a fight.

On the 19th all the armies were grouped about Gaylesville, in the rich valley of the Chattooga, abounding in corn and meat, and I determined to pause in my pursuit of the enemy, to watch his movements, and live on the country. I hoped that Hood would turn toward Guntersville and Bridgeport. The Army of the Tennessee was posted near Little River, with instructions to feel forward in support of the cavalry, which was ordered to watch Hood in the neighborhood of Will's Valley, and to give me the earliest notice possible of his turning northward. The Army of the Ohio was posted at Cedar Bluff, with orders to lay a pontoon across the Coosa, and to feel forward to Centre and down in the direction of Blue Mountain. The Army of the Cumberland was held in reserve at Gaylesville, and all the troops were instructed to draw heavily for supplies from the surrounding country. In the mean time, communications were opened to Rome, and a heavy force set to work in repairing the damages done to our railroads. Atlanta was abundantly supplied with provisions, but forage was scarce, and General Slocum was instructed to send strong foraging-parties out in the direction of South River and collect all the corn and fodder possible, and to put his own trains in good condition for further service.

A Wary Foe.

Hood's movements and strategy had demonstrated that he had an army capable of endangering at all times my communications, but unable to meet me in open fight. To follow him would simply amount to being decoyed away from Georgia, with little prospect of overtaking and overwhelming him. To remain on the defensive would have been bad policy for an army of so great value as the one I then commanded, and I was forced to adopt a course more fruitful in results than the naked one of following him to the South-west. I had previously submitted to the commander-in-chief a general plan, which amounted substantially to the destruction of Atlanta and the railroad back to Chattanooga, and, sallying forth from Atlanta through the heart of Georgia, to capture one or more of the great

Atlantic seaports. This I renewed from Gaylesville, modified somewhat by the change of events.

On the 26th of October, satisfied that Hood had moved westward from Gadsden across Sand Mountain, I detached the Fourth corps, Major-General Stanley, and ordered him to proceed to Chattanooga and report to Major-General Thomas at Nashville.

Subsequently, on the 30th of October, I also detached the Twenty-third corps, Major-General Schofield, with the same destination, and delegated to Major-General Thomas full power over all the troops subject to my command, except the four corps with which I designed to move into Georgia. This gave him the two divisions under A. J. Smith, then in Missouri, but *en route* for Tennessee, the two corps named, and all the garrisons in Tennessee, as also all the cavalry of my military division, except one division under Brigadier-General Kilpatrick, who was ordered to rendezvous at Marietta.

Defence of the Railroad.

Brevet Major-General Wilson had arrived from the Army of the Potomac to assume command of the cavalry of my army, and I despatched him back to Nashville with all dismounted detachments, and orders as rapidly as possible to collect the cavalry serving in Kentucky and Tennessee, to mount, organize, and equip them, and to report to Major-General Thomas for duty. These forces I judged would enable General Thomas to defend the railroad from Chattanooga back, including Nashville and Decatur, and give him an army with which he could successfully cope with Hood should the latter cross the Tennessee northward.

By the 1st of November, Hood's army had moved from Gadsden, and made its appearance in the neighborhood of Decatur, where a feint was made; he then passed on to Tuscumbia and laid a pontoon-bridge opposite Florence. I then began my preparations for the march through Georgia, having received the sanction of the commander-in-chief for carrying into effect my plan, the details of which were explained to all my corps commanders and heads of staff departments, with strict injunctions of secrecy. I had also communicated full details to General Thomas, and had informed him I would not leave the neighborhood of Kingston until he felt perfectly confident that he was entirely prepared to cope with Hood should he carry into effect his threatened invasion of Tennessee and Kentucky. I estimated Hood's force at thirty-five thousand infantry and ten thousand cavalry.

Crippling the Enemy.

I moved the Army of the Tennessee by slow and easy marches on the south of the Coosa back to the neighborhood of the Smyrna camp-ground, and the Fourteenth corps, General Jeff. C. Davis, to Kingston, whither I repaired in person on the 2d of November. From that point I directed all surplus artillery, all baggage not needed for my contemplated march, all the sick and wounded, refugees, etc., to be sent back to Chattanooga; and the Fourteenth corps above-mentioned, with Kilpatrick's cavalry, was put in the most efficient condition possible for a long and difficult march. This operation consumed the time until the 11th of November, when, everything being ready, I ordered General Corse, who still remained at Rome, to destroy the bridges there, all foundries, mills, shops, warehouses, or other property that could be useful to an enemy, and to move to Kingston.

At the same time the railroad in and about Atlanta and between the Etowah and the Chattahoochee was ordered to be utterly destroyed. The garrisons from Kingston northward were also ordered to draw back to Chattanooga, taking with them all public property and all railroad stock, and to take up the rails from Resaca back, saving them, ready to be replaced whenever future interests should demand.

The railroad between the Etowah and the Oostanaula was left untouched, because I thought it more than probable that we would find it necessary to reoccupy the country as far forward as the line of the Etowah.

Atlanta itself is only of strategic value as long as it is a railroad-centre; and as all the railroads leading to it are destroyed, as well as all its foundries, machine-shops, warehouses, dépôts, etc., etc., it is of no more value than any other point in Northern Georgia; whereas the line of the Etowah, by reason of its rivers and natural features, possesses an importance which will always continue. From it all parts of Georgia and Alabama can be reached by armies marching with trains down the Coosa or the Chattahoochee Valley.

All Communication Cut Off.

On the 12th of November my army stood detached and cut off from all communication with the rear. It was composed of four corps: the Fifteenth and Seventeenth, constituting the right wing, under Major-General O. O. Howard; the Fourteenth and Twentieth corps, constituting the left wing, under Major-General H. W. Slocum—of an aggregate strength of sixty thousand infantry; one cavalry division, in aggregate strength five thousand five hundred, under Brigadier-General Judson Kilpatrick; and the artillery reduced to the minimum, one gun per one thousand men.

The whole force was moved rapidly, and grouped about Atlanta on the 14th of November.

In the mean time, Captain O. M. Poe had thoroughly destroyed Atlanta, save its mere dwelling-houses and churches, and the right wing, with General Kilpatrick's cavalry, was put in motion in the direction of Jonesboro and McDonough, with orders to make a strong feint on Macon, to cross the Ocmulgee about Planters' Mills, and rendezvous in the neighborhood of Gordon in seven days, exclusive of the day of march. On the same day General Slocum moved with the Twentieth corps by Decatur and Stone Mountain, with orders to tear up the railroad from Social Circle to Madison, to burn the large and important railroad-bridge across the Oconee, east of

Madison, and turn south and reach Milledgeville on the seventh day, exclusive of the day of march. In person I left Atlanta on the 16th, in company with the Fourteenth corps, Brevet Major-General Jeff. C. Davis, by Lithonia, Covington, and Shady Dale, directly on Milledgeville. All the troops were provided with good wagon-trains loaded with ammunition and supplies, approximating twenty days' bread, forty days' sugar and coffee, a double allowance of salt for forty days, and beef cattle equal to forty days' supplies. The wagons were also supplied with about three days' forage in grain. All were instructed by a judicious system of foraging to maintain this order of things as long as possible, living chiefly if not solely upon the country, which I knew to abound in corn, sweet potatoes, and meats.

Atlanta Doomed.

My first object was of course to place my army in the very heart of Georgia, interposing between Macon and Augusta, and obliging the enemy to divide his forces to defend not only those points, but Millen, Savannah, and Charleston. All my calculations were fully realized. During the 22d, General Kilpatrick made a good feint on Macon, driving the enemy within his intrenchments, and then drew back to Griswoldville, where Walcutt's brigade of infantry joined him to cover that flank, while Howard's trains were closing up and his men scattered breaking up railroads. The enemy came out of Macon and attacked Walcutt in position, but was so roughly handled that he never repeated the experiment. On the eighth day after leaving Atlanta—namely, on the 23d—General Slocum occupied Milledgeville and the important bridge across the Oconee there, and Generals Howard and Kilpatrick were in and about Gordon.

Rescuing Prisoners.

General Howard was then ordered to move eastward, destroying the railroad thoroughly in his progress, as far as Tennille Station, opposite Sandersville, and General Slocum to move to Sandersville by two roads. General Kilpatrick was ordered to Milledgeville and thence move rapidly eastward to break the railroad which leads from Millen to Augusta, then to turn upon Millen and rescue our prisoners of war supposed to be confined at that place.

I accompanied the Twentieth corps from Milledgeville to Sandersville, approaching which place on the 25th we found the bridges across Buffalo Creek burned, which delayed us three hours. The next day we entered Sandersville, skirmishing with Wheeler's cavalry, which offered little opposition to the advance of the Twentieth and Fourteenth corps, entering the place almost at the same moment.

General Slocum was then ordered to tear up and destroy the Georgia Central railroad from Station 13 (Tennille) to Station 10, near the crossing of the Ogeechee, one of his corps substantially following the railroad, the other by way of Louisville, in support of

Kilpatrick's cavalry. In person I shifted to the right wing, and accompanied the Seventeenth corps, General Blair, on the south of the railroad till abreast of Station 9½ (Barton)—General Howard in person, with the Fifteenth corps, keeping farther to the right and about one day's march ahead, ready to turn against the flank of any enemy who should oppose our progress.

Gallant Kilpatrick.

At Barton I learned that Kilpatrick's cavalry had reached the Augusta railroad about Waynesboro, where he ascertained that our prisoners had been removed from Millen, and therefore the purpose of rescuing them, upon which we had set our hearts, was an impossibility. But as Wheeler's cavalry had hung around him, and as he had retired to Louisville to meet our infantry, in pursuance of my instructions not to risk battle unless at great advantage, I ordered him to leave his wagons and all encumbrances with the left wing, and, moving in the direction of Augusta if Wheeler gave him an opportunity, to indulge him with all the fighting he wanted. General Kilpatrick, supported by Baird's division of infantry of the Fourteenth corps, again moved in the direction of Waynesboro, and, encountering Wheeler in the neighborhood of Thomas's Station, attacked him in position, driving him from three successive lines of barricades handsomely through Waynesboro and across Brier Creek, the bridges over which he burned, and then, with Baird's division, rejoined the left wing, which in the

MAP SHOWING THE ROUTE TAKEN BY SHERMAN IN HIS MARCH THROUGH GEORGIA.

mean time had been marching by easy stages of ten miles a day in the direction of Lumpkin's Station and Jacksonboro.

The Seventeenth corps took up the destruction of the railroad at the Ogeechee near Station 10, and continued it to Millen, the enemy offering little or no opposition, although preparations had seemingly been made at Millen.

On the 3d of December the Seventeenth corps, which I accompanied, was at Millen; the Fifteenth corps, General Howard, was south of the Ogeechee, opposite Station 7 (Scarboro); the Twentieth corps, General Slocum, on the Augusta railroad, about four miles north of Millen, near Buckhead Church; and the Fourteenth corps, General Jeff. C. Davis, in the neighborhood of Lumpkin's Station, on the Augusta railroad.

Aiming for Savannah.

All were ordered to march in the direction of Savannah, the Fifteenth corps to continue south of the Ogeechee, the Seventeenth to destroy the railroad as far as Ogeechee Church; and four days were allowed to reach the line from Ogeechee Church to the neighborhood of Halley's Ferry on the Savannah River. All the columns reached their destination on time, and continued to march on their several roads— General Davis following the Savannah River road, General Slocum the middle road by way of Springfield, General Blair the railroad, and General Howard still south and west of the Ogeechee, with orders to cross to the east bank opposite "Eden Station," or Station No. 2.

As we approached Savannah the country became more marshy and difficult, and more obstructions were met in the way of felled trees where the roads crossed the creek-swamps on narrow causeways. But our pioneer companies were well organized, and removed these obstructions in an incredibly short time. No opposition from the enemy worth speaking of was encountered until the heads of the columns were within fifteen miles of Savannah, where all the roads leading to the city were obstructed more or less by felled timber, with earthworks and artillery. But these were easily turned and the enemy driven away, so that by the 10th of December the enemy was driven within his lines at Savannah. These followed substantially a swampy creek which empties into the Savannah River about three miles above the city, across to the head of a corresponding stream which empties into the Little Ogeechee.

The City Invested.

These streams were singularly favorable to the enemy as a cover, being very marshy and bordered by rice-fields, which were flooded either by the tide-water or by inland ponds, the gates to which were controlled and covered by his heavy artillery. The only approaches to the city were by five narrow causeways—namely, the two railroads, and the Augusta, the Louisville, and the Ogeechee dirt roads—all of which were commanded by heavy ordnance, too strong for us to fight with our light field-guns. To assault an enemy of unknown strength at such a disadvantage appeared to me unwise, especially as I had so successfully brought my army, almost unscathed, so great a distance, and could surely attain the same result by the operation of time.

I therefore instructed my army commanders to closely invest the city from the north and west, and to reconnoitre well the ground in their fronts respectively, while I gave my personal attention to opening communication with our fleet, which I knew was waiting for us in Tybee, Wassaw, and Ossabaw sounds.

In approaching Savannah, General Slocum struck the Charleston railroad near the bridge, and occupied the river-bank as his left flank, where he had captured two of the enemy's river-boats, and had prevented two others (gunboats) from coming down the river to communicate with the city; while General Howard, by his right flank, had broken the Gulf railroad at Fleming's and Way Station, and occupied the railroad itself down to the Little Ogeechee near Station 1, so that no supplies could reach Savannah by any of its accustomed channels.

Ample Supplies.

We, on the contrary, possessed large herds of cattle, which we had brought along or gathered in the country, and our wagons still contained a reasonable amount of breadstuffs and other necessaries, and the fine rice-crops of the Savannah and Ogeechee rivers furnished to our men and animals a large amount of rice and rice-straw.

We also held the country to the south and west of the Ogeechee as foraging-ground.

Still, communication with the fleet was of vital importance, and I directed General Kilpatrick to cross the Ogeechee by a pontoon-bridge, to reconnoitre Fort McAllister, and to proceed to St. Catharine's Sound in the direction of Sunbury or Kilkenny Bluff, and open communication with the fleet. General Howard had previously, by my direction, sent one of his best scouts down the Ogeechee in a canoe for a like purpose. But more than this was necessary. We wanted the vessels and their contents, and the Ogeechee River, a navigable stream close to the rear of our camps, was the proper avenue of supply.

Quick Work.

The enemy had burned the road-bridge across the Ogeechee, just below the mouth of the Camochee, known as "King's Bridge." This was reconstructed in an incredibly short time in the most substantial manner by the First Missouri Reserves, Fifteenth corps, under the direction of Captain Reese of the Engineer Corps, and on the morning of the 13th December the second division of the Fifteenth corps, under command of Brigadier-General Hazen, crossed the bridge to the west bank of the Ogeechee, and marched down with orders to carry by assault Fort McAllister, a strong inclosed redoubt manned by two companies of artillery and three of infantry, in all about two hundred men, and mounting twenty-three guns *en barbette* and one mortar.

General Hazen reached the vincinity of Fort McAllister about one P. M., deployed his division about the place, with both flanks resting upon the river, posted his skirmishers judiciously behind the trunks of trees whose branches had been used for abattis, and about five P. M. assaulted the place with nine regiments at three points, all of them successfully. I witnessed the assault from a rice-mill on the opposite bank of the river, and can bear testimony to the handsome manner in which it was accomplished.

Up to this time we had not communicated with our fleet. From the signal-station at the rice-mill our officers had looked for two days over the rice-fields and salt marsh in the direction of Ossabaw Sound, but could see nothing of it. But while watching the preparations for the assault on Fort McAllister we discovered in the distance what seemed to be the smoke-stack of a steamer, which became more and more distinct, until at about the very moment of the assault she was plainly visible below the fort, and our signal was answered.

At the Fort.

As soon as I saw our colors fairly planted upon the walls of McAllister, in company with General Howard, I went in a small boat down to the fort, and met General Hazen, who had not yet communicated with the gunboat below, as it was shut out to him by a point of timber. Determined to communicate that night, I got another small boat and a crew, and pulled down the river till I found the tug Dandelion, Captain Williamson, U. S. N., who informed me that Captain Duncan, who had been sent by General Howard, had succeeded in reaching Admiral Dahlgren and General Foster, and that he was expecting them hourly in Ossabaw Sound. After making communications to those officers and a short communication to the War Department, I returned to Fort McAllister that night, and before daylight was overtaken by Major Strong of General Foster's staff, advising me that General Foster had arrived in the Ogeechee near Fort McAllister, and was very anxious to meet me on board his boat. I accordingly returned with him, and met General Foster on board the steamer Nemaha, and, after consultation, determined to proceed with him down the sound, in hopes to meet Admiral Dahlgren. But we did not meet him until we reached Wassaw Sound, about noon. I there went on board the admiral's flag-ship, the Harvest Moon, after having arranged with General Foster to send us from Hilton Head some siege ordnance and some boats suitable for navigating the Ogeechee River.

Admiral Dahlgren very kindly furnished me with all the data concerning his fleet and the numerous forts that guarded the inland channels between the sea and Savannah. I explained to him how completely Savannah was invested at all points save only the plank-road on the South Carolina shore, known as the "Union Causeway," which I thought I could reach from my left flank across the Savannah River. I explained to him that if he would simply engage the attention of the forts along Wilmington Channel at Beaulieu and Rosedew, I thought I could carry the defences of Savannah by assault as soon as the heavy ordnance arrived from Hilton Head.

On the 15th the admiral carried me back to Fort McAllister, whence I returned to our lines in the rear of Savannah.

Surrender Refused.

Having received and carefully considered all the reports of division commanders, I determined to assault the lines of the enemy as soon as my heavy ordnance came from Port Royal, first making a formal demand for surrender. On the 17th a number of thirty-pounder Parrott guns having reached King's Bridge, I proceeded in person to the headquarters of Major-General Slocum on the Augusta road, and despatched thence into Savannah, by flag of truce, a formal demand for the surrender of the place, and on the following day received an answer from General Hardee, refusing to surrender.

In the mean time, further reconnoissances from our left flank had demonstrated that it was impracticable or unwise to push any considerable force across the Savannah River, for the enemy held the river opposite the city with iron-clad gunboats, and could destroy any pontoons laid down by us between Hutchinson's Island and the South Carolina shore, which would isolate any force sent over from that flank.

I therefore ordered General Slocum to get into position the siege-guns and make all the preparations necessary to assault, and to report to me the earliest moment when he could be ready, while I should proceed rapidly round by the right and make arrangements to occupy the Union causeway from the direction of Port Royal. General Foster had already established a division of troops on the peninsula or neck between the Coosahatchie and Tullifinney rivers, at the head of Broad River, from which position he could reach the railroad with his artillery.

Preparing for an Assault.

I went to Port Royal in person and made arrangements to reinforce that command by one or more divisions under a proper officer, to assault and carry the railroad, and thence turn toward Savannah until it occupied the causeway in question. I went on board the admiral's flag-ship, the Harvest Moon, which put to sea the night of the 20th. But the wind was high and increased during the night, so that the pilot judged Ossabaw Bar impassable, and ran into Tybee, whence we proceeded through the inland channels into Wassaw Sound, and thence through Romney Marsh. But the ebb-tide caught the Harvest Moon, and she was unable to make the passage. Admiral Dahlgren took me in his barge, and, pulling in the direction of Vernon River, we met the army-tug Red Legs, bearing a message from my adjutant, Captain Dayton, of that morning, the 21st, to the effect that our troops were in possession of the enemy's lines, and were advancing without opposition into Savannah, the enemy having evacuated the place during the previous night.

Admiral Dahlgren proceeded up the Vernon River in his barge, while I transferred to the tug, in which I proceeded to Fort McAllister, and thence to the rice-mill, and on the morning of the 22d rode into the city of Savannah, already occupied by our troops.

Hardee Escapes.

I was very much disappointed that Hardee had escaped with his garrison, and had to content myself with the material fruits of victory without the cost of life which would have attended a general assault. The substantial results will be more clearly set forth in the tabular statements of heavy ordnance and other public property acquired, and it will suffice here to state that the important city of Savannah, with its valuable harbor and river, was the chief object of the campaign.

With it we acquired all the forts and heavy ordnance in its vicinity, with large stores of ammunition, shot and shells, cotton, rice, and other valuable products of the country. We also gain locomotives and cars, which, though of little use to us in the present condition of the railroads, are a serious loss to the enemy, as well as four steamboats gained, and the loss to the enemy of the iron-clad Savannah, one ram, and three transports blown up or burned by them the night before.

Formal demand having been made for the surrender, and having been refused, I contend that everything within the line of intrenchments belongs to the United States, and I shall not hesitate to use it, if necessary, for public purposes. But, inasmuch as the

SAVANNAH, GEORGIA.

inhabitants generally have manifested a friendly disposition, I shall disturb them as little as possible consistently with the military rights of present and future military commanders, without remitting in the least our just rights as captors.

Our Army in Savannah.

After having made the necessary orders for the disposition of the troops in and about Savannah, I ordered Captain O. M. Poe, chief engineer, to make a thorough examination of the enemy's works in and about Savannah, with a view to making it conform to our future uses. New lines of defences will be built, embracing the city proper, Forts Jackson, Thunderbolt, and Pulaski retained, with slight modifications in their armament and rear defences. All the rest of the enemy's forts will be dismantled and destroyed, and their heavy ordnance transferred to Hilton Head, where it can be more easily guarded.

Our base of supplies will be established in Savannah as soon as the very difficult obstructions placed in the river can be partially removed. These obstructions at present offer a very serious impediment to the commerce of Savannah, consisting of cribwork of logs and timber heavily bolted together and filled with the cobble-stones which formerly paved the streets of Savannah. All the channels below the city were found more or less filled with torpedos, which have been removed by order of Admiral Dahlgren, so that Savannah already fulfils the important part it was designed in our plans for the future.

In thus sketching the course of events connected with this campaign, I have purposely passed lightly over the march from Atlanta to the seashore, because it was made in four or more columns, sometimes at a distance of fifteen or twenty miles from each other, and it was impossible for me to attend but one. I would merely sum up the advantages which I conceive have accrued to us by this march.

Fruits of the Grand March.

Our former labors in North Georgia had demonstrated the truth that no large army, carrying with it the necessary stores and baggage, can overtake and capture an inferior force of the enemy in his own country; therefore no alternative was left me but the one I adopted—namely, to divide my forces, and with the one part act offensively against the enemy's resources, while with the other I should act defensively and invite the enemy to attack, risking the chances of battle.

In this conclusion I have been singularly sustained by the results. General Hood, who, as I have heretofore described, had moved to the westward, near Tuscumbia, with a view to decoy me away from Georgia, finding himself mistaken, was forced to choose either to pursue me or to act offensively against the other part, left in Tennessee. He adopted the latter course, and General Thomas has wisely and well fulfilled his part of the grand scheme in drawing Hood well up into Tennessee until he could concentrate all his own troops, and then turn upon Hood, as he has done, and destroy or fatally cripple his army. That part of my army is so far removed from me that I leave, with perfect confidence, it management and history to General Thomas.

I was thereby left with a well-appointed army to

sever the enemy's only remaining railroad communications eastward and westward for over one hundred miles—namely, the Georgia State railroad, which is broken up from Fairburn Station to Madison and the Oconee, and the Central railroad from Gordon clear to Savannah, with numerous breaks on the latter road from Gordon to Eatonton and from Millen to Augusta, and the Savannah and Gulf railroad. We have also consumed the corn and fodder in the region of country thirty miles on either side of a line from Atlanta to Savannah, as also the sweet potatoes, cattle, hogs, sheep, and poultry, and have carried away more than ten thousand horses and mules, as well as a countless number of their slaves. I estimate the damage done to the State of Georgia and its military resources at one hundred millions of dollars, at least twenty millions of which has inured to our advantage, and the remainder is simple waste and destruction. This may seem a harsh species of warfare, but it brings the sad realities of war home to those who have been directly or indirectly instrumental in involving us in its attendant calamities.

The campaign has also placed this branch of my army in a position from which other great military results may be attempted, besides leaving in Tennessee and North Alabama a force which is amply sufficient to meet all the chances of war in that region of our country.

Since the capture of Atlanta my staff is unchanged, save that General Barry, chief of artillery, has been absent, sick, since our leaving Kingston. Surgeon Moore, United States army, is chief medical director, in place of Surgeon Kittoe, relieved to resume his proper duties as a medical inspector.

Major Hitchcock, A. A. G., has also been added to my staff, and has been of great assistance in the field and office.

Captain Dayton still remains as my adjutant-general. All have, as formerly, fulfilled their parts to my entire satisfaction.

A Splendid Army.

In the body of my army I feel a just pride. Generals Howard and Slocum are gentlemen of singular capacity and intelligence, thorough soldiers and patriots, working day and night, not for themselves, but for their country and their men.

General Kilpatrick, who commanded the cavalry of this army, has handled it with spirit and dash to my entire satisfaction, and kept a superior force of the enemy's cavalry from even approaching our infantry columns or wagon-trains. His report is full and graphic. All the division and brigade commanders merit my personal and official thanks, and I shall spare no efforts to secure them commissions equal to the rank they have exercised so well. As to the rank and file, they seem so full of confidence in themselves that I doubt if they want a compliment from me; but I must do them the justice to say that, whether called on to fight, to march, to wade streams, to make roads, clear out obstructions, build bridges, make "corduroy," or tear up railroads, they have done it with alacrity and a degree of cheerfulness unsurpassed. A little loose in foraging, they "did some things they ought not to have done," yet, on the whole, they have supplied the wants of the army with as little violence as could be expected and as little loss as I calculated. Some of these foraging-parties had encounters with the enemy which would in ordinary times rank as respectable battles.

The behavior of our troops in Savannah has been so manly, so quiet, so perfect, that I take it as the best evidence of discipline and true courage. Never was a hostile city, filled with women and children, occupied by a large army with less disorder, or more system, order, and good government. The same general and generous spirit of confidence and good feeling pervades the army which it has ever afforded me especial pleasure to report on former occasions.

I avail myself of this occasion to express my heartfelt thanks to Admiral Dahlgren and the officers and men of his fleet, as also to General Foster and his command, for the hearty welcome given us on our arrival at the coast, and for their ready and prompt co-operation in all measures tending to the result accomplished.

Your obedient servant,
W. T. SHERMAN, *Major-General*.

President Lincoln's Christmas Present.

When Savannah was evacuated General Sherman sent this brief message to President Lincoln:

"I beg to present to you as a Christmas gift the

city of Savannah, with one hundred and fifty heavy guns, plenty of ammunition, and twenty-five thousand bales of cotton."

To which the President responded:

"Many, many thanks for your Christmas gift—the capture of Savannah. When you were about to leave Atlanta for the Atlantic coast, I was anxious, if not fearful; but feeling that you were the better judge, and remembering that 'nothing risked, nothing gained,' I did not interfere. Now, the undertaking being a success, the honor is all yours, for I believe none of us went farther then to acquiesce. And, taking the work of General Thomas into account, as it should be taken, it is indeed a great success. Not only does it afford the obvious and immediate military advantages, but in showing to the world that your army could be divided, putting the stronger part to an important new service, and yet leaving enough to vanquish the old opposing forces of the whole—Hood's army—it brings those who sat in darkness to see great light. Please make my grateful acknowledgments to your whole army, officers and men."

General Sherman is most famous as the hero of the "march to the sea," but in military importance that movement was of less consequence than his campaigns just before and after. To use his own words: "Were I to express my measure of the relative importance of the march to the sea and of that from Savannah northward, I should place the former at one and the latter at ten or the maximum."

CHAPTER XXI.

Brilliant Campaign of the Carolinas.

Leaving Savannah, General Sherman moved his army northward, and put the finishing strokes upon his magnificent achievements, which were one continuous series of successes from the time he started on his great march toward Atlanta. Following is his interesting account of his campaign through the Carolinas:

> Headquarters of the Military Division of the Mississippi,
> Goldsboro, N. C., April 4, 1865.

General: I must now endeavor to group the events of the past three months connected with the armies under my command, in order that you may have as clear an understanding of the late campaign as the case admits of.

I have heretofore explained how, in the progress of our arms, I was enabled to leave in the West an army under Major-General George H. Thomas of sufficient strength to meet emergencies in that quarter, while in person I conducted another army, composed of the Fourteenth, Fifteenth, Seventeenth, and Twentieth corps and Kilpatrick's division of cavalry, to the Atlantic slope, aiming to approach the grand theatre of war in Virginia by the time the season

CAMPAIGN OF THE CAROLINAS. 451

would admit of military operations in that latitude. The first lodgment on the coast was made at Savannah, strongly fortified and armed, and valuable to us as a good seaport, with its navigable stream inland.

Refitting the Army.

Nearly a month was consumed there in refitting the army and in making the proper disposition of captured property and other local matters; but by the 15th of January I was all ready to resume the march. Preliminary to this, General Howard, commanding the right wing, was ordered to embark his command at Thunderbolt, transport it to Beaufort, South Carolina, and thence by the 15th of January make a lodgment on the Charleston railroad at or near Pocotaligo. This was accomplished punctually, at little cost, by the Seventeenth corps, Major-General Blair, and a dépôt for supplies was established near the mouth of Pocotaligo Creek, with easy water-communication back to Hilton Head.

BRIG.-GEN. A. TERRY.

On the 18th of January I transferred the forts and city of Savannah to Major-General Foster, commanding the Department of the South, imparted to him my plans of operation, and instructed him how to follow my movements inland by occupying in succession the city of Charleston and such other points along the sea-coast as would be of any military value to us. The combined naval and land forces under Admiral Porter and General Terry had, on the 15th of January, captured Fort Fisher and the rebel forts at the mouth of Cape Fear River, giving me an additional point of security on the seacoast. But I had already resolved in my own mind, and had so advised General Grant, that I would undertake at one stride to make Goldsboro, and open communication with the sea by the Newbern railroad, and had ordered Colonel W. W. Wright, superintendent of military railroads, to proceed in advance to Newbern, and to be prepared to extend the railroad out from Newbern to Goldsboro by the 15th of March.

"Forward, March!"

On the 19th of January all preparations were complete, and the orders of march were given. On the 25th a demonstration was made against the Combahee ferry and railroad-bridge across the Salkahatchie, merely to amuse the enemy, who had evidently adopted that river as his defensive line against our supposed *objective*, the city of Charleston. I reconnoitred the line in person, and saw that the heavy rains had swollen the river, so that water stood in the swamps for a breadth of more than a mile at a depth of from one to twenty feet

Not having the remotest intention of approaching Charleston, a comparatively small force was able, by seeming preparations to cross over, to keep in their front a considerable force of the enemy disposed to contest our advance on Charleston. On the 27th I

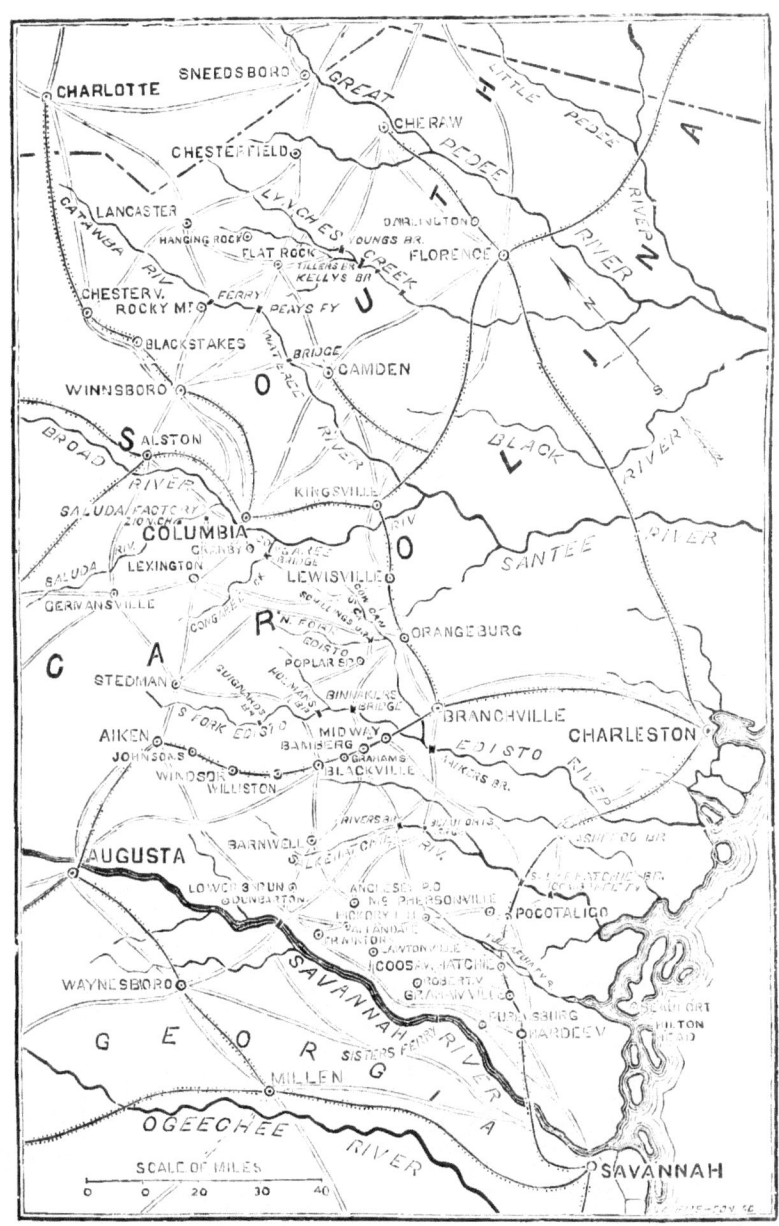

MAP SHOWING THE ROUTE OF SHERMAN'S ARMY THROUGH SOUTH CAROLINA

rode to the camp of General Hatch's division of Foster's command, on the Tullifinney and Coosahatchie rivers, and directed those places to be evacuated, as no longer of any use to us. That division was then moved to Pocotaligo to keep up the feints already begun, until we should, with the right wing, move higher up and cross the Salkahatchie about River's or Broxton's Bridge.

The Seventeenth and Fifteenth corps drew out of camp on the 31st of January, but the real march began on the 1st of February. All the roads northward had for weeks been held by Wheeler's cavalry, who had, by details of negro laborers, felled trees, burned bridges, and made obstructions to impede our march. But so well organized were our pioneer battalions, and so strong and intelligent our men, that obstructions seemed only to quicken their progress. Felled trees were removed and bridges rebuilt by the heads of columns before the rear could close up.

Driving the Enemy.

On the 12th the Seventeenth corps found the enemy intrenched in front of the Orangeburg bridge, but swept him away by a dash, and followed him, forcing him across the bridge, which was partially burned. Behind the bridge was a battery in position, covered by a cotton and earth rampart, with wings as far as could be seen. General Blair held one division (Giles A. Smith's) close up to the Edisto, and moved the other two to a point about two miles below, where he crossed Force's division by a pontoon-bridge, holding Mower's in support. As soon as Force emerged from the swamp the enemy gave ground, and Giles Smith's division gained the bridge, crossed over, and occupied the enemy's parapet. He soon repaired the bridge, and by four P. M. the whole corps was in Orangeburg, and had begun the work of destruction on the railroad. Blair was ordered to destroy this railroad effectually up to Lewisville, and to push the enemy across the Congaree and force him to burn the bridges, which he did on the 14th; and without wasting time or labor on Branchville or Charleston, which I knew the enemy could no longer hold, I turned all the columns straight on Columbia

Early on the morning of February 16th the head of the column reached the bank of the Congaree opposite Columbia, but too late to save the fine bridge which spanned the river at that point. It was burned by the enemy. While waiting for the pontoons to come to the front we could see people running about the streets of Columbia, and occasionally small bodies of cavalry, but no masses. A single gun of Captain De Grass's battery was firing at their cavalry squads, but I checked his firing, limiting him to a few shots at the unfinished State-house walls and a few shells at the railroad dépôt, to scatter the people who were seen carrying away sacks of corn and meal that we needed. There was no white flag or manifestation of surrender. I directed General Howard not to cross directly in front of Columbia, but to cross the Saluda at the factory, three miles above, and afterward Broad River, so as to approach Columbia from the north. Within an hour of the arrival of General Howard's head of column at the river opposite Columbia the head of column of the left wing also appeared.

Capture of Columbia.

In anticipation of the occupation of the city, I had made written orders to General Howard touching the conduct of the troops. These were to destroy absolutely all arsenals and public property not needed for our own use, as well as all railroads, dépôts, and machinery useful in war to an enemy, but to spare all dwellings, colleges, schools, asylums, and harmless private property. I was the first to cross the pontoon-bridge, and in company with General Howard rode into the city. The day was clear, but a perfect tempest of wind was raging. The brigade of Colonel Stone was already in the city, and was properly posted. Citizens and soldiers were on the streets and general good order prevailed.

General Wade Hampton, who commanded the Confederate rear-guard of cavalry, had, in anticipation of our capture of Columbia, ordered that all cotton, public and private, should be moved into the streets and fired, to prevent our making use of it. Bales were piled everywhere, the rope and bagging cut, and tufts of cotton were blown about in the wind, lodged in the trees and against houses, so as to resemble a snow-storm. Some of these piles of cotton were burning, especially one in the very heart of the city near

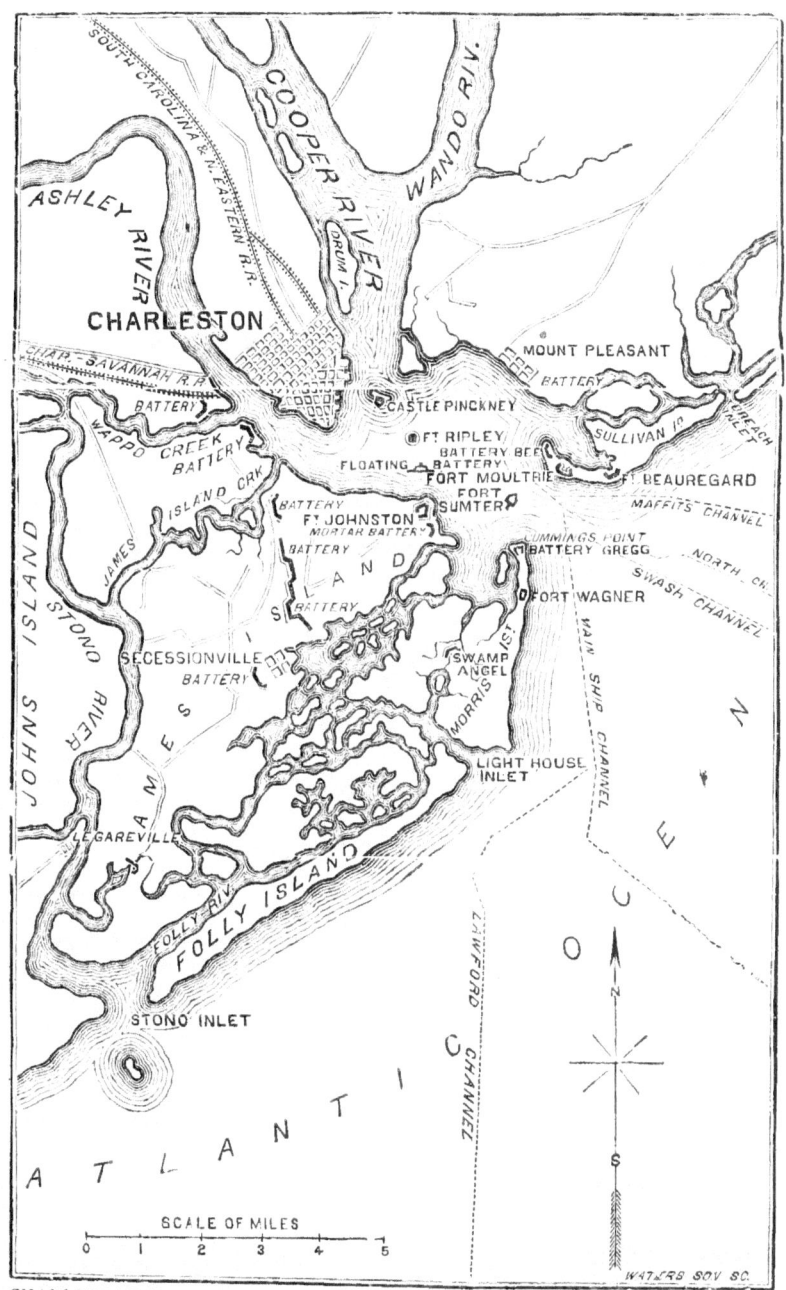

CHARLESTON HARBOR AND ITS APPROACHES, SHOWING FORTS SUMTER AND WAGNER, JAMES ISLAND, Etc., Etc.

the court-house, but the fire was partially subdued by the labor of our soldiers. During the day, the Fifteenth corps passed through Columbia and out on the Camden road. The Seventeenth did not enter the town at all, and the left wing and cavalry did not come within ten miles of the town.

Before one single public building had been fired by order, the smouldering fires set by Hampton's order were rekindled by the wind and communicated to the buildings around. About dark they began to spread, and got beyond the control of the brigade on duty within the city. The whole of Wood's division was brought in, but it was found impossible to check the flames, which by midnight had become unmanageable, and raged until about four A. M., when, the wind subsiding, they were got under control.

The Town Fired by Confederates.

I was up nearly all night, and saw Generals Howard, Logan, Wood, and others laboring to save houses and to protect families thus suddenly deprived of shelter and of bedding and wearing apparel. I disclaim on the part of my army any agency in this fire, but, on the contrary, claim that we saved what of Columbia remains unconsumed. And, without hesitation, I charge General Wade Hampton with having burned his own city of Columbia, not with a malicious intent or as the manifestation of a silly "Roman stoicism," but from folly and want of sense in filling it with lint, cotton, and tinder. Our officers and men on duty worked well to extinguish the flames; but others not

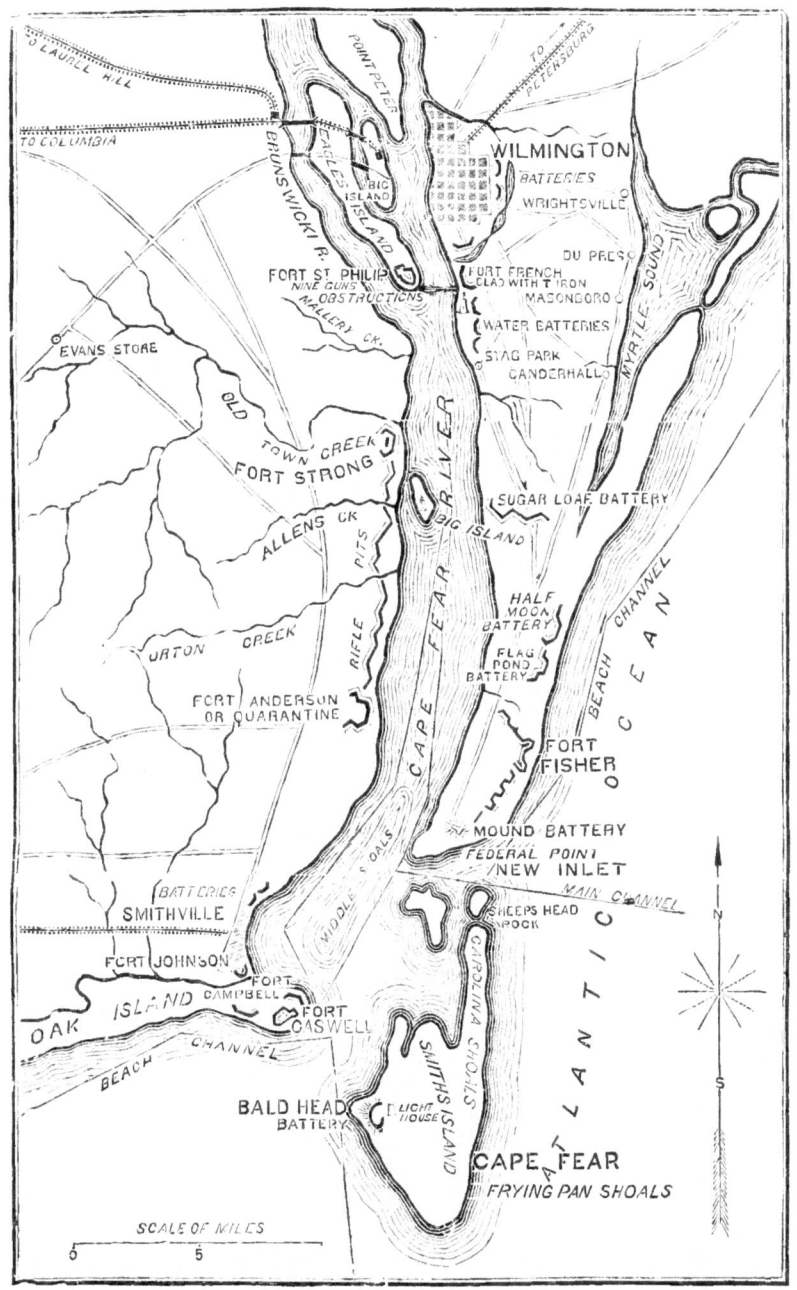

MAP SHOWING THE ENTRANCE TO CAPE FEAR RIVER AND APPROACHES TO WILMINGTON, N. C.

on duty, including the officers who had long been imprisoned there, rescued by us, may have assisted in spreading the fire after it had once begun, and may have indulged in unconcealed joy to see the ruin of the capital of South Carolina. During the 18th and 19th the arsenal, railroad dépôts, machine-shops, foundries, and other buildings were properly destroyed by detailed working-parties, and the railroad track torn up and destroyed to Kingsville and the Wateree bridge and up in the direction of Winnsboro.

Without unnecessary delay the columns were again put in motion, directed on Fayetteville, North Carolina, the right wing crossing the Pedee at Cheraw and the left wing and cavalry at Sneedsboro. General Kilpatrick was ordered to keep well on the left flank, and the Fourteenth corps, moving by Love's Bridge, was given the right to enter and occupy Fayetteville first. The weather continued unfavorable and the roads bad, but the Fourteenth and Seventeenth corps reached Fayetteville on the 11th of March, skirmishing with Wade Hampton's cavalry, that covered the rear of Hardee's retreating army, which, as usual, had crossed Cape Fear River, burning the bridge. During the march from the Pedee, General Kilpatrick had kept his cavalry well on the left and exposed flank.

Hampton's Sudden Attack.

During the night of the 9th March his three brigades were divided to picket the roads. General Hampton, detecting this, dashed in at daylight and gained possession of the camp of Colonel Spencer's brigade and the house in which General Kilpatrick and Colonel Spencer had their quarters. The surprise was complete, but General Kilpatrick quickly succeeded in rallying his men on foot in a swamp near by, and, by a prompt attack, well followed up, regained his artillery, horses, camp, and everything, save some prisoners whom the enemy carried off, leaving their dead on the ground.

The 12th, 13th, and 14th were passed at Fayetteville, destroying absolutely the United States arsenal and the vast amount of machinery which had formerly belonged to the old Harper's Ferry United States arsenal. Every building was knocked down and burned, and every piece of machinery utterly broken up and ruined, by the First regiment Michigan Engineers, under the immediate supervision of Colonel O. M. Poe, chief engineer. Much valuable property of great use to an enemy was here destroyed or cast into the river.

Up to this period I had perfectly succeeded in interposing my superior army between the scattered parts of my enemy. But I was then aware that the fragments that had left Columbia under Beauregard had been reinforced by Cheatham's corps from the West and the garrison of Augusta, and that ample time had been given to move them to my front and flank about Raleigh. Hardee had also succeeded in getting across Cape Fear River ahead of me, and could therefore complete the junction with the other armies of Johnston and Hoke in North Carolina.

Johnston in Front.

And the whole, under the command of the skilful and experienced Joe Johnston, made up an army superior to me in cavalry, and formidable enough in artillery and infantry to justify me in extreme caution in making the last step necessary to complete the march I had undertaken. Previous to reaching Fayetteville, I had despatched to Wilmington from Laurel Hill Church two of our best scouts with intelligence of our position and my general plans. Both of these messengers reached Wilmington, and on the morning of the 12th of March the army-tug Davidson, Captain Ainsworth, reached Fayetteville from Wilmington, bringing me full intelligence of events from the outer world.

All the signs induced me to believe that the enemy would make no further opposition to our progress, and would not attempt to strike us in flank while in motion. I therefore directed Howard to move his right wing by the new Goldsboro road, which goes by way of Falling Creek Church. I also left Slocum and joined Howard's column, with a view to open communications with General Schofield, coming up from Newbern, and Terry from Wilmington. By subsequent reports I learned that General Slocum's head of column had advanced from its camp of March 18th, and first encountered Dibbrell's cavalry, but soon found its progress impeded by infantry and artillery. The enemy attacked his head of column, gaining a temporary advantage, and took three guns and caissons of General Carlin's division, driving the two leading brigades back on the main body. As soon as General Slocum realized that he had in his front the whole Confederate army, he promptly deployed the two divisions of the Fourteenth corps, General Davis, and rapidly brought up on their left the two divisions of the Twentieth corps, General Williams. These he arranged on the defensive, and hastily prepared a line of barricades. General Kilpatrick also came up at the sound of artillery and massed on the left. In this position the left wing received six distinct assaults by the combined forces of Hoke, Hardee, and Cheatham, under the immediate command of General Johnston himself, without giving an inch of ground, and doing good execution on the enemy's ranks, especially with our artillery, the enemy having little or none.

Johnston's Rapid Move.

Johnston had moved by night from Smithfield with great rapidity and without unnecessary wheels, intending to overwhelm my left flank before it could be relieved by its co-operating columns. But he "reckoned without his host." I had expected just such a movement all the way from Fayetteville, and was prepared for it. By four P. M. of the 20th a complete and strong line of battle confronted the enemy in his intrenched position, and General Johnston, instead of catching us in detail, was on the defensive, with Mill Creek and a single bridge to his rear. Nevertheless, we had no object to accomplish by a battle, unless at an advantage, and therefore my general instructions were to press steadily with skirmishers alone, to use artillery pretty strongly on the wooded space held by the enemy, and to feel pretty strongly the flanks of his position, which were, as usual, covered by the endless swamps of this region of country.

Thus matters stood about Bentonville on the 21st of March. On the same day General Schofield entered Goldsboro with little or no opposition, and General Terry had got possession of the Neuse River at Cox's Bridge, ten miles above, with a pontoon-bridge laid and a brigade across; so that the three armies were in actual connection, and the great object of the campaign was accomplished.

BRIG.-GENERAL SCHOFIELD.

On the 21st a steady rain prevailed, during which General Mower's division of the Seventeenth corps, on the extreme right, had worked well to the right around the enemy's flank, and had nearly reached the bridge across Mill Creek, the only line of retreat open to the enemy. Of course there was extreme danger that the enemy would turn on him all his reserves, and, it might be, let go his parapets to overwhelm Mower. Accordingly, I ordered at once a general attack by our skirmish-line from left to right.

Quite a noisy battle ensued, during which General

Mower was enabled to regain his connection with his own corps by moving to his left rear. Still, he had developed a weakness in the enemy's position of which advantage might have been taken; but that night the enemy retreated on Smithfield, leaving his pickets to fall into our hands, with many dead unburied, and wounded in his field hospitals. At daybreak of the 22d pursuit was made two miles beyond Mill Creek, but checked by my order.

MAJOR-GENERAL E. O. OR.

General Johnston had utterly failed in his attempt, and we remained in full possession of the field of battle.

General Slocum reports the losses of the left wing about Bentonville at 9 officers and 145 men killed, 51 officers and 816 men wounded, and 3 officers and 223 men missing, taken prisoners by the enemy; total, 1247. He buried on the field 167 rebel dead and took 338 prisoners.

General Howard reports the losses of the right wing at 2 officers and 35 men killed, 12 officers and 289 men wounded, and 1 officer and 60 men missing; total, 399. He also buried 100 rebel dead and took 1287 prisoners.

The cavalry of Kilpatrick was held in reserve, and lost but few, if any, of which I have no report as yet. Our aggregate loss at Bentonville was 1646.

It was all-important that I should have an interview with the general-in-chief; and, presuming that he could not at this time leave City Point, I left General Schofield in chief command, and proceeded with all expedition by rail to Morehead City, and thence by steamer to City Point, reaching General Grant's headquarters on the evening of the 27th of March. I had the good fortune to meet General Grant, the President, Generals Meade, Ord, and others of the Army of the Potomac, and soon learned the general state of the military world, from which I had been in a great measure cut off since January. Having completed all necessary business, I re-embarked on the navy steamer Bat, Captain Barnes, which Admiral Porter placed at my command, and returned *viâ* Hatteras Inlet and Newbern, reaching my own headquarters in Goldsboro during the night of the 30th. During my absence full supplies of clothing and food had been brought to camp, and all things were working well.

A Crowning Success.

I have thus rapidly sketched the progress of our columns from Savannah to Goldsboro, but for more minute details must refer to the reports of subordinate commanders and of staff officers, which are not yet ready, but will in due season be forwarded and filed with this report. I cannot, even with any degree of precision, recapitulate the vast amount of injury done the enemy or the quantity of guns and materials of war captured and destroyed. In general terms, we have traversed the country from Savannah to Goldsboro, with an average breadth of forty miles, consuming all the forage, cattle, hogs, sheep, poultry, cured meats, corn-meal, etc. The public enemy, instead of drawing supplies from that region to feed his armies, will be compelled to send provisions from other quarters to feed the inhabitants.

Of course, the abandonment to us by the enemy of the whole seacoast from Savannah to Newbern, North Carolina, with its forts, dockyards, gunboats, etc., was a necessary incident to our occupation and destruction of the inland routes of travel and supply; but the real object of this march was to place this army in a position easy of supply, whence it could take an appropriate part in the spring and summer campaign of 1865. This was completely accomplished on the 21st of March by the junction of the three armies and occupation of Goldsboro.

In conclusion, I beg to express in the most emphatic manner my entire satisfaction with the tone and temper of the whole army. Nothing seems to dampen their energy, zeal, or cheerfulness. It is impossible to conceive a march involving more labor and exposure, yet I cannot recall an instance of bad temper by the way or hearing an expression of doubt as to our perfect success in the end. I believe that this cheerfulness and harmony of action reflects upon all concerned quite as much real honor and fame as "battles gained" or "cities won," and I therefore commend all—generals, staff, officers, and men—for these high qualities, in addition to the more soldierly ones of obedience to orders and the alacrity they have always manifested when danger summoned them "to the front." I have the honor to be your obedient servant,

W. T. SHERMAN, *Major-General Commanding.*

MAJOR-GENERAL H. W. HALLECK, *Chief of Staff, Washington City, D. C.*

CHAPTER XXII.

Surrender of Johnston to Sherman.—Capture of Fifty Thousand Men.

THE closing act in General Sherman's superb career was his capture of the entire Confederate army under Johnston. We give the account of it in his own words:

On the 15th day of April, 1865, I was at Raleigh in command of three armies, the Army of the Ohio, the Army of the Cumberland, and the Army of the Tennessee; my enemy was General Joseph E. Johnston of the Confederate Army, who commanded fifty thousand men, retreating along the railroad from Raleigh by Hillsboro, Greensboro, Salisbury, and Charlotte. I commenced pursuit by crossing the curve of that road in the direction of Ashboro and Charlotte; after the head of my column had crossed the Cape Fear River at Aven's Ferry, I received a communication from General Johnston, and answered it, copies of which I most promptly sent to the War Department, with a letter addressed to the Secretary of War, as follows:

"HEADQUARTERS MILITARY DIVISION OF THE MISSISSIPPI,
IN THE FIELD, RALEIGH, N. C., April 15, 1865.

"GENERAL U. S. GRANT AND SECRETARY OF WAR: I send copies of a correspodence to you with General

Johnston, which I think will be followed by terms of capitulation. I will grant the same terms General Grant gave Lee, and be careful not to complicate any points of civil policy. If any cavalry has started toward me, caution them to be prepared to find our work done. It is now raining in torrents, and I shall await General Johnston's reply here, and will prepare to meet him in person at Chapel Hill.

"I have invited Governor Vance to return to Raleigh with the civil officers of his State. I have met ex-Governor Graham, Messrs. Badger, Moore, Holden, and others, all of whom agree that the war is over, and that the States of the South must resume their allegiance, subject to the Constitution and laws of Congress, and must submit to the national arms. This great fact once admitted, the details are of easy arrangement.

"W. T. SHERMAN, *Major-General.*"

I met General Johnston in person at a house five miles from Durham Station, under a flag of truce. After a few preliminary remarks he said to me, since Lee had surrendered his army at Appomattox Courthouse, of which he had just been advised, he looked upon further opposition by him as the greatest possible of crimes; that he wanted to know whether I could make him any general concessions, anything by which he could maintain his hold and control of his army and prevent its scattering, anything to satisfy the great yearning of their people; if so, he thought he could arrange terms satisfactory to both parties. He wanted to embrace the condition and fate of all the armies of the Southern Confederacy to the Rio Grande—to make one job of it, as he termed it.

I asked him what his powers were—whether he could command and control the fate of all the armies to the Rio Grande. He answered that he thought he could obtain the power, but he did not possess it at that moment; he did not know where Mr. Davis was, but he thought if I could give him the time he could find Mr. Breckenridge, whose orders would be obeyed everywhere, and he could pledge to me his personal faith that whatever he undertook to do would be done.

Can Johnston Fill the Contract?

I had had frequent correspondence with the late President of the United States, with the Secretary of War, with General Halleck, and with General Grant, and the general impression left upon my mind was that if a settlement could be made consistent with the Constitution of the United States, the laws of Congress, and the proclamation of the President, they would not only be willing, but pleased, to terminate the war by one single stroke of the pen.

I needed time to finish the railroad from the Neuse bridge up to Raleigh, and thought I could put in four or five days of good time in making repairs to my road, even if I had to send propositions to Washington; I therefore consented to delay twenty-four hours, to enable General Johnston to procure what would satisfy me as to his authority and ability as a military man to do what he undertook to do; I therefore consented to meet him the next day, the 17th, at twelve, noon, at the same place.

We did meet again: after a general interchange of courtesies he remarked that he was then prepared to satisfy me that he could fulfil the terms of our conversation of the day before. He then asked me what I was willing to do; I told him, in the first place, I could not deal with anybody except men recognized by us as "belligerents," because no military man could go beyond that fact. The attorney-general has since so decided, and any man of common sense so understood it before; there was no difference upon that point as to the men and officers composing the Confederate armies. I told him that the President of the United States by a published proclamation had enabled every man in the Southern Confederate army, of the rank of colonel and under, to procure and obtain amnesty by simply taking the oath of allegiance to the United States and agreeing to go to his home and live in peace. The terms of General Grant to General Lee extended the same principles to the officers of the rank of brigadier-general and upward, including the highest officer in the Confederate army—viz. General Lee, the commander-in-chief. I was therefore willing to proceed with him upon the same principles.

No White Slaves.

Then a conversation arose as to what form of government they were to have in the South? Were the States there to be dissevered, and were the people to be denied representation in Congress? Were the people there to be, in the common language of the people of the South, slaves to the people of the

GENERAL ROBERT E. LEE.

North? Of course I said, "No; we desire that you shall regain your position as citizens of the United States, free and equal to us in all respects, and with representation upon the condition of submission to the lawful authority of the United States as defined by the Constitution, the United States courts, and the authorities of the United States supported by those courts." He then remarked to me that General Breckenridge, a major-general in the Confederate army, was near by, and if I had no objection he would like to have him present.

I called his attention to the fact that I had on the day before explained to him that any negotiations between us must be confined to belligerents. He replied that he understood that perfectly. "But," said he, "Breckenridge, whom you do not know, save by public rumor, as Secretary of War, is, in fact, a major-general; I give you my word for that. Have you any objection to his being present as a major-general?" I replied, "I have no objection to any military officer you desire being present as a part of your personal staff." I myself had my own officers near me at call, and was willing to grant what I claimed for myself.

Breckenridge came a stranger to me, whom I had never spoken to in my life, and he joined in the conversation; while that conversation was going on a courier arrived and handed to General Johnston a package of papers; he and Breckenridge sat down and looked over them for some time, and put them away in their pockets; what they were I know not, but one of them was a slip of paper, written, as General Johnston told me, by Mr. Reagan, Postmaster-General of the Southern Confederacy; they seemed to talk about it *sotto voce*, and finally handed it to me;

I glanced over it; it was preceded by a preamble and closed with a few general terms; I rejected it at once.

Important Conference.

We then discussed matters—talked about slavery, talked about everything. There was a universal assent that slavery was as dead as anything could be; that it was one of the issues of the war long since determined; and even General Johnston laughed at the folly of the Confederate Government in raising negro soldiers whereby they gave us all the points of the case. I told them that slavery had been treated by us as a dead institution—first by one class of men from the initiation of the war, and then from the date of the Emancipation Proclamation of President Lincoln, and finally by the assent of all parties.

As to reconstruction, I told them I did not know what the views of the Administration were. Mr. Lincoln up to that time, in letters and by telegrams to me, encouraged me by all the words which could be used in general terms to believe not only in his willingness, but in his desires, that I should make terms with civil authorities, governors, and legislators, even as far back as 1863. It then occurred to me that I might write off some general propositions, meaning little or meaning much according to the construction of parties—what I would term " glittering generalities "—and send them to Washington, which I could do in four days. That would enable the new President to give me a clue to his policy in the important juncture which was then upon us, for the war was over; the highest military authorities of the Southern Confederacy so confessed to me openly, unconcealedly, and repeatedly. I therefore drew up the memorandum (which has been published to the world) for the purpose of referring it to the proper executive authority of the United States, and enabling him to define to me what I might promise, simply to cover the pride of the Southern men, who thereby became subordinate to the laws of the United States, civil and military.

Grim Terms of War.

I made no concessions to General Johnston's army or the troops under his direction and immediate control; and if any concessions were made in those general terms, they were made because I then believed, and now believe, they would have delivered into the hands of the United States the absolute control of every Confederate officer and soldier, all their muster-rolls, and all their arms. It would save us all the incidental expense resulting from the military occupation of that country by provost-marshals, provost-guards, military governors, and all the machinery by which alone military power can reach the people of a civilized country. It would have surrendered to us the armies of Dick Taylor and Kirby Smith, both of them capable of doing infinite mischief to us by exhausting the resources of the whole country upon which we were to depend for the future extinguishment of our debt, forced upon us by their wrongful and rebellious conduct.

I never designed to shelter a human being from any liability incurred in consequence of past acts to the civil tribunals of our country, and I do not believe a fair and manly interpretation of my terms can so construe them, for the words "United States courts," "United States authorities," "limitations of executive power," occur in every paragraph. And if they seemingly yield terms better than the public would desire to be given to the Southern people, if studied closely and well it will be found that there is an absolute submission on their part to the Government of the United States, either through its executive, legislative, or judicial authorities. Every step in the programme of these negotiations was reported punctually, clearly, and fully by the most rapid means of communication that I had.

All the Fruits of Victory.

And yet I neglected not one single precaution necessary to reap the full benefits of my position in case the Government amended, altered, or absolutely annulled those terms. As those matters were necessarily mingled with the military history of the period, I would like at this point to submit to the committee my official report, which has been in the hands of the proper officer, Brigadier-General Rawlings, chief of staff of the army of the United States, since about the 12th instant. It was made by me at Manchester, Va., after I had returned from Savannah, whither I went to open up the Savannah River and reap the fruits of my negotiations with General Johnston, and to give General Wilson's force in the interior a safe and sure base from which he could draw the necessary supply of clothing and food for his command. It was only after I had fulfilled all this that I learned, for the first time, through the public press, that my conduct had been animadverted upon, not only by the Secretary of War, but by General Halleck and the press of the country at large.

I did feel hurt and annoyed that Mr. Stanton coupled with the terms of my memorandum, confided to him, a copy of a telegram to General Grant which he had never sent to me. He knew, on the contrary, that when he was at Savannah I had negotiations with civil parties there, for he was present in my room when those parties were conferring with me, and I wrote him a letter setting forth many points of it, in which I said I aimed to make a split in Jeff. Davis's dominions by segregating Georgia. Those were civil negotiations, and, far from being discouraged from making them, I was encouraged by Secretary Stanton himself to make them.

Righteous Indignation.

By coupling the note to General Grant with my memorandum he gave the world fairly and clearly to infer that I was in possession of it. Now, I was not in possession of it, and I have reason to know that Mr. Stanton knew I was not in possession of it. Next met me General Halleck's telegram, indorsed by Mr. Stanton, in which they publicly avowed an act of perfidy—namely, the violation of my truce, which I had a right to make, and which, by the laws of war and by the laws of Congress, is punishable by death and no other punishment.

Next, they ordered an army to pursue my enemy, who was known to be surrendering to me, in the presence of General Grant himself, their superior officer; and, finally, they sent orders to General Wilson and to General Thomas—my subordinates, acting under me on a plan of the most magnificent scale, admirably executed—to defeat my orders and to thwart the interests of the Government of the United States. I did feel indignant; I do feel indignant. As to my honor, I can protect it. In my letter of the 15th of April I used this language: "I have invited Governor Vance to return to Raleigh, with the civil officers of his State." I did so because President Lincoln had himself encouraged me to a similar course with the governor of Georgia when I was in Atlanta. And here was the opportunity which the Secretary of War should have taken to put me on my guard against making terms with civil authorities, if such were the settled policy of our Government. Had President Lincoln lived, I know he would have sustained me.

After the War.

The foregoing narrative by General Sherman throws a clear light on his action—an action which was disapproved at Washington. He was anxious to stop the flow of blood, and was willing to be magnanimous toward a fallen foe.

Then followed the grand review of the troops in Washington, and on May 30, Sherman took leave of his army in general orders. In the reorganization of the army Grant became general and Sherman lieutenant-general. When Grant became President, Sherman was elevated to the highest military office, which he retained until his retirement in February, 1884.

Appropriately, we may close this part of our volume with Charles De Kay's striking poetical tribute to the brilliant commander, whose achievements went far toward saving the Union at the time of greatest peril:

> Rumble and grumble, ye drums,
>   Shrill be your throat, O pipes!
> Writhe, blood-red flag, in your mourning band,
>   Serpent of harlequin stripes!
>   But, stars in the banner's blue!
>   Smile, for the war-chief true
> Up from the myriad hearts of the land
>   Comes—to your haven comes.
>
> Guns that sullenly boom,
>   Mourn for the master's hand
> Dreadful, uplifting the baton of war
>   While your hurricane shook the land!
>   Marching, marching, battle and raid,
>   Gay and garrulous, unafraid,
> Sherman drove with his brilliant star
>   A dragon of eld to its doom.
>
> Pass, O shade without stain!
>   Sunsets that grimly smile
> Shall paint how your signal flags deploy
>   Battalions, mile on mile—
>   Horsemen and footmen, rank on rank,
>   Sweeping against the foeman's flank,
> Howling full of the strange mad joy
>   Of slaughter and fear to be slain!

BOOK III.

GENERAL SHERMAN'S DEATH AND OBSEQUIES.

CHAPTER XXIII.

Fatal Illness.—The Giant Shorn of his Strength.—Anxiety throughout the Nation.

GENERAL SHERMAN's last illness began on the 10th of February. It was hoped that his iron constitution would stand firmly against the attack, and that the hero of many well-fought battles would not have to surrender yet to death. The strongest man is finally weak; the bravest soul must some time be vanquished; the great general's foe this time was more formidable than ranks bristling with steel. The veteran of hot campaigns had met an enemy too strong to be defeated.

At 1.15 A. M. a messenger left General Sherman's house in New York on the run to the nearest druggist. He carried a message to Senator Sherman, saying, "Papa is much worse." It was signed "SHERMAN."

At 1.20 A. M. R. T. Sherman sent the following despatch to Senator John Sherman, brother of the general: "Papa is very much worse. You had better come."

At a quarter-past eleven Dr. Alexander, through the general's son, handed out the following bulletin, showing the result of a consultation of physicians:

"The result of the consultation of Drs. Alexander and Janeway shows that there has been no improvement in General Sherman's condition.

"DR. ALEXANDER."

All day the battle between death and General Sherman was waged with varying fortune. The bedside of the aged sufferer was surrounded by the members of his family and loving friends, and all that medical science could suggest to ward off the encroachments of the insidious disease which had attacked his face was done.

The chances were against him. It was his second attack of erysipelas, and much more severe than the first one. His many years—he celebrated his seventy-first birthday on the previous Sunday—had weakened his iron constitution, and it was certain that he had little reserve force with which to battle against it. But his brother and his children, remembering how he had come forth victorious from many a forlorn hope before, refused to lose heart or to admit that his case was hopeless, and at noon, as if in answer to their faith, he began to rally from his sinking spell.

Each succeeding hour brought encouraging news

from the sick chamber, and at six o'clock Dr. R. H. Green, who had been at his bedside all the afternoon, said that there was no immediate danger of death. But he held out small hopes of his recovery. Senator Sherman clung to the belief that he would get well, but postponed his intended return to Washington.

Surrounded by his Children.

All of General Sherman's family, with the exception of his son, the Rev. T. E. Sherman, who was studying in the Jesuit institution in the island of Jersey, and who was notified by cable of his father's condition, watched by his bedside. His friend, Dr. and Lieutenant-Colonel Charles T. Alexander of the army, was in constant attendance upon him. Shortly after midnight it was noticed that his condition had changed for the worse and that he was steadily growing weaker His face and neck were badly inflamed, and any motion seemed to be quite painful. But, as a general thing, he did not suffer much. He lay in a state of semi-coma, and could only be roused at long intervals to partake of medicine or nourishment. In his conscious moments he seemed to be aware of the danger of his situation, but he bore his pains and faced the menacing death with the same simple courage which had always marked his strong character. He waited without trepidation for the dread visitor that had often confronted him on the battle-field, and whose coming now had no terrors.

He lay in the front room of his residence, on the

second floor. The shades were drawn tightly down, and no noise was permitted to reach him. A notice at the door warned callers not to ring the bell, and a special attendant was placed there to answer the questions of inquirers, who came in great numbers, and to receive the shoals of telegrams which came from all parts of the country. One of these, from President Harrison, making anxious inquiry, was answered by Mr. P. T. Sherman, but most of them were answered only by the hourly bulletins which were sent out by the doctors or by young Mr. Sherman.

Once in a while the general became slightly delirious, and it seemed as if the disease had attacked the brain, which was the complication to be feared. But he would rally from these attacks and hope would return again.

The Worst Feared.

As the morning wore on the physicians lost courage, intimating that he would not live another twenty-four hours, and declared that there was no possible hope.

"General Sherman is suffering from facial erysipeias," said Dr. Alexander, "coupled with slow fever. It is a simple disease, but difficult to treat, which makes it a dangerous one. It is bad enough for a younger man, who has the strength and vigor to withstand its insidious attack, but the general has not the constitution that he once had. I do not anticipate any crisis in this case, for erysipelas does its work by slowly undermining the strength of the patient until he has none left to do battle with it."

Among the callers at the house who were admitted were General Thomas Ewing, General O. O. Howard, and Lieutenant Treat of his staff.

The reports were discouraging during the morning hours, but about noon their tenor changed and the doctors began to report an improvement. The following bulletins will tell the story of the day:

"11.50—No change for the better. General Sherman continues to grow weaker."

"2 P. M.—General Sherman was worse this morning, and his condition was considered critical. During the day his condition has improved considerably."

"6.15 P. M.—General Sherman's condition has not changed in the least since last bulletin. Still improving, very slowly."

"9 P. M.—General Sherman is resting easily. His family are confident that he will live through the night."

He Knew his Friend.

General Ewing, who left the house at eventide, said that the physicians were feeling much more hopeful, though there had been no decided improvement in his condition. "General Sherman is fully as strong now as he was at six o'clock this morning," he said, "and when he is aroused from his lethargy seems to be entirely intelligent and free from hallucination. He has been in a state of semi-coma for a long time.

"I have been sitting by his bedside for a full hour. His face and neck are much swollen and somewhat inflamed, so that he moves his head with difficulty and pain. I asked the general if he recognized me. He replied, 'Hello, Ewing! is that you?' He appeared to have considerable difficulty in speaking on account of the mucus in his throat and the stiffness of his muscles. I do not apprehend his death to-night."

Thousands of his old friends all over the country were praying for his recovery, but there appeared to be very little hope that the hero who saved Shiloh, and the genius which performed the impossible and marched two thousand miles to the sea against the prognostications of military men the world over, would do more than linger for a few hours or days, at the most, before he laid down his colors to the one enemy who is unconquerable.

President Harrison having telegraphed to New York for information concerning the condition of General Sherman, received a telegram from Mr. P. T. Sherman, saying that his father's condition was critical, but that there was a slight improvement. General Schofield also received a telegram from Mr. Sherman saying, "My father's condition is still critical, but the doctors are hopeful."

Sympathy from the Grand Army.

The State Department, Grand Army of the Republic, in annual session in Boston, sent the following despatch to the daughter of General Sherman: "The Massachusetts Department of the Grand Army of the

Republic, in convention assembled, watches with solicitude the condition of the last of the three great leaders of the Union army, and that he may speedily be restored to health is the earnest desire of his comrades."

The illness of General Sherman was the sole topic in New York and throughout the country. The earlier reports from his bedside suggested the possibility of his recovery from the attack, but later on February 12th bulletins were put up here and there which indicated that his family had really given up hope.

A Touching Scene.

In front of all the bulletin-boards in the city throngs were assembled during the entire day, but perhaps the most suggestive and touching exhibition of the interest in the great general was shown in front of the bulletin which one of the newspapers put up early in the afternoon. That was a bulletin from the son of Sherman, in which it was stated that the family had given up all hope of the general's recovery.

Not many moments after it was put up there came in the throng two persons who stopped and read the bulletin. One of them was a man who leaned heavily upon his cane, whose white hair was shown beneath his tall beaver hat, and whose complexion, swarthy and yet clear and indicating abundant health, was that seemingly of a native of the tropics. This was Hannibal Hamlin, and he was leaning upon the arm of his son, General Hamlin. He was unrecognized by the crowd. He stood for a moment, read the bulletin, and then said: "I am afraid my old friend, General Sherman, has reached the number of his days."

Ex-Vice President Hamlin seemed to be deeply affected. His relations with General Sherman had been most cordial, and in the early part of the war the great general had no stronger friend in the Administration than Mr. Hamlin showed himself to be. Although he was ten years older than Sherman, yet he displayed a vigor which the general had not shown in the last year or two.

The lights and the flitting shadows in the deathchamber of the old warrior, who was slowly passing away, were carefully watched during the entire night by a score of newspaper-men, and every bulletin issued by Drs. Alexander and Janeway was quickly wired all over the continent.

Death Expected.

Two policemen were on duty outside, and everything was kept as quiet as possible in the neighborhood. The electric bell was removed from the door, so that its jingling would not disturb the rest of the sick man, and instructions were given not to admit any one except relatives and personal friends.

The next bulletin said that death was only a question of a few hours. Simultaneously with this came a despatch from P. Tecumseh Sherman, the general's son, and it was addressed to President Harrison, informing him that death was momentarily expected. From then on the house remained in comparative darkness. The solitary policeman silently paced in front of the residence, occasionally answering the queries of passers-by with the stereotyped answer, "Sinking rapidly." When the early morning wagons came rattling down the street a wave of the hand from the officer on duty caused them to slacken their pace, and they crept by in silence, avoiding that noise of wheels on the pavements so disagreeable to sick persons.

The scenes about General Sherman's residence this morning strongly suggested those of six years before, when the death of General Grant was momentarily expected. The newspapers of New York and Brooklyn were represented, some having two or three reporters present. On the street corners were groups of men waiting apparently to get the latest information from the sick-room. Conversation was carried on in whispers, as if fearful of disturbing the dying warrior, though half a block removed from his bedside. Inside the storm-doors of the front entrance a young man scrutinized each card handed in, and none but the most intimate family friends were admitted. All others merely left their cards and withdrew.

CHAPTER XXIV.

Battling with the Foe.—A Gallant Fight for Life.

ALL through the day, Thursday, February 12th, General Sherman was wrestling with an invincible foe. What a battle it was which was waged in the home of the grim old soldier! Death never tackled a tougher adversary. It caught him by the throat and tried to strangle him; it burned in his veins with consuming fire; it stole stealthily into the seat of his intellect. But he met it at every point and wrestled with it mightily. He was like a tough and sturdy oak, swayed but unbroken by the storm.

It was not that the general feared death. It had no terrors to him, with his beloved wife awaiting him on the other side. But he wanted to see Tom before he went. He was determined to shake hands with his first-born, his beloved, who had grown apart from him in his religion, but for whom his heart still beat loyally.

He would not die till Tom came, he had said before his case got desperate, and he set all the powers of his indomitable will to the task of living until the Rev. Father Sherman came across the sea and clasped him in his arms once more. And this resolution never left him, conscious or delirious.

It was that which made him last beyond the expectation of his physicians and turned his case into a marvel.

And "Tom" left Queenstown the day before in a desperate race with death. Could he possibly win? At times it seemed as if he might. It was Sherman that saved the lost battle of Shiloh. It was Sherman that performed the "impossible" march to the sea. A man of miracles, would his unconquerable will hold death itself back when hope itself seemed madness?

It was like Shiloh.

The story of the day—what pen will ever tell it? What a drama it was in the home of the dying soldier! Hope and despair, hope and despair, chased each other in rapid succession across the stage, and each hour had its special expectation. Like fast-fluctuating tides the flickering life changed all the way from a seeming certainty of death within the hour to the semblance of sure recovery. The doctors had disagreed a score of times, and the partial hopes of friends often built high the ramparts of expectation, but the outcome of it all was the edict of the men of science that death was a certainty and only a matter of time.

The fright of the early morning, when all nature was at ebb tide and General Sherman's life-force with it, was succeeded after daybreak by a period of hope. The danger of immediate death grew less patent, and the doctor said that at the worst he would live for several hours. The fever was not so high nor the coma so complete. The brain was still unattacked by inflammation. Could it be possible to avert the catastrophe, after all?

New Danger.

After a time the doctors were able to alter the diet to beef tea, considerable of which was administered with success, and the stimulating and strengthening effects of which were noticeably felt.

But now a new danger was made manifest. Mucus collected upon the lungs, which General Sherman did not have the power to relieve himself of, and there was danger of his choking to death. At times he started up and tried to rise, but his limbs refused their office. The physicians sought in every way to relieve him, but it seemed in vain, and matters were at a desperate stage.

Without the house a guard was constantly in attendance telling each inquirer that hope had almost fled. Sturdy workingmen with their tin buckets paused to ask after the general, and ladies and gentlemen in fine carriages rolled up to the curb and sent in their cards or went in themselves to ask personally how went the tide of battle.

Eleven o'clock, and the tide at its lowest ebb. General Sherman was dying, the doctors said. All hope was gone. He had been unconscious some time. His lungs were full. His face was purple. His breath came in short, quick gasps. Mucus rattled in his throat. The dew of death gathered on his wrinkled forehead as fast as it could be wiped away. Finis seemed written on the seamed face. Only the will remained unconquered. Tom had not come!

Pathetic Scene.

The weeping family were gathered about the bedside. The gentle Rachel had her arms about her father. The Senator stood leaning on the headboard looking into the face of his elder brother. The private secretary, who had been hastily summoned from his vacation, and the grizzled friend, General Tom Ewing, were weeping a little apart. The doctors bent over the knotted form, fighting as stubbornly as the general himself.

But Tom had not come! The old soldier had not yet surrendered. Again he rallied his forces mightily, and the fortunes of war were again in his favor.

A sudden fit of coughing freed his lungs of a large quantity of mucus. He was given a stimulant, and the effect was astonishing. The doctors, who had sent out bulletins to the effect that he could not live another hour, were now putting forth promising bulletins. A despatch was sent to President Harrison by Senator Sherman saying: "The improvement of General Sherman at one o'clock to-day justifies a faint hope that he will recover."

When the doctor left the house he said that nothing but the marvellous vitality of General Sherman kept him alive. All through the afternoon hope lived again, but it was at one o'clock, only two hours after he had seemed to be fairly within the gates of death, that the most marvellous exhibition of General Sherman's will-power was manifested. For some time he had been half sitting up, and striving earnestly to rid himself of the incubus on his lungs. He was conscious, but frequently wandered off into delirium. Now he made a sturdy effort to rise, and, assisted by the doctors, succeeded in walking across the room and sat down in a chair. The exercise seemed to help him, and when he reached his bed again he seemed clearer and more vigorous than he had been for twenty-four hours.

Encouraging News.

News of this wonderful exhibition was given to the newspaper-men by General Horatio C. King, who was greatly elated by it. It was promptly confirmed by Secretary Barrett and General Ewing, who thought it meant recovery. The doctors said no to this, and hinted at fears of pneumonia.

There was a fresh alarm at nightfall, coupled with most alarming bulletins, and carriages rattled up from every direction bringing persons who had been hastily summoned. But the prophets of disaster again reckoned without their host, and at ten o'clock the general was again pronounced out of immdiate danger.

He was resting quite easily, though breathing with difficulty. He was quite conscious and knew those present. He had gotten rid of much of the troublesome mucus. At times he had a bandage over his eyes to shade them from the light. He still appeared

SENATOR JOHN SHERMAN.

to have a good deal of strength and vitality. If he could hold out forty-eight hours longer, the doctors held out hopes of his ultimate recovery. His will was resolute.

Senator John Sherman, who spent the previous night at the house of Mrs. Hoyt, his niece, decided to remain at the Sherman residence.

At eleven o'clock the servants closed the storm-doors and drew down the blinds. Policeman Brown was called to the basement door by Private Secretary Barrett, and requested to hold until morning all telegrams and messages which arrived after midnight, and give the family rest.

On his Feet for a Moment.

At eleven o'clock in the evening the general again demonstrated his extraordinary will-power, according to Lieutenant Fitch, by arising from his bed and walking halfway across the room. He was unable to speak, but appeared to recognize those who were in the room.

When he reached the middle of the floor he stopped and tottered. He was at once supported back to bed, and when he lay down appeared to be very much exhausted.

Early, at twenty-five minutes after five in the morning, the general's son, P. T. Sherman, sent this despatch to the President:

"My father is growing steadily worse. It appears to be only a question of hours. I have given up all hope."

Senator Sherman at one o'clock in the afternoon sent this telegram to President Harrison:

"The improvement of General Sherman at one o'clock to-day justifies a faint hope of his recovery."

The medical bulletin at 8.30 P. M. said: "General Sherman's condition is very critical. He is gradually growing weaker."

Profound sympathy was awakened for the dying hero, and from all parts of the country came messages showing how deeply the nation was moved.

Prayer in Washington.

In the course of the opening prayer on February 12th the chaplain of the United States Senate, referring to General Sherman's illness, said:

"Look in mercy upon Thy servant around whose sick bed so many hearts lovingly gather, and in this time of anxiety give support and grace. Oh, that the peace of God which passeth all understanding may keep his heart and mind as he casts himself upon the mercy of God!

"If it so please Thee, spare this life, so long preserved, sanctify this affliction, and grant that, as we move among the dying and the dead, we may so live that when this mortal life shall end we may enter upon the life that never ends."

Thursday night was a grateful relief to the worn-out family, for the general slept peacefully, and those who had been up all the night before were able to retire and get much-needed rest. He was awakened every hour and given nourishment, which seemed to strengthen him considerably, and about half-past six in the morning he again rose from his bed and sat for a few moments on a chair while a nurse made his bed. At eleven o'clock he again got out of bed, and his attendants had considerable trouble in keeping him in bed, especially as he was suffering somewhat from his long-time enemy—asthma—and was anxious to assume an upright position.

The Father's Heart.

At no time during the day was he delirious, and though his mind was not at all active, it was quite clear and he understood all that was said to him. He seemed to have but one consuming wish, and that was to see Tom. Several times he asked for him and for "Cump," the younger son. There were some things he wished to talk about, but weakness would not permit it.

The house in West Seventy-first street looked peaceful enough at sunrise. All signs of the hurry and disorder which prevailed the day before were absent. At seven o'clock a smiling housemaid came to the door and announced that the general had passed a quiet and restful night. He had taken considerable nourishment and had slept well, and was at that time asleep. The doctors were very much encouraged.

When the tin-pail brigade came and asked its questions, the solitary officer was able to give encouraging news, and many a "Thank God!" was uttered as the questioners turned away.

General Sherman's illness attracted a great deal of interest, and wherever bulletins were posted hundreds of people stopped to learn the latest tidings. So great was the interest throughout the country that the Western Union Telegraph Company found it necessary to send bulletins of his condition to eighteen thousand offices. One did not realize what a popular hero " Uncle Billy " was until his peril showed how universal was the feeling about him.

The first official news of Friday was brought out at eight o'clock by the general's private secretary, whose face wore a hopeful look. He was inclined not to promise too much, but he showed that the hopes entertained were shared in even by the conservative doctors, who had no intention of putting forth any rainbow statements.

No Loss meant a Gain.

At nine o'clock the following bulletin, the first of the day, was issued:

"9 A. M.—After consultation this morning the physicians find that General Sherman has lost nothing during the night."

This was as far as the doctors would go officially, but they admitted privately that no loss meant a gain. The erysipelas had nearly all disappeared, and the great peril now was from pneumonia, which had not developed, but still threatened. If they could keep the patient from going backward until one or two o'clock this morning, they said, there would be substantial basis for hope. There was slight œdema in one of the lungs, but the other was entirely free. He was still somewhat troubled by the accumulation of mucus in one lung, but it was not to the alarming extent as on the day before.

At eleven o'clock Senator Sherman sent the following telegram, which was given to the press in lieu of a bulletin:

"To the Hon. Redfield Proctor, *Secretary of War, Washington, D. C.:*

"Telegram received. General Sherman passed a good night. Asthma, his old disease, his chief trouble. Heart and lungs performing their functions. We are much encouraged and hope for recovery. He has every care which love, sympathy, and human skill can render, for which we all are profoundly grateful."

At twelve M. General Thomas Ewing appeared, and said that for the last fourteen hours the patient's condition had been easy and that he had been resting quietly.

The Crisis Passed.

"We all think," said General Ewing, "that the supreme crisis has been passed." The following bulletin was given out later:

"1.20 P. M.—After a consultation the physicians say there has been no change in General Sherman's condition since this morning."

The afternoon was void of news. The doctors did not put out a bulletin for several hours, and no news was looked upon as equivalent to good news. The early hours of morning were the ones looked for with apprehension. It is then, when all nature seems to be at an ebb, that danger is to be feared. If those hours could be reached and passed in safety and pneumonia kept at bay, the doctors said they could then begin to talk of hope.

The chief danger from erysipelas they declared to be past. The swelling was going down and the action of the muscles was growing more normal. General Sherman was out of pain, and if his strength could be kept up there was a good prospect of recovery.

Kind Inquirers.

There were many callers at the house during the afternoon, but no one save the members of the family were permitted to see the sufferer. Among the telegrams of sympathy or inquiry received were ones from Governor Hill, ex-President Cleveland, and Governor Fitzhugh Lee of Virginia.

Evening brought an increase of fever, and with it an increase of anxiety. It was felt that the steady drain on the resources of the aged man was slowly undermining his vitality, and while no alarming symptoms were developed, all felt that he was slowly growing weaker. The elation which had marked the hours of sunshine disappeared, and the family shut themselves away from the newspaper-men and were chary of information, saying that they cared only to speak in case of a marked change for better or for worse.

The doctors were non-committal and evasive. They could give no good news; they would not advance any further prognostications. The doughty old sufferer had belied their prophecies too many times. At nine o'clock a servant-girl was sent in a hurry to the drug-store. The general had a bad turn, and it looked as if he was sinking.

An Alarming Bulletin.

The doctors were at the bedside. The consultation was the longest which had been held, and the countenances of the physicians showed that the situation was extremely critical. At ten o'clock they issued a bulletin which was truly ominous. It was as follows:

"10 P. M.—After consultation the doctors say there is no change for the better."

A member of the household spoke frankly. "The general is undoubtedly growing weaker," he said, "and this gives the family food for anxiety, for even the most stubborn vitality must yield in time. Yet there is no marked change in his condition. He rests easily and is not troubled by mucus. It is his extreme and growing weakness that causes the chief anxiety."

CHAPTER XXV.

The Struggle Ended.—The Great Warrior's Last Battle.

GENERAL SHERMAN died at ten minutes of two o'clock on Saturday, February 14th, aged seventy-one years and five days.

His end was peaceful—it could not have been more so. He had been totally unconscious all the morning, and had ceased to struggle long before the coming of the end. The immediate cause of death was said to be the filling of his lungs with mucus, which he had not strength to throw off. He had fought so long as a particle of strength remained, and even at the close his iron will was not vanquished. He was not ready to go until his son "Tom" had come home to him. But death beckoned and he had to go.

All the morning he lay dying, his family grouped about his bed. His struggles, which had been painful when he returned to that semi-consciousness which showed the proud, unconquered spirit that still lived within him, were pitifully weak now. With all hopes gone the family prayed only for a speedy end. For hours they stood grouped about the bed, watching and waiting for the end. Several times it seemed as if it had come, but once more the spirit struggled back and death was beaten off again.

But at ten minutes of two there came a change. The color and the look which are noticeable only when death comes suddenly spread over the drawn face, disfigured with iodine, and the nurse, who had been bending over him listening to the last faint flutterings of his heart, quickly straightened up and said, "He is dead."

Remarkable Coincidence.

Thus, thirty hours after the last admiral of the United States, Admiral Porter, the last general, his friend for many years, passed away.

The last general of our army; the last of the great heroic figures who filled the eye of the public in the bloody era that is past; the last of the idols whom the tattered remnant of the armies of the sixties loved to follow and to worship, William Tecumseh Sherman, was gone, and with him one of the strongest links that still connected the people of America with an epoch which all would willingly forget save for the mighty debt of gratitude which the present generation owes to the heroes of that past and passing one.

Not the least of the battles fought by Sherman was the one with disease and death. It was a battle to be proud of. It was an exhibition of American pluck and grit and unconquerable determination in which the least of Americans must feel a reflected pride. Brief, compared to the long-enduring struggle of the hero Grant, it was yet long enough to show the metal of the man, who had but one reason for caring to remain on earth—a wish to clasp his absent son in loving arms.

Oh, what a rare and sweet example of parental love! Who would have looked for it in the grim old soldier who had hid this love behind a crusty exterior for ten long years? About the last word which his lips uttered was his cry for "Tom" on Friday. But he could not hold out till the coming of that son. The forces against him of disease and age were too mighty. But he held off the end with wonderful power and vigor, and died as he had lived, with an unvanquished spirit.

The Last Ebb of Life.

The beginning of the end was about six o'clock the evening before. The tide of life, which had risen and fallen so many times, and which during the day had passed the flood-mark of hope, began its final ebbing, which, to the eyes of the professional watchers, would never be stayed again. It was a question now of hours only. How long could the sturdy frame withstand the gnawing teeth of his disease? Time only could give the answer.

The family, who had begun to smile and talk cheerily of recovery, now grew haggard again. Hope vanished. They read the story in the eyes of the silent doctors. They knew that the last rally had been held and that the standard of life must be lowered. Well, let it come! It was better than this agony of waiting. None but the family and the professional attendants were admitted to the sick-room. The forehead and other parts of the face affected by erysipelas had been anointed with iodine.

The general was speechless now, and utterly unconscious. All the energies of his being were concentrated on the one desperate task of breathing, and all efforts to assist this operation seemed to have no effect. "No better" was the repeated report from the chamber of sickness; and no better meant the constant sapping of the depleted store of strength.

Fast Sinking.

At four o'clock in the morning it seemed as if he were sinking to the end, and again the family were summoned. The trained nurse who had zealously attended him, and who for more than twenty-four hours had refused to take sleep or rest, did all that a nurse could do to minister to his wants. Two hours before this the doctors said "Not yet," and some of the family had left the house, but they were hastily called back, and all came expecting that he would scarce survive the rising of the sun.

It was Dr. Alexander who first noticed a change for the worse. It was slight, to be sure, but the trained eye of the friend and physician saw an ominous significance in it.

Then this bulletin came from the general's house: "The physicians after consultation declare that the general's condition is now hopeless. He is dying, and the end is near." There was no mistake about it this time, as before.

Dr. Alexander, who brought this bulletin to the

telegraph-office, added significantly to the reporters assembled, "There will be no more bulletins."

The erysipelas had again set in, and bronchitis had also attacked the sick man. At half-past nine another report came from the house through a friend of the general. He said that the dying man was in no physical pain. It was somewhat difficult for him to breathe, but otherwise he was not suffering.

From ten o'clock on General Sherman continued to fail. At twenty minutes past eleven it was stated that his death was but a question of minutes. There were many callers during the morning. Only immediate friends were admitted. The others merely left their cards. At twenty-five minutes past eight o'clock Senator Sherman telegraphed to his family at Washington that the general was still alive, but only partially conscious.

Death only a Question of Minutes.

He was apparently without pain, but his breathing was labored and his strength diminishing. At ten minutes past twelve P. M. Thomas Ewing, Jr., said that no further bulletins of General Sherman's condition would be issued. Death was only a question of minutes, he said.

At a quarter to twelve a carriage and a pair drove up to the door with a caller, who was Mrs. U. S. Grant. She did not leave her carriage, but upon being told that there was not the slighest hope for the general, was deeply affected and immediately drove away. There was nothing to do now but wait for the end, and the family waited with beating hearts. In the general's office in the basement were a number of military gentlemen, including Generals Howard, Slocum, Stewart L. Woodford, and the commander of Grant Post of Brooklyn.

About the bedside were grouped the general's two unmarried daughters, Misses Lizzie and Rachel Sherman, his son Philemon T., Lieutenant and Mrs. Fitch, Lieutenant and Mrs. Thackara, Senator John Sherman, Mrs. Colgate Hoyt, Dr. Alexander, and General Thomas Ewing. The nurse sat at the bedside watching the pinched lip of the dying man.

In the windows in front the shades were up and the curtains slightly parted. The policeman paced in front and kept the noises at a distance, save the loud detonation of the blasters who were at work in a lot across the way. A hush seemed to fall upon the street.

The End had Come.

Suddenly the watchers on the opposite sidewalk saw the curtains pulled together and the shades drawn down. A moment later General Ewing appeared bareheaded at the door and waved his hand. "It is all over," he said.

In another moment the electric spark was flashing over the land the news. Sherman was dead! His spirit had joined the great majority with his many old comrades, and had met the gentle spirit of his wife at last. He had marched from Atlanta to the sea. He had crossed the dark, dark river. Let the fife shriek and the drum sound the deathless song that was written for him, and will never die so long as martial music lives.

> "Bring the good old bugle, boys, we'll have another song—
> Sing it with a spirit that will start the world along—
> Sing it as we used to sing it, fifty thousand strong,
> While we were marching through Georgia.
>
> "'Hurrah! hurrah! we bring the jubilee!
> Hurrah! hurrah! the flag that makes you free!'
> So we sang the chorus from Atlanta to the sea,
> While we were marching through Georgia."

Those who were present in the room said that the end was so quiet as to be almost imperceptible. It was not until the nurse looked up and spoke the simple words, "He is dead," that his daughters knew that they were fatherless.

> "'Halt!' breathed a muffled voice;
> 'Ensheath thy sword, lay down thine arms.
> No more the battle's bugles or alarms
> Shall rouse thy lion's heart. Rejoice!'
> Yet, spite Death's mandate low,
> Despite a nation's woe,
> Sherman marched on—
> Marched on triumphantly,
> As when he led his armies to the sea—
> Marched on!
>
> "O Death! thou couldst not stay
> A hero, dauntless set upon his way
> To a new planet, toward eternal peace;
> Thou couldst not touch him, save with pain surcease:
> For while thou spakest, even,
> Sherman marched on—to heaven.
> Where, then, thy sting, O Death? since he
> Has heard God's roll-call. Where thy victory,

O grave? since he has made reply.
  Can Sherman die?
Nay; glory-girded, one more battle won,
  He has marched on.

"Choke back your sobs, O men!
He has out-tripped the sun—what then?
The Spring, that cometh soon, will let
Her gently falling tear-drops wet
  His new-made grave.

"Nature will weep, but men—men do not weep the brave.
Lay his sheathed sword upon his breast;
After life's burning warfare peace is best.
Let dust to dust return; *nothing can shroud
The soul of Sherman.* Be not overbowed
With grief; rather let joy exult;
For even Death's grim "Halt!"
  His purpose could not stay;
  He saw the coming day,
And 'neath the sunrise marched, as toward the sea,
  Marched—marched—to immortality."

Messages of Sympathy.

The following telegrams were received by the family of General Sherman:

To Hon. John Sherman: Convey to your brother's bereaved family our tenderest sympathy. A very great man has gone.   James G. Blaine.

To P. T. Sherman: In this hour of affliction you have my deepest sympathy. The memory of General Sherman will be for ever cherished by the American people as one of their most valued possessions.
  B. F. Tracy.

Governor Pattison of Pennsylvania sent the following message to P. T. Sherman: "I desire to express the sincere sympathy of the people of Pennsylvania for the family of General Sherman, of whose death I have just been advised. His patriotic, faithful, and invaluable services to his country will ever be gratefully remembered."

MISS SHERMAN: Deep and heartfelt sympathy for the irreparable loss both to you and to America.
H. M. STANLEY.

General Joseph E. Johnston, Sherman's great foe, sent the following:

To the MISSES SHERMAN: Intelligence of General Sherman's death grieves me much. I sympathize deeply with you in your great bereavement.

To MISS RACHEL SHERMAN: The nation mourns and sympathizes with you in all your great sorrow. Your illustrious father's death is to Mrs. Morton, our children, and myself the loss of a personal friend, to whom we were devotedly attached.
LEVI P. MORTON.

To the MISSES SHERMAN: The death of my old commander causes deep sorrow to myself and household. Our sympathy is with his family in their great affliction. JOHN M. HARLAN.

To the HON. JOHN SHERMAN: We mourn with the family and kindred of General Sherman. He was beloved by me and my family with the warmest personal affection. I expect to reach the Fifth Avenue Hotel Monday. R. B. HAYES.

To HON. JOHN SHERMAN: Please accept for yourself and the members of your family sympathy in the bereavement you suffer in the loss of the general commander, who was my dearest friend.

J. M. SCHOFIELD.

The following is the President's message to the family of General Sherman:

EXECUTIVE MANSION, Washington, Feb. 14, 1891.— To HON. JOHN SHERMAN, New York: I loved and venerated General Sherman, and would stand very near to the more deeply afflicted members of his family in this hour of bereavement. It will be as if there were one dead in every loyal household in the land. I suggest the body be borne through Washington and lie in state for one day in the rotunda of the Capitol. Please advise me of any arrangements made. BENJAMIN HARRISON.

Upward of three thousand telegrams were received within twenty-four hours, expressing the sympathy felt in all parts of the land, and the high appreciation in which General Sherman was held by all classes of his countrymen.

There is something impressive in the sight of a great nation moved by a common feeling. As in the old days of the war the whole North was sometimes thrilled and overjoyed by the news of victory, so now the country was affected by a common sorrow.

And the grief was not entirely confined within geographical lines. In all parts of the land there was mourning for the hero whose war record was one of the most brilliant written in the annals of the republic. The hills of New England, the Rockies in the West, and the vales of the South might well have been draped in black.

CHAPTER XXVI.

A Nation in Mourning.—Tributes of Love and Respect.

PRESIDENT HARRISON had just finished his luncheon and was walking up stairs to his office when the bulletin announcing the death of General Sherman reached the White House. The telegraph operator handed the despatch to Private Secretary Halford, who hastened to inform the President, and met him on the stairway. The President was very much shocked. He served under General Sherman in the famous march to the sea, and the friendship begun at that time had been strengthened by their close association ever since. General Sherman never visited Indianapolis while General Harrison was there without spending many hours in his society, and even greater intimacy had existed between them since the President's election. The last time they were together was on January 27th, when General Sherman called at the White House in company with General Schofield. In the words of Mr. Halford, "The President had the greatest love and admiration for General Sherman, and is sorely grieved at his death."

A few minutes after reading the bulletin the President received a brief telegram from Senator Sherman announcing his brother's death. He thereupon sent for

General Lewis A. Grant, who was acting as Secretary of War, and Major-General Schofield, and gave instructions for full military honors for the dead soldier, and made several suggestions in regard to the character of the general order announcing General Sherman's death to the army. He also prepared a message to Congress on the same subject and issued the following executive order:

It is my painful duty to announce to the country that General William Tecumseh Sherman died this day at 1.50 oclock P. M., at his residence in the city of New York. The Secretary of War will cause the highest military honors to be paid to the memory of this distinguished officer. The national flag will be floated at half-mast over all public buildings until after the burial, and the public business will be suspended in the executive Departments at the city of Washington and in the city where the interment takes place on the day of the funeral, and in all places where public expression is given to the national sorrow during such hours as will enable every officer and employee to participate therein with their fellow-citizens. BENJAMIN HARRISON.

Executive Mansion, Washington, D. C., February 14, 1891.

An Ideal Soldier.

The message to Congress is as follows:

To the Senate and House of Representatives:

The death of William Tecumseh Sherman, which took place to-day at his residence in the city of New

York at 1.50 o'clock P. M., is an event that will bring sorrow to the hearts of every patriotic citizen. No living American was so loved and venerated as he. To look upon his face, to hear his name, was to have one's love of country intensified. He served his country, not for fame, not out of a sense of professional duty, but for love of the flag and of the beneficent civil institutions of which it was the emblem.

He was an ideal soldier, and shared to the fullest the esprit de corps of the army; but he cherished the civil institutions organized under the Constitution, and was only a soldier that these might be perpetuated in undiminished usefulness and honor. He was in nothing an imitator. A profound student of military science and precedent, he drew from them principles and suggestions, and so adapted them to novel conditions that his campaigns will continue to be the profitable study of the military profession throughout the world.

His genial nature made him a comrade to every soldier of the great Union army. No presence was so welcome and inspiring at the camp-fire or commandery as his. His career was complete; his honors were full. He had received from the Government the highest rank known to our military establishment and from the people unstinted gratitude and love.

No word of mine can add more to his fame. His death has followed in startling quickness that of the admiral of the navy, and it is a sad and notable incident that when the Department under which he served shall have put on the usual emblems of mourning four of the eight executive Departments will be simultaneously draped in black, and one other has but to-day removed the crape from its walls.

BENJ. HARRISON.

Executive Mansion, Feb. 14, 1891.

General Army Order.

The Acting Secretary of War issued a general order to the army announcing the death of General Sherman. It included the President's message to Congress and the executive order issued by him to the executive Departments, and ordered that the War Department be draped in mourning for the period of thirty days, and that all business be suspended therein on the day of the funeral.

This was accompanied by another order issued by Adjutant-General Kelton, by command of Major-General Schofield, as follows:

On the day of the funeral the troops at every military post will be paraded and this order read to them, after which all labors of the day will cease. The national flag will be displayed at half-staff from the time of the receipt of this order until the close of the funeral. On the day of the funeral a salute of seventeen guns will be fired at half-hour intervals, commencing at eight o'clock A. M. The officers of the army will wear the usual badges of mourning, and the colors of the several regiments and battalions will be draped in mourning for a period of six months. The day and hour of the funeral will be communicated to department commanders by telegraph, and by them to their subordinate commanders. Other necessary orders will be issued hereafter relative to the appropriate funeral ceremonies.

Imposing Obsequies in New York.

General Sherman's funeral began in New York on February 19th, and ended in St. Louis on the 21st.

But once has New York seen a greater funeral pageant, and that was when General Grant was borne to his tomb in Riverside Park. Twenty thousand men, it is said, followed the remains of General Sherman as they were carried through the streets, decorated with emblems of mourning and thronged with mourners eager to participate in the last honors to the hero of the "March to the Sea."

The day was wellnigh perfect, and from first to last no serious accident, no untoward incident, detracted from the beauty and impressiveness of the pageant. The bright sunshine, which made the metal helmets of the soldiers glitter as they marched and sent the light flashing from swords and guns, relieved the sombreness of the funeral cavalcade, and gave the procession the appearance of bravery which befitted a great soldier's funeral. Everything seemed suited to the occasion and to the man, and Nature and the nation joined in doing honor to the great Union captain.

Sympathetic Crowds.

An hour or more before the hour set for the moving of the procession the streets along which it was to pass began to fill, and at two o'clock they were densely packed. Tens of thousands crowded every available place, and some, women as well as men, stood for hours, that they might see "Sherman's funeral." The interest manifested was intense, and the comments on the dead hero heard on every hand were always appreciative, although sometimes uncouth.

The first thing that the waiting thousands saw were the mounted police that forced the crowd back to the sidewalks, leaving the street free for the vast procession. Not far behind them came the regular troops, mounted and on foot, marching with the precision which marks the veteran. Then followed, drawn by four black horses, the caisson on the top of which rested the coffined remains of General Sherman, the simple casket covered with the flag of the United States.

Behind the caisson came the carriages of the mourners, the President, Cabinet, and other distinguished attendants, and these were followed by the Loyal Legion, the Grand Army, and the National Guard. The procession made a striking picture as its various and contrasting sections passed slowly down Fifth avenue, and it compelled the comment that the hero of Atlanta was worthily escorted. In the marching line was a committee of twelve men from the Confederate Veteran Camp of New York, and one of the honored pall-bearers was General Joseph E. Johnston, one of the greatest of the Confederate commanders.

The Solemn Knell.

As the procession moved church-bells tolled slowly, and from St. Thomas's, near Central Park, down to Old Trinity, their solemn music gave notice that General Sherman's funeral escort was marching. At intervals cannons boomed, salutes of seventeen guns having been fired at half-hour intervals from Fort Wood on Bedloe's Island, Fort Hamilton, Fort Wadsworth, Fort Schuyler, Governor's Island, Willett's Point, and from the recruiting dépôt on David's Island.

The mourning decorations were not, as a rule, elaborate, but they were tasteful, and such as General Sherman would have been likely to approve, comprising mainly flags crape bordered. One of these, which hung from one of the Vanderbilt houses, bore the names of all the battles in which General Sherman fought. Nearly every house passed by the procession bore some evidence of sorrow, and from some floated several flags bearing the insignia of mourning. There was no ostentation; there was also no neglect. The mourning decorations, like the pageant, were impressive, but they were not oppressive through excessive sombreness.

The Casket Open during the Forenoon.

The casket remained open during the forenoon for any distinguished visitors that might arrive from the hotels. At 10.30 none but some intimate friends and old veterans had come in to take a last look at their old commander. A few minutes before eleven o'clock a large floral shield was received at the house from

A NATION IN MOURNING. 521

West Point cadets. The shield was six feet in height and four feet broad. It was made of white and blue immortelles, and bore the inscription, "William Tecumseh Sherman, from his West Point boys, Class of 1840." At the top of the shield was the American eagle worked in blue immortelles, and at the bottom a sword and scabbard in the same flower. The base of the shield was made of white calla lilies. At eleven o'clock Secretaries Proctor and Rusk drove up to the house in a carriage and passed in at the front door.

At eleven o'clock many other distinguished guests arrived at the house. Among the number were General O'Beirne and General Romer. Shortly after them Secretary Blaine walked up Seventy-first street, arm-in-arm with General Thomas Ewing. President Harrison would not look upon the remains of the general. The family sent an invitation to him this morning at the Fifth Avenue Hotel, but the President kindly replied that he preferred to keep with him the remembrances of the general while alive. He did not wish to see him in death, when their associations had been so warm and genial.

At noon every doorstep along the street was crowded with interested spectators and windows were filled with expectant faces. The street was kept free from pedestrians, but the side-streets were crowded with the forming troops and citizens.

About 12.25 the caisson, draped in black and drawn by four horses, was drawn up in front of the Sherman house. The horses were mounted by regulars and an army officer was in charge. Behind the caisson was an orderly leading the black charger which bore the military trappings of the general. A black velvet covering almost hid the horse from view, but the boots and saddle were plainly conspicuous.

The services of prayer began promptly on the hour. At five minutes to twelve a Father left the general's late residence and entered No. 77 Seventy-first street, and summoned the boy choir of St. Francis Xavier. The services were over at 12.30. The prayers were read by Rev. Father Sherman.

There were about one hundred and fifty persons present at these ceremonies. The greater number were relatives, but there were many close friends as well, among them being Mrs. Grant and Senator Cameron.

The reading of the service and the singing together did not occupy more than fifteen minutes. During that time no one was permitted to enter the house. There were large crowds of people all along the street and on the house-stoops, but they maintained the utmost order, and by their silent, composed demeanor manifested their respect for the dead general.

As the hour of two drew near the scene in the immediate neighborhood was one full of life. Mounted officers and orderlies dashed through the streets, the polished trimmings of their horse equipments flashing in the bright sunlight, and their yellow- and scarlet-lined capes flying in the breeze.

VETERANS SALUTING THE FUNERAL TRAIN.

Drooping Flags.

Flags at half-staff in almost countless numbers fluttered from windows of every house in the vicinity.

Ex-President Cleveland and Chauncey M. Depew arrived at the house together about 1.30. Soon after came Governor Pattison of Pennsylvania and Major-General Snowden, with their staff, and following them were Governor Bulkley and staff and Lieutenant-Governor Jones. Ex-President Hayes was accompanied by Joseph H. Choate.

The Senate committee arrived in a body, wearing the usual signs of mourning, and after them came the large committee of the House. It was close on to two o'clock when President Harrison, with Lieutenant Ernst, his aide-de-camp, reached the house. Following were the remaining members of the Cabinet.

Mourning Decorations.

The hour at which the head of the funeral procession was to move from Seventy-first street was two o'clock, but long before that time spectators began to take up their places along the route of march. Every house in the block where General Sherman lived so long was tastefully decorated with draped flags. Along Fifty-seventh street, from Broadway to Fifth avenue, nearly every house was draped, and up to noon the work of decoration continued. Fifth avenue from the Plaza at Central Park to the Arch at Washington Square presented a bewildering array of draped and half-masted flags. The club-house of the Seventh Regiment Veterans was handsomely draped, and the Union League Club building presented an elaborate display of black. Especially noticeable were the sombre decorations of the big hotels along the line. The big wholesale houses on Broadway had their flags at half-mast, and the smaller stores were tastefully draped. The side-streets were similarly decorated.

Forming the Procession.

The first move toward the formation of the procession was at 1.58. General Howard came out on the front steps of the general's residence and ordered the caisson, which had been withdrawn, to come up. At that instant a detailed squad of the Sixth Cavalry formed to the left of the house in the middle of the street. The caisson came up in front of the house at exactly two o'clock. Generals Howard, Slocum, Johnston, and other military dignitaries formed two lines on the walk and made a passageway to the caisson. As the pall-bearers left the house an army band out toward Central Park began playing a funeral march.

Six lieutenants appeared in the doorway bearing on their shoulders the casket of the general. Slowly they bore their burden to the awaiting funeral carriage. All heads were then bared, and silence reigned from one end of the street to the other. This was at 2.05. A marching order was given and the caisson moved out toward Eighth avenue. The private carriage of General Butterfield was then driven to the door, and Generals Schofield, Howard, Slocum, and Schofield's aide entered. The pall-bearers were then seated in their respective carriages in quick succession, and were ready to fall into line.

The members of the family then entered their carriages, and the friends, governors, senators, and other notables followed in the order previously announced.

The procession at 2.45 had moved down Eighth avenue for some distance, but the movement was very slow. Out on the side-streets were hundreds of carriages waiting for a place in the immense procession.

As the caisson bearing the body rumbled over the pavement through the sunlit street into Eighth avenue the vast crowds stood with uncovered heads, reverently watching the starry folds of the American flag enveloping the casket. More than one veteran wept as the body of his old commander was borne past him. The sidewalks, the roof-tops, every window, swarmed with watching humanity. As the cortège passed down the avenue there fell in behind it the Military Order of the Loyal Legion of the United States and officers of the army and navy, among them being representatives of the Ohio Commandery, of which General Sherman was a member. Then came the Grand Army of the Republic, followed by the West Point cadets.

The next in line was the National Guard, under command of General Louis Fitzgerald. Among the veterans were the Confederate Veterans' Camp of the city of New York, riding in carriages, and after them came, in carriages, representatives of the Chamber of Commerce and the New York Historical

Society, of the Common Councils of Boston and Brooklyn, the Union League Club, and other bodies. Altogether, fully fifteen thousand men were in line.

The whole line of the long route was thronged on sidewalks, on house-tops, and in every window with reverent spectators, who stood in silence with bare heads as the body of the dead general was borne past them. The route was lined with seventeen hundred policemen, and the most perfect order was maintained. As the procession moved slowly along the church-bells began to toll, and through the whole route the mournful sound of the bells continued as it wended its way to its destination. There were many funeral dirges played, but none struck with keener force on the listening ears than "Marching through Georgia," played in half time, as arranged for the occasion.

In New York especially General Sherman was a favorite. The achievements of the man, his blunt yet kind demeanor, his downright integrity, and honesty of purpose, his commanding figure, which, wherever he went, associated him with the heroic deeds of the nations' patriots, all served to endear him to the hearts of the people, and awake profound regret at his death.

New York honored itself in the memorable tribute she paid to the dead soldier. The assemblage of persons from distant places told how strong a hold Sherman had upon the love and admiration of his countrymen. He had made his place in the nation's history. He was a magnificent figure in the wonderful panorama of our national life and deeds. It was fitting that his obsequies should be nothing less than a national demonstration.

CHAPTER XXVII.

Final Obsequies of General Sherman.—Grand Procession of Troops and Civic Bodies.

ON February 21st, St. Louis bade an impressive farewell to the soldier whose military genius was excelled by none and equalled by few.

For the first time in several days the sun shone out gloriously, but its rays fell upon a city draped in mourning. The hearts of the people were saddened, and with one accord all manner of men abandoned their earthly pursuits and assembled along the line of the funeral procession to do homage to the honored dead. As early as 6.30 o'clock in the morning the Union Dépôt was thronged with people awaiting the arrival of the Sherman funeral train. As the morning advanced the crowd became larger, and each train as it entered the dépôt deposited load after load of human freight, which added to the throng until the dépôt became almost impassable.

When the hands of the big clock pointed to 8.20 o'clock a squad of police marched to the dépôt, and soon the immense crowd was under control. In a few minutes the funeral train appeared, and the ponderous iron horse slowly rolled into the station. The dull black engine looked duller, blacker, and heavier than ever before, its sombre drapings of mourning adding to the dismal effect.

For miles the streets were lined with solid walls of people, standing at least a dozen deep, and the evidences of affection in which his fellow-townsmen held General Sherman were abundant on all sides. The city was draped in mourning. Evidences of individual sorrow were also abundant, and badges of ribbon and crape fluttered from every coat-lapel. The grief of those in the procession was not alone genuine, but apparent to every one. His comrades of Ransom Post marched in hollow square about the caisson.

The Historic Thirteenth.

Following the caisson were the handful of survivors of the old Thirteenth Infantry, a small and grief-stricken body of men, following their old leader over a road which they too must travel at no very far distant day

There were, besides, thousands of veterans of the war, members of the Grand Army of the Republic, old and grizzled comrades-in-arms of the dead general. Slowly they walked, and only too plainly was it written that the ravages of time were fast depleting the ranks of the preservers of the Union. Yet none of them were so feeble that they would admit, even to themselves, that they were taxing their strength in following Sherman to Calvary, even as they had followed him to Savannah.

Arrival of the Funeral Train.

The funeral train arrived at just half-past eight. As it crossed the bridge a salute from a near-by battery announced its approach. Emerging from the tunnel, it was compelled to proceed slowly while the police cleared the tracks of people. On the dépôt platform was Governor Francis with his staff and the members of the General Reception Committee, headed by Messrs. James C. Yeatman and Henry Pitchcock.

After an exchange of greetings the governor and representatives of the General Committee and Ransom Post, G. A. R., were introduced to the members of the Cabinet and Lieutenants Fitch and Thackara.

Meantime, outside, the military companies were moved into position. The caisson on which the body was to be borne from the train to its resting-place was standing on Poplar street, at the entrance of the carriage-way. It was from Battery E, First Artillery, and was under Lieutenant Wilson, with Sergeant Cannon in immediate charge. It was drawn by six bay horses. The riders were the men who worked the Hotchkiss gun at the battle of Wounded Knee Creek during the recent Indian war. They belonged to the Seventh Cavalry, known as the "Fighting Seventh." Their names were Privates Mallory, Ryan and Krauss. The body-bearers were eight sergeants. Four of them— Sergeants Connelly, Lang, Hennessey and Siegber— were from the Seventh Cavalry. The other four— Sergeants Hunneman, Lavay, French and Donohugh —were from Battery E, First Artillery.

The Riderless Horse.

In front of the caisson, on Poplar street, was the Twelfth Infantry, from Fort Leavenworth, under command of Colonel Townsend, drawn up in line facing the dépôt. On the opposite side of the street were the members of Ransom Post, who were to act as guard of honor. The horse that was to be led behind the caisson, equipped with the dead general's saddle, bridle, boots and spurs, stood next to the caisson. He was a black horse belonging to Troop D, Seventh Cavalry, of Fort Riley, Kansas, and was brought from there especially for this purpose. It was led by Sergeant George H. Rathguber. The hearse on this occasion was not covered with a black cloth, as was done in the general parade in New York.

Removal of the Body from the Train.

At a quarter-past ten an open barouche drove into the carriage-way. All of the floral pieces brought from New York and those received during the trip were put in this carriage, to be conveyed to the cemetery. General Merritt and staff arrived at the dépôt at half-past ten. At this hour the adjacent streets and Twelfth street bridge were fairly black with people. The police had all they could to keep room enough for the procession to move in.

Immediately after the arrival of General Merritt and staff preparations were made to remove the body from the car where it had rested during its long journey. The eight body-bearers took up positions at the car-door, four on each side. Directly behind them, six on a side stood the honorary pall-bearers. They were: Military—Major-General John Pope, Brevet Major-General Amos Beckwith, Brevet Major-General A. J. Smith, Brevet Major-General John W.

Turner, Brevet Major-General Willard Warner, Brevet Brigadier-General John W. Barriger, Commander Charles S. Cotton, U. S. N.; Citizens—Judge Samuel Treat, Colonel George E. Leighton, Colonel Charles S. Parsons, Byron Sherman, Esq., Daniel B. Harrison, Isaac Sturgeon, and Thomas E. Tutt.

A Silent Throng.

Ranged in line on each side of the carriage-entrance were the military and public officials who had accompanied the remains from New York, General Merritt and staff, and Governor Francis and staff. Three comrades of Ransom Post entered the funeral car and assisted the six sergeants in charge to lift the casket out through the car-door to the shoulders of the waiting pall-bearers. As the end of the flag-covered oaken box was passed through the door every head was uncovered and silence reigned supreme. Slowly and carefully the precious burden was taken from the car and placed on the shoulders of the stalwart sergeants.

As they started with slow step out through the carriage-way to the waiting caisson, the Twelfth Infantry presented arms, flags were dipped and the regimental band played Pleyel's well-known hymn. Many, many hearts were touched by the sight, and veterans and comrades of the dead soldier could be seen crying on all sides. Generals Howard and Slocum were so overcome they could not speak for several minutes. The casket was placed lengthwise on the caisson and strapped in place. On it were placed the hat and sword of him who lay inside. The delivery of the remains to the St. Louis body-guard relieved the six sergeants who had accompanied it from New York of all further care.

The Procession.

When the fastening of the casket was finished, Colonel L. Townsend gave the order to march, and the Twelfth Infantry wheeled into line and marched up Eleventh street to the corner of Clark street. Here they halted. The open carriage with the floral pieces followed directly behind. Then the order was given by Lieutenant Wilson, and the caisson, with its sacred burden, moved slowly up Eleventh street to a place next the carriage containing the flowers. On each side of the caisson walked the four military body-bearers. Directly the caisson started the four hundred members of Ransom Post, who had made up the guard of honor, marched up in two columns, one going to one side and the other on the opposite side of the caisson. The saddle-horse bearing the riding equipments of the general was led just behind the caisson and between the columns of Ransom Post.

Meanwhile the immediate members and relatives of the Sherman family had filled coaches, and were now driven into a place in the procession next to the guard of honor. Behind the family were carriages in which were the people who had come from New York to attend the funeral. In the first coach were Secretary and Mrs. Noble, Judge Hough and Major Ran-

FINAL OBSEQUIES.   535

dolph; in the second, Secretary Rusk, Assistant Secretary Grant, Charles A. Greeley, Captain Kingsbury; the third carriage contained ex-President Hayes, General Schofield, Governor Stannard, and Lieutenant Anderson; the fourth, Generals Howard, Slocum, and Broadhead and Lieutenant Howard; the fifth, General Alger, James E. Yeatman, Colonel McCreary, and General James D. Moore. When these carriages had taken their proper places in the line, General Merritt with his staff galloped to the head of the procession, which was at the corner of Clark avenue and Eleventh street. At just ten minutes after eleven, all division commanders having reported everything ready, General Merritt gave the order to march.

Great Popular Demonstration.

The funeral column was made up of six divisions, composed of the regular military escort, as provided by army regulations, and Grand Army posts, Loyal Legion, Sons of Veterans, civic societies, State militia of Missouri and Ohio, and Legislatures of Missouri, Illinois, and Kansas, governors of States and staffs, unorganized bodies, and citizens in carriages and on foot. The route of the procession from the dépôt to Calvary Cemetery, a distance of nearly eight miles, was through some of the principal streets and avenues. After starting from the junction of Eleventh street and Clark avenue, the cortège moved up Eleventh street to Market, through Market to Twelfth, and through Twelfth to Pine street. The route was through the business section.

The stores were closed, but the windows of nearly all the big blocks were filled with spectators, and the sidewalks were filled with crowding, surging masses of humanity. While there was no disorder (in the full sense of the word) in the streets mentioned, the jam of people coming in from the various intersecting streets when the procession started was something terrific. Strong men and weak women were swept along by this human tidal wave until they were brought to a standstill by the crowds that already had possession of every inch of available standing-room.

The march to the cemetery from the dépôt was through some of the principal streets of the city. The route laid out was through Eleventh, Market, Twelfth, and Pine and Grand avenue, thence out Florissant avenue to Calvary Cemetery. The entrance to the cemetery was by the rear gate. The larger part of the military remained outside of the cemetery.

The Scene at the Cemetery.

When the caisson entered the gates of the cemetery most of the troops remained outside of the cemetery. On account of the large number of carriages occupied by Grand Army men, members of the Loyal Legion, and the Sons of Veterans who were unable to endure the fatigue of the entire march of nearly eight miles, and for whom carriages were provided at the corner of Grand and Eastern avenues, the road from the entrance to the cemetery to the grave was soon blocked, and many of those who occupied carriages and near the end of the procession were obliged to leave them some distance from the gate and walk to the grave. This caused some delay, and it was not until half-past two o'clock that all who had been assigned places took their positions about the open grave, which was lined inside with flags.

A short distance to the south was the brave Thirteenth, to the east members of the G. A. R., and directly around it to the north were grouped Senator Sherman, the Misses Sherman, P. T. Sherman, Colonel Hoyt Sherman, Lieutenants Thackara and Fitch and their wives, Judge and Mrs. P. B. Ewing, General and Mrs. Thomas Ewing, General and Mrs. Nelson A. Miles, Secretary and Mrs. Noble, Secretary and Mrs. Rusk, Assistant Secretary Grant, ex-President Hayes, General Schofield, General Howard, General Slocum, and others. After all had taken their positions the eight sergeants, acting as body-bearers, lifted the casket from the caisson and bore it reverentially to the grave, when all that was mortal of General Sherman was lowered to its last resting-place. The casket was draped with flags and was bare of any floral tributes.

The Services at the Grave.

The services were of the simplest character and were conducted by Rev. Thomas Ewing Sherman, all assembled at the grave standing with uncovered heads. As the casket was being lowered the regimental band played Pleyel's hymn. Father Sherman read the Catholic service, one of the selections being "I am the resurrection and the life," offered a fervent prayer, and the services were at an end. As the services progressed many about the grave were visibly affected, and when the flags surrounding the casket were removed the sounds of low sobbing were heard. At three o'clock the closing of the grave took place, and the buglers of the Seventh Calvary sounded "Taps," "Lights out." Salutes were fired by the Thirteenth Infantry, followed by three salvos of artillery, which was stationed some distance to the east. Wreaths and branches of evergreens were then placed upon the grave by loving hands. The funeral party and troops returned to the station and the many thousands of citizens dispersed to their homes.

Thus was laid to rest by the side of his wife and two sons, one of whom was his "soldier boy," General William Tecumseh Sherman

Description by an Eye-witness.

The following graphic recital of the events attending the last obsequies is from the pen of an eye-witness of the wonderful spectacle:

The scene at the St. Louis Union Dépôt as early as six o'clock was one of great animation, and by the time the funeral train arrived the crowd rivalled in numbers the largest ever seen in this city. Every few minutes, from 6.40 A. M. to 10 o'clock, a train would roll in bearing a company or regiment of milltia under arms and in full uniform, besides numerous civilians and State dignitaries from other States. Committees were promptly on hand to meet and escort them to their respective places, and notwithstanding the push and jam of the crowd, there was but little confusion in readily carrying out the programme that had been previously arranged. With the marching and counter-marching of the incoming troops, with their glistening bayonets, the scene just before the arrival of the funeral train vividly called to mind the excitement attending upon the movements of an army during the war.

It was early announced that the funeral train, which was expected at 7.30 o'clock, would not arrive till 8.25, so there was no anxious waiting upon the part of the committees appointed to meet it. A few minutes after eight o'clock Colonel Brodhead, chairman of the reception committee, and a number of the members of his committee, assembled in the ladies' waiting-room of the dépôt, and were soon joined by Governor Francis and several other prominent gentlemen. They proceeded to a position just outside the main entrance, where they were joined by General Merritt.

Dense Crowd.

Promptly at 8.30 the funeral train was sighted slowly approaching around the curve at the east end of the yards. Its approach was announced by a salute. The crowd that now lined both sides of the track to a depth of several feet became anxious to catch a view of the train, and were with great difficulty pressed back by the police, who were stationed every few feet along the track.

The engine drawing the train was No. 8 of the Bridge and Tunnel Company. It was heavily draped in black, and on the headlight was placed an engraving of the dead general surrounded by a band of black, while over the engine was fastened a United States flag draped with crape. Slowly, with muffled bell, the engine pulled past the main entrance, revealing one after another the eight heavily and tastefully draped coaches composing the funeral train, till the locomotive reached the Twelfth street bridge.

Impressive Scene.

Immediately following the engine was the funeral car, with the doors of each side pushed back, revealing the interior. The floor was covered with a handsome carpet, and in the centre was a catafalque, on which rested the black walnut casket covered with a silk flag, while on the top of it lay the dead general's sword and hat. At the head of the casket were a number of beautiful floral emblems, and at the foot, on a stand, were the saddle, bridle, boots, and other riding equipments of the dead hero. The interior of the car was entirely covered with black cloth. On each side of the catafalque stood erect the guard of honor, composed of the following past commanders of Ransom Post, who went on to meet the train at Indianapolis: John B. Harlow, J. G. Butler, Smith P. Galt, and A. G. Peterson.

The commercial strife of a great city was arrested

for a few hours when the people of St. Louis ranged themselves in line and paid reverence to the remains of William Tecumseh Sherman. Outwardly this aspect of mourning was preserved throughout the day, save for the activity of the restless ones, who, having satisfied their curiosity, set about other business. No one can gainsay the affection and respect felt for General Sherman by the mass of the multitude who forsook their customary vocations. It was shown in the deep and reverential silence maintained while the procession passed—in the eagerness of the many whom a mere military show does not summon from their homes.

The spectacle offered by the funeral procession was most impressive and significant. Two generations of men and women blocked the sidewalks along Pine street and Grand avenue for many miles. For the older generation war had been a horrible reality; for the younger it was but an historical episode. But young and old were perhaps equally impressed by the solemnity of it all.

The murmur of expectation caused by the distant sound of approaching troops was stilled when the first horseman advanced, and silence fell upon the multitude assembled to the west of where the procession had gotten under way. All was in harmony with the occasion. Early in the morning the clouds lowered forbiddingly, and there seemed small hope that the wretched weather of the past week would be broken. But just before eleven o'clock—the hour set for the order to march—the sun absorbed the mist and shone cheerfully enough, and a light breeze bore away the smoke and the lingering fog. The streets had been washed clean by the heavy rains; the air was fresh and bracing. It was excellent marching weather.

Bronzed Veterans.

The sight of trained soldiers is always an inspiring one. In line was a regiment of the regular army, a regiment made up of cavalry, artillery, and infantry—bronzed and weatherbeaten men, most of them, who formed a dignified and solemn escort to the remains of the old commander. The troops showed service, and when the broken companies of the Seventh Cavalry rode by the spectators were reminded that war is even yet a reality and that these men had fought at Wounded Knee.

No more melancholy procession than a military funeral finds its way to a cemetery. Neither crape nor coffin was needed to emphasize the mournfulness of that march to the grave. The impression of sorrow is conveyed in the slow steps of the soldiers, in the sad strains of bugles which were moulded for inspiring melody, and in the sullen tone of muffled drums. As the escort moved west there came a sound even more doleful than these. It was the tolling of the bell in the tower of St. John's Catholic church at Sixteenth and Chestnut streets. It began before the escort was under way, and clanged a cheerless accompaniment to the slow and monotonous tramp of the troops. Then one of the military bands struck up a funeral march, and people easily affected felt glad that the sun was shining.

Tokens of Grief.

Since the war in which Sherman fought there has perhaps occurred nowhere in the West so imposing a public ceremony. In the matter of mere numbers there has been no such body of men in line in St. Louis since the encampment of the Grand Army of the Republic. It was not singular, then, that the railways brought to this city thousands of strangers, who, swelling the local population, made sightseers thankful that the route to the cemetery was so long. Otherwise the pavements and the windows along the line of march would scarcely have accommodated the crowds.

They stretched for miles up Pine street and along Grand avenue, and the streets at their intersection were blocked with well-filled wagons. Mourning was displayed in many windows, and while the procession was under way St. Louis and its people showed innumerable tokens of sincere grief. There was something more than this visible in the attitude of the older spectators. They realized that another link in the chain of events between '61 and '91 had been broken—that another paragraph was prepared for American history. And they took their way thoughtfully to their homes, never to forget the mournful scenes of the day.

Seldom has St. Louis ever made such a display of

visible tokens of its sorrow. Perhaps it has never been more universally draped in mourning. Both in the business portions and the residence neighborhoods there was a general display of funeral hangings. The stately buildings on the down-town streets and the small and unpretentious shops removed from the business centre were alike draped. On the public buildings the sombre materials were unsparingly used. Along parts of the route of the funeral pageant every building was made to testify to the general sadness. In every part of the city the same mournful scenes were presented. The drapery and other emblems varied in quality, quantity, and perhaps in taste and skill of arrangement, but whether it was the black calico draping of the small shop or the cashmere, serge, bombazine, bunting, or broadcloth of the richer houses, it none the less testified to the popular esteem in which the city held the dead hero.

Flags in Graceful Folds.

Many liberally disposed persons incurred great expense in this work of love and reverence, though they occupied houses in unfrequented streets, where their displays were hidden from general view. The materials used in the principal down-town thoroughfares and in the wealthier residence neighborhoods were all costly.

The piers of the basement section of the Government building were heavily shrouded with black, and the upper stories were hung with the same materials, secured with black rosettes. The City buildings were all elaborately draped with black materials and flags. In the windows everywhere were portraits of Sherman in black frames. Large flags gracefully arranged in folds or looped up with black bands were used as drapery on many of the big business buildings and on private dwellings. On others there were many small flags with crape sashes.

A large flag with a heavy black bar extending diagonally across it floated over Washington avenue near Seventh street. Broad bands of mourning were stretched lengthwise across several buildings on that street, and a large number of the windows were handsomely decorated. Black and white feathers tastefully grouped, and sheaves of wheat and rye with appropriate inscriptions, made many of the large windows on the principal streets attractive.

The banks, the railroad offices, big wholesale houses, hotels, and other large edifices, all bore some mournful tribute to the dead man. It was all done hurriedly, but none the less tastily.

The wealthy residents on the streets and avenues through which the funeral procession passed had their palatial abodes put in mourning costume by skilled decorators and designers. The work was not elaborate, but it was rich, costly, and in keeping with the homes. Many of these houses were not draped, however, either because of the short time allowed for the work after it was known what route the funeral procession would take or because of a question of propriety.

Myriads who Honor the Hero.

The hotels were all so well filled that many of the late-comers to the city could not obtain rooms, but myriads came for the day only, and the numbers who sought accommodations at the hotels furnished no fair standard by which to estimate the entire number of strangers in the city. By noon the population had bounded from its ordinary limit at half a million to very much nearer six hundred thousand, and citizens and strangers were out early, side by side, seeking the most advantageous point possible from which to view the procession. Hundreds of country relatives and friends found comfortable quarters in the houses of citizens within view of the line of march, but there were myriads who were less fortunate. Train-load after train-load rolled into the dépôt from every point of the compass during the first half of the day.

The day had scarcely begun when the earliest arrivals were landed, and soon there were in all of the down-town streets little, broken, irregular lines of men and women wandering about till time for the pageant to move. In a short time these processions became denser and broader. A little later armed and uniformed lines of men gave variety to the scene. Soon they were all over the down-town district. They no longer moved in thread-like lines; the sidewalks were no longer broad enough to hold them. Every house except those along the line of march seemed to give up its occupants to join the strangers in the wild rush hither and thither, jostling and pushing to get in the streets from which the column could be seen, and afterward to get good standing-places there.

Martial Dirges.

Then there was a blare and clash of bands, and the big crowd increased its struggle to get the vantage-points. Hundreds of them took to the street-cars and were quickly transported far out along the line. Hundreds of others did not understand the necessity of going early, and as a result the jam was so great in many of the down-town streets that the street-cars were delayed or stopped entirely when the procession was forming.

All kinds of vehicles were moving in the direction of Pine street long before the cortège was to move. Trucks of all kinds, licensed and unlicensed vender-wagons and carts rigged out with rows of wooden benches, light wagons, carriages, coaches, and cabs, were called into use to give the anxious people an opportunity to see the uniformed line. But many of them were disappointed.

The windows, roofs, and balconies were lined with people before the procession moved. And still others came pushing and crowding, creeping under wagons and crowding between vicious horses. They rushed pellmell one way in expectation of finding a vacant place, and then dashed back again when they discovered that there was no such place in sight. Pale-faced, ill-clad women, gayly-dressed girls, clerks, workingmen. and merchants crowded together and conversed while the line moved.

CHAPTER XXVIII.

Glowing Eulogies upon the World-Renowned Commander.

When the President's message announcing General Sherman's death reached the Senate, discussion of the subject under consideration (the Copyright bill) was suspended, and Mr. Hawley, of Connecticut, offered the following:

Resolved, That the Senate receives with profound sorrow the announcement of the death of William Tecumseh Sherman, late general of the armies of the United States.

Resolved, That the Senate renews its acknowledgment of the inestimable services which he rendered to his country in the day of its extreme peril, laments the great loss which the country has sustained, and deeply sympathizes with his family in its bereavement.

Resolved, That a copy of these resolutions be forwarded to the family of the deceased.

Mr. Hawley said:

"Mr. President, at this hour the Senate, the Congress, and the people of the United States are one family. What we have been daily expecting has happened: General Sherman has received and obeyed his last order. He was a great soldier by the judgment of the great soldiers of the world. In time of peace he had been a great citizen, glowing and abounding with love of country and of all humanity. His glorious soul appeared in every look, gesture, and word. The history of our country is rich in soldiers who have set examples of simple soldierly obedience to the civil law and of self-abnegation. Washington, Grant, Sheridan, and Sherman lead the list. Sherman was the last of the illustrious trio who were by universal consent the foremost figures in the armies of the Union in the late war. Among the precious traditions—to pass into our history for the admiration of the old and the instruction of the young—was their friendship, their most harmonious co-operation without a shadow of ambition or pride. When General Grant was called to Washington to take command of the armies of the Union his great heart did not forget the men who stood by him."

Beautiful Tribute by Hawley.

Here Mr. Hawley read the letter from Grant to Sherman (written at that time), expressing thanks to him and McPherson as the men to whom, above all others, he owed his success, and Sherman's letter in reply saying that General Grant did himself injustice and them too much honor.

Mr. Hawley closed his remarks (his voice frequently giving way from grief and emotion) by reading the following passage from Bunyan's *Pilgrim's Progress:*

"After this it was noised about that Mr. Valiant-for-Truth was taken with a summons. When he understood it he called for his friends and told them of it. Then said he: 'I am going to my fathers; and though with great difficulty I got hither, yet now I do not repent me of all the trouble I have been at to arrive where I am. My sword I give to him that shall succeed me in my pilgrimage, and my courage and skill to him that can get them. My marks and scars I carry with me, to be a witness for me that I have fought His battles who will now be a rewarder.' When the day that he must go hence was come, many accompanied him to the river-side, into which as he went, he said, 'Death, where is thy sting?' and as he went down deeper he said, 'Grave, where is thy victory?' So he passed over, and all the trumpets sounded for him on the other side."

From Senator Morgan.

Mr. Morgan said: "On this occasion of national solemnity I would lead the thoughts and sympathies of the American Senate back to those days in our history when General Sherman was, by a choice greatly honorable to his nature, a citizen of the State of Louisiana, and presided over a college for the instruction of Southern youths in the arts of war and the arts of peace. These were not worse days than some we have seen during the last half of this century. In those days, notwithstanding the then conditions of the South, in view of its institutions inherited from the older States of the East, every

American was as welcome in Louisiana and the South as he was elsewhere in the Union. We are gradually and surely returning to that cordial state of feeling which was unhappily interrupted by the Civil War.

"Our fathers taught us that it was the highest patriotism to defend the Constitution of the country. But they had left within its body guarantees of an institution that the will of the majority finally determined should no longer exist, and which put the conscience of the people to the severest test. Looking back now to the beginning of this century and to the conflict of opinion and of material interests engendered by these guarantees, we can see that they never could have been stricken out of the organic law except by a conflict of arms. The conflict came, and it was bound to come, and Americans became enemies, as they were bound to be in the settlement of issues that involved so much of money, such radical political results, and the pride of a great and illustrious race of people. The power rested with the victors at the close of the conflict, but not all the honors of the desperate warfare. Indeed, the survivors are now winning honors, enriched with justice and magnanimity, not less worthy than those who fell in battle, in their labors to restore the country to its former feeling of fraternal regard and to unity of sentiment and action, and to promote its welfare.

"The fidelity of the great general who has just departed in the ripeness of age and with a history marked by devotion to his flag was the true and simple faith of an American to his convictions of duty. We differed with him and contested campaigns and battle-fields with him, but we welcome the history of the great soldier as the proud inheritance of our country. We do this as cordially and as sincerely as we gave him welcome in the South as one of our people when our sons were confided to his care in a relation that (next to paternity) had its influence upon the young men of the country.

Supreme Devotion.

"The great military leaders on both sides of our Civil War are rapidly marching across the borders to a land where history and truth and justice must decide upon every man's career. When they meet there they will be happy to find that the honor of human actions is not always measured by their wisdom, but by the motives in which they had their origin I cherish the proud belief that the heroes of the Civil War will find that, measured by this standard, none of them, on either side, were delinquent, and they will be happy in an association that will never end, and will never be disturbed by an evil thought, jealousy, or distrust. When a line so narrow divides us from those high courts in which our actions are to be judged by their motives, and when so many millions now living and increasing millions to follow are to be affected by the wisdom of our enactments, we will do well to give up this day to reflection upon our duties and (in sympathy with this great country) to dedicate the day to his memory. In such a retrospect we shall find an admonition that an American Senate should meet, on this side of the fatal line of death, as the American generals meet on the other side, to render justice to each other and to make our beloved country as happy, comparatively, as we should wish the great Beyond to be to those great spirits.

From Senator Manderson.

Mr. Manderson said that as the hours of the last few days passed away he had not had the heart to make such preparation for the event which all feared and dreaded as might seem to be meet and appropriate. He had been afraid to prepare anything that might be in the nature of a post-mortem tribute. It seemed like a surrender to the enemy. The death of General Sherman came (although one might have been prepared for it) as the unexpected. It was a day of mourning and grief. Here, at the capital of the nation, lay the body of the great admiral, the chief of the navy; and in New York was being prepared for the last sad rites the body of the greatest military genius which the nation had produced. General Sherman had been not only great as a military leader, but he had been great as a civilian. Who was there that had heard him tell of the events of his wonderful career who had not been filled with admiration and respect for his abilities? It seemed to him that General Sherman was perhaps the only man in the North who in the early days of the war seemed to appreciate what the terrible conflict meant.

It was recollected how it was said in 1861 that he must be insane to make the suggestions which he made. These suggestions were so startling to the country that he (Mr. Manderson) did not wonder that men doubted General Sherman's sanity. Like men of great genius, he seemed to have lived in that debatable ground existing between the line of perfect sanity and insanity.

After a review of General Sherman's military career, opening at Shiloh and closing at Atlanta, Mr. Manderson read General Sherman's letter to the mayor and common council of Atlanta, beginning, "We must have peace, not only at Atlanta, but in all America." In conclusion, Mr. Manderson said:

The Model Citizen.

"General Sherman was estimable as a citizen, and as fully appreciated the duties of a civilian as he was admirable as a soldier. But this strife which we have watched for the past few days has ceased. The conflict has ended. The nation has witnessed it. Sixty millions of people have stood in silence, watching for the supreme result. Death, ever victorious, is again a victor. A great conqueror is himself conquered. Our captain lies dead. The pale lips say to the sunken eye: 'Where is thy kindly glance?' And no answer is returned."

Mr. Davis said he could hardly trust himself to speak. He had been a soldier under General Sherman, and had received acts of kindness from him when he was a subaltern. As the years had gone by and the widening avenues of life had opened up ways of promotion, that acquaintance had ripened into friendship, and, he might say, into intimacy. He had first seen General Sherman at the siege of Vicksburg, twenty-eight years ago, when he was the very incarnation of war, but to-day that spirit had taken up its rest in the everlasting tabernacle of death. It was fit that the clangor of the great city should be hushed in silence, and that the functions of government should be suspended while the soul of the great commander was passing to Him who gives and Him who takes away. No more are heard the thunders of the captains and the shoutings. The soul of the great warrior had passed, and was standing in judgment before Him who was the God of battles and was also the God of love.

Mr. Pierce, as one of the soldiers who had served under General Sherman in the Army of the Tennessee, gave some reminiscences of the war and paid a glowing eulogy to his old commander.

The Eloquent Evarts.

Mr. Evarts said that the afflicting intelligence of the death of General Sherman had touched the Senate with the deepest sensibilities—that that grief was not a private grief, nor was it limited by any narrower bounds than those of the whole country. The affection of the people toward its honorable and honored men did not always find a warm effusion, because circumstances might not have brought the personal career, the personal traits, the personal affectionate disposition of great men to the close and general observation of the people at large. But of General Sherman no such observation could be truly made. Whatever of affection and of grief Senators might feel was felt, perhaps, more intensely in the hearts of the whole people. To observers of his death, as they had been of his life, General Sherman had been yesterday the most celebrated living American.

He was now added to that longer and more illustrious list of celebrated men of the country for the hundred years of national life. One star differed from another star in glory, but yet all of the stars had a glory to which nothing could be added by eulogy and from which nothing could be taken away by detraction. They shone in their own effulgence, and borrowed no light from honor or respect. It had been said already that General Sherman was the last of the commanders. If those who had passed out of life still watched over and took interest in what transpired in this world (and no one doubted it), what great shades must have surrounded the death-bed of General Sherman! And who could imagine a greater death-bed for a great life than that which has been watched over in a neighboring city during the week? It had been reserved for him (Mr. Evarts), at the declining hour of the day, as a Senator from the State which General Sherman had honored by his residence, and in which he had died, to move, out of respect for his memory, that the Senate do now adjourn.

The resolutions were then adopted unanimously, and, on motion of Mr. Hawley, the presiding officer was requested to appoint a committee of five Senators to attend the funeral of General Sherman. The Senate then, at 5 o'clock, adjourned till Monday at 11 A. M.

In the House of Representatives.

The President's message announcing General Sherman's death was received in the House about three o'clock. Speaker Reed, after consultation with Mr. Cutcheon of Michigan and a few others, decided, in view of the near expiration of the Congress, and of the necessity of getting the appropriation bills over to the Senate as soon as possible, that it would not be advisable to lay the message before the House until near the usual time of adjournment. It was then referred to the Committee on Military Affairs, which will report appropriate resolutions of respect and recommend that the House take part in the funeral services if that be in consonance with the feelings of the family.

General Cutcheon, chairman of the Committee on Military Affairs, referred feelingly to the fact that General Sherman's death removed the last of the three great Union generals. Mr. Cutcheon served under General Sherman only a short time, but was attached to General Burnside's command when General Sherman came to its relief.

"I regard General Sherman," said Mr. Cutcheon, "as the greatest strategist developed by the war. I should say that Grant was the greatest in his firmness and his unfaltering courage and confidence in his ability to succeed. He was also great in his spirit of magnanimity. Sherman knew more of the art and science of war. Sheridan was the most brilliant fighter. Sherman was also great as a patriot and as a man. This passage from his memoirs, I think, is the key to the character of the whole man: it was at the outbreak of the war, when Sherman was in Louisiana: 'On no earthly account will I do any act or think any thought hostile to or in defiance of the old Government of the United States.'"

Warm Tribute from Mr. Blaine.

Members of the Cabinet spoke feelingly of the death of General Sherman. Secretary Blaine said he could remember him personally from the time he was graduated at West Point, fifty years ago, when he was himself a schoolboy of ten years.

"For more than thirty years," continued Mr. Blaine, "by reason of family connections, I had known him very intimately. Of his many and great qualities on his public side I do not care to speak. General Sherman's military history is a part, and a large part, of the proudest annals of the nation. He did not grow less in the intimacy of private life or by the fireside in his own home. He had the kindest of hearts and the most chivalric devotion to those he loved. He was one of the warmest friends to those for whom he professed friendship. He was frank, just and magnanimous. He spoke and wrote with a freedom that almost seemed reckless, and oftentimes was misunderstood, as when he wrote his own memoirs. His death seemed premature. Seeing him very often, I had discovered no decay in the acuteness of his senses except in a slight loss of hearing. I saw him last summer at Bar Harbor for a considerable period, and his brightness of talk and his enjoyment of life, especially with the young, seemed as natural and marked as ever, but at the same time I had in some way gained the impression in talking with him that he had no expectation of a long life."

Secretary Noble's Panegyric.

Secretary Noble said: "I feel a great personal grief at the loss of General Sherman, my friend for many years. I was born in Lancaster, where he was. His father was my father's friend, and while I retain for him the admiration that all Americans and the whole world must, I feel that one has gone from me by whose approval my personal action in life has been greatly influenced. I served under him in the war, and had been honored by his friendship and personal intercourse in St. Louis, New York, and Washington since. His military achievements in the service of the republic are a part of the history of our country; but great as his talents as a commander were, they were equalled by the beautiful traits of his character that made him the instructive companion, the genial friend, and wise counsellor that he was. He was as tender and kind in private life as he was great and successful in war. His literary taste was most wonderful, and his memory, not only of events and facts, but even of figures and statistics, was unfailing.

"His love for his comrades-in-arms was like that of a father for his children. His love embraced all our people. Among the first events in my official life here was a visit from General Sherman, voluntarily made in behalf of General Joseph Johnston, of whom he spoke in the highest terms. He was as ready to support any man when friendly to the Government as he was uncompromising to all its enemies. He was as grand a patriot as ever lived, and I believe that his services, his speeches, and examples will have a happy influence upon our country through all its history. This is no time nor place to attempt to speak of all that was valuable and admirable in the career and character of General Sherman. May God bless and console his family, and raise up other men like him for the support and protection of our republic!"

A Man of "Pure Gold."

Postmaster-General Wanamaker said: "I had only ten years' personal acquaintanceship with General Sherman, but even a much shorter time would have drawn me to him closely. He never seemed to me like an old man, and always woke up in me all the boy that was in me. I was never where he was that I could get near to him that we did not put our arms around each other. The ring of his words and ways showed that he was made of pure gold. No man that I ever knew combined in such a degree the courage of a lion, the loving gentleness of a woman, and the simplicity of a child. The sunset of his career has been as gorgeous and beautiful as the glory of his great campaign."

Attorney-General Miller said: "In General Sherman's death the world has lost the first of its military men. At least there is no one surviving at all comparable to him, unless it be the great German marshal Von Moltke. He was not only a great soldier, but he was wise in all public affairs. He was, perhaps, the first to appreciate, or at least the first to announce, the magnitude of the nation's task in suppressing the great rebellion. In this he was ahead of his contemporaries, and, as usual with men ahead of the times, he was thought to be wild, not to say crazy. Events, however, more than justified his declarations. I have met General Sherman a good many times, but had no close relations with him. One thing especially struck me in the great Centennial review in New York. There he stood by the side of the President. No matter what else might be claiming his attention, he never failed to take off his hat and salute the flag. He might let the men pass without recognition, but never the flag. Very few men have ever been so close to the hearts of the people of the United States as General Sherman.

From Old Comrades.

General Henry W. Slocum, in speaking of General Sherman, said that he felt that he had lost his best friend. In Sherman's famous march General Slocum was in command of the left wing, and the friendship then formed survived the war and became stronger with each succeeding year. He and General Sherman were much together of late years. At public dinners which they both attended it was always to be noticed that the two veterans seemed to enjoy, fully as much as anything, getting together and talking over the interesting story of the war.

General Slocum joined Sherman's expedition at Atlanta, and was with it from that time until the close of the war. Every other day General Sherman rode with him. On these occasions General Sherman, who was a great talker, was as entertaining a companion as could well be imagined. His conversation covered a wide range of subjects, but touched lightly on the one subject which at that time possessed the greatest interest, not only for General Slocum, but for the whole country—the march itself and what was expected of it.

General Sherman's appearance at this time, General Slocum says, was about the same as it was in later years. He was angular, nervous, but giving every one the impression of being a man of great determination. At the same time he was of a sanguine temperament.

"From the time he started on the expedition," said General Slocum, "he never seemed for a moment to doubt that it would ultimately prove successful. Nothing seemed to shake his faith in this respect. He never discussed his plans with me to any extent. It was not his habit to discuss them with his subordinates. He preferred saying little about what he intended to do until it became necessary. His self-reliance was remarkable."

The Army Idolized Him.

With his troops, General Slocum said, General Sherman was exceedingly popular. This was perhaps but natural, as he had led them to success, and a commander in such a position generally is popular. While possibly he was not generous with his men, he was always just, and this fact they recognized and honored him for. His sense of justice caused him to be severe in his treatment of those who failed to do their duty. He always looked well after the welfare of those under his command, and was never above having a pleasant word for his men. Yet he was none the less a soldier, a man of deeds.

Speaking of the feeling of the Southern people against General Sherman, which was probably stronger than that felt against any other Northern general, General Slocum said that it had never been General Sherman's wish or intention to cause any unnecessary suffering to the people in the country through which he was marching. For the burning of Columbia he was in no way responsible. Yet he was charged with it, with much bitterness, by the Southern people. As a matter of fact, the inhabitants of the place were themselves to blame for its burning. They had filled the streets with cotton, and when Sherman's army marched in, thinking to propitiate the soldiers, they had waylaid them with whiskey, which they gave to them in tin cups, as much as they would take, until every ugly fellow in the ranks was still uglier and half drunk.

Sorrows of War.

"General Sherman," said General Slocum, "always expressed great regret at the suffering caused by the burning of Columbia. He talked with me about it at the time, and frequently spoke of it after the war. Nothing was further from his intentions than that the city should be burned. He strove to burn everything useful to the Confederates; nothing else. When we first crossed into South Carolina, we found we were walking on torpedoes planted in the road, and the troops did some burning on their own account, but General Sherman put a stop to it as soon as possible."

One of the most astonishing things about General Sherman, General Slocum declared, was his memory. He never seemed to forget anything which he met with, and which he thought might at any future time be of use to him. Having been stationed at Charleston before the war, he seemed to have the whole topography of the State at command. Frequently he was able to give information which was not found on the map which General Slocum had with him. When asked how he came to know some particular thing about the country, he would say that he had noticed it several years before.

Tribute from General Howard.

Major-General O. O. Howard, commanding the Division of the Atlantic, was much affected by the death of his old comrade and friend. He talked for a few moments regarding the dead commander, and his voice trembled as he spoke.

"General Sherman," he said, "has permitted me during the last two years in which I have been stationed in the vicinity of his home to be particularly intimate with him. He never seemed like a fellow-officer so much as like a father or elderly friend. So to-night my heart bleeds at his loss. When did I first meet him? I think it was shortly before the first battle of Bull Run, and after that I was with him at Chattanooga and on the march to the sea. My personal acquaintanceship with him did not really begin until 1863."

Reminiscences by General King.

Said General Horatio C. King: "The announcement of General Sherman's death is a great shock to me, as I have had a strong hope that he would pull through. I regard it as one of the greatest privileges of my life that I have been favored with the close friendship of General Sherman. He was the most interesting conversationalist I have ever met, and his fund of reminiscences was seemingly inexhaustible. I shall never forget the first address he made at one of our army reunions held in Philadelphia, June 6, of the Centennial year. The meeting was in the Academy of Music. He made quite a long and patriotic off-hand address, in which he counselled tenderness toward the South. 'Let us,' he said, 'forgive and forget—provided they will do the same.'

"General Sherman has felt of late years that his

strength was being too strongly taxed by the incessant social demands upon him. He never could refuse his old Western associates, but I had some difficulty to persuade him that he had as many friends in the East. At Saratoga Springs in 1887 he gave me a most laughable scoring for my persistence. He said: 'By the law of our land, which is the only king we worship, I was turned out to grass, and I was told that I could spend the rest of my days in peace and retirement. I sought refuge in the city of St. Louis; I found but little peace there. But I read, I think in Dr. Johnson, that peace and quiet could only be had in a great city or forest—in Nature's wilderness. I therefore sought it in New York City.' Then General Sherman told his famous story of Captain Bonneville. Bonneville, it seemed, wanted peace and quiet. He asked for two years' leave of absence, and got it, and he went out to the mountains where Salt Lake now is. He caught beavers and otter and fished, and the Crows came and cleaned him out, and he kept out of the way for two years more. He was reported dead. He went to the adjutant-general and reported, but the adjutant says: 'Bonneville is dead.'—He says: 'I am not dead.'—'Oh yes,' said the adjutant, 'you are dead; you are as dead as a mackeral. Go away from here and don't disturb the record.'

"Sherman is the last of the great triumvirate of generals—Grant, Sherman and Sheridan—for in that order they will always be named; yet to my thinking Sherman possessed the highest military genius, and as a strategist had not his equal in the war of the rebellion."

Tributes from Abroad.

Lord Wolseley, who is believed to be the best informed man in the British army, said: "I join the people of the United States in their regret at General Sherman's death, for his loss is not confined to America, but is shared by all military people."

Asked what he thought of Sherman as a military commander, Lord Wolseley replied that it was a difficult matter for an outsider to make comparisons, but, speaking purely from a military point of view, he undoubtedly would place Sherman at the head of all the Northern commanders as a strategist. Sherman showed great power, and in this he excelled all others, while in the achievements for which he was most famous—notably his march to the sea—he displayed a dash combined with strategical skill that at once proved his great power.

Colonel Hugh McCalmont, C. B., who has seen much service in India, and who was the officer commanding the Fourth (Royal Irish) Dragoon Guards at Dublin, said with great feeling that in his judgment Grant would not have been able to break down the heroic opposition of Lee if it had not been for the genius of Sherman, whose march to the sea was the grandest thing of its kind in history. He especially admired Sherman because he was a pukka general (pukka in India means real, genuine), also because he was a soldier solely, having resolutely refused to go in for politics.

One of the most accomplished and best-read staff officers in the British army is Colonel S. F. Maurice, of the Royal Artillery, at present professor of Military Art and History at the Staff College. He said: "I have long considered the Atlanta campaign of Sherman as one of the most valuable lessons in war furnished by our time. The feature of Sherman's career which has always impressed me with the most interest as a man was the generosity with which, after he had himself opposed Grant's arrangements for the Vicksburg campaign, he immediately afterward on the spot and at the time confessed himself in the wrong, and used all his military genius to point out the skill, foresight and importance of what Grant had done. The mode in which Sherman talked to influential politicians and others of those very achievements of Grant became the starting-point of Grant's great career. To a large extent the United States owe to Sherman's generosity of character and to his military clearness of vision the ultimate selection of Grant as the general who carried their armies to success."

Similar tributes from Von Moltke and other great military heroes show the estimate placed upon the renowned commander who now lies in death, "his martial cloak wrapped around him."

Milton Keynes UK
Ingram Content Group UK Ltd.
UKHW040058180324
439604UK00007B/1101